Nuclear Proliferation after the Cold War

Nuclear Proliferation after the Cold War

Edited by Mitchell Reiss
and Robert S. Litwak

Published by The Woodrow Wilson Center Press
Distributed by The Johns Hopkins University Press

Woodrow Wilson Center Special Studies

The Woodrow Wilson Center Press
Editorial Offices
370 L'Enfant Promenade, S.W.
Suite 704
Washington, D.C. 20024-2518 U.S.A.
telephone 202-287-3000, ext. 218

Distributed by
The Johns Hopkins University Press
Hampden Station
Baltimore, Maryland 21211
order department telephone 1-800-537-5487

Cover design by Meadows and Wiser Graphic Design, Washington, D.C.

Printed in the United States of America

∞ Printed on acid-free paper.

9 8 7 6 5 4 3 2 1

Library of Congress Cataloging-in-Publication Data

Nuclear proliferation after the Cold War / edited by Mitchell Reiss
    and Robert S. Litwak.
        p.   cm. — (Woodrow Wilson Center special studies)
    Includes index.
    ISBN 0-943875-64-1 (hardcover : acid-free paper). — ISBN
0-943875-57-9 (pbk. : acid-free paper)
        1. Nuclear nonproliferation. I. Reiss, Mitchell. II. Litwak,
Robert. III. Series.
JX1974.73.N813   1994
327.1'74—dc20   94-22717
                                                            CIP

The Woodrow Wilson International Center for Scholars

The Center is the living memorial of the United States of America to the nation's twenty-eighth president, Woodrow Wilson. The Congress established the Woodrow Wilson Center in 1968 as an international institute for advanced study, "symbolizing and strengthening the fruitful relationship between the world of learning and the world of public affairs." The Center opened in 1970 under its own board of trustees.

Woodrow Wilson Center Special Studies

The work of the Center's Fellows, Guest Scholars, and staff— and presentations and discussions at the Center's conferences, seminars, and colloquia, often deserve timely circulation as contributions to public understanding of issues of national and international importance. The Woodrow Wilson Center Special Studies series is intended to make such materials available by the Woodrow Wilson Center Press to interested scholars, practitioners, and other readers. In all its activities, the Woodrow Wilson Center is a nonprofit, nonpartisan organization, supported financially by annual appropriations from the Congress, and by the contributions of foundations, corporations, and individuals. Conclusions or opinions expressed in Center publications and programs are those of the authors and speakers and do not necessarily reflect the views of the Center staff, Fellows, trustees, advisory groups, or any individuals or organizations that provide financial support to the Center.

Contents

Acknowledgments

This volume stems from an international conference sponsored by the Division of International Studies of the Woodrow Wilson International Center for Scholars in December 1992 as part of a multi-year project on nuclear nonproliferation. U.S. government officials from the legislative and executive branches, foreign diplomats, technical experts, and regional analysts participated in the two days of discussion.

The editors would like to express their gratitude to the following individuals who commented on the formal presentations: R. Jeffrey Smith, Gordon Oehler, Rose Gottemoeller, James Leonard, Ho Young Ahn, Virginia Foran, Zachary Davis, Will Tobey, Ellen Laipson, James Schear, Fred McGoldrick, and Janne Nolan. The papers presented at the conference have been revised in light of these comments and updated to take account of subsequent developments. In addition, we appreciate the contributions by Joseph Nye, Daniel Poneman, Norman Wulf, and Randy Rydell in the final panel session on defining and coordinating U.S. nonproliferation policy.

Both the conference and this book were made possible through the generous support of the Ford Foundation. We would like to thank especially Shepard Forman and Geoffrey Wiseman for their encouragement and advice during the organization of the conference.

At the Woodrow Wilson Center, Director Charles Blitzer and Deputy Director Samuel F. Wells, Jr., offered unstinting support and key advice at every stage. Deep and special thanks go to Michele Carus-Christian, Bonnie Terrell, Maria Farnon, Leanne MacDonald, Michael Rubin, and Catherine Fellows for doing all of the logistical and coordinating work involved in staging an international conference and preparing the manuscript for publication. We also appreciate the help provided by our colleagues Jane Mutnick, Monica Marsolais, Traci Nagle, and Constantine Symeonides-Tsatsos.

Finally, we are indebted to Joseph Brinley and Carolee Walker of the Woodrow Wilson Center Press for their efficient and timely support of this project.

Introduction

Mitchell Reiss and Robert S. Litwak

The end of the cold war has fundamentally transformed the calculus of nuclear threat. The world no longer lives in fear of a superpower confrontation leading to nuclear holocaust. And yet, even as this paramount danger recedes, others have arisen in the post-cold war era that confound efforts to create a "new world order." The revelations in the aftermath of the Gulf War about Saddam Hussein's secret nuclear program and the continuing crisis over North Korea's circumvention of international safeguards underscore the challenges confronting the nonproliferation regime. In the former Soviet Union, uncertainties persist about the security of nuclear weapons and the long-term nuclear intentions of the successor states. President Bill Clinton and other senior administration officials have identified nuclear proliferation as the foremost threat to U.S. national security interests.

This volume is intended to illuminate current policy issues for the reader by providing important background and analysis. It is divided into two parts—the first focusing on specific country and regional case studies, the second exploring the significance of new technologies and the responses of key international institutions to proliferation challenges. Space limitations precluded the inclusion of contributions on additional important subjects, such as nuclear terrorism and prospects for a comprehensive test-ban treaty. This volume could also have discussed the proliferation of other weapons of mass destruction—chemical and biological weapons and ballistic missiles. Again, space constraints are part of the reason these subjects were omitted. But the primary reason is that these weapons represent threats that ultimately differ in magnitude from the threats presented by nuclear weapons. This has been demonstrated by the use of both chemical weapons and ballistic missiles in the Iran-Iraq War and, more recently, by the use of Scuds in the Gulf War. None of these occasions evoked anywhere near the type of international response and outrage that would have followed the use of even a single nuclear weapon. Indeed, the primary source of concern over the dissemination of ballistic missiles is the possibility of placing a nuclear warhead on top of one.

Part I, devoted to particular country and regional case studies, opens with an examination of the Iraqi nuclear program by Gary Samore in chapter 1. He argues that the case of Iraq represented "a near massive failure" of the international nonproliferation regime—a policy failure averted only by Saddam Hussein's invasion of Kuwait, which created the postwar conditions for the destruction of Iraq's nuclear program. Samore observes that Iraq highlighted the danger that a country could circumvent its Nonproliferation Treaty (NPT) safeguards obligations by developing and building clandestine nuclear facilities entirely outside its declared nuclear program. The international community responded to revelations about Iraq's nuclear program by strengthening International Atomic Energy Agency (IAEA) safeguards and export controls to correct weaknesses that Iraq had exploited, increasing international pressure on other countries suspected of NPT violations (such as Iran and North Korea), and placing renewed emphasis on political solutions to nuclear proliferation problems in the Middle East and South Asia.

In chapter 2, Shahram Chubin writes that given the diffusion of knowledge and engineering skills having nuclear applications, as well as the growth of industrial infrastructure useful for nuclear weapons development, it would be wise not to place too much emphasis on "the politics of denial"—that is, on the technical aspects of nuclear nonproliferation. He argues that as capabilities are enhanced, "political will becomes even more important, indeed becomes the chief determinant of the decisions on whether to 'go' or not go toward nuclear weapons." His chapter surveys the attitudes and policies of those regional states—

notably, Iran, Iraq, Israel, Libya, and Algeria—that either are reputed to have nuclear weapons programs or are considered proliferation risks. He also addresses the prospects for regional arms control (including proposals for the creation of a nuclear free zone) and the role that extraregional states might play in promoting nonproliferation. Chubin concludes that Iran is "the most difficult proliferator . . . because its incentives to acquire nuclear weapons are so diffuse, being animated by global ambitions as much as by regional threats."

Israel's policy of "deterrence through uncertainty" is examined by Shai Feldman in chapter 3. Feldman notes that successive Israeli governments, irrespective of their composition, have adhered to Israel's policy of avoiding any reference to the precise state of its nuclear capacity, thereby demonstrating a remarkable degree of constancy and broad political support. Israel's ambiguous stance has produced an effective deterrent vis-à-vis its Arab adversaries, while avoiding a crisis in relations with the United States over nuclear nonproliferation. The desire to maintain the benefits of this calculated policy of nuclear ambiguity accounts for Israel's refusal to accede to the NPT. Moreover, Israel considers the NPT a highly deficient instrument for arresting nuclear proliferation in the Middle East and elsewhere. In this chapter, Feldman explores a range of proposed arms control and confidence-building measures for the Middle East, as well as the evolving regional nuclear environment, from the perspective of Tel Aviv. He concludes that any multilateral arms control agreement would have to include all Middle East countries from North Africa to Iran and that compliance would have to be verified by the application of extremely intrusive measures conducted by the parties themselves.

In chapter 4, Steven Miller assesses the unprecedented nonproliferation challenges raised by the disintegration of the Soviet Union into fifteen newly independent states. Miller notes that the USSR left behind a legacy of some thirty thousand nuclear weapons and an extensive and far-flung nuclear infrastructure for the production and maintenance of these weapons. This chapter provides a comprehensive picture of proliferation risks (while avoiding either undue alarmism or unwarranted risks) and describes actions and policies to contain them. Miller argues that the successful consolidation of the Soviet nuclear arsenal would entail five steps: (1) relocation of all Soviet nuclear weapons in Russia; (2) removal of all nuclear weapons from troubled or potentially troubled areas of Russia; (3) provision of safe and secure transport and interim storage for all weapons so relocated or removed; (4) dismantlement of all excess nuclear weapons as quickly as possible; and (5) arrangement of the safe disposition of the fissile material produced by the dismantlement process. A comprehensive Western nonproliferation policy toward the former Soviet Union should also include the encouragement of all the newly independent states to promptly join the NPT and their acceptance of IAEA safeguards for all nuclear reactors. Miller concludes that the likelihood of nuclear proliferation in the former Soviet Union will be heavily influenced by the character of the regional order that emerges; the emergence of a conflict-prone regional order—particularly one in which Russia is menacing—will create conditions in which some successor states are likely to find the nuclear option attractive.

Chapter 5, authored by Robert Carlin, discusses what is known and not known about North Korea's nuclear program and intentions. Carlin argues that an examination of these topical and controversial questions yields "several types of answers: some technical, some political, some that are known in Pyongyang, and some that Pyongyang itself may not even understand. . . . In the final analysis, what observers think about the North's nuclear program is, to a large extent, a function of what they think they know about North Korea." What is often depicted in the West as a narrowly focused problem—namely, how to stop the North's nuclear weapons program—is viewed by the Pyongyang regime within the broader political context of its evolving relations with the outside world. In reviewing the North's "serious and surprisingly steady" policy of economic experimentation and opening to the outside (including the initiation of a dialogue with Seoul), Carlin notes that these developments serve as a necessary backdrop for understanding the pace and direction of Pyongyang's nuclear policies. Indeed, they provided the logic for the regime's eventual acceptance of IAEA inspections in January 1992, as well as for the related conclusion of a bilateral nonnuclear agreement with South Korea the previous month. As this volume goes to press, the dispute between the United States and North Korea over the contravention of the latter's IAEA responsibilities continues. By providing an analysis of the Pyongyang regime's nuclear capabilities and the "political prism" through which it views the external world, this chapter should contribute to the ongoing public discussion of this important foreign policy concern.

China's nuclear and missile export policies—and the particular challenge they pose to the Clinton administration—are examined by Shirley Kan and Zachary Davis in chapter 6. Given the higher priority accorded nonproliferation by President Bill Clinton, they anticipate a less conciliatory approach toward China on nonproliferation issues and greater efforts to reverse China's policy of exporting technology useful for developing nuclear weapons and missiles. Kan and Davis argue that a new strategy is needed to move China from its currently "ambiguous" nonproliferation policy to full membership in the international nonproliferation regime. Of specific concern to the United States and its allies has been Chinese nuclear and missile cooperation with Pakistan and Iran. Belated Chinese accession to the NPT in August 1991 stemmed from Beijing's desire to deflect criticism of its nuclear export policy, especially in the aftermath of the Tiananmen Square massacre, and to secure most-favored nation (MFN) trade status from the United States. One positive indication of the direction of China's nonproliferation policy has been its acquiescence to the United Nations and the IAEA to address NPT noncompliance by Iraq and North Korea. In light of continuing questions about Beijing's relationships with Pakistan and Iran, the central issue facing the Clinton administration, according to Kan and Davis, is "whether, and how, to use the powerful but double-edged sword of trade to improve Chinese compliance with international nonproliferation norms."

Nuclear proliferation concerns about India and Pakistan—two regional powers that have neither signed the NPT nor accepted IAEA safeguards—are addressed by Brahma Chellaney and Ali T. Sheikh, respectively, in chapters 7 and 8. Since the U.S. cutoff of military and economic assistance to Pakistan in 1991 because of its nuclear program, Pakistani dilemmas in the nuclear field have further sharpened. As Sheikh notes, Pakistan is both unable to proceed with its nuclear program and unwilling to unilaterally roll back the program without reciprocity from India. Pakistan's proposal for a five-power conference on South Asia's nuclear future was partially motivated by its desire to win a resumption of American aid. Despite reports that the air force and army now favor flexibility on the nuclear issue, domestic pressure in Pakistan to continue with its nuclear program has been fueled by the

hawkish public posturing of political leaders for electoral considerations. Sheikh argues that India's continued policy of nuclear
ambiguity, coupled with its refusal to enter into regional and
international arrangements, not only reflects India's own historical concerns but also indicates New Delhi's perception that Pakistan may be forced to accede to U.S. pressure without gaining
any concessions from India. Given the existing political realities
and the complexities of the India-Pakistan nuclear equation, he
advocates a series of confidence-building measures on the Helsinki and Conference on Security and Cooperation in Europe
(CSCE) models as a promising starting point.

In chapter 7, Chellaney focuses on India's nuclear incentives
and disincentives, domestic and external constraints on its proliferation-related activities, Indian nuclear diplomacy, and the
prognosis for regional security in the subcontinent. He observes
that, unlike the dedicated weapons programs pursued by Pakistan and China, India's nuclear weapons capability derives from
its civilian atomic research and that the military plays an insig-
nificant role in nuclear policy-making relative to the elected civilian authorities, notably the prime minister and the cabinet secretariat. He argues that India's long-term nuclear calculations
remain centered on China and that Beijing's rising military
spending and its nuclear modernization program are serving to
reinforce obstacles to a regional nonproliferation regime in South
Asia. Despite a weapons capability demonstrated two decades
ago, India still does not appear close to building a nuclear arsenal.
"Only one major possible development in the next few years,"
Chellaney writes, "could trigger such a decision: evidence of
overt weaponization by Pakistan." Although the end of the cold
war has witnessed an improvement in U.S. relations with India,
Washington will not be able to translate increased influence into
an ability to coax New Delhi into signing the NPT. India's emergence as a potential second-tier supplier means that Washington
may seek to bring India into the Nuclear Suppliers Group and
the Missile Technology Control Regime. Chellaney concludes that
India's nuclear diplomacy will remain aimed at "deflecting outside pressure on the country to enter into regional nonproliferation arrangements or accept controls that would impinge on the
country's nuclear weapons option."

David Fischer in chapter 9 addresses the case of South Africa
in light of former President F. W. de Klerk's startling revelation
in March 1993 that South Africa had constructed six nuclear

bombs but had destroyed them before signing the NPT in July 1991. Fischer details the evolution of the South African nuclear program from the 1974 decision to develop atomic weapons to the actual fabrication of nuclear devices during the 1980s. He notes that the purpose of the nuclear program was not deterrence per se, given the absence of an overt external threat, but rather the creation of a "political weapon" for pressuring the United States to intervene in South Africa should the white regime be threatened militarily. De Klerk's subsequent nuclear turnabout was not solely a response to the end of the cold war, the withdrawal of Cuban troops from Angola, and the tripartite agreement on the independence of Namibia. More fundamentally, it was part of his overall strategy to transform South Africa's domestic and foreign policies—the major elements of which included the end of apartheid within South Africa and the replacement of a policy of regional destabilization by one of regional cooperation. Fischer observes, "The paramount conclusion to be drawn from the South African case is that it has demonstrated . . . that nuclear proliferation is reversible." More sobering, it also demonstrated that a state with "a reasonably sophisticated scientific and technical infrastructure can build an arsenal of relatively simple nuclear weapons without detection or testing."

In chapter 10, Mónica Serrano examines the Latin American nonproliferation regime with a particular focus on the Argentine-Brazilian nuclear interaction. This chapter features an overview of the main trends that have led to the creation of a nonproliferation regime in Latin America. After an analysis of the key Argentine-Brazilian bilateral relationship, she identifies those relevant lessons that can be derived from the Latin American experience. Serrano notes that during the negotiations over the 1967 Treaty of Tlatelolco, the emergence of two diverging views on denuclearization became clear: the "rigorous" view supported by the Mexican delegation, which was closer to U.S. interests on nonproliferation, and the view shared by Argentina and Brazil deriving from the incorporation of nuclear energy issues in their respective national security agendas. An important factor facilitating the eventual Brazilian-Argentine nuclear rapprochement was the return of democratic rule to both countries in 1989. Partly motivated by their interest in removing a potential source of friction in their relationships with the United States, Argentina and Brazil have taken a number of steps to affirm their commitment to "nondiscriminatory nonproliferation" (e.g., the appointment of joint representatives to the IAEA, their participation as observers during the 1990 NPT Review Conference, and a series of confidence-building measures involving the exchange of information on their respective nuclear programs). Yet, she argues, these decisions have been clearly linked to external pressures, and there is not sufficient evidence to support the view that they have been fully endorsed by the military. That said, the conditions and the progress achieved by the Latin American regime offer a solid basis for cautious optimism.

Part II examines both the influence of technology on nuclear proliferation and the responses of key institutions, such as the IAEA, to the new challenges of the post-cold war era. The former topic has been surprisingly neglected in the literature. At a time when many analysts correctly note the increasing ease with which a country can acquire a nuclear weapons capability, these chapters persuasively argue that new technologies can also be employed to prevent or retard the spread of nuclear weapons.

In chapter 11, "The Impact of New Technologies on Nuclear Weapons Proliferation," Amy Sands takes a broad overview of how new technologies will influence efforts to prevent nuclear weapons spread in the coming years. Sands notes that efforts aimed at denying militarily sensitive technology to certain countries have been frequently denigrated by critics yet have been successful in slowing countries' march toward nuclear weapons; she also notes that these efforts are more politically palatable than other nonproliferation options, such as sanctions and the use of military force.

Sands usefully creates a taxonomy of new technologies: (1) those that directly relate to developing nuclear weapons, such as new methods to obtain fissile material; (2) dual-use items, such as computers; and (3) delivery systems, in particular, ballistic missiles. Sands argues that technologies in the first category will be too complex and sophisticated to be profitably absorbed by potential proliferators. Dual-use technologies will be much more helpful, assuming that they can be acquired and maintained. Although most states of proliferation anxiety already have the means of delivering a bomb, technologies relating to guidance or propulsion systems could upgrade existing capabilities.

Interestingly, Sands cautions that the "greatest technological threat" for nuclear proliferation derives from the improved scientific, technical, and engineering infrastructure and capabilities in the developing world. Countries that possess this technological base will be better able to take advantage of decades-old technologies (e.g., Iraq's advances on electromagnetic isotope separation technology) for their nuclear weapons and ballistic missiles programs.

Sands's conclusion, that "new technologies will have a significant impact on the spread of nuclear weapons but will actually serve more strongly as *inhibitors* than as facilitators of nuclear proliferation," persuasively challenges the conventional wisdom. These technologies will improve existing information-collection capabilities, verification, data integration, and response capabilities. Advances in these areas offer hope of making nuclear weapons-related activities in suspect countries more transparent. This, in turn, will "improve verification capabilities, facilitate confidence-building measures, and possibly, because of fear of being discovered, inhibit nuclear weapons development programs." Should a country nonetheless acquire nuclear weapons, these technologies will also improve response capabilities for "real-time searching, seizure, and destruction of sensitive nuclear materials and nuclear weapons."

Joseph F. Pilat in chapter 12, "Responding to Proliferation: A Role for Nonlethal Defense?," states that military responses to the spread of weapons of mass destruction are a poor basis for a nonproliferation policy. When technology denial, security assurances, export controls, IAEA safeguards, conventional military assistance, and other approaches fail to halt a country's acquisition of a nuclear weapons capability, Pilat explains how "nonlethal defenses or "disabling technologies" can expand the menu of options for decision makers while minimizing the risk of hostilities. Aside from obvious measures such as covert action or special operations designed to destroy nuclear facilities or nuclear arms, new technologies under development would "disrupt, degrade, or destroy a wide set of targets, with minimum physical damage and no intentional casualties."

Pilat offers an intriguing look at how these technologies might work: "disruption of information, communications, command and control, and other systems by advanced computer viruses, electromagnetic disturbances, and deception; disruption of advancing forces by jellifying fuel and inhibiting combustion in the engines of tanks and armored personnel vehicles, crystallizing the tires of military vehicles and stalling the vehicles with anti-traction polymers and lubricants; and destroying air forces by embrittling or otherwise weakening airframes and spraying polymer adhesives on runways." Moreover, these measures can be utilized across a "continuum ranging from preconflict to high-intensity conflict at the strategic level."

To many, Saddam Hussein's secret nuclear program represented a failure of the IAEA and the international safeguards regime. Less well publicized was the massive failure of Western intelligence communities to detect the scale and sophistication of Iraq's nuclear ambitions.

In chapter 13, "Can the Intelligence Community Keep Pace with the Threat?," Jeffrey Richelson answers in the affirmative and also explains how U.S. intelligence efforts to prevent nuclear proliferation can be improved. Richelson first outlines the scope of the problem and the means currently available to the intelligence community. Information-collection targets include identification of personnel, location of facilities, what is inside these facilities, what leaves these facilities (communications and emissions), suppliers of nuclear-related technology, and the international banking transactions used to finance purchases of advanced technology. Information is gathered in these areas by various means: nuclear intelligence (NUCINT), imagery intelligence (IMINT), signals intelligence (SIGINT), communications intelligence (COMINT), and human intelligence (HUMINT).

Richelson states that further efforts in developing networks of informants in certain countries (e.g., Iran, Iraq, North Korea), although difficult, could be enormously beneficial to nonproliferation efforts. "Technical collection has already improved due to the increased sensor capabilities of U.S. imagery satellites," but these can be improved still further. "More frequent monitoring and processing of nuclear weapons programs, suppliers, and financial communications links" would increase chances of detection. A larger slice of the intelligence budget for nonproliferation efforts would help. Yet Richelson wisely cautions that the "hardware" can do only so much; the "software" also needs to be improved—more and better analysts would be welcome.

A forceful indictment of the IAEA is provided by David Kay, who documents an array of agency sins in chapter 14, "The IAEA: How Can It Be Strengthened?" Kay discounts the wisdom of creating a new institution to replace the IAEA, however, and instead urges a "reinvigorated IAEA" to help combat what he sees as the growing threat of nuclear proliferation. Kay recommends specific steps to strengthen both the IAEA safeguards system and the agency as a whole. He argues that it is necessary to change an organizational culture and management ethos that is too timid when conducting inspections; to extend safeguards procedures and approaches beyond materials accountancy and control of declared nuclear material to detect clandestine nuclear activities (or at least make such activities more costly and difficult); to reallocate limited budgetary resources to concentrate on those countries of particular proliferation concern; to equip inspectors with more sophisticated equipment; to make routine inspections more like special inspections, with greater freedom of movement among sites to be inspected; to insist on greater exchange of design information on nuclear facilities and on nuclear-related exports to certain countries; and to increase the IAEA's resources after ten years of zero budgetary growth.

In the concluding chapter, Mitchell Reiss provides an assessment of the state of the international nonproliferation regime after the cold war. Reiss addresses two central questions: How has the problem of nuclear proliferation changed? Is the spread of nuclear weapons more or less likely than before?

Reiss surveys both the positive and the negative developments of the past few years and analyzes the trends that have appeared. On balance, he judges that "efforts to prevent nuclear weapons spread stand at least as good a chance as before." Placing this view in historical context, he concludes, "The task of preventing the spread of nuclear weapons after the cold war will be very much like it was during the cold war—a pattern of quiet, gradual, and incremental successes punctuated by a few very public failures." The end of the cold war will not dissuade a small number of states from inaugurating or continuing efforts to construct nuclear arms. Their success and, to a lesser extent, their strivings will have serious ramifications for regional security and international stability. Whatever new challenges emerge or whatever accomplishments are realized during the next decade, the only certainty is that the problem of nuclear proliferation will not disappear.

Part I

Country and Regional Case Studies

Chapter 1

Iraq

Gary Samore

Overview

The revelations about Iraq's nuclear weapons program in the aftermath of the Gulf War were a strong shock to the international nonproliferation regime. As inspectors from the International Atomic Energy Agency (IAEA) began to sift through the rubble of Iraqi facilities and to examine Iraqi nuclear documents, it soon became obvious that Iraq's nuclear weapons program was far greater and more advanced than previously imagined. Despite growing suspicions about Iraq's nuclear ambitions in the late 1980s, its massive violations of the Nonproliferation Treaty (NPT) and safeguards went undetected, either by the IAEA or by national intelligence services. Moreover, prewar efforts by the United States and other countries to wean Saddam Hussein away from his nuclear ambitions, through a policy of diplomatic pressure and economic incentives, were revealed as ineffective. Even worse, much of Iraq's nuclear weapons program was based on extensive imports of Western equipment and materials, often obtained by circumventing export controls.

In hindsight, the case of Iraq represented a massive failure of the international nonproliferation regime and national nonproliferation policies; disaster was averted only by Saddam's invasion of Kuwait, which created the conditions for the destruction of Iraq's nuclear weapons program. This near-disaster shook confidence in the sanctity of the NPT, the effectiveness of IAEA safeguards, the strength of national and international export controls, and the effectiveness of national intelligence and policy instruments to detect efforts to acquire nuclear weapons and to deter countries from pursuing the acquisition of nuclear weapons. It gave ammunition to critics, who asserted that the nonproliferation regime was a hollow shell and in need of radical overhaul.

In response, the international community moved to correct perceived shortcomings in the safeguards and in the export control regimes that had been exposed by Iraq. IAEA safeguards have been strengthened to enhance the agency's authority and ability to inspect undeclared nuclear facilities, using special inspections and other techniques, such as environmental monitoring. In addition, the United Nations (UN) Security Council asserted its intention to take action in the case of a safeguards violation found by the IAEA. In the area of export controls, these lessons stimulated greater cooperation in enforcement and intelligence-sharing among suppliers and helped to cement consensus within the Nuclear Suppliers Group (NSG) to extend international controls to cover nuclear-related dual-use items. Most of these measures had been under consideration before 1991, but the shock of Iraq helped to build the necessary political consensus for action.

In addition to strengthening the regime, the international community reacted to the warning of Iraq by focusing greater attention on potential "Iraqs"—other countries suspected of violating or planning to violate their NPT obligations, countries such as North Korea and Iran. A strong international coalition has pressured North Korea to implement its NPT safeguards obligations and to complement international inspections with a regional regime, including bilateral inspections with South Korea and additional restrictions on nuclear activity, such as a ban on reprocessing and enrichment.

The lessons of Iraq also helped to stimulate greater international interest in trying to untie the Gordian knot blocking the establishment of nonproliferation arrangements in South Asia and the Middle East. Both regions present formidable problems of rolling back advanced nuclear programs in Israel, India, and Pakistan, which are intertwined with deeply felt convictions of national security and stature. Nonetheless, Iraq underscored the need to seek a political solution to nuclear proliferation in the Middle East and to give increased attention to South Asia as the region closest to an open nuclear arms race. Moreover, the end of the cold war has helped to facilitate international and regional arms control efforts in both regions. Although substantial progress to resolve the nuclear issue in either the Middle East or South Asia is unlikely in the near term, a number of interesting proposals have been put forward, including ideas for "capping" existing nuclear programs, and regional parties have shown some increased willingness to talk, both to each other and to outside parties.

The Case of Iraq

The United States originally began to suspect Iraq's nuclear intentions back in the mid-1970s when Iraq used its newfound oil wealth to obtain large turnkey projects from Western European suppliers, mainly France and Italy. This suggested that Iraq might be seeking to develop the basis for a plutonium route to the bomb. In response, the United States successfully persuaded European suppliers to limit additional assistance to Iraq and supported a rigorous safeguards regime for the Osirak research reactor.

By the early 1980s, concern about Iraq's nuclear ambitions had dissipated, due to Israel's destruction of the Osirak reactor (the only source of significant plutonium production in Iraq), Iraq's preoccupation with the war with Iran, and the growing reluctance of suppliers to provide nuclear assistance. During 1988–89, however, there were increasing indications that Iraq was trying to revive its nuclear weapons ambitions. In particular, evidence became available that Iraqi procurement agents were seeking to obtain equipment and materials useful for gas centrifuge development, which would enable Iraq to pursue the uranium route to the bomb.

The response, from the United States and other countries, was to organize efforts to break up Iraqi smuggling rings and to apply direct diplomatic pressure on Baghdad by warning Iraq that its relations with the outside world would be damaged if Iraq did not cease suspicious nuclear activities. Iraq, of course, steadfastly denied that it had any intention of acquiring nuclear weapons or violating its obligations under the NPT.

The conventional wisdom at the time, which was shared by all key countries, was that Iraq's gas centrifuge program was at a relatively early stage of research and development and that the combination of export controls and political pressure had time to contain the threat. Even after Iraq invaded Kuwait in August 1990, the only perceived short-term threat was that Iraq might be able to make some kind of crude nuclear device by diverting a small quantity of safeguarded highly enriched uranium (HEU) research reactor fuel, which it had acquired from France and the USSR.

After the war, it gradually became clear that Iraq's nuclear weapons program was far larger and more advanced than the world realized. In particular, Iraq had invested tremendous resources in a calutron or electromagnetic isotope separation (EMIS) program that put it only a few years away from building nuclear weapons. In hindsight, it is clear that Iraq's nuclear weapons program had probably reached the stage where export controls and political measures alone could not have stopped it.

Ironically, Saddam's invasion of Kuwait created the opportunity to short-circuit his nuclear ambitions. During the war, coalition partners destroyed and damaged many key nuclear installations, including the two calutron production complexes at Tarmyia and Ash-Sharqat. After the war, the UN imposed an extensive nuclear disarmament regime, embodied in UN Security Council Resolutions 687, 707, and 715.

Resolution 687 authorized the IAEA, with the assistance of the UN Special Commission, to conduct unlimited inspections in Iraq and to "destroy, remove, or render harmless" facilities and equipment associated with Iraq's nuclear weapons program. Resolution 707 required Iraq to cease all nuclear activities until the terms of 687 were fulfilled. Resolution 715 imposed on Iraq a long-term monitoring system, including challenge inspections and sharp restrictions on nuclear activities, such as a ban on all reprocessing and enrichment programs.

Implementation of these resolutions has been impressive, despite constant Iraqi efforts to frustrate and obstruct international inspections. To date, there have been twenty-one nuclear inspections, scrutiny of many Iraqi nuclear documents, removal of key materials, such as the French-supplied HEU, and destruction of key equipment and facilities, such as the nuclear weapons complex at Al-Atheer. At this point, it is unlikely that any significant nuclear facilities have escaped detection and neutralization, although we will probably never be able to say with confidence that every scrap of equipment has been eliminated. Gaps also remain in our knowledge of Iraq's procurement system and external sources of technical information, but Iraq has recently begun to provide procurement documentation, which the IAEA is evaluating for accuracy and completeness.

Despite this progress, most observers believe that Saddam Hussein continues to harbor ambitions to revive Iraq's nuclear capability, along with his conventional forces and other weapons of mass destruction. Even the most rigorous application of UN Security Council Resolution 687 will not destroy Iraq's basic technological and economic infrastructure, including dual-use equipment, which could be used to revive Iraq's nuclear program. Moreover, Iraq still retains its most valuable nuclear asset: skilled scientists and engineers who possess the knowledge necessary to reconstruct Iraq's nuclear weapons program in the future.

Accordingly, the chief challenge for the IAEA and the UN Special Commission is implementation of an effective long-term monitoring system under Security Council Resolution 715, which includes environmental-monitoring techniques, resident inspectors, challenge inspections, and a system for monitoring and tracking dual-use imports. As economic sanctions against Iraq are lifted, the ability of the IAEA and the UN Special Commission to ensure that Iraq's nuclear ambitions remain in check will depend heavily on the continued willingness of the UN Security Council to enforce long-term monitoring, including the threat to reimpose sanctions and, if necessary, use force to deter or defeat a revival of Iraq's nuclear weapons program. In the longer term, progress toward regional arms control arrangements, such as a freeze on production of fissile material and the eventual establishment of a nuclear weapons free zone (NWFZ) in the Middle East, may help to provide additional political constraints on Iraq's nuclear ambitions.

Lessons of Iraq for IAEA Safeguards

The IAEA safeguards system has focused primarily on detecting the diversion of a significant quantity of nuclear material from peaceful to military purposes. In a country that is an NPT party with full-scope safeguards, this means that IAEA safeguards are intended to verify that no significant amount of nuclear material is available for the acquisition of a nuclear device.

Iraq highlighted the danger that a country could circumvent its NPT safeguards obligations by developing and building clandestine nuclear facilities entirely outside of its declared nuclear program. In addition, Iraq demonstrated that the IAEA needed to be able to draw from information outside its own resources, including intelligence from member states, in order to determine whether a country is violating its safeguards commitments. Finally, Iraq underscored the need to reaffirm the IAEA's authority to refer safeguards violations to the UN Security Council, which is empowered to address international treaty violations.

In response, the IAEA Secretariat and the IAEA Board of Governors have taken several steps to strengthen safeguards. Most important, at the December 1991 and February 1992 meetings of the IAEA Board of Governors, the board affirmed the IAEA's statutory authority to request a "special inspection" of undeclared nuclear facilities if the director general believes that such an inspection is necessary for the agency to fully verify that all nuclear materials are under safeguards. In making such a determination, the director general has announced that the agency will rely on all available information, including information from member states.

On a political level, the relationship between the IAEA and the UN Security Council has also been reaffirmed. If a country refuses the request for a special inspection, the director general is entitled to report this refusal to the UN secretary general, and the board, on finding that a country is in noncompliance with its safeguards obligations, is required to report this fact to the UN General Assembly and Security Council for appropriate action. For its part, the Security Council, in a statement by heads of government in January 1992, asserted the importance of the IAEA safeguards system and stated that the members of the council would take "appropriate measures" if notified of a safeguards violation by the IAEA.

Beyond breathing new life into the "special inspection" provision, the IAEA is in the process of taking measures to improve the IAEA's ability to detect clandestine nuclear activity. In February 1992, the board approved a measure to call on member states to provide the IAEA with advanced information on the design of planned nuclear facilities and modifications of existing facilities. The board has also approved arrangements for nuclear suppliers to provide the IAEA with information on imports and exports of nuclear material and equipment, information that can yield clues to possible undeclared nuclear activity.

In addition to stimulating specific safeguards measures, Iraq also provided a "culture shock" for the IAEA. However unfairly, the IAEA found itself under attack as incompetent or, even worse, naive and afraid to question suspected proliferators. With the support of the international community, the agency has developed a healthier, tougher, and more skeptical attitude. Certainly, the agency's performance in Iraq has demonstrated its ability to carry out difficult inspections under harsh conditions. International confidence in the IAEA has been strengthened due to the agency's performance in Iraq and its use of innovative approaches to implement full-scope safeguards in countries that had previously operated unsafeguarded facilities, such as North Korea and South Africa.

In addition, the agency has become more active in developing novel measures to deal with new safeguards challenges. This is especially evident in the IAEA's efforts to verify the nuclear inventories of countries like South Africa and North Korea, which have operated unsafeguarded nuclear facilities before accepting full-scope safeguards, and countries like Iran, which are suspected of violating their safeguards obligations. In these cases, Director General Hans Blix has sought a political commitment to allow the agency to "visit" any facility it requests, and agency inspectors are using a variety of technical measurements and the study of historical records to implement full-scope safeguards. In addition, the IAEA is examining the use of new technologies, such as environmental monitoring, to enhance its ability to detect undeclared nuclear activities.

Lessons of Iraq for Export Controls

The international export control system focuses on regulating commerce in especially designed and prepared nuclear material and equipment, as defined in the Zangger or NPT Exporters Committee trigger list and the Nuclear Suppliers Group guidelines. Iraq highlighted the danger of a country that evades the intent of these controls by obtaining raw materials, dual-use equipment, and technology to use in manufacturing its own nuclear capability, such as components for calutrons and gas centrifuge machines. In addition, Iraq's successful establishment of clandestine procurement networks around the world exposed some embarrassing loopholes and enforcement problems in various national export control systems. Finally, Iraq illustrated how difficult it is in a closed society to determine whether dual-use technology has been diverted from civilian to military use.

Responding to these lessons, the key nuclear suppliers revived the Nuclear Suppliers Group, which held its first formal meeting in twelve years at the Hague in March 1991. In the intervening years, there had been a number of informal meetings of some NSG parties to discuss matters of common concern, but there had been no consensus to hold a formal meeting, partly because some NSG members feared that developing countries would strongly oppose the appearance of a suppliers cartel. Even before the Gulf War, concern about Iraq's procurement activities had helped to overcome these objections among suppliers. As additional revelations about Iraq came to light, suppliers realized that the regime needed reinforcement and expansion.

The key nuclear suppliers have rejected the argument made by some that Iraq discredited peaceful nuclear cooperation as an essential element of the regime, but the lesson of Iraq did help to reinforce international acceptance of stricter conditions for peaceful cooperation. By the time of the March 1992 meeting in Warsaw, the NSG had been able to reach agreement on a regime designed to prevent the export of nuclear-related dual-use items to nuclear weapons programs or unsafeguarded nuclear facilities. The NSG also declared a common policy of requiring full-scope safeguards as a condition for significant nuclear supply, which is an important measure to deny the benefits of peaceful nuclear cooperation to countries that have not joined the nonproliferation regime. The Zangger Committee has continued its work to refine and update its trigger lists, including work to control chemical enrichment and EMIS technology. The lesson of Iraq also stimulated efforts by key countries, such as Germany, to tighten controls and improve enforcement and supported a greater willingness among suppliers to share intelligence and enforcement efforts.

Drawing from the increased interest in export controls caused by Iraq, President George Bush proposed in May 1991 that the

United States, Russia, France, the United Kingdom, and China meet to discuss common guidelines for both conventional arms transfers and exports of weapons of mass destruction technology to the Middle East. After a series of meetings, the five countries agreed in May 1992 to a set of guidelines related to weapons of mass destruction, including nuclear technology. Although China was not prepared to join the other four countries in agreeing to require full-scope safeguards as a condition of supply for nuclear cooperation, the five did agree to "exercise restraint" in the transfer of sensitive nuclear facilities, technology, and weapons-usable materials. In addition, the five agreed not to export equipment and materials that could be used in the manufacture of nuclear weapons-usable materials (i.e., dual-use items) except when satisfied that the items in question would not contribute to the development of nuclear weapons or to unsafeguarded nuclear activities. Thus, China committed itself to observe, in principle, nuclear export rules that approximate some of the NSG guidelines.

Further efforts to formally engage China in the international regime, however, have proved unsuccessful. Protesting U.S. arms sales to Taiwan, China has withdrawn from further meetings of the permanent members of the UN Security Council on the Middle East and continues to pursue nuclear sales to countries without full-scope safeguards (in the case of Pakistan) and to countries of dubious nonproliferation credentials (in the case of Iran). The collapse of the Soviet Union poses an even greater challenge to the international export regime. Despite efforts by the states of the former Soviet Union to develop and install effective export control systems, the potential for leakage and smuggling of nuclear expertise, technology, and even nuclear materials remains high. In addition, the economic hardships caused by the collapse of the Soviet Union have increased pressures for nuclear sales abroad, as in the case of Russia's agreement to provide nuclear power and research reactors to Iran.

Iraq also serves as a reminder of the limits of export controls as an instrument of nonproliferation policy. For exporters, high-technology sales to developing countries are seen as a mechanism to achieve both political influence and commercial gain. Although there may be agreement to bar any nuclear or dual-use assistance to suspicious nuclear programs, it is much more difficult to achieve international agreement to totally embargo all dual-use exports, especially if there is little concrete evidence that items sold for civilian uses are being diverted or if the information on a country's nuclear ambitions is ambiguous. Inevitably, as developing countries expand their industrial and scientific infrastructure, the utility of export controls begins to diminish.

Preventing Future Iraqs

In addition to strengthening the regime, the international community reacted to the lessons of Iraq by focusing greater pressure on countries suspected of violating or planning to violate their NPT obligations, such as North Korea and Iran. The UN Security Council's action to disarm and punish Iraq—a country found in violation of its NPT commitments—created a clear precedent for concerted international action and a strong warning to those suspected of disregarding their NPT commitments.

THE DEMOCRATIC PEOPLE'S REPUBLIC OF KOREA (DPRK)

North Korea was widely seen as the next major challenge for the NPT regime and as a test case for the IAEA's strengthened safeguards system. Despite its accession to the treaty in 1985, North Korea refused to implement full-scope safeguards, and unlike the case of Iraq before the Gulf War, there was indisputable evidence that North Korea had developed unsafeguarded facilities that could contribute to the development of a nuclear weapons capability. Accordingly, pressure on North Korea was stepped up throughout 1991, including thinly veiled references to Security Council action if North Korea did not fulfill its NPT safeguards obligations. North Korea, however, claimed that it could not conclude a full-scope safeguards agreement until its concerns about the "U.S. nuclear threat" were addressed.

By the end of 1991, North Korea began to respond to a combination of increasing international pressures and unilateral gestures from the United States and the Republic of Korea (ROK), including the withdrawal of U.S. nuclear weapons from South Korea and Seoul's willingness to suspend the U.S./ROK joint military exercise "Team Spirit" in 1992. In early 1992, the DPRK finally signed and ratified a full-scope safeguards agreement with the IAEA, and the agency began conducting inspections in May 1992 to verify the completeness and accuracy of North Korea's declared inventory of nuclear material, including a small quantity of plutonium. To reinforce its bona fides, the DPRK also volunteered to let the IAEA "visit" any site it requested. In addition, North and South Korea reached an agreement in December 1991 on a Denuclearization Declaration, which included provisions for a bilateral inspection regime to complement IAEA safeguards and a ban on reprocessing and enrichment facilities.

Despite this apparent breakthrough in late 1991 and early 1992, North Korea emerged as an even greater issue in 1993 when it threatened to withdraw from the NPT after the IAEA found it in noncompliance with its safeguards agreement. Based on analysis of samples taken during its rigorous inspections of North Korea in 1992, the IAEA detected "discrepancies" suggesting that North Korea had produced more plutonium than the small amount declared to the IAEA. In addition, the United States provided evidence to the IAEA from satellite imagery showing apparent North Korean efforts to disguise and conceal two nuclear waste sites, which might contain evidence of additional reprocessing.

In late 1992, the IAEA sought access to the suspect waste sites under the terms of the DPRK's voluntary offer to accept IAEA "visits" at any site. When the DPRK refused, claiming that the sites were "military facilities unrelated to its nuclear program," IAEA Director General Blix formally requested a special inspection in December 1992. North Korea rejected the IAEA request, and the IAEA Board of Governors met in a historic special meeting in February 1993, giving the DPRK one month to comply with the IAEA's request. In March, North Korea responded by announcing its intention to withdraw from the NPT, citing as reasons the U.S. "nuclear threat" and the IAEA's "partiality." Undeterred, the IAEA board met again in April, finding North Korea in noncompliance with its safeguards obligations and reporting this noncompliance to the UN Security Council. Supporting the IAEA's authority, the UN Security Council adopted a resolution on May 11, 1993, calling on North Korea to honor its nonproliferation obligations and requesting member states to assist in this effort.

On this basis, the United States subsequently engaged in lengthy negotiations with North Korea in an effort to persuade North Korea to remain in the NPT, to cooperate with the IAEA, to comply with full-scope safeguards, and to implement the North-South Denuclearization Declaration. In the course of formal U.S.-DPRK talks in New York in June and in Geneva in July, as well as numerous working-level meetings in New York, North Korea agreed to "suspend" its withdrawal from the NPT, refrain from additional reprocessing, and accept IAEA inspections required to maintain continuity of safeguards. The United States offered to improve relations with North Korea if it complied with its nonproliferation obligations but declared that the United States would end the talks and seek Security Council sanctions if North Korea violated any of these commitments.

Whatever the ultimate outcome of the U.S.-DPRK talks, the North Korean case established several essential precedents for a stronger post-Iraq safeguards system. First, it signaled a greater willingness by intelligence services to provide information to the IAEA and helped to legitimize the use of such information by the IAEA in the application of safeguards. Second, the IAEA Board of Governors affirmed that special inspections are an integral part of a country's full-scope safeguards obligations under the NPT and strongly supported the director general's authority to request special inspections on the basis of personal judgment. Finally, the North Korean case marked the first time that the UN Security Council took action against a country found in noncompliance with its safeguards agreement by the IAEA Board of Governors.

IRAN

Iran represents a different challenge for the international community. As far as one can tell, Iran's strategy seems to be the acquisition of a broad-based nuclear infrastructure under safeguards and not—at least not yet—the development of clandestine nuclear facilities as in the cases of North Korea or Iraq. Dating back to the shah, Iran has had an interest in developing nuclear energy for peaceful purposes. Nonetheless, there is a strong basis for suspecting that the Iranian leadership is interested in developing a nuclear weapons capability, both as a hedge against the possible revival of Iraq's program and as a route to Iran's larger ambitions of becoming the dominant power in the region.

Although it is difficult to organize an international coalition on the basis of suspicion, the lesson of Iraq has helped to persuade most nuclear suppliers not to provide any substantial assistance to Iran until it has become clear that Iran intends to live up to its NPT commitments. In addition to Western suppliers,

Argentina, India, and Pakistan have apparently decided against cooperation with Iran. China has provided some research equipment to Iran, such as a zero-power research reactor and a calutron, but this equipment is not capable of producing any significant quantity of nuclear weapons material. Although China and Russia have agreed in principle to build power reactors in Iran, it remains unclear whether political, technical, and financial obstacles to these sales can be overcome. In any event, these projects would take many years to complete and would provide no direct technical contribution to a weapons capability. Without external assistance in the fuel cycle area, Iran's nuclear program can make only slow progress.

Moreover, the international community has tried to put Iran on notice that any effort to move in the direction of acquiring nuclear weapons will have severe consequences for Iran's relations with the outside world. It is hard to read the thinking in Tehran, but it appears that at least some Iranians are well aware of this danger and have made efforts to reassure the world that Iran does not seek to acquire nuclear weapons. Many Iranians believe that the treatment of Iraq could be repeated against them if a nuclear weapons program comes to light. Partly to deflect suspicions about its nuclear program, Iran agreed in June 1992 to allow the IAEA to "visit" any site that it requested. The IAEA made a surprise visit in November 1993. Not surprisingly, given the state of Iran's nuclear development, the IAEA found nothing untoward, but the precedent may prove valuable in the future if concrete evidence does emerge of unsafeguarded facilities in Iran.

Arms Control in the Middle East and South Asia

Finally, Iraq helped to focus international attention on the need to seek regional political solutions to the extremely difficult issues of nuclear proliferation in South Asia and the Middle East. In the Middle East, the example of Iraq served two purposes. First, from an Arab standpoint, initiation of a regional arms control process was seen as essential to sustain political support for the UN Security Council Resolution 687 restrictions on Iraq and to avert criticism that Iraq was being singled out while other nuclear weapons programs in the region went unchecked. Second, from an Israeli standpoint, Iraq drove home the point that ultimately a political solution would be necessary to end the threat of nuclear proliferation in the region. In particular, it did not appear credible that Iraq's long-term capabilities could be denied, either by restrictions on its basic industrial and scientific development or by repeated military action.

Thus, the parties in the region were relatively amenable to some discussion of regional nonproliferation issues in the aftermath of the Gulf War. To stimulate ideas for consideration, President Bush announced a package of arms control ideas for the Middle East in May 1991. In the nuclear area, the United States proposed that the countries in the region agree to implement a verifiable ban on the production of nuclear weapons usable material, as a first step toward the establishment of an NWFZ. The president also reiterated longstanding U.S. support for all countries in the region to accede to the NPT and to place all nuclear facilities under IAEA safeguards.

Not surprisingly, the U.S. suggestion for a nuclear materials production ban did not entirely please all sides. Some Arabs were concerned that a "freeze" might grant Israel a permanent nuclear advantage, since Israel was assumed to have already produced a substantial quantity of nuclear materials. Some Israelis feared that acceptance of a "freeze," which would require the shutdown of operations at the Dimona nuclear reactor, would only escalate demands for Israel to join the NPT or accept an NWFZ.

Nonetheless, the revival of the Arab-Israeli peace process in 1991 did provide the opportunity to initiate multilateral Arms Control and Regional Security (ACRS) talks among some regional states and outside parties. The ACRS process has included both plenary sessions, alternating between Washington and Moscow, and a series of "international events," such as a verification workshop held in Cairo in July 1993. These talks provide a valuable forum for discussions on a range of potential confidence-building measures and possible arms control agreements in the region, but it is important not to raise unrealistic expectations for near-term success, especially in the nuclear area.

Establishment of an NWFZ in the region is a key long-term objective, since it will not likely be possible until a secure settlement of the Arab-Israeli conflict has been achieved. In fact, premature efforts to "solve" the nuclear problem could easily complicate the search for peace and encourage efforts to link other issues, such as implementation of the Chemical Weapons Convention (CWC) or extension of the NPT, to a nuclear solution. If substantial progress is made on the Arab-Israeli front, however, and if the nuclear programs of Iran and Iraq are stymied, it may be possible to secure some concrete interim steps in the nuclear area.

South Asia remains the region where the danger of an open nuclear arms race and where potential nuclear escalation of a local war is greatest. In two respects, Iraq helped to focus renewed efforts to break the longstanding diplomatic stalemate between India and Pakistan on nuclear issues. Pakistan has offered to take steps only on a reciprocal basis with India, including joining the NPT and establishing an NWFZ in the region, whereas India continues to insist that neither the NPT nor a South Asian NWFZ addresses broader issues of global equality and India's larger security concerns, such as China.

First, the greater international focus on nonproliferation and the strengthening of the regime that followed in the wake of Iraq has put India more on the defensive. Aware of its political isolation on this issue and the danger of potential economic penalties, India has, at least, tried to exhibit more flexibility and may be willing to take some interim steps to restrict its own nuclear program short of its longstanding demand for global disarmament. Second, the reaction to Iraq helped to reinforce in both India and Pakistan a clear sense that the international community would be strongly opposed if either openly declared its nuclear capabilities or contributed to proliferation by assisting other countries.

Even more than the example of Iraq, the end of the cold war may offer some new opportunities for diplomacy in South Asia. Freed from the constraints of the cold war, the United States and other declared nuclear weapons states have greater flexibility and incentive to undertake unilateral arms control steps and to pursue global arms control measures, such as a Comprehensive Test Ban, Convention on the Cutoff of Fissile Material Production, and more formal arrangements for Negative Security Assurances and No First Use pledges. Progress in these areas can provide new openings to restrain the nuclear weapons programs in India and Pakistan. For example, India and Pakistan might be persuaded to refrain from testing and to suspend further production of unsafeguarded fissile material, pending the negotiation of nondiscriminatory and universal treaties in these areas.

Conclusion

Iraq's near-acquisition of nuclear weapons, along with the end of the cold war, raised the priority of nuclear proliferation on the international agenda and created concerns that the nonproliferation regime was in danger of collapse. Some warned that Iraq was a harbinger of the future and that the world was poised on the brink of an epidemic of nuclear proliferation. The international community responded to the revelations about Iraq's nuclear program in three ways. First, IAEA safeguards and export controls were strengthened to correct weaknesses that Iraq had exploited. Second, international pressure was increased on other countries suspected of NPT violations, such as North Korea and Iran. Third, renewed attention was paid to seeking political solutions to the nuclear proliferation problems in the Middle East and South Asia.

In fact, only a handful of countries present serious nuclear proliferation concerns today. If anything, the number has dwindled in the last two years, due to developments entirely independent of Iraq. In Latin America, Argentina and Brazil have reached an agreement to implement both bilateral and IAEA full-scope safeguards and are moving to bring the Treaty of Tlatelolco into force. South Africa has joined the NPT and accepted full-scope safeguards, opening the way for the establishment of an NWFZ in all of Africa.

Despite all of these achievements, however, much remains to be done. Perhaps the most important task facing the regime is extension of the NPT in 1995. There is a good chance to achieve indefinite extension if attempts to hold extension hostage to regional disputes or global disarmament schemes can be defeated. Adequate technical assistance, political support, and financial resources must be provided to enable the IAEA to meet its expanded mandate and growing safeguards obligations. Implementation of export controls requires constant attention, both to deny technology to countries with suspect records and to extend peaceful nuclear cooperation to those with proven nonproliferation credentials. We also need to persuade additional countries, especially China and the states of the former Soviet Union, to join the export control regime.

Of all the country-specific proliferation issues, Ukraine and North Korea are clearly the most important, both in terms of implications for regional security in Europe and the Far East and in terms of consequences for the global regime. The January 1994 agreement among the United States, Russia, and Ukraine to remove and dismantle nuclear warheads on Ukrainian territory is a significant achievement, which clears the way for Ukraine to join the NPT as a nonnuclear weapons state, but it remains unclear whether the agreement can be implemented, given domestic political factors in both Kiev and Moscow and the persistent sources of suspicion and tension between the two. The resolution of the North Korean issue is also in doubt. Diplomatic efforts by the United States and others have succeeded in freezing the situation, but it is uncertain whether North Korea can ultimately be persuaded and pressured to give up its nuclear weapons option and rejoin the regime.

Gains in Latin America and Africa must be consolidated by ensuring complete implementation of IAEA full-scope safeguards in Argentina, Brazil, and South Africa and by supporting the establishment of regional regimes to complement and support IAEA safeguards. In the Middle East, a successful strategy must maintain a strong international coalition to prevent the revival or emergence of a nuclear weapons capability in Iraq and Iran while encouraging dialogue and confidence-building measures in the region to improve long-term prospects for the establishment of a regional NFWZ that includes Israel. The solution to nuclear proliferation in South Asia also represents a long-term problem. However, success in dampening regional tensions between India and Pakistan, as well as engaging India in a broader multilateral arms control process, could improve prospects for controlling nuclear developments in the region.

Ultimately, the solution to these nuclear proliferation problems is political. Export controls and threats of sanctions are important holding actions, but the most important objective in the long term is to convince countries that it is not in their own interests to acquire nuclear weapons. Inevitably, this means addressing the underlying motivations—those of security and status—that drive countries to seek nuclear weapons in the first place. On these issues, Saddam Hussein provided an invaluable service to the international community. By serving as a warning of what might have been, he has given the international community greater reason and resources to deal with the threat.

The views expressed here are solely those of the author and do not necessarily reflect those of the Department of State or the U.S. government.

Chapter 2

The Middle East

Shahram Chubin

The first crises just before, and just after, the cold war were in the Middle East. Each had global ramifications, but the more recent one also had a strong nuclear dimension to it. This chapter deals with the prospects for nuclear proliferation in that region. Given the record, modesty is called for. In the past we have systematically predicted a faster pace of proliferation than has, in fact, occurred. We have been and remain unsure about the relative importance of technical and political considerations or the weight of global and regional elements in states' decisions. Generally, since the 1970s our emphasis has been on nonsignatories to the Nonproliferation Treaty (NPT) and on the close relationship between a large nuclear energy program and the requirements for nuclear weapons, that is, on how a large "peaceful" program could generate significant amounts of fissile material (within the rules, as Albert Wohlstetter and others noted), which could be diverted fairly quickly into a weapons program.

Iraq was a surprise, a signatory that cheated by simply not declaring nuclear materials and facilities rather than diverting from safeguarded sites. Indeed, the latter were used to divert attention and reassure outsiders. Since then, there has been much emphasis on NPT signatories that might be avoiding their obligations. Today there is a certain tendency to overcompensate for this failure by seeing cheating proliferators everywhere and generalizing the case. This is understandable on two levels: bureaucrats cannot afford to be caught short twice, and the risks of exaggeration are small compared with another failure. Academics likewise sense their time has come—their fifteen minutes of fleeting glory is at hand.

Nonproliferation is a global and principally a South-South issue, not a subject for unilateral U.S. policy or a North-South confrontation. It is not a subject suited to a crusade. The Iraqi case should not be generalized, precisely because it was so exceptional: Iraq was rich, ambitious, with a grievance and able to camouflage its crash program under cover of the conventional war it was fighting. The need for a multileveled policy to deal with the variety of motives impelling states toward nuclear weapons cannot be a shortcut for convenience or from exasperation. Policy that is patient, firm, and broad-based will be more effective in producing results.

Predictions are hazardous but acquire in retrospect heuristic value. One example suffices. An analyst in 1977 looked at "a very probable 1990 descendant" of the Middle East situation as he saw it:

> A deployed Israeli nuclear force with a minimum 30–40 devices of various kiloton yields atop mobile SRBM's, supersonic fighter-bombers and possibly cruise missiles and RPV's . . .
>
> An Arab nuclear force of 10–15 devices in the twenty kiloton range deployed in Egypt, Syria and Iraq, deliverable by mobile Scaleboard SRBM's and medium-range bombers with or without air-launched cruise missiles, and subject to centralized command and control . . .
>
> An Iranian nuclear force of 20–30 weapons in the twenty-kiloton range carried by supersonic fighter bombers . . .
>
> Though Iranian proliferation may be induced by weapons programs in the Arab-Israeli theater, Iranian planning and deployments are likely to be primarily directed toward the Indian subcontinent and the Soviet Union and only collaterally toward the Persian Gulf countries. The strategic linkages between the Iranian-Iraqi-Saudi relationship on the one hand, and the Arab-Israeli nuclear context on the other will be tenuous and purposely de-emphasized by

Iran, which would have no interest in becoming involved in an Arab-Israeli nuclear exchange.[1]

The striking point about this prediction is how far the *political* (as opposed to technical) characteristics have turned out differently. Israel has not changed its "bomb in the basement" approach; the "Arabs" have never been more disunited; one has made peace while the others have been at virtual war for a decade; and Iran (which has yet to finish one power reactor) is focused primarily on the Persian Gulf and Arab-Israeli fronts and has seen the United States, rather than the now defunct USSR, as the principal threat for the past dozen years.

Although on the face of it, the durability of conflict apparently makes political extrapolations relatively safe, leaving only the question of technical capability unclear, the reality is different. Not only threat perceptions but also priorities and alignments are susceptible to change; it is the political dimension of proliferation decisions that should preoccupy us. If, as seems likely over the coming years, the diffusion of knowledge and engineering skills having nuclear applications appears inexorable—and with it the growth of infrastructure useful for nuclear weapons development—it would be wise not to put too much emphasis on the technical side or on policies of "denial." As capabilities are enhanced, political will becomes even more important, indeed becomes the chief determinant of the decisions on whether to "go" or not go toward nuclear weapons. This chapter concentrates on the factors bearing on political will.

The Politics of the Middle East

The Middle East is considered one of the most sensitive regions from the point of view of proliferation, with states relatively low in capability but high in risk. Proliferation here could threaten nearby Europe and the security of allies (Israel and Turkey), as well as access to the region's oil resources. Islamic fundamentalism, which has been growing in the region, is a source of concern, and it, together with the absence of democracy, is seen as a potentially destabilizing force. The region is seen as alien, not sharing and even hostile to Western values and opposed to the Western order (political, economic, and cultural) in which the inhabitants perceive themselves victims and dispossessed.

As viewed from the West, the absence of democracy is not simply an abstract issue concerning values; it affects and reflects societies that are more prone to use force domestically and have fewer checks on its use externally. Insecure, unstable, and illegitimate, these states have succession problems and are more politically volatile than democratic states. Furthermore, closed, secretive societies are the reverse of what is needed to build trust and confidence, namely openness and transparency between states.

The scene of repeated wars, the Middle East is also one of the most militarized areas in the world, whether by reference to gross military or per capita expenditures, arms imports, manpower under arms, or concentration of weapons of mass destruction and missiles. There clearly is some relationship among the type of society, militarization, and propensity for the use of force: insecurity stimulates the need for arms and military leaders, and the latter seek to buttress their standing by resorting to arms.

The West tends to see the differences in values and systems and the hostility of some in the region to Israel and the West as especially dangerous. There is much loose talk about irrational leaders, crazy states, undeterrable threats, and different pain thresholds. The specter of an "Islamic bomb" or nuclear-armed terrorists is easily conjured up from this complex of alien values and hostility, leading some to advocate decapitation strategies. Exaggerating differences can be counterproductive, making acquisition more desirable to other states and eroding restraints on use by demonizing the "enemy."

The Middle East is riven by multiple axes of overlapping conflict: Arab-Israel, Arab-Arab, Arab-Iran—to name a few. The wars in the region in the past decade have included at least one of each type. Thus, there is no dominant but several conflicts or arms races at any one time. There is always the potential for a domino effect, including nuclear proliferation. Consider the probable reactions of Egypt, Syria, and Iran if Iraq had acquired and kept a nuclear capability; it would have been much more severe than it has been to Israel. To some extent, then, the "fear of being second" vis-à-vis others still exists in the region separate from Israel's position or lead.

Political instability and change can fundamentally reorient a state, making it overnight a candidate for nuclear proliferation. Consider Iran's reorientation in 1979, which changed a state with strong incentives for good ties with the West to one adamantly rejecting any ties. Algeria today constitutes a potentially similar case. Political change in Egypt could alter most regional calculations. Similarly, such change can alter alliances and regional priorities.

Another characteristic of the region is its asymmetries in wealth, population, size, and military potential. Especially important here is Israel, which has sought to compensate for its lack of space and population by acquiring advanced armaments, including nuclear weapons, to maintain a qualitative edge. This, at least on some level, is bound to act as a goad to other states, which, refusing to accept permanent "inferiority," seek equivalent arms. A similar dynamic was evident in Iraq's policies of 1988–90 and now in the Persian Gulf (so far without nuclear arms) in the policies of the Arab states vis-à-vis Iran and Iraq. Asymmetries may encourage nuclear weapons as the ultimate "equalizer."

Repeated conflicts, political instability, and large arms stocks make the outbreak of wars likely. The nuclearization of the Middle East contains special dangers because it threatens to involve Western interests and allies directly. How has this been affected by the end of the cold war, and what is the regional setting?

After the Cold War

The effect of the end of the cold war on nuclear proliferation has been uneven. The legacy of nuclear weapons during those tensions and in contributing to their end remains ambiguous. Nuclear weapons were held (or "used") by the West to offset and deter superior conventional forces. Possession of nuclear weapons infused restraint into every superpower encounter. A code of conduct evolved. It became clear that the principal and possibly only utility of nuclear weapons was in deterring other nuclear weapons. With the end of the cold war, arms control between the two principal nuclear powers will reduce the stocks of nuclear weapons and contribute to the impression that they are of limited value in day-to-day diplomacy. This has already been evident in the focus on new attributes of power, such as economic issues.

In the post-cold war era, the risks of nuclear war have shifted to the peripheries. The threat now is of a nuclear arms race (or war) between two southern states or between a large and a new (or aspiring) nuclear power, rather than between two nuclear giants. The threat is different in another way: one cannot assume a "rational-actor" model for all of these states, and the risk of unauthorized or accidental use is higher than it was between the superpowers.

The motives of regional states have not been fundamentally affected by the ending of the cold war. Regional tensions and instabilities remain. There is no shared feeling that the use of force is counterproductive or abhorrent. The bloc structure that contained local conflicts in Europe did not have a similar effect in the Middle East. But the end of the Soviet Union has taken away a dependable provider of arms, or a diplomatic supporter to some states (such as Syria), leaving the United States as the unchallenged power in the region. This unipolar world, together with its possible impact in favoring Israel, was evoked as a threat and criticized by Saddam Hussein (in a speech to other Arab states in Amman in January 1990) and may well have been a factor in his subsequent calculations. The new fluidity of international politics might have given the impression of new regional vacuums, with things "up-for-grabs," something that someone like Saddam Hussein would see as an opportunity and invitation to act.

Uncertainty about access to arms or the means to balance Israel could lead to one of two responses: a willingness to compromise and negotiate, or a search for countermeasures such as unconventional arms or nuclear weapons. The end of the cold war may have encouraged a search for such alternatives, a direction that might have been accelerated by the overwhelming victory of the United States in the conventional war against Iraq. The Persian Gulf War may have reinforced the conclusion that since the conventional means are unavailable and probably ineffectual, better to go for nuclear weapons to deter the United States or Israel. An additional motive is the high cost of conventional weapons; the expectation that nuclear weapons could substitute for (or improve on) expensive and hard-to-get conventional weapons would imply lowering the threshold of the use of nuclear weapons.

There has been much speculation about whether countries like Iran, Syria, Algeria, or Libya could obtain nuclear weapons components, technology, or expertise from the disintegration of the Soviet Union and thus speed up any national programs they might have. Doubtless, efforts have been made in this regard, just as the United States and Germany have sought to provide the means to keep nuclear experts employed in Russia. At the same time there is now a greater consciousness about nonproliferation and more resources devoted to it. National intelligence agencies, tighter legislation, and improved international cooperation all make attempts to evade controls more problematic, especially for specifically targeted "sensitive countries."

For states like Iran and Syria, the end of the cold war could be the beginning of a new era of insecurity, with the United States unbalanced by any other power, interventionist and discriminatory in its policies. Syria's regional allies—Egypt and the Gulf states—encourage a diplomatic effort, whereas Iran foresees disappointment and looks for a military option. Iran sees the dangers of a U.S. presence in the Persian Gulf, a U.S.-engineered peace process that leaves Arab demands unsatisfied, and a position for itself as a a champion of Moslem causes if it plays its cards right and builds up militarily.

But there are other trends at work. The end of the cold war came at a time of great regional change, reinforcing this change. The two Gulf wars were indicative of a shift if not of priorities then of realities: Iran and Islam became players on the Middle Eastern scene, and Iraq demonstrated the hollowness of Arab nationalism, not only in the attack against Kuwait but also in the sham that this was linked with Palestine. The *intifadah*, meanwhile, took the issue from the hands of the Arab states that had more or less ignored the Palestine issue during the latter phases of the Iran-Iraq War. The upshot was that the Arab world was more differentiated than before, less susceptible to appeals, and more resistant to the pressures of conformity on one issue.

The issues of democratization, economic performance, and the role of Islam have come to the fore everywhere. In Egypt, fundamentalism looms large as a critic of policies; in the Gulf states, the oil boom is over, and attempts at the slow opening up of the political systems have started. In Syria, Iran, and Libya, economic problems limit the ambitions and resources available for foreign affairs. Economic failure and corruption are at the root of the problems in Algeria. Throughout the region, the opportunity costs of armaments are rising, and the willingness to indulge in external adventures or crusades is declining.

The tensions between domestic pressures and limited resources on the one side and discontent, regional sources of conflict and rivalry on the other are difficult to reconcile. What appears predictable is that the current window provided by the exhaustion of local parties, the pressure on resources, and the sense of standing at a new phase in the region's destiny could be cruelly shattered if not properly used. The growth of fundamentalism, the repression of movements tending toward democratization, and the frustration of young and unemployed populations that feel discriminated against by an insensitive North could change the balance of forces identified above and lead to a world filled with nuclear weapons in the late 1990s.

The Middle East and Proliferation

A shift to domestic priorities may not be forthcoming immediately, but it will remain a background pressure nonetheless. The decline of Arab nationalism means decreased external-regional pressures to align or take rhetorically extreme positions on issues. Both will be moderating factors in regional security. The same cannot be said for two other factors: the spread of the weapons of mass destruction and the tighter linkage of the Persian Gulf states (especially Iran) with the Arab-Israeli balance. Since the Paris conference on chemical weapons in 1989 and latterly through President Hosni Mubarak's proposal for a zone free of weapons of mass destruction, Arab states have sought to link the renunciation or banning of chemical and biological weapons to the banning of nuclear weapons.

The second factor, linking Iran to the Arab-Israeli balance, was exemplified by Saddam Hussein's use of missiles against Israel during the second Gulf war. Future arms control efforts will have to take into account a wider geographic zone, introducing definitional problems and new actors.

A third factor is the multiplicity of rivalries in the region. Many of these overlap, suggesting that settlement of any one issue does not necessarily detract from the incentives for ensuring security through nuclear weapons for the others or for the generally insecure environment. At any given time, states have to consider threats from numerous sources:

Israel—the Arab states and Iran
Iraq—Israel, Iran, and the other Arab states
Iran—Israel, the Arab states, the United States, and India/Pakistan
Turkey—the Arab states and Iran

What is lacking here is the pattern of confrontation that existed between the superpowers—or between two clearly defined rivals like India and Pakistan. Lacking this binary structure, it is not clear how nuclear weapons would contribute to ultimate security or what specific role is envisaged for them.

In this context there are grounds for supposing that nuclear weapons, whatever their presumed military function, are sought for political rather than military purposes.[2] Insurance, leverage, an amplified voice, and an injection of caution in crises that might stem from a muffled and ambiguous program are the immediate aims, rather than a logical doctrine of use, targeting, delivery, control, and safety. This applies in the cases mentioned above, even without clear or overwhelming threats. If correct, this type of general incentive to acquire an option may be difficult to discourage by reference to the limits of proportional deterrence, the vulnerability of small installations, the costs of modernization, or the need for second-strike capabilities (command and control, safety measures). But lacking urgency or focus, these incentives may be easier to derail by simply raising the costs of reaching the goal.

IRAQ

What does Saddam Hussein's attempt to acquire nuclear weapons tell us about proliferation in the Middle East, and what does it suggest for nonproliferation policy? There has been much fixation on the technical aspects and little discussion of Iraq's motives. Iraq had a "surprisingly systematic and sophisticated clandestine program largely built upon indigenous scientific and technical resources and supplemented by a select international procurement network."[3] Iraq was able to pursue its own parallel program for enrichment and to supplement it by importing components. The program was undoubtedly helped by the transfer of sensitive technology; and purchases of components, including those of dual-use, from a variety of sources helped mask its intentions. Furthermore, Iraq's approach was comprehensive, involving simultaneously work on delivery systems and design components. It was close to being able to construct one or two bombs a year. All estimates had been incorrect by greatly underestimating Iraq's capability and progress.

It turned out that a state with a modest technological base like Iraq could in a relatively short period produce nuclear weapons.

A report a decade before, analyzing Iraq's capabilities with reference to basic indigenous resources needed to achieve nuclear status (excluding ability to design and make weapons), had concluded that relative to India (56 percent) and Pakistan (27 percent), Iraq rated 9 percent versus Libya's 6 percent.[4] Iraq, with a reported expenditure of some $10 billion and a cadre of some ten thousand specialists, was able to come very close to the bomb.[5] Iraq is not typical; it is relatively rich and comes closer to the model of a garrison state than most other states. On the other hand, its manpower base certainly does not compare to that of Iran or Egypt.

A final word on the technical side: Iraq's program was detected only because of its defeat and only then because of defectors' information and unprecedentedly intrusive inspections. Neither information from satellite reconnaissance nor information from periodic safeguards was adequate to reveal the scope of the program. If anything, the safeguards regime tended to allay doubts. What did Iraq think it was doing? What did Saddam Hussein have in mind?

Iraq had long sought Arab leadership in rivalry with Egypt and Syria. Its domestic politics, where a Sunni Arab minority dominated the state, made it gravitate toward pan-Arab causes. At the same time it was frustrated by geography, which limited its access to the Persian Gulf and put it between two strong, non-Arab neighbors—Iran and Turkey. Reconciling its ambitions, location, and resources has been a costly and lengthy business for Iraq, whose war with Iran was part of this quest. During that war, Iraq discovered the value of missiles as terror weapons, used chemical weapons without a serious international response, and built up its armed forces and military base beyond those of its neighbors. Otherwise, it emerged from the war bankrupt, its ambitions intact and animated by a new sense of grievance. This complaint was twofold, against the Arab states of the peninsula for lack of appreciation for its role as "defender of the eastern flank" and against Israel for its attack on Osirak in June 1981, which destroyed its developing nuclear program.

In retrospect, the Israeli action appears to have been justified; at the time it appeared less so to some experts.[6] While it set back Iraq's nuclear ambitions, it also focused them and gave them a sense of urgency that had been lacking before. Whereas Iraq started a long-term program from the mid-1970s and used its membership in the International Atomic Energy Agency (IAEA) to allay suspicions (while buying hot cells and other dubious nuclear materials), the war with Iran militarized the society and gave Iraq the impetus to look to its ultimate security.

After the war, Iraq again wrapped itself in the mantle of Arab nationalism, depicting its armed forces as Arab rather than simply Iraqi forces. Saddam Hussein's alarm at the changes in international and regional politics, which he saw approaching with the decline of the USSR, and the subsequent threats by Israel, which he suspected of planning another Osirak (in April 1990), need little elaboration. He continued his crash program on nuclear weapons, which the war interrupted and then stopped. Saddam had acquired the capability to make one or two bombs a year and had been developing a missile—the Badr 200—for their delivery. With such a small stock the nuclear program would have been vulnerable for some time to come, perhaps explaining Saddam's sensitivity to hints of Israeli preventive attacks.

Why and for what did Iraq want nuclear weapons? Nuclear weapons would emphatically affirm Iraq's leadership in the Arab world—they would be a ticket not only to regional power but to any negotiations involving Israel. Second, they could deter the Israeli threat. Third, they insured against the revival of any threat in the future from nearby Iran. Fourth, they might be useful to deter any Western threat to, or intervention in, Iraq.

Iraq's immediate aim had been to threaten the use of missiles and mass destruction weapons to "burn Israel" in order to protect what remained of a fledgling nuclear program. Saddam's long-range or eventual intention had been to use his nuclear weapons to protect Iraq from external attack while freeing his conventional forces for use at will. Iraq, it will be recalled, had built up all elements of its forces (air force *and* missiles; conventional forces *and* chemical weapons *and* nuclear weapons). The utility of his conventional forces is clear: coercion and the assertion of regional dominance. This would have entailed the annexation of Kuwait, the threat of renewed fighting vis-à-vis a submissive Iran, and the intimidation of the Arab peninsula states (who would have been prepared to pay for "protection," as Kuwait had traditionally done), and then and only then move against Israel.

The role of nuclear weapons in such a strategy is unclear. Did Saddam believe that his nuclear weapons would deter any threat or use by Israel, leaving the field free for conventional weapons? Did he believe that his nuclear weapons would deter intervention by the United States, whether in the Gulf or against Israel? Did he believe that nuclear weapons could compensate for his numerical disadvantages compared with Iran, act as a deterrent against Israel and the United States, and serve as a legitimizing factor in Arab and domestic politics? What sort of nuclear doctrine did he envision: proportional deterrence against the United States? Last resort against Iran? Disarming strike against Israel? We cannot know, and one doubts that these issues were thought through.

What of Iraq's behavior during the war in 1991? The most notable issue was the failure to use chemical weapons. Explanations for nonuse vary from the technical-practical (problems of mounting warheads, command and control, speed of allied attack) to the political. In the last category was uncertainty given the allies' ambiguity about likely responses, which could have encompassed a like-for-like exchange of chemical weapons, or an escalatory nuclear response, or a widening of war aims to include the destruction or occupation of Baghdad, regime-decapitation, and/or a serious war crimes effort. We do not know for certain why Iraq failed to use chemical weapons. Nor can we infer from this nonuse much about nuclear doctrine. What needs to be emphasized is that in the crunch, Iraq was careful, not suicidal, although clearly its misreading of international politics invited doubts about its rationality.

Iraq is now being forcibly disarmed in the areas of nuclear weapons, chemical weapons, and missiles with a range of over 150 kilometers. There is much to be learned from the monitoring program, especially loopholes that must be tied up to prevent a repetition of a program that exploits ambiguity and inconsistency in national laws, definitions of dual-use items, commercial greed, and multiple sources to bypass controls. Equally important is the need to consider whether such an enforced regime can endure in only one country in the region, and whether, as envisaged in the empowering UN resolution, this cannot be widened into a regional system of arms control, encompassing both the Gulf and the Arab states closer to Israel.

ISRAEL

Unlike all of the other major regional states, Israel is a member of the IAEA but not a member of the NPT; unlike most of them, it is suspected of having a highly developed nuclear program and enough material to construct many bombs at short notice. Unlike its neighbors, it also has plausible security motives for seeking nuclear weapons, although this is neither to commend nor to condemn that decision. Here at least one can infer a policy from the assumed bomb-in-the-basement capability. Ambiguity has its uses, especially in making plain Israel's determination to ensure its own defense. The policy of neither denying its capability too insistently nor manipulating it too blatantly has not been easy, but it has served its purpose. The policy has credibly served to remind the Arab states that as a last resort in the face of an overwhelming Arab conventional onslaught, Israel was prepared to "go nuclear." As long as this has been the message, it has been credible without being provocative. The "shadow effect" of Israel's nuclear weapons surely has influenced the calculations of Arab states both in their war aims and in their willingness to recognize the fact of Israel and its right to exist—subject to negotiations.[7]

Another function of nuclear weapons for Israel was as an implicit warning to the former USSR against involvement in a regional conflict on the Arab side, specifically against use of nuclear weapons in that regard. Whether Israeli nuclear weapons could have deterred Soviet aid to the Arab states short of nuclear weapons is doubtful. But Israel's ability to cover some Soviet targets must have registered and increased the incentives for restraint. With the end of the cold war and the USSR, this function is no longer necessary, assuming that China is not a candidate to replace the Soviet Union.

There have been temptations at times to lower the nuclear threshold, to see if nuclear weapons could be made to cover a wider spectrum of threats than simply the ultimate one. Especially in light of the increasing burden and cost of conventional forces, it has sometimes been argued that Israel ought to threaten nuclear use against major conventional attacks or at least to keep the question of response ambiguous enough to cover them. This argument has been rejected, although the debate as to what else nuclear weapons can do besides deter other nuclear weapons and act as a last-resort weapon continues.

Nuclear weapons have figured in the debate about territory as well. One of the arguments for occupying additional land has been as a buffer for depth, since conventional defense was impossible without it. Some have argued that an explicit Israeli acknowledgment of nuclear weapons would make territorial expansion less necessary (and by extension, withdrawal possible).[8] If the choice were presented in this way—an Israeli renunciation of nuclear weapons and insistence on additional territorial depth or an Israeli retention of nuclear weapons and withdrawal from most of the occupied territories—there is little doubt what most Palestinians would prefer.[9]

Israeli nuclear weapons have been diplomatically directed at the United States as well as the Arab states. It would be difficult to deny the leverage that a state can get when bargaining for arms or diplomatic support when it can credibly threaten to resort to nuclear weapons. When that state is not just any state but one enjoying special relations with Washington (and the American people), it is clear that nuclear weapons have served to influence the relationship and to cement these ties. The United States has been ambivalent about Israel's type of proliferation, which serves to some extent to inhibit a resort to force even at the conventional level. Yet there can be no doubt that whatever the asymmetries impelling the Israeli decision, an acceptance of Israel's lead and U.S. acquiescence in it will furnish the pretext for other regional states (besides Iraq) to attempt to match it or to justify their own programs by reference to it.

Several wars and the fact of Israel's nuclear weapons have influenced Arab states into recognition that Israel is here to stay, leaving only the modalities and forms for negotiation. Together with the changes in the region outlined earlier, Arab incentives to organize coalitions for new wars are slim to nonexistent. Therefore, is Israel's nuclear weapons status a continuing necessity, and does it serve its original purpose?

One could argue that the diminished threat of an Arab coalition or eastern front reduces the traditional military threat faced by Israel. On the other hand there is a new threat—that of missiles and chemical weapons. The linkages noted earlier complicate deterrence. With Iran able—or soon able—to hit Israel from afar, the problem of deterrence is different from that of deterring say, Syria. In initiating an attack, the latter has to take into account the full weight of Israel's retaliatory power, on the ground and in the air. Deterring Iran is more difficult, since this same capability cannot be harnessed for retaliation; it will be harder, for example, to retaliate against missile attacks with air attacks or ground incursions.

There is an additional problem posed by the introduction of chemical weapons and missiles into the equation, which have served to blur thresholds. This is especially the case if an attempt is made to link chemical and nuclear weapons, as Saddam's Iraq tried to do. In theory, Syria could acquire chemical weapons as a first step toward development of a nuclear capability and then use a chemical weapons umbrella to advance the "achievement of true strategic parity with Israel by nullifying Israel's nuclear monopoly"[10]—something very similar to what Saddam tried to do. The combination of mass destruction and nuclear weapons could allow Arab states to change the unwritten rules that have governed interactions between Israel and the Arab states; chemical weapons and missiles against population centers could be used to deter air attacks on nuclear facilities, or nuclear weapons could be used to deter a response, freeing chemical weapons for first use. Weapons that deter the use of Israel's conventional forces offensively change the nature of deterrence substantially.

Recognition of the changed nature of the region—its expansion and potential nuclearization—has affected the Rabin government's approach to peace negotiations. An agreement with Syria, which has few good choices (alliance with Iran or Iraq? how to replace weapons that are lost?), is the best approach. Agreement with Syria would substantially reduce the threat from Iran. Even Iran would find it difficult to be "more Arab than the Arabs," and more practically, Tehran relies on good relations with Syria for access to Israel through Lebanon.

For Israel the current period is an important one. Numerous domestic issues have to be solved, and water sharing, demographic problems, and the like demand attention and make a claim on resources. The regional context could deteriorate if alignments change, which could happen from one day to the next in a region where policy is the result of individuals, rather than institutions or consensus. A Syrian-Iraqi-Iranian axis could emerge if no progress is made toward peace, or if all three states are cold-shouldered because of their current limited means. Egypt, for all its solidity, is not as stable as Washington believes and hopes. Closer to home, the development of Hamas in the Gaza may spread to the occupied territories if Islamic fundamentalism appears to be the only way out of stillborn peace negotiations. Thus the Israeli-Palestine, Gaza-Jericho agreement of September 1993 offers a way to defuse these pressures, especially if it is built upon.

The only way that new weapons of mass destruction can be limited and the incentives not to follow Israel toward nuclear weapons dulled is by improved political relations, which include confidence building and arms control measures. Measures that reinforce the current moderate order in the Arab world and contribute to the demise of Arab nationalism are necessary. The time for improved relations between the main parties has seldom been better because none is in an especially advantageous position. Whether or not the result will be the dismantling of Israel's nuclear program, the fact that this is formally unacknowledged makes it easier to deemphasize. South Africa is an analogous case; regional and domestic political transformations reduced the need for nuclear weapons as a last-resort weapon. An opening up of the Israeli program at some point could serve a similar function in the Middle East. Israel is on record as supporting a nuclear free zone in the area as long as it is the product of negotiations among the parties concerned.

IRAN

Iran, another potential proliferator, is unusual in lacking strong ties to any power and in having no constituency of its own, but it remains intent on playing some sort of international role.

Under the shah, Iran had begun an ambitious nuclear power program. Four reactors had been ordered: two 1,200–megawatt reactors from Germany (Kraftwerkunion) and two 900–megawatt ones from France (Framotome). The anticipated startup dates were 1982–83 and 1984–85, respectively. Iran had also bought into Eurodif, a European consortium for enriching uranium. Iran was in the category of states having reprocessing facilities, and it was calculated that it would have separable plutonium for three to six nuclear bombs by 1984. Moreover, by the early 1990s it was estimated that Iran would have some 3,220 kilograms of plutonium (for reloads of mixed plutonium and uranium oxide [MOX] fuel), equivalent to 371 bombs.[11] Iran was said to be training some ten thousand scientists and engineers for an anticipated increase in its program, which it justified by the need for energy and access to modern science and technology. Furthermore, Iran was cooperating with countries like Argentina in the nuclear field. No one doubted that Iran under the shah was creating the foundation for what could become a nuclear option.[12]

The scale of Iran's nuclear program was large, and it is doubtful that these goals would have been met; manpower shortages and financial constraints alone would have arrested development.

It is, however, worth summarizing the forces operating on Iran at that time for and against a decision to go toward nuclear weapons capability. *In favor* were prestige, leverage against the United States, a hedge against the USSR, a hedge against India/Pakistan, and an assertion of leadership in the Persian Gulf area. *Against* were the risks of endangering a good security relationship with the United States, the risks of antagonizing and inviting preventive attacks by the USSR, and the risk of diluting conventional military predominance by starting the nuclearization of the region. There were no strong or urgent security incentives for going toward nuclear weapons and several strong reasons for not doing so. Perhaps the strongest reason against was the security relationship with the United States, a relationship that might be endangered by such a decision, intended ironically to increase Iran's security.

Iran's program was interrupted by the revolution and war with Iraq. In the closing years of the war and since, the Islamic Republic of Iran (IRI) has sought to revive the program, insisting on economic grounds and on an earlier commitment by Germany to complete the half-finished reactors at Büshehr. Germany has been unwilling to allow its companies to do so. Iranian authorities have since declared the necessity for building a large nuclear program as part of their postwar reconstruction, principally to meet their power-generation needs. They have also justified it by reference to the need for access to modern science and technology and have insisted on their peaceful intent by noting their adherence to the NPT and to regular inspections by the IAEA.[13]

The United States and its allies are in no mood for favors on this issue. With the lesson of Iraq and experience of terrorism still fresh, regulations have been tightened, scrutiny improved, and international coordination intensified. After Iraq, adherence to the NPT and periodic inspections are not grounds for reducing doubts about intent. And Iran gives cause for doubt. Statements have been made (not at the highest level) suggesting that Iran has the same right as Israel to possess nuclear weapons. The pattern of Iran's purchases has also been suspicious: attempts to buy reactors from Argentina and India may have been stopped by U.S. pressure, but other attempts to purchase plants from China and Russia have been successful. Iran is reported to have tried to cooperate in the nuclear field with Pakistan or, more accurately, to get access to that country's work in the field.[14] There are also rumors of joint cooperation with South Africa, which has yielded a large quantity of uranium concentrate. So far there are no signs that Iran has managed to obtain unsafeguarded enriched uranium. However, it appears likely that Iran will, finances permitting, build up a nuclear industry, ostensibly under safeguards but with the possibility of undeclared facilities operating alongside. By the end of the century, if not before, Iran might have access to fissile material and some nuclear weapons. This might occur sooner or on a larger scale if more resources are put into it or if Iran gains access to materials, components, or manpower specialized in this field, perhaps from the Commonwealth of Independent States (CIS), perhaps by cofinancing projects with another state. Even with tighter controls and the lessons of Iraq, there are suspicions that Iran, with its experience of evading the arms embargo and of setting up clandestine purchasing networks for arms in the 1980s, might be able to do the same for nuclear materials in this decade.

The United States has insisted that any cooperation or trade with Iran in the nuclear field should be avoided, with or without safeguards. It has so far managed to stop several deals and will no doubt continue to use its undoubted leverage to prevent future trade in this area.

Iran is suspected of harboring nuclear ambitions and is believed to want nuclear weapons for the following reasons:

1. To become the dominant power in the Persian Gulf and thus to intimidate its neighbors
2. To inhibit a U.S. presence and reduce U.S. access to the region in general and the Gulf in particular
3. To assert its leadership in the Moslem world and especially to activate a new eastern ("resistance") front aligned against Israel and intended to threaten Israel

It is clear that the IRI's political goals are very far removed from those of its predecessor and that the strategic picture has also changed. For the latter, the U.S. connection was an incentive *not* to acquire such weapons, whereas for the IRI, it is a major motivator. Conversely, whereas the USSR was a major security problem (incentive) in the 1970s, it is not the same sort of problem in the 1990s. Iran in the earlier period had not witnessed a major war in over a century, its conventional arms were adequate for regional contingencies, and relations with most of its neighbors and the international community were good. Its ambition was for increased status, and better economic growth was considered an important part of this. By contrast the IRI is an international pariah, relations with neighbors are at best wary, allies are non-existent, sources of conventional arms are uncertain, its economy is stagnant, its population is a burden, and its ambitions are unlimited. These ambitions are for leadership, first, of the "Moslem world" and, second, of the dispossessed or oppressed internationally. This implies a rejection of the current Western-dominated international order and an eventual confrontation with its upholders.

On both specific and general grounds, whether in the Gulf, in the Middle East as a whole, or internationally, Iran clearly places itself in opposition to U.S./Western interests and values. It seems reasonable to infer from Iran's statements, its past actions, the pattern of its current acquisitions (in which there is a considerable overlap between potential civilian and military applications), its suppliers, and its unfulfilled ambitions that this is a state intent on acquiring nuclear weapons. Equally, nuclear weapons in the hands of such a state might be considered a catastrophe, not necessarily because of their frivolous use, but because of what this would do to other states' incentives, especially Turkey, because of the impact for U.S. security commitments in the region, because of how Israel might react, and because of uncertainty about how safe, secure, and reliable these nuclear weapons would be and what doctrine, if any, would govern their use.

Seen from Iran's view, things look different. The past decade has seen two wars in the Persian Gulf and two interventions by outside powers, one aimed at the IRI and another at Iraq. Force clearly remains important in international affairs, and it is one of the principal components of U.S. power. If Iran is to play a major international role, it must be an equal of the great powers; an important element of equality is nuclear weapons. Second, Iran has access to no reliable source of advanced conventional arms and has to rely on itself for defense. An additional reason may be the recognition that nuclear weapons can act as an equalizer insofar as countries like Iran cannot hope to catch up with the new conventional precision technologies. Third, the United States remains hostile to the IRI and treats it in a discriminatory manner, whether in regard to arms sales, technology transfers, or nuclear controls. It supplies other Gulf states with arms. The United States supports Israel, ignores its nuclear program, and proposes arms control measures and moratoria that freeze Israel's lead by ignoring it (e.g., President George Bush's May 1991 proposals). This selectivity regarding arms control demonstrates U.S. support for Israel. Fourth, Iran needs nuclear weapons to match those of Israel. Fifth, Iran cannot be certain that Iraq will not again seek nuclear weapons—after all, its technical cadre remains intact. Finally, nuclear weapons may substitute for other achievements and divert attention from domestic failures.

In essence, the incentives for nuclear weapons are (1) to form part of any independent state's arsenal; (2) to compensate for conventional weaknesses; (3) to deter U.S. intervention; (4) to match Israel's capabilities; (5) to hedge against an Iraqi program; and (6) to provide an ersatz source of legitimacy. None of these is immutable; there is no urgent overriding military threat or rationale (as in the Israeli and Pakistani cases) but multiple reasons, some of which include status-equity and "global" ambitions and others that concern questions of self-reliance and access to conventional weapons. The specific motives—to deter U.S. intervention or to hedge against a new Iraqi program—could be reduced by improved relations with the United States and/or transformation of the IRI, and there are alternative means of reassuring Iran (and the world) about the state of the Iraqi program and of gaining domestic support.

Political change and evolution are possible and need to be worked on. The path to acquiring nuclear weapons can be made difficult, costly, and risky, especially if it entails a kind of crash program that sees an arms buildup across the board, like that of Iraq. A broad-based civilian program like that of India is harder to tackle, but it is also a lengthier process that gives time to work on the political incentives. Progress on Arab-Israeli issues would deprive Iran of one of its strongest potential cards—dissatisfaction with the West for its role in this issue. More transparency and a deemphasis on nuclear weapons by Israel would weaken the argument for the need to balance that state. This still leaves several areas of potential unrest that might favor fundamentalism and play to Iran's strengths. But even though the past decade has seen the growth of fundamentalism as an opposition force, especially as secular models (Arab socialism and Arab nationalism) have failed, it has also shown that Islamic unity is not around the corner. There is no natural unity or axis among states that are highly differentiated in terms of resources, political systems, history, and even culture. The past decade has seen at least two wars among them and several border and other conflicts. States as different as Turkey and Saudi Arabia may favor the West, whereas Iran, Syria, and Libya—not obvious allies—oppose it. Unity is more likely to come about from Western/Northern policies that treat all these states in the same way and act as if Islamic unity and hostility toward the West are inevitable. In short, policies can exacerbate the problem or contribute to reducing the incentives for nuclear weapons (as well as making attainment of nuclear weapons more difficult).

Iran is a particularly difficult case because its motives are general and diffuse, not sharp and tangible. Furthermore, its experience in the 1980s has habituated it to hardship, reinforced its belief in the need for self-reliance, and accentuated its self-image as a long-suffering martyr. One additional problem is that Iran has relatively little to lose, since it is already subject to embargoes and surveillance and treated as a pariah generally. Sanctions have their place, but cornering states does not necessarily improve their receptivity to dialogue. On the other hand, in the case of Iran, its past policies have discouraged any appearance of rewards. Its sense of grievance and its continuing diffuse international ambitions will not be easy to handle without leading to a zero-sum game.

LIBYA, ALGERIA, AND TURKEY

Libya has long been considered a potential proliferator. Colonel Muammar Qadafi is known as an international troublemaker and was reported some years ago as having sought to purchase a bomb and later as having invested in Pakistan's nuclear effort to create an "Islamic bomb." Soviet cooperation with Libya did not turn out to be as extensive or careless as some had anticipated, and Libya today has only a small nuclear program, far from a nuclear weapons capability. Libya's initial interest was a characteristically naive one: it sought a bomb to increase its influence in Arab politics, to pose as a defender of the Arabs against Israel. Its current and prospective economic situations do not suggest that resources will be available for heavy investment in a nuclear program, nor is there a large, skilled, indigenous manpower pool available. Libya's policies regarding missiles and chemical weapons have focused attention on the country. Its support for terrorism has led to its current embargo, with little dissent from most of the Arab world (the exception being Egypt, which fears the economic consequences for its workers' remittances). Libya does not seem to be a serious candidate for proliferation: neither its capabilities nor its potentialities make it one. Furthermore, events have essentially sidelined Libya as an actor in regional politics, and no amount of effort at leadership and exhortation is likely to make it a central player in the Arab-Israel area.

Algeria has recently been cited as a proliferation risk. Its unannounced acquisition of a reactor from China, its failure so far to sign the NPT, and its tardy acceptance of inspections suggest to some a hidden motive. What would be the motive? Algeria has not signed the NPT, probably for reasons to do with equity and with its self-image as a revolutionary Third World state and nonaligned leader. Given that the socialist government signed the deal with China several years ago (1987), the motivation was apparently a desire for access to modern technology. Algeria has a "technically advanced"[15] manpower base, which presumably could benefit from such equipment. But where is the motive for nuclear weapons? Algeria does not have poor relations with any of its neighbors in the Maghreb. It has not been in the forefront of the radicals in the fight against Israel. It has few claims or pretensions putting it into conflict with the great powers. In short, reconciling Algeria's political context with the estimates and alarmism of those looking at Algeria's nuclear program is difficult. Admittedly, the possibility that the country may be taken over by fundamentalists casts a different light on issues, but this was not the concern of analysts who began the furor over Algeria's alleged aims well before developments changed the political context.

Algeria's original decision may have been to acquire technology and perhaps to confirm or seek a leadership role among the nonaligned. Political change (as in the case of Iran) reveals the dangers: decisions made at one time can take effect at another. A new regime may look at the world differently, put a different priority on acquiring nuclear weapons, and pursue them for quite different ends. Any progress made by its predecessor toward such a capability, however inadvertent, may then contribute to new and unforeseen ends. The implication of this is unwelcome, suggesting that a strategy of technology denial may be safer in those regions where political stability is elusive.

Turkey is the only country to which the West has strong formal security commitments. It is not an obvious candidate for nuclear weapons primarily because this connection—which encompasses the North Atlantic Treaty Organization (NATO) and the West European Union (WEU) and perhaps also one day the European

Union—forms a solid bilateral foundation with the United States. The health of this relationship, the sympathy and harmony existing between Ankara and Washington, and the vitality of the security commitment are critical elements influencing how Turkey will react to current and future security problems. Surrounded by unstable and largely unfriendly states (Syria, Iraq, and Iran, among others), Turkey is now no longer concerned about Soviet aggression but rather about the instability and conflicts of the successor states adjacent to it. Wars in the Caucasus, Georgia, and Azerbaijan involve bordering regions and Turkic peoples with whom Turkey retains links and sympathy. Managing the transition in the former Soviet republics will not be easy and may involve military commitments.

In the Middle East, Turkey has formalized diplomatic relations with Israel. It remains the only officially secular Moslem state, which causes resentment in Iran. Syria and Iraq feel vulnerable to Turkey's potential control of their water sources and support a Kurdish guerrilla group (the PKK) for counterleverage. Thus, Turkey is surrounded by instabilities and potential conflicts—the Balkans, the Caucasus, and the Middle East. Although there is no one dominant threat, there are many smaller ones. None of these would impel Ankara to go for nuclear weapons. Things could change quickly, however. An Iranian or Iraqi program would test Turkey's restraint and put pressure on the U.S./NATO strategy and the explicit extension of positive security guarantees. Unless these were forthcoming, and relations with the West were good and felt to be dependable in Ankara, there would be the risk that one proliferating state would encourage a breakout by others. Pan-Turkic ambitions would not dictate movement toward nuclear weapons unless the U.S. connection were in doubt. This is thus another case where commitments and alliances are an effective nonproliferation policy.

Policy Implications

Greater sensitivity to the issue of proliferation is leading toward more comprehensive and intrusive inspections. Confidence, shaken after the Iraqi surprise, will require tighter controls and tougher safeguards, implying greater demands on nonnuclear states. There is already a tendency abroad to focus on those NPT parties that are considered "sensitive" (likely to have the motive

to cheat), such as Iran, Syria, and Libya; the United States seeks
to prevent any sort of nuclear cooperation, safeguarded or not,
with such states.

At the same time, technology levels are inexorably increasing,
putting science and technology within reach of states that were
very distant from it two decades ago. While general scientific
knowledge is being diffused, some technologies associated with
nuclear weapons capabilities also threaten to become more
widely available; eventually, these could pose particular problems
for safeguards, such as the laser-isotope enrichment process,
which is harder to detect and inspect, and cruise missile technology, which will make the delivery of nuclear weapons more
accurate. On the more hopeful side, the growth of nuclear power
worldwide has stopped, and power plants are at best being replaced, if not actually in decline (the main exception is in the
Pacific rim).

Both the diffusion of technology and greater awareness of the
risks of proliferation require stricter safeguards, yet such a policy
is unlikely to work because it is selective and lacks the necessary
international consensus. Indeed, unilateral or coercive nonproliferation measures by the United States are likely to create new
or to reinforce old incentives for proliferation by other states. In
general, those states most susceptible to technology denial will
be those least developed and hence those of minimal concern.
Denial is not a viable long-term strategy for the more serious
candidates and threatens to aggravate incentives to proliferate.
However, denial definitely has some role in policy, and it can,
above all, buy time for political strategies to work or for political
equations to change. What of political will, the other dimension
of proliferation? What can be done to influence motives? Generally, in dealing with advanced countries like Germany, Sweden,
and Japan, there is little focus on capability, which is more or less
assumed; rather, the political-security context is emphasized.
With developing countries, the focus has been on technology
controls, in part because such controls are doable. But these
states are not identically motivated, any more than they are similarly endowed. Most do not aspire to a global role; some have
specific and understandable security motives. Some, like India,
are willing to pay a high price for nuclear weapons and have had
a long-term security strategy. "Drifting" governments, as some
have called them, would like to have nuclear weapons but are
sensitive to the price to be paid, and thus can be influenced.

Most of them are motivated by regional considerations, and it is there that policy should focus. Recognizing the political dimension implies that governments will be treated differently but not necessarily that some will be singled out for coercion. The broadest possible consensus, without watering down safeguards needs, implies coalition building in international institutions and the avoidance of confrontation, which would threaten to change the subject to a bilateral one. It will be important to create disincentives, reasons for moderation and something to lose from confrontation or evasion of international norms. There will be tensions surrounding the need to retain nuclear weapons as part of an overall arsenal, because their importance increases as their number decreases with arms control; similarly, there is a balance to be struck between the need to deemphasize the role of nuclear weapons in the new era and the requirements of the commitments and security assurances that many states may require as a price for renouncing nuclear weapons.

On another level, there is the problem of nuclearization and regional conflicts. Nuclear weapons might be used, or threatened, as a shield to cover aggression by conventional forces. Regional aggressors may believe that nuclear weapons will deter external intervention, especially since outside powers will have difficulty in making nuclear threats in distant areas where extended deterrence lacks credibility. In light of Washington's vast conventional superiority demonstrated by Desert Storm, local states might want to rely on nuclear weapons to deter any intervention, thus compensating for conventional inadequacies and seeking some form of equalizer.[16]

It is worth seeing the world from the view of some proliferators. To them, the new world order looks like one in which the United States is free to pursue its own interests and vendettas. This power is unchecked and even dominates the UN, which is harnessed to U.S. ends; witness the aggressive nonproliferation policy and the campaign against Libya. U.S. policy is, as always, partial; interest in nonproliferation and arms control is selective, oblivious to Israel's policies but targeted against those of Syria and Iran. Thus President Bush's May 1991 arms control proposal addressed only future proliferation, not the proliferation that already exists as a result of Israel's possession of nuclear weapons. Similarly, attempts to tighten safeguards and inspections for states parties to the NPT while ignoring the status of nonparties like Israel suggest a policy that is partial. U.S. arms-transfer policies that increase conventional arms sales to the Arab states of the peninsula and to Israel but that seek to stop sales to Iran and Syria do not suggest an unbiased approach. Yet the U.S. role is crucial, not just as a catalyst in regional discussions, but as the state with the most to offer the international community in efforts to enhance the effectiveness of safeguards. Increasingly, these will depend on information, especially satellite intelligence, received from national governments. Such information will make it possible for the IAEA to request "targeted" inspections of specific sites that may be undeclared by host states. National intelligence inputs will thus be an important part of a future safeguards regime. To ask states to submit to such inspections on the information provided by other nations requires that the latter enjoy a reputation for impartiality and integrity. Otherwise there is the risk that such information might be doctored, selective, or vindictive or offered simply for "fishing expeditions." If only for the future of the safeguards system and the imperative of maximizing support for more stringent measures, the United States should attempt to see the effect that a coercive and biased approach has on the receptivity of states like Syria and Iran.

IRAN

The Islamic Republic of Iran, for a variety of reasons, is high on everyone's list of disliked states. After a near-miss with Iraq, it is easy to see why there is little inclination to give Tehran the benefit of the doubt. This has led some to argue that the "lesson" of Iraq is the futility of trying to woo, moderate, or appease this type of regime. The conclusion is that only coercive policies will be understood and that the best and only reassurance for the United States would be the removal of these regimes from political power. The longevity of the regimes in Syria (since 1970), Libya (since 1969), and Iraq (since 1968) gives little grounds for hope in this respect.

Apart from the fact that the Islamic Republic may indeed survive for another decade or two, making unremitting hostility toward it unproductive, there are other reasons for a less emotional response. This type of "coercion-only" policy will simply accentuate the tendency of the regime to develop its siege mentality, driving it into a corner and perhaps into alliance with other pariahs, but in any case making it less responsive to dialogue and accommodation. Second, we cannot be sure that this approach will be effective in achieving its ends. There is at least a finite chance, given Iran's location and presumed interest in nuclear weapons, that it will be able to gain access to several kilograms of fissile material through leakage (theft or purchase) from the nearby southern republics of the Commonwealth of Independent States. Enough enriched uranium to make several bombs (one bomb needs fifteen to twenty-five kilograms) would certainly speed up Iran's nuclear weapons program and shortcut the otherwise formidable engineering bottlenecks that exist. (Even then Iran would still need to weaponize the materials and design a bomb.) Still, if appreciable fissile material turned up in Iran undetected, the country could be well on the way to a nuclear weapons capability, rendering the West's continued sanctions policies irrelevant. Third, given the possibility of such leakage, it would be imprudent to drive Iran into a corner by a sanctions-only policy that would deprive the West of the ability to influence, in a kind of socialization process through strategic dialogue, how Iran might view those weapons and the type of doctrine it might adopt. The opportunity to help moderate the possibly uninformed or half-formed ideas about the utility or use of these weapons should be actively sought. To conceive a sanctions policy as an end in itself is to misconceive a tool intended to delay and impose costs on the prospective target. The time thus bought, if it is to be useful, must be used to increase political dialogue.

On the one hand it is getting harder and costlier to proliferate: more and better resources are available through better detection, better equipment, better coordination, and more diplomatic muscle. A global norm of nonproliferation is emerging, backed up by a threat of possible UN-mandated action. On the other hand, the diffusion of technology, as well as of science and education together with the mobility of labor, means that the spread of capabilities is only a matter of time. A fixation on the technical side will therefore be a losing battle.

Because of resource constraints that prohibit a crash program, Iran will more likely creep toward nuclear capability, making it sensitive to cost and susceptible to pressure. A firm decision has not yet been made and hence is subject to reversal. Doubtless the attitudes of the superpowers and other powers toward nuclear weapons will influence Iranian judgments about relative utility and cost-effectiveness. The same applies to regional developments. Combating the proliferation of nuclear weapons is a multileveled exercise. It has technical/political, regional/global, rhetorical/practical, and unilateral/multilateral components.

THE RELATIONSHIP AMONG VARIOUS TYPES OF ARMS AND ARMS CONTROL

Attempts to ban nuclear weapons without reference to their potential functions and relations with other types of arms, conventional and unconventional, seem unrealistic. The converse is also the case: attempts to ban unconventional weapons without reference to nuclear weapons would also appear to be doomed. The Arab states are on record as linking their adherence to the chemical weapons convention with Israel's adherence to the NPT.[17] At the same time, whereas some believe that Israel's nuclear weapons are intended for deterrence and as a last-resort weapon, others think the weapons appear as instruments of coercion and a symbol of inequality. Basic asymmetries are a reality; the question is whether they need be an independent cause for blocking an improvement of political relations. Progress in political relations could reduce their importance and eventually perhaps the perceived necessity of the maintenance of nuclear weapons as an option. In this sense the "peace process" is part of nonproliferation policy. It could lead to dialogue, and more transparency. Threats of surprise attack could be reduced, military deployments constrained, and confidence increased. In the meantime, U.S. measures that have the effect of favoring one side or reducing the leverage of the other will not increase Washington's credibility as a potential mediator.

Progress in the Arab-Israel dispute will reduce Iran's potential for disturbance and its regional constituency. Syria's adherence to an agreement may see a reduction and/or elimination of the Iranian presence in Lebanon. A positive U.S. role will make it harder to argue that the United States is anti-Moslem and a slave to Israeli dictates. This will not end Iran's nuclear ambitions, but it will reduce the credibility of the claim that Iran intends to serve Moslem purposes. Progress on arms control will inescapably involve outside powers.

REGIONAL ARRANGEMENTS AND OUTSIDE POWERS

Besides framing arms control initiatives and arms transfer policies, outside powers will inevitably be called on to support, finance, and guarantee an eventual arrangement. These guarantees may well have to be security guarantees to compensate for the "loss" of security or the "risk" of departing from past policy, that is, for renouncing nuclear weapons or territory. To be effective, such guarantees will have to be extended to all parties and agreed on by all sides. Implicit in them will be agreement on the relationship between regional security and the outside powers' roles and the conditions under which their involvement would be activated.

In the Persian Gulf the same issues exist. Here, encouraging regional dialogue may be one way of avoiding direct contact but stimulating discussion about arms control and of providing a framework in which chemical and nuclear weapons and missiles can be linked to arms control in the Arab-Israel area. The relationship between conventional and other forms of arms will need to be discussed and restraints suggested that meet both Israel's need to deal with asymmetries and other states' need for a sense of equality. The United States has left regional dialogue to the local parties but kept in the wings its informal security commitment to Kuwait and Saudi Arabia. If arms control is to succeed, a regional security arrangement or forum will have to be encouraged. Within it the role and function of outside powers as arms suppliers, and guarantors, will inevitably arise. The United States has not been active or imaginative in promoting security in the Persian Gulf. Containing Iran may be satisfying and a palliative, but it alone does not solve the problem. Involving Iran or engaging it perhaps through the Gulf Cooperation Council (GCC), the Middle East peace process, or the UN Committee on Disarmament in multilateral arms control discussions might be a start toward defining the terms and conditions of outside power involvement in the region. The Arab states feel the need for external guarantees, whereas Iran and Iraq feel threatened by this. Discussions on this subject could result in a reduction in the perceived threat and a decline in the incentive for nuclear weapons.

The Linkages between Arab-Israel and the Persian Gulf

With modern weapons bringing distant targets within reach and likely to become more accurate over time, and with the political linkages established between the fate of Moslems and Arabs in Gaza and the West Bank and Moslems in the Persian Gulf, there is an increased need to deal with both areas simultaneously—especially in terms of arms control. In this sense the definition of *region* has expanded. The relationships with other regions, such as South Asia or the Caucasus, are also potentially important but need not impede concentration on the strategic interactions between these two areas. At the least, the sequence of measures will have to be coordinated and the measures themselves made similar in content.

NUCLEAR AND OTHER FREE ZONES

Progress in peace negotiations could permit steps toward denuclearization of the area. Israel is not opposed in principle as long as these steps include direct discussions for their achievement. Egypt and Iran originally supported a Middle East nuclear free zone, and the subject has seen revived interest.[18] Measures that increase confidence could be built on to reduce the need for large or provocatively deployed forces or preemption and targeting doctrines that keep populations hostage.

Because the legacy of conflict has heightened suspicion and doubt, there will be a need for special measures, including safeguards and inspections that go beyond those of the IAEA, to instill the kind of confidence necessary for acceptance of any agreement by all parties. Although they will have to be worked out by the states themselves, there will be a need for an outside power as catalyst, facilitator, underwriter, and guarantor. Here again its role as potential provider of intelligence for implementing strict and relevant inspections means that the outside power's impartiality must be above suspicion.

Conclusion

Potential proliferators in the Middle East are a mixed bag in terms of capability and motives. Some, like Israel, have clear-cut security incentives, whose needs could be met by a combination of improved relations with its neighbors and external guarantees. Because of the threat of general nuclearization and the rise of other needs, Israel's incentive to compromise in negotiations appears high. The Arab states have similar incentives for flexibility. The threat of Algeria and Libya seeking nuclear weapons appears exaggerated and can be handled relatively simply given the economic problems of both states. They do, however, require sensitive treatment so that they and other Moslems do not feel that they are being singled out for special attention.

In general, the end of the cold war, the Iraqi crisis, and the passing of Arab nationalism increase the opportunities for progress in regional relations. Although new weapons are complicating the calculations about the utility and function of nuclear weapons, the incentives for the latter are not increasing. This could change, especially if tensions continue, if the West gangs up on the Arabs, if fundamentalism spreads, or if access to conventional arms appears vital and unavailable. Much depends on regional and especially internal political dynamics, which cannot be predicted, but at the moment the omens are auspicious.

The most difficult proliferator is Iran, in part because its incentives to acquire nuclear weapons are so diffuse, being animated by global ambitions as much as by regional threats. They are sought as much for an expression of the Revolution's vitality and for a defiant assertion of equality as for any specific purpose. Wars and interventions in the Gulf and the U.S. survival as the only superpower, which is seen by Iran as a threat, are incentives to seek compensating power or leverage. Positive incentives, as well as the erection of more obstacles, and the imposition of more sanctions are required. Evenhandedness in the Arab-Israel negotiations and in arms control proposals would help, as would efforts to bring Iran into discussions on arms control. Incentives for proliferation surely increase the more isolated and beleaguered a nation becomes, even—perhaps especially—if this condition is virtually invited by the state itself. Involving such states at more levels of international and regional relations would be helpful, not the least in ventilating them to the true winds of change in these domains.

As Hedley Bull observed, nuclear proliferation is one area where "the goals of international order and of international justice or equal treatment are in conflict with one another." To make this order based on this explicit inequality more solid requires the support of the largest possible number of states for its legitimation.[19] Widening the consensus thus requires political coalition-building of the most basic sort. Early recourse to muscular threats of enforcement action by the UN Security Council is provocative and unwise until the patient, and vigilant, fostering of alternatives is exhausted.

Notes

1. Paul Jabber, "A Nuclear Middle East: Infrastructure, Likely Military Postures, and Prospects for Strategic Stability," *ACIS Working Paper*, no. 6

(Los Angeles: UCLA Center for Arms Control and International Security, 1977), pp. 37–38.

2. Ted Greenwood, "Discouraging Proliferation," in Ted Greenwood et al., *Nuclear Proliferation Motivations, Capabilities, and Strategies for Control* (New York: Council on Foreign Relations, 1977), p. 27.

3. Hans Blix, "Verification of Nuclear Proliferation: The Lesson of Iraq," *Washington Quarterly* 15, no. 4 (Autumn 1992): 58.

4. U.S. Senate, Committee on Foreign Relations, Subcommittee on Arms Control, *Analysis of Six Issues about Nuclear Capabilities of India, Iraq, Libya, and Pakistan* (Washington, D.C.: Government Printing Office, 1982), pp. 37–39.

5. See Rolf Ekeus, "The Iraqi Experience and the Future of Non-Proliferation," *Washington Quarterly* 15, no. 4 (Autumn 1992): 69, and John M. Deutch, "The New Nuclear Threat," *Foreign Affairs* 71, no. 4 (Fall 1992): 128.

6. Among several views, see Jed Snyder, "The Road to Osiraq: Baghdad's Quest for a Bomb," *Middle East Journal* 37, no. 4 (Autumn 1983): 565–93, and Shai Feldman, "The Bombing of Osiraq—Revisited," *International Security* 7, no. 2 (Fall 1982): 114–42.

7. I agree with George Quester, who makes the same point in "Nuclear Weapons and Israel," *Middle East Journal* 37, no. 4 (Autumn 1983): 560. See also his "The Future of Nuclear Deterrence," *Survival* 34, no. 1 (Spring 1992): 87.

8. Quester, "Nuclear Weapons and Israel," p. 559.

9. See Geoffrey Kemp, *The Control of the Middle East Arms Race* (Washington D.C.: Carnegie Endowment, 1991).

10. See Avigdor Haselkorn, "Arab-Israeli Conflict: Implications of Mass Destruction Weapons," pp. 131–35.

11. Albert Wohlstetter et al., *Moving toward Life in a Nuclear Crowd*, final report prepared for the Arms Control and Disarmament Agency, CDA/PAB-263 (Los Angeles: Pan Heuristics, 1976), pp. 15, 76, 153, 159, 252.

12. For two discussions of the shah's program, see Anne Hessing Cahn, "Determinants of the Nuclear Option: The Case of Iran," in Onkar Marwah and Ann Schulz, eds., *Nuclear Proliferation and the Near Nuclear Countries* (Cambridge, Mass.: Ballinger, 1975), chapter 8, and George Quester, "The Shah and the Bomb" (unpublished paper, 1975).

13. For a discussion of Iran's program, see Leonard Spector, *Nuclear Ambitions* (Boulder: Westview Press, 1990), chapter 12. See also Anthony Cordesman, *Weapons of Mass Destruction in the Middle East* (London: Brassey's, 1991), chapter 2. For more recent accounts, see this author's paper for Science Application International Corporation's Center for National Security Negotiations Conference on Nuclear Proliferation, Arden House, November 1991. For a fuller discussion and citations, see the monograph by this author for the Carnegie Endowment: *Iran's National Security Policy* (Washington, D.C.: Brookings, 1993). See also L. Spector, "Is Iran Building a Bomb?" *Christian Science Monitor*, December 31, 1991.

14. See David Albright and Mark Hibbs, "Spotlight Shifts to Iran," *Bulletin of the Atomic Scientists*, March 1992, pp. 9–11.

15. Blix, "Verification of Nuclear Proliferation," p. 64.

16. For a discussion of some of these issues, see Walter Slocombe, "The Nuclear Factor in the Post Cold War Era," in Thomas Marshall and Jerome Paolini, eds., *What Future for Nuclear Forces in International Security?* (Paris, France: CNSN-IFRI Workshop, 1992), pp. 31–48.

17. See Statement of Arab Foreign Ministers Meeting in Damascus, Syrian Arab Republic Radio, July 25, in BBC/ME/1443/A/1-2, July 27, 1992. See also Syrian Foreign Minister's Statement, Syrian Arab TV, ME/1503/A/8, October 5, 1992. For an earlier statement by Egypt, see the comments of Osamah al-Baz, Director of the President's Office of Political Affairs, MENA, November 15, in ME/1232/A/8, November 18, 1992.

18. See, in particular, "Effective and Verifiable Measures Which Would Facilitate the Establishment of a Nuclear Weapon Free-Zone in the Middle East" (report of a group of experts for the secretary general, Department of Disarmament Affairs, Study Series no. 22, 1991). See also Geoffrey Kemp, *The Control of the Middle East Arms Race* (Washington, D.C.: Carnegie Endowment, 1991). Other sources include Paul Power, "Preventing Nuclear Conflict in the Middle East: The Free Zone Strategy," *Middle East Journal* 37, no. 4 (Autumn 1983): 617–35, and "Building toward Middle East Peace," Policy Paper no. 1, Working Group Reports from *Cooperative Security in the Middle East* (Moscow, October 1991), published by University of California, Institute of Global Conflict and Research (January 1992).

19. Hedley Bull, *The Anarchical Society: A Study of Order in International Politics* (London: Macmillan, 1977), p. 243. For citation, see p. 300.

Chapter 3

Israel

Shai Feldman

Israel's Nuclear Policy

Comprehending Israel's approach to nuclear arms control requires ascertaining the rationale of its nuclear policy. This is because its approach to preventing nuclear proliferation in the Middle East is affected by considerations that have led it to develop a nuclear potential in the first place and then to surround such potential with maximum ambiguity.[1]

David Ben-Gurion, Israel's founding father and its first prime minister, seems to have urged the development of a nuclear potential in the framework of the state's general efforts to acquire a qualitative edge over its quantitatively superior Arab adversaries. As such, this development reflected Ben-Gurion's impression that a nuclear potential could serve as a "great equalizer," providing the Jewish state with some capacity to face the threat presented by the Arabs' larger numbers.[2] It also became an important part of his concept of cumulative deterrence: namely, that an evolving Israeli track record of successfully confronting the Arabs and defeating their efforts to destroy the Jewish state would eventually produce an Arab perception that Israel could not be defeated militarily and must be accommodated politically.[3] Implicitly, the development of Israel's nuclear potential was intended to contribute to such a track record and thus become part of its peace policy.

From the outset, Israel surrounded its nuclear policy with a high degree of ambiguity.[4] To date, it is not clear how far Ben-Gurion intended for Israel to advance along the path of developing its potential or when, and if, critical junctions along the road were crossed. Indeed, similar if not greater ambiguity continues to surround the evolution of Israeli thinking in the nuclear realm. Thus, it is not clear whether Israeli decision makers ever considered such a potential as relevant beyond its contribution to the state's general and cumulative deterrence. Consequently, it is impossible to ascertain whether such a capability was ever considered as potentially providing "specific deterrence": namely, the capacity to deter specific challenges and threats. All assertions to the contrary regarding the evolution of Israel's nuclear policy remain highly speculative.

Publicly, Israel adhered to a policy of avoiding any reference to the precise state of its nuclear capacity. Its declaratory policy on this issue was limited to repeated statements to the effect that Israel "would not be the first to introduce nuclear weapons to the Middle East," although senior Israeli officials, such as Foreign Minister Yigal Allon, sometimes added that Israel would "not be the second, either."[5] Presumably, the latter supplement was designed to dispel any Arab illusion that they might ever enjoy a nuclear monopoly in the Middle East. Indeed, this ambiguous nuclear policy was followed by successive Israeli governments, irrespective of their composition, demonstrating a remarkable degree of constancy and tacit bipartisan support.

Such ambiguity seems to have served a number of strategic as well as internal imperatives. First, it seems to have been designed to produce effective "deterrence through uncertainty."[6] Thus, the Arab states' inability to rule out the possibility that Israel might possess an operational nuclear capability and might use it in retaliation was expected to deter them from posing threats to Israel's existence and survival.

Second, Israel's implicit policy helped avoid a clash with the United States. After making a significant contribution to global nuclear proliferation in the framework of the Eisenhower administration's "Atoms for Peace" program, Washington attempted to prevent the further spread of nuclear arms. Whereas some U.S. administrations—notably those of Presidents Dwight Eisenhower, John Kennedy, and Lyndon Johnson—have raised the nuclear issue with successive Israeli governments, Israel's ambiguous policy helped prevent an explicit clash with Washington on this matter.[7] Indeed, Israel's nuclear ambiguity may have also provided a continuous incentive for U.S. conventional arms supplies to Israel. Such supplies may have been partly designed to ensure that Israel would remain strong enough conventionally so that it would refrain from "going nuclear."[8]

Third, Israel's ambiguous policy may have been designed to avoid encouraging its neighboring Arab states to seek a countervailing nuclear capability. The argument here seems to have been that if Israel adopted an explicit nuclear deterrence policy, Arab leaders would face intolerable domestic pressures to do the same, even if they considered such efforts to be too costly and technically uncertain and even if they regarded such a capability to be largely irrelevant to *their* strategic objectives. Thus, Israel's ambiguous nuclear posture could provide the Arab leaders with a capacity for "plausible deniability." As long as they could confess uncertainty regarding Israel's nuclear potential, they could continue to resist domestic pressures to produce "a response."

Also, Israel's ambiguous nuclear policy seems to have served the requirements of maintaining domestic consensus and support for its general defense policy. Among the policy elite, the ambiguous policy originally served as a compromise between those advocating greater reliance on nuclear deterrence and those claiming that such deterrence was irrelevant to the Middle East or counterproductive for Israel. Moshe Dayan seems to have been the most outspoken among the former, whereas Yigal Allon seems to have been the most explicit among the latter. The compromise reached between the two camps seems to have been that the potential would be developed but that reliance on it for specific deterrence would be limited by its ambiguous nature.[9]

More generally, the ambiguous posture helped prevent the development of a public debate regarding Israel's nuclear policy. This ensured not only the maintenance of domestic consensus but also a high degree of "policy autonomy" for those involved in tailoring the development of Israel's nuclear potential. In the absence of reliable information regarding the state of Israel's nuclear activities, a debate about its nuclear policy could not be conducted. And in the absence of public debate, the individuals navigating Israel's nuclear future could remain largely immune to external checks and controls.

Finally, Israel's nuclear ambiguity may have been designed to prevent it from developing a complacency resulting from excessive reliance on the nuclear option. This results from a widely shared Israeli judgment that nuclear options are irrelevant to most of the challenges it faces and that conventional forces must therefore continue to compose the central pillar of Israel's security.

 Indeed, the ambiguity surrounding Israel's nuclear potential was maintained despite some clear costs: first, the credibility of its general nuclear deterrence was somewhat limited as long as Israel's neighbors remained uncertain regarding its capability; second, the development of a coherent nuclear doctrine was hindered by the absence of open debate; third, the ability to conduct a direct or indirect strategic dialogue with Israel's neighbors—or to communicate specific threats or threat perceptions—remained constrained by secrecy; and finally, the process of socializing the Arab publics to Israel's permanence in the region was delayed by the limited capacity to project Israel's nuclear potential as contributing to such permanence.[10]

Nuclear Arms Control: Israel's Approach

THE NUCLEAR NONPROLIFERATION TREATY

Israel's refusal to sign the 1968 Nonproliferation Treaty (NPT) seems to have resulted from a number of considerations. Primarily, successive Israeli governments probably regarded such signature as contradicting the capacity to maintain Israel's ambiguous nuclear posture. Indeed, they seem to have considered that until there was conclusive evidence that the Arab states had reconciled themselves to Israel's existence and were willing to coexist peacefully with the Jewish state, Israel must continue to enjoy whatever measure of "deterrence through uncertainty" could be derived from its ambiguous nuclear posture.

In this context, becoming an NPT signatory would have closed a deterrent option before the dangers that had brought about the development of the deterrent could be eliminated. Closely related to this is the perception that the treaty isolates the nuclear dimension artificially, that is, without regard to conventional and other threats.

In addition, Israel considered the NPT to be a highly deficient instrument for arresting nuclear proliferation in the Middle East and elsewhere. And it did not want to contribute anything to the illusion that this was not the case. Indeed, three related short-comings of the NPT regime seemed to become the focus of Israeli concern. First, under the terms of the treaty, an NPT signatory can develop a full nuclear fuel cycle and can stockpile large quantities of plutonium, as long as these stockpiles and the facilities involved are subjected to periodic inspections by the International Atomic Energy Agency (IAEA). This raises the possibility that after accumulating such stockpiles of weapons-grade materials over a number of years, a state could then withdraw from the NPT—having given appropriate notice of its intention to do so, in accordance with the mechanisms defined in the treaty.

Second, the verification system adopted to ensure compliance with the NPT was considered extremely deficient. IAEA inspections were confined to declared facilities, and prior notice was given to the inspected state regarding prospective visits. Thus, no provisions were made for surprise visits to suspected facilities. Indeed, the IAEA also lacked any independent or otherwise meaningful intelligence-gathering capabilities for identifying suspected facilities. In addition, inspectors' considerations of future access were perceived as also limiting the extent to which inspections of declared facilities would be conducted rigorously. Thus, a country could develop a full-scale military nuclear capability right under the nose of IAEA inspectors, as Iraq was conclusively shown to have done.

The absence of painful sanctions, to be applied automatically in case a clear violation of the treaty was identified, also significantly reduced the credibility of the NPT. Under the regime's present structure, properly motivated signatories cannot be deterred from cheating.

Moreover, Israel considered itself at an inherent disadvantage regarding the NPT-IAEA regime. First, the more numerous and vast Arab countries were far better positioned to hide large-scale, forbidden nuclear facilities. Here, also, Iraq serves as an excellent example: its efforts and facilities for uranium enrichment through the electromagnetic isotope separation route were never discovered by the IAEA or by any of the Western intelligence agencies, including Israel's. Had Saddam Hussein avoided invading Kuwait—with his defeat leading to intrusive nuclear inspections—Iraq might have been able to acquire an operational nuclear capability. The fact that it had done so might not have been discovered before such efforts were completed.

Finally, during the past twenty years, Israel became increasingly uneasy about all UN-related international organizations, since the "one-state, one-vote" rule adopted by such bodies meant that the more numerous Arab states could always muster an Arab-Third World majority against the Jewish state. Israel suspected that such near-automatic majority could further protect Arab states from international sanctions, even if they were found to be violating the terms of the NPT.

THE NUCLEAR FREE ZONE PROPOSALS

The transformation of the Middle East into a nuclear weapons free zone (NWFZ) was proposed, in different versions, by Egypt (since 1974) and Israel (since 1980). On a number of occasions, the UN General Assembly adopted the idea, approving by large majorities a version similar to the one proposed by Egypt.[11] The main difference between the Israeli and Egyptian texts concerned the mechanism by which a nuclear weapons free zone should be established in the Middle East.

The Egyptian draft resolution called for the establishment of a Middle East nuclear weapons free zone without elaborating a mechanism for establishing such a zone. Indeed, it did not even suggest that a formal agreement creating such a zone should be negotiated *among* the region's states. Rather, it implied that these states should simply comply with the limitations stipulated by the creation of the zone. Thus, the Egyptian approach did not envisage that a change in political relations among the region's states should accompany the establishment of a nuclear weapons free zone in the Middle East.

In contrast, the Israeli draft resolution, first proposed on October 31, 1980, called "upon all states of the Middle East and non-nuclear-weapon states adjacent to the region, which are not signatories to any treaty providing for a nuclear-weapons-free-zone, to convene at the earliest possible date a conference with a view to negotiating a multilateral treaty establishing a nuclear-weapon-free zone in the Middle East."[12] The Israeli proposal's focus on the negotiating mechanism was quite intentional. Primarily, it resulted from the conviction that Israel should not surrender the deterrent effect of its nuclear potential unless Arab acceptance of Israel's existence in the region would allow them to negotiate with the Jewish state. Thus, the negotiating process was seen as an essential part of the efforts to build mutual confidence among the region's states, without which an NWFZ could not be established.

Indeed, some Israelis may have originally regarded Israel's consent to establish an NWFZ as a bargaining chip designed to obtain Arab recognition through their willingness to negotiate with the Jewish state. In this context, the Arab states' participation in direct negotiations with Israel was the price they would have to pay to constrain Israel's nuclear potential via the establishment of an NWFZ.

At the same time, it is possible that some Israelis who supported Israel's NWFZ proposal insisted on the aforementioned linkage because they assumed that the Arab states would never agree to take part in such negotiations. Based on this assumption, they may have argued that Israel was presented with an opportunity to appear favorably disposed toward the establishment of a nuclear weapons free zone with very little danger that Israel would ever have to confront the dilemmas involved in the establishment of such a zone in terms of its impact on Israeli deterrence.

The second distinction between the two proposals was found in their different approaches to the NPT and to IAEA safeguards. The Egyptian nuclear weapons free zone proposal suggested that pending the establishment of such a zone in the Middle East, the region's states should adhere to the stipulations of the NPT and subject all their nuclear facilities to IAEA safeguards. Some Egyptian formulations regarded NPT signature as the avenue for establishing the NWFZ. The Israeli approach to these matters was the opposite and regarded the possibility of an NWFZ as a substitute for the NPT. Israel's attitude on this issue seemed to be based on the aforementioned view that the IAEA safeguards system—designed to verify compliance with the NPT—was highly deficient. Consequently, it insisted that credible and intrusive verification measures must be negotiated by the region's states.

Israel's preference for the establishment of a *negotiated* NWFZ over participation in the NPT regime seemed to be based on the following considerations. First, the establishment of an NWFZ negotiated directly by all relevant parties in the region, including Iraq, Iran, and Libya, which form the focus of Israel's current nuclear proliferation concerns, would require a fundamental political transformation in the region. Only such a basic transformation in its neighbors' approach would allow Israel to reconsider the role of its nuclear potential in the state's grand strategy.

Second, a negotiated NWFZ would allow Israel to insist that the verification system attached to its establishment be sufficiently intrusive to prevent further proliferation. Thus, it would avoid the two main deficiencies of current NPT and IAEA stipulations: allowing the accumulation of weapons-grade material and refraining from short notice and challenge inspections. An NWFZ could include a complete ban on the production and stockpiling of plutonium and enriched uranium and could allow for a much more effective verification system.

Indeed, Israel could then insist that rather than delegating the task of such verification to an international organization, the parties to the agreement would conduct such verification themselves, in much the same manner that Americans and Russians currently monitor the various arms control and confidence-building agreements that they concluded in recent years. Even if a third party, such as the IAEA or teams of U.S. and Russian inspectors, did take part in such verification, the arrangements could stipulate significant participation by inspectors who are nationals of the region's states. In particular, it would be important to ensure that any challenge inspection would include experts from the country presenting the challenge.

In this context, an obvious question concerns the relationship between Israel's call for a negotiated NWFZ and the multilateral discussions on Middle East Arms Control and Regional Security (ACRS) launched in Moscow in early 1992. In principle, these talks could eventually provide the framework for negotiating the establishment of a regional NWFZ. However, much would have to be accomplished in the framework of these discussions, as well as in the context of the Israeli-Syrian bilateral talks, before these multilateral negotiations could focus on the establishment of an NWFZ in the Middle East.

Such prior progress is necessary because the region's states must first create a political and strategic environment that could make possible an NWFZ in the region. From the standpoint of most Arab states, the resolution of the political-territorial dispute with Israel seems to be a prerequisite to the establishment of a *negotiated* NWFZ. Syria, for example, is unlikely to agree to intrusive verification measures that include the participation of Israeli inspectors, without a prior resolution of its conflict with Israel.

Indeed, throughout 1992 Syria continued to boycott all Middle East multilateral negotiations conducted in the framework of the Moscow process, including the ACRS talks.[13]

From Israel's standpoint, the various bilateral and multilateral negotiations currently being conducted would have to address its motivations for developing a nuclear potential in the first place, namely, Israel's rejection by its Arab and Moslem neighbors and the strategic asymmetries characterizing its relationship with them. In this context, two problems would have to be addressed.

First, in comparison with the surrounding Arab states, Israel continues to suffer from a quantitative inferiority in the realm of standing conventional forces, exposing the Jewish state to surprise attack.[14] In the framework of the bilateral and multilateral talks currently being conducted, various security arrangements and confidence-building measures would have to be concluded in order to diminish Israel's fears of surprise attack.

These measures would have to include arrangements and mechanisms similar to those already adopted in Europe and the Middle East: the establishment of demilitarized and limited-forces zones; the reciprocal stationing of early-warning stations; the sharing of satellite intelligence data; the creation of mechanisms for mutual prenotification regarding large-scale military exercises and major military movements; the establishment of "hot lines" for effective communication between defense leaders and local commanders, allowing rapid resolution of incidents and uncertainties regarding unusual military activities; and the stationing of U.S. peacekeeping forces.

However, to reduce Israel's concerns to the extent that it would feel comfortable enough to diminish its reliance on nuclear deterrence, the surrounding Arab states would have to diminish their reliance on huge standing conventional forces and would have to adopt a ratio of reserves and standing forces similar to that adopted by the Israeli Defense Forces. To be sure, such changes in the Arab militaries would have to be implemented gradually, in order to avoid sharp economic, social, and political dislocations; however, the complex territorial and political components of an Arab-Israeli compromise are unlikely to be implemented overnight. These various stabilizing measures could be negotiated in the near future and implemented in concert over time.

The second problem that would need to be addressed is the participation of a number of key states currently remaining outside the multilateral negotiating process. Although in the conventional realm it is possible to establish a rationale for negotiating arms control between Israel and the Arab states surrounding it—Egypt, Jordan, Syria, and Lebanon—such limited negotiations would make very little sense in the realm of nuclear weapons and ballistic missiles. In the latter areas, the prime sources of concern are precisely the countries located on the region's periphery—Iraq, Iran, Libya, and Algeria. With appropriate delivery capabilities, these states' nuclear programs could affect Israel's security.[15] Without applying effective constraints to these countries, nuclear proliferation in the Middle East would not be arrested. Thus, if an NWFZ is to be established, the participation of these states would have to be ensured.

Whereas this second condition may seem self-evident, the first—linking the establishment of an NWFZ to the application of arms control and confidence building in the conventional realm—could be mistakenly interpreted as a sign of reduced Israeli commitment to the establishment of such a zone. Paradoxically, such a linkage arises from a very positive development in the region's strategic environment, namely, the Madrid process designed to resolve the Arab-Israeli dispute.

It is noteworthy that when Israel first proposed the establishment of an NWFZ, a comprehensive Middle East peace process, involving the surrounding Arab states, was considered a dream. Such a process is now reality. Understandably, however, the focus of Arab demands in these negotiations is Israel's withdrawal from all territories conquered in the 1967 War. The implication of launching negotiations to establish a Middle East NWFZ under current circumstances is that Israel would be asked to give up simultaneously the deterrent effect of its nuclear potential and the defensive advantage of its control of the West Bank and the Golan Heights.

It is extremely difficult to see how Israel could assume the risks entailed in making such far-reaching concessions in both realms at the same time. Indeed, to meet even a large part of the Arab states' territorial demands, let alone to meet all these demands, Israel would have to increase rather than diminish its reliance on all elements of its general deterrence.[16] Since the Arab states attach priority to resolving the political dispute and to gaining Israel's withdrawal, confidence-building measures should be applied parallel to such withdrawal; the new "peace and security" regime should register a positive track record before launching serious efforts to establish an NWFZ. Such a sequential approach would increase the likelihood that Israel would be prepared to assume the risks entailed in the establishment of such a zone and would diminish the odds that the Middle East negotiations would become overloaded.

Arms Control in the Middle East: The New Nuclear Agenda

THE NEW NUCLEAR ENVIRONMENT

Israel's future approach to nuclear arms control in the Middle East is likely to be affected not only by the aforementioned recent positive changes in the regional environment but also by the new dangers of nuclear proliferation in the Middle East. From Israel's standpoint, two related sources of risk are involved. The first concerns the various nuclear programs that are currently being launched throughout the region. In this context, Israel continues to be concerned about Iraq's nuclear threat, which comprises the following: (a) the combination of Saddam Hussein's determination and his proven skills in managing a complex nuclear program; (b) Iraq's financial and other resources; (c) uncertainties as to whether all Iraqi nuclear facilities have been uncovered by the inspections conducted in the framework of UN Resolution 687;[17] and (d) certainties regarding the fact that Iraq's expert manpower in the nuclear realm has remained intact.

Iran is a second source of concern, given the thick fog surrounding its nuclear efforts. Such concern is only marginally affected by the fact that Iran is an NPT signatory and must subject its nuclear facilities to full-scope IAEA safeguards. The main elements of the perceived Iranian nuclear threat are the following: (a) a number of statements made by Iranian leaders during the past two years, indicating every intention to develop an advanced nuclear capability;[18] (b) the availability of sufficient financial resources and trained manpower, including nuclear scientists and engineers who have been trained abroad; (c) reported efforts to reconstruct the nuclear program established by the shah, with particular efforts applied to completing the German-made nuclear reactors in Bushire and to purchasing a nuclear reactor from

China;[19] (d) uncertainties regarding suspected nuclear installations reportedly being established in Esphahan and Ghazvin, and the possibility that such facilities might include enrichment and reprocessing plants;[20] (e) confusion over the nature of assistance possibly provided to the Iranian nuclear program by Pakistan and China; and (f) the absence of an appropriate inspection regime such as the one currently applied to Iraq.

Libya, Algeria, and Syria currently compose a far smaller risk in the nuclear realm, but considerable uncertainties still surround the efforts made by the first two to establish an infrastructure in this field. In this context, it remains unclear how much progress Muammar Qadafi has made in developing the Libyan nuclear science center that was reported to include a ten-megawatt reactor.[21] Nor can the secrecy with which Algeria has surrounded the construction of its Chinese-made nuclear reactor be easily reconciled with its repeated declarations regarding the completely benign nature of its nuclear program.[22] Indeed, some suspicion is already developing that Algeria may next attempt to construct a reprocessing plant to produce weapons-grade plutonium. Thus, a number of countries on the region's perimeter are a growing source of Israeli concern in the nuclear realm.

Israel also does not remain indifferent to the initial steps taken by Syria to establish a nuclear infrastructure by purchasing a mini-reactor from China and by reportedly negotiating the purchase of nuclear facilities from India.[23] Israel also acknowledges that Egypt continues to enjoy considerable professional expertise in the nuclear realm. Its nuclear research center in Inshass was the first established in the Arab world, training hundreds of nuclear scientists and engineers. Recently, Egypt moved to improve its nuclear capability by signing an agreement to purchase from Argentina an additional research reactor.[24] Egypt is an NPT signatory, and all its nuclear facilities are subject to full-scope safeguards. There is no evidence that Egypt has deviated from its strategic decision to refrain from developing a military nuclear capability. In terms of the professional expertise available, Egypt certainly maintains an "option" to do so. But in the absence of facilities for uranium enrichment or plutonium reprocessing, such a change of direction would take years to implement.

A second—and more immediate—Israeli fear is that an Arab or Moslem state might import a "quick fix" nuclear capability. In the aftermath of the breakup of the Soviet Union, such concern centers on the possibility that in the chaos surrounding the breakup, control over some nuclear warheads would be lost, creating the danger that they might be smuggled and sold clandestinely in the Middle East. Additional concerns focus on the possibility that the deteriorating economic conditions in the Commonwealth of Independent States (CIS) would lead some of its nuclear engineers and weapons designers to prefer employment in the Middle East.[25]

It is extremely difficult to estimate the probability of these dangers.[26] For the moment, it seems that the mix of assistance, incentives, and warnings provided by the United States to the CIS has considerably diminished the odds that control over warheads would be lost.[27] Similarly, a set of external incentives and internal enforcement seems to have reduced the likelihood of a major brain drain, and there is at any rate some question as to the dangers that might have been involved in such a drain. Currently, it seems that the bottlenecks in Middle East nuclear programs result not from a shortage of expertise but rather from existing export controls exercised by most nuclear suppliers—blocking the transfer of materials and devices that are essential for constructing enrichment and reprocessing facilities.

Another source of danger entailed in the current state of affairs in the CIS—one that cannot be easily dismissed—is the possibility that plutonium or enriched uranium will be stolen and sold to a Middle East client.[28] The nuclear fuel-cycle in the CIS is now estimated to include some 150 tons of plutonium and over 1,000 tons of enriched uranium.[29] Even conservative assumptions about the current state of accounting, safety, and security procedures in the CIS cannot rule out that a very small amount of such materials could be smuggled.[30] This is particularly the case given the fact that less than 10 kilograms of plutonium or 25 kilograms of enriched uranium are needed to construct a nuclear device. Even small-scale material leakage from the CIS may have enormous strategic consequences in the Middle East. Although the difficulties of safely transporting such materials are considerable, smugglers might be prepared to compromise such safety in exchange for appropriate financial gains.

The main implication of this new nuclear environment—involving the enormous uncertainties surrounding the evolving nuclear programs in the region, as well as the risks of clandestine nuclear leakage from the CIS—is that to be effective, a nuclear arms control regime in the Middle East would have to include extremely intrusive verification measures. In turn, such measures would have to allow surprise and detailed inspections of any suspected facility, as well as careful monitoring of all direct and indirect routes from the CIS to the Middle East.

CAPPING: U.S. AND EGYPTIAN PROPOSALS

The difficulties entailed in applying the more ambitious objectives of nuclear arms control in the Middle East, such as universal adherence to the NPT, application of IAEA safeguards to all nuclear facilities in the region, and/or the transformation of the Middle East into an NWFZ, led the Bush administration to propose an interim objective: a verified freeze on the production of weapons-grade nuclear materials in the Middle East. The proposal, announced on May 29, 1991, in the framework of the "Bush Initiative" on arms control in the Middle East, stipulated that the production of separated plutonium and enriched uranium in the region should be banned.[31]

It should be noted that the Bush proposal does not apply to any preexisting stockpiles of fissionable materials in the region, nor does it address the long-standing ambiguity surrounding Israel's activities in the nuclear realm. In the latter respect, it may contrast with another proposal to end the production of weapons-grade nuclear material in the Middle East, a proposal developed by a number of senior Egyptian analysts. The latter proposal was first communicated informally to Israeli analysts in the immediate aftermath of the Gulf War. Later, it found explicit expression in an article published in *Al-Ahram* on April 28, 1991, by Ambassador Sallah Bassiouny, then director of the National Center for Middle East Studies in Cairo.[32] It was also presented in a paper delivered by Abdel Monem Said Aly of the Al-Ahram Center for Political and Strategic Studies at a conference held in Moscow in October 1991.[33]

This Egyptian production-freeze proposal differs in one key respect from the proposal advanced by President George Bush: the Egyptian proposal contains, as a first step toward implementing the freeze, a "transparency" stipulation, which would require Israel to declare that it possesses a nuclear stockpile.[34] The rationale for this Egyptian demand may be that a verifiable nuclear freeze cannot be implemented unless an agreement is first reached regarding the levels being frozen.

In informal communication, U.S. officials have rejected this notion, arguing that verifying a freeze requires only that the absence of further production is ensured. Accordingly, they suggest that verification of such a freeze should focus on production facilities, if they exist, and should not require that present inventories and past activities, to the extent that they existed, be declared.[35] Concurrently, some Israelis fear that Egypt's quest for nuclear transparency might be designed merely to "smoke out" Israel's nuclear potential, in the hope that the resulting international pressure might compel Israel to sign the NPT.[36] Although Israel has so far refrained from reacting to any of the "freeze" initiatives, it is likely to find the U.S. version less risky than the Egyptian proposal.

It seems that for Israel to accept any version of nuclear capping, it would have to be assured that the freeze would not be implemented unless all the region's states would accept its stipulations and, in light of the aforementioned changes in the region's nuclear environment, that the freeze would be accompanied by adequate verification measures. These measures would have to be implemented by the parties themselves, for much the same reasons mentioned above regarding the possible transformation of the region into an NWFZ. Only in such fashion could Israel be assured that the freeze might become an effective vehicle for preventing the regional spread of nuclear weapons.

Also, Israel would have to be promised that the steps taken in the framework of implementing the proposal would not result in any erosion of Israeli deterrence. At the technical level, this means that any step that might erode Israel's nuclear potential would be avoided. At the political level, prior agreement that Israel's acceptance of a freeze would not lead to immediate demands for it to assume additional obligations in the nuclear realm would have to be obtained. Indeed, Israel would need to be assured that progress from the "freeze" phase to the implementation of the more ambitious goals included in the Bush Initiative, such as adherence to the NPT and the transformation of the region to an NWFZ, would be linked to a political timetable; these steps would be implemented only after agreements resolving the Arab-Israeli disputes were completed. In this way, the agreements and their associated confidence-building measures would acquire a positive track record over a considerable length of time before the next steps in the nuclear realm would be attempted.

Finally, Israel's acceptance of such a "freeze" would probably require a prior U.S.-Israeli agreement, involving a U.S. commitment to act effectively to prevent further nuclear proliferation in the Middle East and to support Israeli deterrence and preventive measures if these efforts fail.

UNILATERAL PREVENTION

Pending circumstances that allow the effective application of multilateral nuclear nonproliferation measures, such as adherence to the NPT, the establishment of a Middle East NWFZ, or the implementation of a "freeze" on the production of weapons-grade materials, Israel is likely to continue to pursue unilateral prevention. This policy was adopted in the late 1970s and focused on arresting Iraq's nuclear buildup. Its climax was the bombing of Iraq's French-built Osirak nuclear research reactor in Tuwaitha, near Baghdad, on June 5, 1981.[37]

The premise underlying this preventive policy is that the acquisition of nuclear weapons by Arab states—before the Arab-Israeli conflict has been resolved and the Middle East has been stabilized—would threaten Israel's very existence. Thus, every effort should be made to arrest nuclear proliferation in the region in the interim.

Israel's preventive policy has been explicitly stated by its government. After the bombing of Osirak, it stated, "Under no circumstances would we allow the enemy to develop weapons of mass destruction against our nation; we will defend Israel's citizens in time, with all the means at our disposal."[38] The statement was soon crowned "the Begin doctrine," not only because it was viewed as such by numerous observers worldwide but also because it was repeated by different Israeli leaders.[39] Publishing the doctrine was intended to dissuade Iraq, as well as other Arab countries that might consider emulating Baghdad, from attempting to develop a nuclear weapons capability.

In a postraid news conference, Prime Minister Menachem Begin also clarified the connection between Israel's approaches to nuclear proliferation and peace by noting that its announced preventive doctrine applied only to its enemies.[40] The statement implied that the doctrine would not be applied to Egypt, which had signed a peace treaty with Israel in 1979. Much later, in response to considerable international criticism of the 1981 bombing, particularly at the UN and during the annual meetings of the IAEA, Israel also promised to avoid destroying "peaceful nuclear installations."

Yet these clarifications have not diminished Israel's continuous commitment to do everything possible to prevent dangerous nuclear buildups in the Middle East. The deputy chief of staff of the Israel Defense Forces (IDF), General Amnon Shahak, recently noted: "Even a delay of one week is important, and a delay of ten years is excellent. The State of Israel should invest all its energy and efforts in order to prevent the development of a nuclear capability in an Arab country." He stressed that in his view, "all means are legitimate in pursuing this objective."[41] Thus, Israel's preventive doctrine concerning the acquisition of nuclear weapons by its remaining adversaries remains in effect.

PROLOGUE: THE RABIN GOVERNMENT'S APPROACH

Since entering office in July 1992, the new Israeli government, headed by Prime Minister Yitzhak Rabin, made a number of decisions reflecting its approach to arms control in the Middle East. First, it decided to permit European participation in the multilateral working group on "Security and Arms Control in the Middle East." This was in contrast to the previous Israeli government's reservations regarding such possible participation. Second, it opened a direct dialogue with the Egyptian government on arms control issues, thus transcending both governments' previous habit of confining themselves to presenting their conflicting approaches to the U.S. government.

Third, the Israeli Cabinet decided to join the Chemical Weapons Convention (CWC) as an original signatory, without preconditions. This reversed the position of Israel's former government, which had presented a number of prerequisites to its signature, such as universal Arab participation in the CWC regime and prior agreement on specific verification measures.

Fourth, by early November 1992, Israeli and Jordanian negotiators agreed on an agenda for future bilateral peace talks between the two countries. The joint document elaborates the two governments' "mutual commitment, as a matter of priority and as soon as possible, to work towards a Middle East free from weapons of mass destruction, conventional and non-conventional weapons." It also states, "This goal is to be achieved in the context of a comprehensive, lasting and stable peace characterized by the renunciation of the use of force, reconciliation and openness."[42]

Finally, in response to suggestions by the Egyptian government and the Bush administration, Israel agreed in late 1992 to define its "visionary goals" for the arms control process in the Middle East. It began to do so in the Israeli-Jordanian joint agenda and continued in the framework of a speech delivered by Foreign Minister Shimon Peres in Paris on January 14, 1993, on the occasion of signing the CWC. Peres announced, "In the spirit of the global pursuit of general and complete disarmament, and the establishment of regional and global arms control regimes, Israel suggests to all the countries of the region to construct a mutually verifiable zone, free of surface-to-surface missiles and of chemical, biological and nuclear weapons." He added: "Arms control negotiations and arrangements should be mutually agreed upon and include all the states of the region. Implementation and verification mechanisms, the establishment of comprehensive and durable peace, should be region-wide in their application. Priority in this process ought to be assigned to systems whose destabilizing potential and effects have been proven through their use in wars and have inflicted mass casualties." Within this context, Israel called on the region's states "to install mutual challenge inspections once peace has been established and endured the test of time."[43]

Although none of these decisions reflect a revolutionary change in Israeli policy, taken together they signal a more positive approach toward arms control. Moreover, a number of themes characterizing the evolution of Israel's approach to nuclear arms control are revealed, particularly in the latter two statements. First, nuclear disarmament should be implemented in a region-wide framework in which all weapons of mass destruction (WMD) are addressed. Second, conventional weapons should be considered as WMD, since their frequent use in the region has resulted in enormous damage. Indeed, the Israel-Jordan agenda represents the first instance of Arab acceptance of this Israeli emphasis. Third, priority in regional arms control negotiations should be given to conventional and chemical weapons, since, to date, all killing in the Middle East has been the result of these weapons. Fourth, the establishment of a comprehensive and durable regionwide peace implies that the purposes of Israel's cumulative deterrence have been obtained. Under such conditions Israel would support the establishment of a WMD-free zone in the Middle East. And finally, verification of compliance with the agreements, including challenge inspections, should not be assigned to a third party, including the UN. Instead, verification should be conducted by the parties themselves on a reciprocal basis.

Conclusion

A number of points regarding Israel's nuclear policy and its approach to nuclear arms control in the Middle East should be derived from this chapter. First, Arab rejection of Israel and Israel's quantitative inferiority in standing conventional forces— exposing it to surprise attack—led to its development of a nuclear option. Thus, a negotiated end of the conflict, accompanied by appropriate security arrangements and confidence-building measures designed to reduce mutual fears of surprise attack, would enable Israel to negotiate the establishment of an NWFZ or a zone free of all WMD in the Middle East.

Second, given the evolving regional nuclear environment, such a zone would have to include all of the countries in the Middle East, from North Africa to Iran, and their compliance with the constraints involved would have to be verified by the application of extremely intrusive measures, conducted by the parties themselves.

Third, until an NWFZ or a WMD-free zone can be established, the production of weapons-grade nuclear material in the Middle East could be capped. But in this case as well, regionwide participation and the application of adequate verification measures would have to be ensured if such a "freeze" is to constitute effective arms control. From Israel's standpoint, it would also be necessary to guarantee that until the Arab-Israeli conflict is resolved, the constraints involved in such a "freeze" do not erode the deterrent effect of Israel's nuclear potential.

Finally, until any of these multilateral nuclear arms control measures can be applied, Israel is likely to continue to adhere to its preventive doctrine. Clearly, however, its ability to apply the doctrine would depend on the specific circumstances surrounding each of the nuclear weapons programs in the Middle East: their location and composition, the extent of their proliferation potential, and the political circumstances prevailing when action is considered.

Notes

1. There is little sense in denying the sensitive nature of the subject matter, and the qualified phrases used here merely reflect this sensitivity. Indeed, such sensitivity also makes it imperative to emphasize that this chapter simply reflects its author's perspective and by no means should be interpreted as reflecting Israeli government policy. Thus, when interpretations of Israeli policy and its rationale are presented, these merely reflect the author's best understanding of the issues involved. Finally, nothing in this chapter should be regarded as indicating anything about the state of Israel's nuclear potential. The author of this chapter confesses total ignorance on this matter, and the ambiguous references to Israel's nuclear potential simply reflect the author's own ambiguity regarding the past and current state of such potential.

2. Indeed, this seems also to be the Arab reading of the purposes of Israel's nuclear deterrent. See Ambassador Sallah Bassiouny, "Israel's Nuclear Option and the Question of Peace," *Al-Ahram*, April 28, 1991.

3. David Ben-Gurion, *Bama'aracha*, vol. 1 (Tel Aviv: Am Oved, 1957), pp. 16, 61–62, 159, 212. See also Avner Yaniv, *Deterrence without the Bomb* (Lexington, Mass.: D.C. Heath and Co., 1987), p. 274.

4. Yair Evron, "Israel and the Atom: The Uses and Misuses of Ambiguity, 1957–1967," *Orbis* 17, no. 4 (Winter 1974): 1326–43.

5. See Yair Evron, *Hadilema Hagarinit Shel Israel* (Israel's nuclear dilemma) (Efaal: Yad Tabenkin, 1987), p. 81.

6. See Shai Feldman, *Israeli Nuclear Deterrence: A Strategy for the 1980s* (New York: Columbia University Press, 1982), p. 10.

7. For an exposé of the factors determining the U.S. approach toward Israel's nuclear potential, see ibid., pp. 192–233.

8. See Evron, *Hadilema Hagarinit Shel Israel*, pp. 79–81. See also Evron, "Israel and the Atom," pp. 1326–43.

9. Evron, *Hadilema Hagarinit Shel Israel*, p. 18.

10. For an elaboration of the advantages of an explicit nuclear posture, see Feldman, *Israeli Nuclear Deterrence*, pp. 7–24.

11. For example, see UN General Assembly Resolution 45\52, titled "Establishment of a Nuclear Weapons Free Zone in the Region of the Middle East," December 4, 1990.

12. "Establishment of a Nuclear-Weapon-Free-Zone in the Region of the Middle East—Israel: Draft Resolution," UN General Assembly, Thirty-fifth session, First Committee, Agenda Item no. 38, October 31, 1980.

13. Aluf Ben, "Syria May Participate in the Next Meeting of the Arms Control Talks," *Ha'aretz*, September 27, 1992.

14. For an exposé of these quantitative asymmetries, see, for example, Shlomo Gazit, ed., *The Middle East Military Balance, 1990–1991* (Tel Aviv: Jaffee Center for Strategic Studies, Tel Aviv University, 1992).

15. See Kenneth R. Timmerman, *Weapons of Mass Destruction: The Cases of Iran, Syria, and Libya* (Los Angeles: Simon Wiesenthal Center, 1992).

16. This point has also been stressed on a number of occasions by Geoffrey Kemp. See his "The Middle East Arms Race: Can It Be Controlled?" *Middle East Journal* 45, no. 3 (Summer 1991): 441–56.

17. "Former UN Inspector Rejects Report That Iraq Has Given up Nuclear Plans," *Jerusalem Post*, September 4, 1992.

18. "Iranian Vice-President: Yes, We Are Working Towards Attaining a Nuclear Bomb," *Hadashot*, November 17, 1991; "Iran: We Guarantee an Atomic Bomb vis-à-vis the Israeli Nuclear Challenge," *Ha'aretz*, November 17, 1992.

19. Elaine Sciolino, "Iran to Get A-Power Reactor from China," *International Herald Tribune*, September 12–13, 1992; Dan Izenberg et al., "Quan: Reactor for Iran Is Not a Nuclear Weapon," *Jerusalem Post*, September 17, 1992; "Iran Conducting Negotiations with China and Russia for the Purchase of Atomic Reactors for Peaceful Needs," *Ha'aretz*, September 24, 1992.

20. In this connection, some concern is also directed at the reported "secret clause" in the agreement reached between France and Iran settling their dispute regarding Iran's investment in Eurodif, the French producer of enriched uranium. Haim Hendwalker, "Secret Agreement between France and Iran Regarding Iran's Demand to Receive Enriched Uranium," *Ha'aretz*, November 13, 1991.

21. See Timmerman, *Weapons of Mass Destruction*, p. 88.

22. "Algeria to Sign Nuclear Pact, Aide Says," *International Herald Tribune*, January 8, 1992.

23. "Beijing to Sell Mini-reactor for Transfer to Syria," *Jerusalem Post*, November 29, 1991; Shefi Gabai, "Syria Authorized by the Atomic Energy Agency to Purchase Reactors," *Ma'ariv*, February 10, 1992.

24. "Egypt Purchasing from Argentina a $60 Million Nuclear Research Reactor," *Ha'aretz*, September 20, 1992.

25. "At Least 500 Soviet Nuclear Experts Emigrated to Libya, Syria, and Iraq," *Ha'aretz*, January 14, 1992; "German Newspaper Reports: Saddam Recruited 50 Nuclear Scientists from CIS," *Ha'aretz*, June 8, 1992.

26. For the view that concern about the odds of nuclear "leakage" from the CIS has been exaggerated, see Stephen M. Meyer "The Post-Soviet Nuclear Menace Has Been Hyped," *International Herald Tribune*, December 16, 1991.

27. For an illustration that worry about warhead safety continues, see Michael R. Gordon, "Keeping an Eye on Warheads," *International Herald Tribune*, July 4–5, 1992.

28. "Soviet Uranium on Sale Abroad," *Jerusalem Post*, January 1, 1992.

29. William J. Broad, "Estimate Rises on Russian Uranium," *International Herald Tribune*, September 12–13, 1992.

30. "German Police Seize Smuggled Uranium," *International Herald Tribune*, October 17–18, 1992; "Bonn Says Seized Uranium Wasn't Suitable for Bombs," *International Herald Tribune*, October 20, 1992. See also William J. Broad, "From Soviet Warheads to US Reactor Fuel," *New York Times*, September 6, 1992.

31. See "Fact Sheet on Middle East Arms Control Initiative," Release from the White House Office of the Press Secretary, Kennebunkport, Maine, May 29, 1991.

32. Bassiouny, "Israel's Nuclear Option." Bassiouny refers to this idea as having been presented by Israelis and Americans at a conference held in Cairo a year earlier.

33. Abdel Monem Said Aly, "Arms Control and the Resolution of the Arab-Israeli Conflict: An Arab Perspective" (paper presented at the conference on "Cooperative Security in the Middle East," Institute of the USA and Canada, Moscow, USSR, October 21–24, 1991).

34. Bassiouny, "Israel's Nuclear Option."

35. Interview with senior State Department officials, summer 1991.

36. For the view that Israel should refrain from greater nuclear transparency, as suggested by Egyptians, see Ze'ev Schiff, "Of What Are the Arabs Afraid," *Ha'aretz*, June 26, 1991. Schiff also argued that Israeli acceptance of the "capping" proposal would lead to U.S. pressures on Israel to sign the NPT. See Ze'ev Schiff, "To Dimona through Iraq," *Ha'aretz*, July 5, 1991.

37. Shai Feldman, "The Bombing of Osiraq—Revisited," *International Security* 7, no. 2 (Fall 1982): 114–42.

38. *Ha'aretz*, June 9, 1981.

39. See Feldman, "The Bombing of Osiraq—Revisited," p. 122.

40. William Claiborne, "Begin Threatens to Destroy Any Reactor Menacing Israel," *Washington Post*, June 10, 1981.

41. Ya'acov Erez and Emanuel Rosen, "Deputy Chief of Staff, General Amnon Shahak-Lipkin: 'All the Means Are Legitimate' to Prevent a Nuclear Capability from an Arab State," *Ma'ariv*, April 17, 1992.

42. "Text of Israel-Jordan Agenda for Talks," *Jerusalem Post*, November 2, 1992.

43. Release by the Ministry of Foreign Affairs, Jerusalem, January 14, 1993.

Chapter 4

The Former Soviet Union

Steven E. Miller

Introduction

The disintegration of the Soviet Union has raised unprecedented nonproliferation challenges.[1] The USSR left behind a legacy of some thirty thousand nuclear weapons and an extensive and far-flung nuclear infrastructure for the production and maintenance of these weapons. The devolution of the Soviet Union into fifteen newly independent states left unsettled the destiny of this vast arsenal and its associated nuclear complex.[2] The Soviet nuclear legacy could plausibly end up safely and securely consolidated in Russia. But it is perhaps equally plausible that the disposition of the Soviet nuclear legacy will contribute to regional and global nuclear proliferation. More than two years after the collapse of the USSR, the question remains unresolved. Indeed, mounting instability in key countries, including notably Ukraine and Russia, as well as growing frictions between them, makes the proliferation risks in the former Soviet Union as worrisome as ever.

This chapter will describe and assess the proliferation risks associated with the demise of a nuclear superpower. Inevitably, this will involve speculation about possible scenarios whose relative likelihood is subject to dispute.[3] Analyzing this subject is impossible without focusing on potential negative outcomes that may be improbable but that cannot be dismissed. The aim in this chapter is to provide a comprehensive picture of proliferation risks while avoiding either undue alarmism or unwarranted nonchalance. Finally, actions and policies intended to contain nuclear proliferation risks in the former Soviet Union will be described.

Types of Proliferation Risks in the Former Soviet Union

The proliferation risks produced by the disintegration of the Soviet Union arise from four features of the post-Soviet landscape. First, the nuclear arsenal and nuclear infrastructure left behind by the USSR were widely distributed geographically. Indeed, until the last year or two, the Soviet Union had weapons deployed in fourteen of its fifteen republics and on the territory of several of its East European allies. However, a substantial consolidation of the nuclear arsenal has already taken place, which removed nuclear weapons from East Europe and from eleven of the Soviet republics.[4] But nuclear weapons remain in three Soviet successor states and are widely distributed throughout Russia. Second, the nuclear custodial system charged with responsibility for the safety and security of the nuclear arsenal and infrastructure is functioning in conditions of political instability and socioeconomic distress. It appears to have performed well so far, but its effectiveness could erode if subjected to further dislocations. Third, almost unnoticed, the demise of the USSR has raised a traditional nonproliferation concern: a number of the newly independent states have inherited nuclear reactors that were completely outside the international safeguards system, and many of these facilities are still not safeguarded. Hence, the option of exploiting spent reactor fuel as a source of fissile material for use in nuclear weapons—which international safeguards are meant to prevent—is available to these states. Finally, the post-Soviet international order in Soviet Eurasia, already less than peaceful, could come to be marked by high levels of insecurity and conflict. This could create incentives for successor states to proliferate.

These four sources of potential trouble lead to three types of nuclear proliferation risks.[5] One is the risk of successor state proliferation—the possibility that the collapse of the USSR could give rise to more than one nuclear-armed state. A second is the risk of nuclear terrorism or other illicit or unauthorized seizure or use of nuclear weapons. And third is the possibility of nuclear spillover: the risk that nuclear weapons or weapons-related items and materials will leak out of the former Soviet Union and contribute to the global spread of nuclear capability. The following sections will discuss each of these risks in turn.

Four Paths to Successor State Proliferation

One proliferation risk raised by the demise of the Soviet Union is the possibility that more than one successor state will opt to acquire a nuclear weapons capability. There are four ways in which this might come about.

1. Gaining custody of Soviet nuclear weapons deployed outside of Russia. Three newly independent states—Belarus, Kazakhstan, and Ukraine—still have strategic nuclear forces deployed on their territories. Indeed, both Ukraine and Kazakhstan have over one thousand nuclear weapons within their borders—enough to make them the third- and fourth-largest nuclear powers, respectively. One or more of these three states could decide to take custody of these weapons.[6]

At present, this is not the declared intention of any of the three governments in question. Quite the contrary, all three have repeatedly pledged to denuclearize their territories and to become members of the Nonproliferation Treaty (NPT) as nonnuclear weapons states. Further, in the May 1992 Lisbon Protocol to the START agreement, which made these three states parties to the START treaty (joining with Russia and the United States), they reiterated these pledges in a formal and legally binding agreement with the United States. In addition, at the January 1994 tripartite Moscow summit, Russia, the United States, and Ukraine signed the Trilateral Statement in which Kiev reaffirmed yet again its commitment to denuclearize and to join the NPT in the shortest possible time.[7]

However, Kazakhstan and especially Ukraine have been slow to ratify the START I/Lisbon Protocol package, the entry into force of START I has been blocked by Ukraine's failure to accede to the NPT, and as of May 1994, implementation of the denuclearization commitment has hardly begun in either country. Moreover, so long as nuclear weapons are stored or deployed within these states, the possibility remains that one or more of the states in question could decide at some point in the future to take control of them. This appears to be a lesser concern in the case of Belarus, which ratified START relatively promptly, voted to accede to the NPT in February 1993, and agreed with Russia that all nuclear weapons will be withdrawn from its territory by the end of 1994; removal of these weapons began in the fall of 1993, and by the end of that year only fifty-four of the original eighty-one SS-25 Intercontinental Ballistic Missiles (ICBMs) remained in Belarus.[8]

But for Kazakhstan and Ukraine, the timetables for denuclearization stretch years into the future. They have both committed to denuclearize within the START implementation schedule, which is seven years from the entry into force of the treaty. Since START has not yet entered force, the deadline accepted by Kiev and Almaty will arrive no sooner than 2001 and will be even later if entry into force is further delayed. In connection with the Trilateral Statement, Ukraine is reported to have reached a confidential agreement with Russia and the United States to eliminate all nuclear weapons from its territory within three years;[9] if measured from the date of signature, this means that Ukraine's denuclearization deadline is January 1997.

As the past several years have vividly demonstrated, a lot can change in three years, and even more in seven. It is possible, for example, that current governments will abandon their present denuclearization policy in response to changing circumstances. None of the three has proclaimed an unconditional commitment to denuclearization. Indeed, in the course of becoming parties to START, they stated explicitly that their national security interests would be taken into account in implementing denuclearization.[10] Thus, a rupture of relations with Moscow, the outbreak of hostilities with Moscow or other neighbors, or perhaps the prevalence of endemic conflict within the former Soviet Union could constitute grounds for reversing course on the nuclear weapons issue.[11]

Further, the governments of Ukraine or Kazakhstan are unlikely to remain unchanged over the next seven years or more. And given the political turbulence being experienced throughout the former Soviet Union, the character of the next governments is highly uncertain; there can be no guarantee that they will regard themselves as bound by the commitments of the present governments. Pro-nuclear weapons sentiment clearly exists in Ukraine,[12] for example. Indeed, since Kiev gained its independence, the tide of Ukrainian opinion has been shifting strongly in the direction of retaining nuclear weapons.[13] There already appears to be wide support in the Ukrainian parliament for keeping nuclear weapons and even more for going slow on denuclearization.[14] It will hardly be surprising if, over the next seven years, such views become predominant in the Ukrainian government, whether it be democratic or authoritarian.

In short, although current governments have promised denuclearization, neither current policies nor current leaders will necessarily survive the implementation timetables presently envisioned.

2. Leakage from the Soviet nuclear arsenal or complex to newly independent states. Any of the Soviet successor states—including Belarus, Kazakhstan, or Ukraine after nuclear weapons are removed from their territories—could acquire nuclear weapons by illicit means from somewhere in the nuclear establishment left behind by the USSR. The custodial system responsible for the safety and security of the nuclear arsenal has so far continued to function remarkably well in difficult political and economic circumstances.[15] But should political instability or economic distress intensify, the nuclear custodial system could erode or break down altogether.[16] This could lead to much greater risk of leakage of weapons or weapons-related materials out of the system to parties seeking nuclear capability. Although most analyses of this problem have focused on the question of nuclear spillover out of the former Soviet Union, there is no reason why this means of nuclear spread could not take place within Soviet Eurasia.

So far, none of the Soviet successor states (other than Russia—and possibly Ukraine) seem strongly or clearly motivated to seek a nuclear weapons capability.[17] But there can be no certainty that this will remain the case indefinitely for all the Soviet successor states. Particularly if the post-Soviet regional order turns out to be malign and conflict-prone, some of these states could come to conclude that nuclear weapons are desirable or necessary to ensure their security. Indeed, Russia's newly independent neighbors will face two conditions that historically have been powerful motivations to acquire nuclear weapons: a potential nuclear adversary and an overwhelming conventional threat.[18] If Russia turns menacing (or is perceived as such), these motivations to acquire nuclear weapons could become irresistible. This point is telling because indications from Moscow are far from reassuring to its neighbors; there are many outspoken Russian proponents of a dominant Russia pursuing an aggressive foreign policy.[19] As the success of the ultranationalist (and, some would say, neo-Facist) Vladimir Zhirinovsky in Russia's December 1993 election indicates, these views are increasingly prominent and influential in the Russian debate.[20] Moreover, not only the Russian debate but also Russian foreign policy is increasingly alarming to the other states of the former Soviet Union; Russia's policy toward the newly independent states appears to be more and more aggressive, and its goal appears to be domination.[21] If this trend should continue or intensify, this could easily push some Soviet successor states toward nuclear acquisition.

In addition, the newly independent states may confront other difficult security challenges, whether disputes with one another or rivalries with other relatively powerful states, such as China or Turkey. Thus, for example, Armenia fits the motivational profile of a potential proliferator: it is locked in a bitter conflict with Azerbaijan, has a long and bloody rivalry with its much more powerful southern neighbor, Turkey (including memories of a genocide earlier in this century), and in general feels encircled by potential enemies. Armenia could be, it has been suggested, the Caucasian Israel.[22] Although some may be more prone than others to seriously consider or to exercise the nuclear option, in theory all fourteen non-Russian successor states could do so, and any among them might be able to amass at least a modest inventory of nuclear weapons by illicit means.

3. Soviet successor states can develop indigenous nuclear weapons programs.   The Soviet successor states will always have the same proliferation option that is available to any other nonnuclear state: they can develop an indigenous nuclear weapons program. As noted, in the coming years, some of these states could well find themselves in a regional setting that provides considerable incentive to do so.

Starting from scratch will be longer, more difficult, and more costly than the proliferation paths described above. In this scenario, the nuclear shortcut provided by the Soviet nuclear legacy is foregone—or at least is not the primary path to a nuclear weapons capability. And it will bring potential proliferators into collision with the international regime of export controls on nuclear commerce, controls intended to make it as difficult as possible for states to develop nuclear weapons capabilities. As the experiences of recent aspiring proliferators attest, this is not an easy path to nuclear weapons.

But there is no reason to suppose that it is beyond the capacities of all the Soviet successor states to adopt this strategy should nuclear acquisition be deemed necessary now or in the future. The larger and wealthier successor states, particularly Ukraine, will undoubtedly possess the financial and technical resources to move in this direction. It is hard to know what the lower threshold of capability would be, but suffice it to say that most of the Soviet successor states possess at least roughly the population of Israel and at least roughly the gross national product and technological level of North Korea—to compare them to two states that are thought to have nuclear weapons programs.

Moreover, some of the Soviet successor states will not be starting from zero. They may, for example, inherit Soviet personnel who could provide useful or necessary expertise. Further, nuclear research centers are located in Armenia, Belarus, Georgia, Kazakhstan, Latvia, Ukraine, and Uzbekistan.[23] More important, four of the newly independent states—Armenia, Kazakhstan, Lithuania, and Ukraine—have nuclear power reactors on their territory. And Belarus, Estonia, Georgia, Kazakhstan, Latvia, Ukraine, and Uzbekistan have research or training reactors within their borders.[24] At present, most of the newly independent states are not members of the NPT, and none has signed a safeguards agreement with the International Atomic Energy Agency (IAEA).[25] In the context of the other proliferation worries associated with the former Soviet Union, this fact has attracted relatively little notice. But in any other setting, the existence of nearly twenty large, unsafeguarded nuclear power reactors, spread across at least five newly independent and not terribly stable states (some of whom have plausible incentives for acquiring nuclear weapons), would be regarded as a crisis for the nonproliferation regime.

Unsafeguarded reactors provide potential access to fissile material, since spent reactor fuel contains extractable plutonium. A notional one-gigawatt-electric reactor will produce about two hundred to three hundred kilograms per year of plutonium in spent fuel.[26] Ukraine—which has by far the largest nuclear power industry of these states—possesses reactors with a combined capacity of some twelve to sixteen gigawatts of electricity.[27] In other words, several thousand kilograms of plutonium in spent fuel are accumulating in Ukraine on an annual basis. Since even primitive weapon designs use no more than five or six kilograms of weapons-grade plutonium,[28] this represents fissile material for some six hundred weapons per year. The same is true, at lower levels of capacity, for the other Soviet successor states with nuclear reactors. What makes this point all the more arresting is that Russia, the supplier of reactor fuel to all these facilities, has been refusing to take back the spent fuel.[29] These states may already have substantial inventories of spent fuel accumulating in cooling pools at their facilities.[30]

Before it can be used to fabricate weapons, plutonium must be separated from spent fuel by reprocessing. This involves cutting the spent fuel rods into pieces, dissolving the contents of the rods in acid, and chemically separating the plutonium. Although handling radioactive and highly toxic materials is not easy, this process should not pose an insurmountable challenge to a determined Soviet successor state.[31]

One of the basic purposes of the IAEA safeguards system is to prevent the diversion to nuclear weapons programs of the fissile material produced by civilian nuclear power reactors. The strict materials accounting procedures and inspection requirements raise a risk of detection that is thought to inhibit or deter diversion. For the time being, and so long as safeguards are not applied to their nuclear power plants, the Soviet successor states do not face this constraint and can divert spent fuel to military purposes with no international accountability. Moreover, even if these states eventually do join the IAEA safeguards system, by the time they do so they will have had ample opportunity to accumulate inventories of spent fuel for use in a weapons program; any material that is not in the initial inventory reported to the IAEA is invisible to the safeguards system.[32] Thus, these states have potential access to significant quantities of fissile material. Were it not for the fact that the other paths to nuclear acquisition for Soviet successor states seem more immediate and more attractive, this would be a preoccupying nonproliferation problem.

4. *The disintegration of Russia as a path to nuclear proliferation.* Should Russia disintegrate, all three of the paths to successor state proliferation described above would come into play, perhaps in exacerbated form—just in a different setting from that which presently exists. Like the Soviet Union, Russia is a multinational state (albeit with a largely Russian population), and it is experiencing centrifugal tendencies. This does not mean that disintegration is inevitable. Indeed, the potential breakaway areas in

Russia are for the most part remote, weak, sparsely populated, and lacking any historical memory of statehood; it will not be easy for them to escape Russia's grasp, nor is this the present objective of most of the regions in question. But Moscow's authority has clearly weakened, and many areas within Russia have already explicitly asserted their desire for autonomy or independence.[33] Disintegration may not be likely, but it could happen. Further, the effort to make it happen could produce civil strife and violence or even civil war.

All three paths to successor state proliferation could be replicated in the event that the Russian Federation breaks into two or more successor states. First, the collapse of Russia could lead directly to successor state proliferation due to the geographic distribution of weapons and facilities. These are scattered from one end of Russia to the other, including in politically disturbed areas that could break from Moscow. One or more newly independent Russian successor states could end up with nuclear weapons on its territory—whether strategic missile fields, air defense units, or even tactical nuclear weapons associated with the army. Indeed, many of Russia's trouble spots are found along its vast southern frontier, an area in which large numbers of such bases and installations are normally found. Because most of the potential breakaway states are so weak relative to Russia, they could feel it imperative to retain a nuclear capability to have any hope of preserving their independence against Russian revanchism.[34] In this way, the splintering of Russia, like the demise of the USSR, has the potential to produce multiple nuclear states.

Second, the collapse of Russia could disrupt or dismember the nuclear custodial system. Depending on where the states seeking independence were located, pieces of this system could be lost. Transportation connections to some facilities or bases could be disturbed or interrupted. For example, a band of autonomous republics—including Mordovia, Chuvashia, Mari, Tatarstan, Udmurtia, and Bashkiria—stands between Moscow and Russian territory in the Urals and eastward and stands astride almost all the east-west land lines of communication (figure 4.1). All but two of the major facilities of the Russian nuclear complex lie east of this cluster of autonomous republics, and parts of the complex lie near or in Mordovia (figure 4.2). Obviously, political disturbances, civil violence, or attempted breakaways in these Russian republics have considerable potential to cause problems for the Russian nuclear establishment. Thus, even Russia—the one

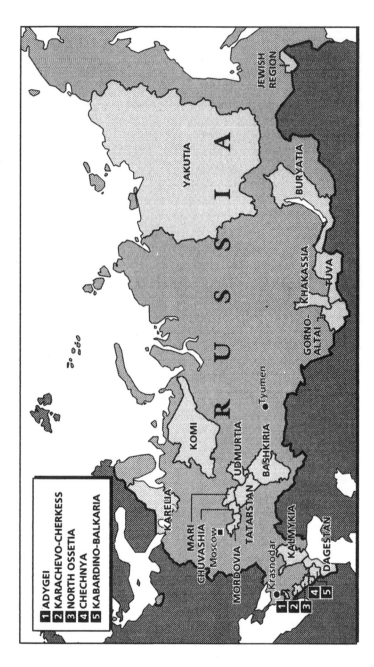

FIGURE 4.1   Autonomous Republics of the Former Soviet Union
SOURCE: *The Economist*, September 5, 1992. Reprinted with permission.

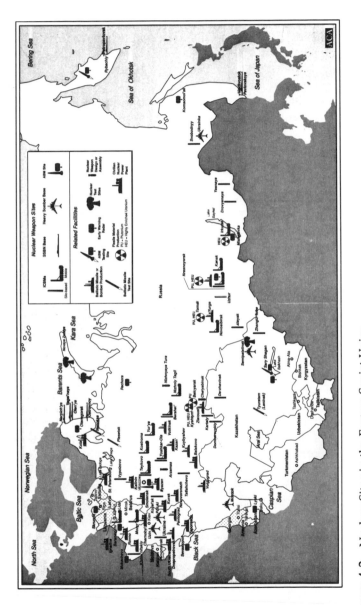

Figure 4.2 Nuclear Sites in the Former Soviet Union
Sources: CIA, DIA, IAEA, NRDC, ACA. Not all listed early warning radars are operational. From *Arms Control Today*, January/February 1992. Reprinted with permission.

Soviet successor state that possesses a full nuclear infrastructure—could be left without a coherent nuclear complex or a fully
functioning custodial system.

This, in turn, could increase the risk of nuclear spread by illicit
means—including possibly to successor states of Russia as well
as of the Soviet Union. There are a variety of reasons why the
nuclear custodial system might erode or break down, and this
could happen even if Russia remains fully intact. But the disintegration scenario is certainly one that could (depending on the
locations and extent of the secession) put enormous stress on the
system. The breakup of Russia could cause the problem of illicit
leakage to become acute.

Third, some Russian successor states, like some Soviet successor states, could inherit unsafeguarded nuclear reactors—not
to mention dedicated nuclear weapons production facilities. In
fact, most Soviet nuclear reactors are located in Russia, and they
are widely scattered. Thus, the same potential head start on an
indigenous nuclear weapons program would exist for Russian as
for Soviet successor states.

Many observers, in and out of Russia, expect the Russian
Federation to disintegrate. The current facts do not fully confirm
that interpretation. But neither do they confidently disconfirm it.
Accordingly, any comprehensive analysis of the proliferation
risks in the former Soviet Union must take into account the possibility of the disintegration scenario.

In sum, there are four routes to nuclear multipolarity in the
former Soviet Union. At present, the first of these—possible seizure by Belarus, Kazakhstan, or Ukraine of the nuclear weapons
deployed on their territory—has attracted the most attention because it poses the most immediate and the largest proliferation
threat. But internal instability and regional instability are likely
to be the hallmarks in the former Soviet Union for years to come,
in which case the nuclear proliferation issue may be not just an
immediate problem but also a lingering concern. And even if all
weapons are removed from Belarus, Kazakhstan, and Ukraine—
no doubt a significant and reassuring step—this closes off only
one of the paths to nuclear capability for Soviet successor states
and hence is not a definitive end to the threat of proliferation in
the former Soviet Union.

Moreover, these paths are not mutually exclusive but can be
pursued in combination. A sensible approach, for example,
would be to combine an indigenous program with as much illicit

access to the Soviet arsenal and complex as possible; in this way, these paths can reinforce one another. They may also reinforce one another in the sense that proliferation by some successor states may increase the incentives of others to proliferate by whatever path is available to them. Thus, in the seven-year timetable for START implementation and for denuclearization of Kazakhstan and Ukraine, any of the four nuclear spread scenarios, or combinations thereof, could plausibly come into play.

Nuclear Terrorism and Other Illicit Use

The erosion or breakdown of the nuclear custodial system in the former Soviet Union could provide opportunities for illicit access not only to states desirous of nuclear weapons but also to nonstate actors.[35] Any number of nonstate actors could seek to grab and exploit nuclear weapons or nuclear materials. The temptation to do so could be especially strong if the deterioration of the system is so severe that nuclear weapons seem to be there for the taking.[36] But even leakage on a smaller scale could be troublesome.

This problem could have several dimensions. One is the misuse of nuclear weapons by nonstate actors within Russia—whether disgruntled nationalists seeking independence from Russia, disillusioned Communists dismayed by their fall from power, or rogue military units hungry for wealth or influence. Another dimension, a variant of the first, is that nuclear weapons could get caught up in civil strife or civil war within Russia. This could involve Moscow in nuclear confrontations with breakaway groups or regions. Finally, international terrorists of whatever stripe could have keen appetites to acquire nuclear capabilities should these become available on the international black market. Little imagination is required to envision the trouble that might ensue if the PLO, or the Red Brigade, or any other highly motivated political group succeeded in obtaining nuclear weapons.

It seems reasonable to posit that the greater the erosion of the nuclear custodial system, the greater the risk of nuclear terrorism. However, some risk of leakage undoubtedly exists even now.

Nuclear Spillover

If the Soviet nuclear legacy is not successfully consolidated and safely controlled, it may contribute to proliferation on a global scale. There is no guarantee that the proliferation effects associated with the demise of the USSR can be contained within the borders of the former Soviet Union.

There are two aspects to this problem.[37] The first is whether the Soviet successor states, including but not limited to Russia, will be willing and able to enforce nuclear export controls that accord with the rules governing international nuclear commerce. Several facts suggest that concern is warranted. For one thing, over the past several years, both before and after the disintegration of the USSR, Moscow made or considered a number of disturbing nuclear export deals, involving sales to non-NPT members and lax observance of the principle that safeguards should precede sales.[38] Another potential problem is that most of the Soviet successor states (with the notable exception of Russia, which inherited the USSR's legal status) are not participants in the international institutions and regimes that regulate international nuclear commerce. Their compliance with rules that they have never formally accepted should not be taken for granted—particularly in view of the desperate economic pressures that may exist. Finally, it is unclear whether all of the Soviet successor states have established legal frameworks for nuclear export controls.[39] But even where such legal frameworks do clearly exist, as in Russia, there is reason to doubt that the governments in question have a true capacity to effectively enforce them, given the new, unsettled, and resource-constrained character of most of these states. In short, damage may be done to the international nuclear nonproliferation regime by nuclear deals undertaken outside the national and international frameworks for controlling such exports.

Second, and more important, if the nuclear custodial system begins to erode and substantial leakage starts to occur, any aspiring proliferator, whether inside or outside Soviet Eurasia, may be able to gain access to weapons-related items and materials or to weapons themselves. The full range of the enormous and comprehensive Soviet nuclear legacy is probably sellable on the international black market: human expertise (the "brain drain" problem), weapons design information, weapons components, fissile material, nuclear weapons, and delivery systems.[40]

Moreover, the threat of leakage appears to be more than hypothetical. Persistent reports of low-grade leakage have appeared in the press in recent months.[41] The most dramatic allegations—sales of nuclear weapons from Kazakhstan to Iran, for example—

have been vigorously denied and are unsubstantiated.[42] Nevertheless, the existing trickle of illicit exports from the Soviet nuclear establishment is distressing evidence that there are those willing to supply nuclear assets on the international marketplace. Should the trickle become a torrent, this would be a nonproliferation disaster.

Containing Proliferation Risks in the Former Soviet Union

The foregoing analysis should indicate that the *potential* proliferation problems caused by the disintegration of the Soviet Union represent the greatest challenge to international efforts to prevent the further spread of nuclear weapons. Failure to cope successfully with this challenge could result in multiple nuclear powers within the former Soviet Union and additional nuclear powers elsewhere, all abetted by a thriving illicit trade in Soviet nuclear assets. This result would do severe, and possibly fatal, damage to the NPT regime. The stakes are clearly very high.

But nothing catastrophic has yet occurred. Nor is it inevitable that the potential problems described above will turn into real crises. The aim of Western policy should be to try, in cooperation with the Soviet successor states, to avert the possible negative outcomes by doing whatever is feasible to facilitate the safe and secure disposition of the Soviet nuclear arsenal.

The four overarching goals of such a program emerge clearly from the description of the sources of the problem. One broad objective is the complete consolidation of the Soviet arsenal to safe and secure locations in Russia. The second is to preserve the integrity of the nuclear custodial system. The third aim is to incorporate the newly independent states into the international nonproliferation regimes so that their nuclear export behavior will conform to international standards and their nuclear facilities will be subject to safeguards. And fourth is to promote the emergence of a peaceful regional order in the former Soviet Union. Some steps have already been taken toward these objectives, but more remains to be done. The discussion that follows outlines the progress so far and the additional efforts that need to be undertaken to achieve these objectives.[43]

CONSOLIDATING THE NUCLEAR ARSENAL

Ideally, the successful consolidation of the Soviet nuclear arsenal would entail five steps: (1) relocation of all Soviet nuclear weapons back into Russia; (2) removal of all nuclear weapons from troubled or potentially troubled areas of Russia; (3) provision of safe and secure transport and interim storage for all weapons so relocated or removed; (4) dismantlement of all excess nuclear weapons as quickly as possible; and (5) safe disposition of the fissile material produced by the dismantlement process. If these five steps can be completed, Russia will be the sole nuclear weapons state to emerge from the demise of the USSR and will have a much smaller nuclear arsenal, safely held in untroubled locations. Some of these steps, notably steps one and three, can and should be accomplished in a relatively short span of time; most likely, these steps would involve several months if implementation is vigorously pursued. Dismantlement, however, could take many years if done at a routine pace and would take several years to complete even if accelerated.[44]

In the short run, the most immediate priorities have been steps one and three; step two could become urgent should instability in Russia intensify. Steps four and five are longer term but are necessary if the excesses of the cold war are to be safely eliminated.

1. Relocation of all Soviet nuclear weapons back into Russia.   This step involves the denuclearization of Belarus, Kazakhstan, and Ukraine. As noted, all three of these states have committed themselves to denuclearization. Hence, assuming they remain willing to translate pledges into actions, the issue here is when and how nuclear weapons will be removed from their territories. So far, however, little tangible progress has been achieved. The main policy aim should be to find ways of accelerating the implementation of this step, to move more quickly than the present timetables require.

This can probably best be accomplished in the context of the START framework.[45] START provides endpoints—including the denuclearization commitment contained in the Lisbon Protocol—that have already been accepted by the five parties to the agreement. Attaining those endpoints more quickly than called for by the treaty will allow the parties to avoid the costs and dangers associated with deployments whose eventual elimination has already been negotiated, and it will accomplish denuclearization in the broader context of treaty implementation that will affect Russian and U.S. forces as well as those deployed in Belarus, Kazakhstan, and Ukraine. One route to this end is for the parties to START to agree that, beginning immediately, nuclear warheads should be removed from all launchers slated for elimination under the agreement and placed in secure central storage. This process should not take more than six months to complete. To facilitate this outcome, the United States should push for the earliest possible exchange of START instruments of ratification. Further, the United States and its Western allies should be prepared to provide financial and technical assistance to facilitate implementation in the former Soviet Union so that logistical choke points and inadequacies do not handicap progress.

But for such efforts to bear fruit, the cooperation of all five parties to START is required. In fact, however, although U.S. policy, particularly during the Clinton administration, has pushed hard for START ratification and for the implementation of denuclearization assistance programs, progress has been slow and disappointing. The largest factor inhibiting progress has been the evident Ukrainian ambivalence about moving forward with denuclearization.

For example, Ukraine became a party to the START I treaty via the Lisbon Protocol, signed on May 23, 1992. But the Ukrainian parliament (Rada) repeatedly postponed consideration of the treaty, thus delaying the ratification process. The Rada did not approve START I until November 18, 1993, and even then it did so in such a conditional fashion that its action suggested problems rather than progress.[46] Among other things, the Rada's START I resolution of ratification asserted ownership of the weapons in Ukraine and repudiated Ukraine's commitment under the Lisbon Protocol to join the NPT as a nonnuclear state in the shortest possible time; it claimed that START I required the elimination of only about 40 percent of the nuclear weapons deployed in Ukraine; and it demanded security guarantees for Ukraine, assurances of adequate denuclearization assistance, and promises of compensation for any warheads removed from Ukrainian territory before START I could enter force. Far from being a breakthrough, the Rada's conditional ratification of START I looked to Moscow and Washington like a renunciation of Ukraine's commitment to denuclearization.

In the aftermath of the Rada vote on November 18, intense diplomatic efforts were undertaken to break the impasse. With the Clinton administration leading the way, the trilateral discussions among the United States, Russia, and Ukraine produced the Trilateral Statement, signed by Bill Clinton, Leonid Kravchuk, and Boris Yeltsin at a summit in Moscow on January 14, 1994.[47] The Trilateral Statement was specifically designed to address a number of the Ukrainian Rada's concerns about security assurances, compensation, and assistance and to promote the commencement of the implementation process for denuclearization. Under enormous international pressure, and prompted by the Trilateral Statement, the Rada approved a new resolution of ratification on February 3, 1994, which rescinds its renunciation of the Lisbon Protocol promise to join the NPT and authorizes the exchange of START I instruments of ratification. However, the Rada still did not act on the question of NPT accession. Since both the United States and Russia have made their own acceptance of START I conditional on Ukraine's accession to the NPT, the Rada's inaction in this regard continues to prevent the entry into force of the treaty.

Thus, although accelerated implementation of START represents one attractive path to denuclearization, as of this writing the policy agenda is still dominated by the struggle to achieve ratification and begin implementation. More than two and one-half years after it was signed, and nearly two years after the signing of the Lisbon Protocol, START I has yet to enter force. Given the record of the past two years, the collapse of START seems about as likely as its accelerated implementation.

A similar tale can be told about efforts to put in place a program of denuclearization assistance. To create a legal framework for the expenditure of U.S. tax dollars on denuclearization activities in the former Soviet Union, it was necessary to negotiate so-called umbrella agreements with each of the countries to receive such assistance. This proved to be a difficult, protracted, and frustrating task, particularly in the cases of Ukraine and Kazakhstan. For example, the Clinton administration was extremely eager to obtain such an agreement with Ukraine and was energetic about pursuing it. But delegation after delegation of Americans passed through Kiev, meeting an exasperating array of objections and complications from Ukraine. At least some American officials involved in the process came to believe that influential figures within the Ukrainian political elite simply did not want to conclude an umbrella agreement and were seeking to stall the denuclearization process as long as possible.[48] It took many months of arduous negotiation, considerable U.S. pressure, and finally, a visit to Kiev by Secretary of State Warren Christopher, before Ukraine finally signed the umbrella agreement on October 25, 1993; and not until December 4 did the United States and Ukraine sign an implementing agreement on assistance for the elimination of strategic nuclear arms.[49] Similarly, Kazakhstan signed an umbrella agreement only on December 13, 1993.

In short, U.S. hopes of rapidly creating a program of denuclearization assistance that would facilitate prompt denuclearization and create financial incentives to move forward have been largely thwarted. More than two years after Congress, in November 1991, voted the first installment of money for denuclearization assistance to the former Soviet Union, not a penny had been spent in Ukraine or Kazakhstan.[50]

The Clinton administration continues to press for progress on START ratification and denuclearization assistance, and it hopes that implementation of warhead removal will begin in 1994 (as called for by the Trilateral Statement). But so far, the smooth and swift elimination of nuclear weapons from Belarus, Kazakhstan, and Ukraine has proven to be an elusive goal.

2. Removal of nuclear weapons from troubled regions of Russia.[51] Considerable attention has been given to the problem of pulling Soviet nuclear weapons back into Russia, but much less attention has been given to the implications of locating the entire enormous Soviet arsenal in a Russia that itself is experiencing both instability and fissiparous tendencies. The violent clash between President Yeltsin and the Russian Parliament in October 1993, the decline in authority of the center and the growing assertiveness of Russia's regions, the rise of extremism, and the ongoing deep economic crisis all attest to the continuing potential for unrest, instability, civil strife, or disintegration in Russia.[52] A comprehensive approach to the proliferation risks in the former Soviet Union cannot overlook this question.

Clearly, removal of nuclear weapons from regions with ethnic conflict, strong independence movements, or high levels of civil strife is desirable. However, this is primarily an issue for authorities in Moscow, because it involves internal deployments on national territory. Presumably Moscow has a strong interest in seeing that nuclear weapons do not get caught up in civil difficulties (much as the Soviet Union, during its last several years of existence, withdrew nuclear weapons from republics in crisis). But Russia could be encouraged to take this factor into account

in its deactivation decisions—for example, in accelerated implementation of START. And insofar as relocation of weapons within
Russia stresses existing transport and storage capacities, Western
assistance should be provided to ease these problems.

There has been, however, no public indication that this consideration has influenced Moscow's behavior. This is understandable, for several reasons. First, some in the Russian political elite
dismiss the disintegration threat on the grounds that it is incon-
ceivable that Moscow would permit some of Russia's regions to
break away. Second, Russia's leaders may fear that acting in a
way that appears to concede that disintegration is a real threat
to the Russian state could be seen as a sign of weakness or a
failure of resolve, thereby undermining Moscow and contributing
to the risk of disintegration. They are unlikely to take steps that
they think will exacerbate this problem. And finally, Russia's
military is unlikely to be enthusiastic about taking a step that
will disrupt its nuclear deployments and diminish its military
capability (much as, earlier, it was reluctant to remove advanced
ICBMs from Belarus, Kazakhstan, and Ukraine because this
would reduce its strategic nuclear capability). Such concerns
could prevent the relocation and consolidation of the nuclear
arsenal within Russia. If so, the proliferation risks of the disintegration scenario, should it come to pass, would remain
considerable.

3. Provision of safe transport and storage.   Full nuclear consolidation entails the movement and at least the interim storage of
thousands of nuclear weapons. It is patently obvious both that
this should be done as safely as possible and that inadequacies
in these areas should not be allowed to inhibit progress toward
full consolidation. Help should be provided as necessary—a fact
long recognized by the United States and other Western powers.

In the United States, the Soviet Nuclear Threat Reduction Act
of 1991 (also known as the Nunn-Lugar Act) authorized $400
million for assistance to the consolidation and dismantlement
process in the former Soviet Union; in each subsequent year,
Congress has approved an additional $400 million annually, for
a combined total so far of $1.2 billion, with a further $400 million
included in the Clinton administration's February 1994 budget
request. Although arguably still larger sums are justifiable, given
the importance of the issue and the U.S. stakes in its satisfactory

resolution, the United States clearly is prepared to devote resources to facilitate the process of moving and dismantling Soviet nuclear weapons.

In addition, the United States has sought to cooperate closely with Russia, Ukraine, Kazakhstan, and Belarus in the design of constructive denuclearization assistance programs. The Bush administration established a safety, security, and dismantlement (SSD) dialogue with the former Soviet Union in the fall of 1991, and the Clinton administration has vigorously continued this practice. The recurrent, even frequent, experts meetings have discussed the full range of relevant issues, identified a number of areas in which assistance is possible and desirable, and negotiated, or attempted to negotiate, implementation agreements to facilitate action in these areas.[53] Thus, during the Bush administration, agreement was reached on the provision of armored blankets to enhance the safety of transport, of accident response equipment, and of transport and storage containers for weapons and for fissile material. Subsequent agreements call for programs to improve the safety of Russian nuclear transport railcars, to provide additional such railcars, to build additional storage for weapons or fissile material, and to improve the nuclear material control and accounting system.[54]

In short, a number of constructive steps in the right direction have been taken. The problem has been the pace of these programs. As noted, much of the Nunn-Lugar money remains unspent. And the implementation of many of the agreed-upon or proposed assistance programs has been sluggish. Several factors have contributed to the difficulty of making prompt and substantial progress on cooperative denuclearization programs. Some of the obstacles have been on the U.S. side. For example, complex legal restrictions governing Department of Defense expenditures mean that it is not easy to spend Nunn-Lugar money. In addition, some of the Nunn-Lugar authorizations did not represent additional allocation to the defense budget but had to be drawn from the existing Defense Department budget—meaning that it cannot be spent except at the expense of other budget items. Hence, not everyone in the department has been enthusiastic about spending this money. Another probable source of delay was the U.S. presidential election in 1992, which diverted high-level attention from these issues for many months; time was also lost in the transition to the new administration in the first half of 1993. And of course, U.S. denuclearization policy has been no more immune than any other government program to the delaying vagaries of bureaucratic politics.[55]

But obstacles in the former Soviet Union have been at least as troublesome. Political instability, bureaucratic infighting, and revolving-door governments in the Commonwealth of Independent States (CIS) have, to varying degrees, made it difficult for the United States to discuss these issues with Moscow, Kiev, Almaty, and Minsk. Moreover, the acute internal crises being experienced in at least Kiev and Moscow have understandably caused those governments to be preoccupied with other problems. Some in Russia have been suspicious of the U.S. enthusiasm for dismantling much of the Soviet nuclear arsenal, because of the obvious element of American self-interest involved; others have been reluctant to open up Russia's traditionally very secretive nuclear complex to nuclear cooperation with the United States. In Kiev, as indicated above, authorities are divided about whether denuclearization is a wise path for Ukraine to follow, and opposition to the Kravchuk government's denuclearization policy has been strong, effective, and a major source of delay. There is also the possibility that these states have seen stalling as an effective bargaining tactic, seeking to gain as much as possible in the way of denuclearization assistance before consenting to progress. And, far from least, some aspects of the denuclearization process depend on cooperation between, or even agreement among, two or more of the four CIS states; this has proven extremely, perhaps even increasingly, difficult to achieve, particularly in the case of Russia and Ukraine.

This constellation of impediments has prevented rapid progress. Thus, a program conceived in the fall of 1991 as an urgent response to an immediate problem limped into 1994 not fully accepted and only partially implemented. Unforgiving critics already condemn this effort as a failure.[56] But proliferation risks in the CIS remain, the benefits from U.S. denuclearization efforts, when successful, are undiminished, and the Clinton administration rightly continues to press hard for progress. It would have been better to have had this all settled a year or two ago; but the programs and aims of U.S. denuclearization initiatives are still desirable (and still in the U.S. interest).

4. *Prompt dismantlement.*   As a result of the Bush-Gorbachev unilateral initiatives of September-October 1991, thousands of

tactical nuclear weapons have been removed to storage from deployed forces. Implementation of START will result in the deactivation of thousands more warheads. The preferred disposition of deactivated weapons is not storage but dismantlement. However, only some of the tactical nuclear weapons are now explicitly slated for dismantlement and only by virtue of reciprocal unilateral initiatives. With respect to strategic nuclear warheads, the START I and II agreements do not require dismantlement. The only formal dismantlement requirement imposed by agreement is found in the Trilateral Statement of January 1994, which states that all nuclear weapons removed from Ukraine to Russia will be dismantled. It would be preferable if Washington and Moscow would make some arrangement, or reach some agreement, that explicitly calls for the dismantlement by both sides of all nuclear weapons removed from active forces.[57] This would establish the political basis for prompt dismantlement. Whether or not such an agreement is ever achieved, however, it appears to be the intention of both the United States and Russia to eliminate a large percentage of the nuclear weapons no longer on active deployment; this will involve the dismantlement of thousands, if not tens of thousands, of nuclear warheads in the coming years.[58]

Such dismantlement needs to proceed as rapidly as possible. Without a concerted effort to make this happen, the dismantlement process could drag on for a decade or more.[59] The United States has been prepared to provide financial and practical assistance to hasten dismantlement. Many of the denuclearization assistance measures reached with Russia, including those aimed at promoting safe transport and storage, were planned to facilitate the smooth functioning of the Russian dismantlement pipeline.[60] One of the key choke points that might delay progress is coping with the fissile material that inevitably results from dismantlement.

5. *Disposition of fissile material.*   The dismantlement process will produce huge quantities of fissile material. Since the difficulty in obtaining significant quantities of fissile material is the basic obstacle for aspiring proliferators, the safe disposition of the inventory produced by the dismantlement process is a critical nonproliferation concern. Highly enriched uranium (HEU) poses an easier problem to solve than plutonium, since HEU can be mixed with lower-grade uranium and used in fuel rods for reactors.[61] The United States has sought to guarantee this result by

agreeing to buy five hundred metric tons of HEU (blended down to reactor-grade uranium hexafluoride) from Russia over the next decade, at a price of approximately $12 billion.[62] Typically, however, it has proven difficult to consummate and implement the deal. Negotiations were begun in the first half of 1992 by the Bush administration; these produced an agreement on February 18, 1993, shortly after President Clinton had taken office. The hope was to move forward quickly on associated implementation agreements, but another year was required to work out all the details; particularly difficult to arrange was the necessary profit-sharing agreement among the four CIS parties to the Lisbon Protocol. The deal appears to have finally been resolved in the context of the Trilateral Statement signed by Presidents Clinton, Kravchuk, and Yeltsin in Moscow in January 1994.[63] If successfully implemented, the HEU deal should go far toward ameliorating one aspect of the fissile material problem.

The long-term disposition of plutonium is a less tractable challenge and is not likely to be settled anytime soon.[64] Hence, at least for an interim period, some form of storage appears to be the most likely solution to the plutonium problem. The United States has been motivated to help Russia address the long-term plutonium storage problem for two reasons. First, it wishes to avoid the possibility that inadequate storage will become a choke-point in the dismantlement process. Second, it is desirable that any long-term plutonium storage facility be as safe and secure as possible. Accordingly, in August 1992, the United States agreed to provide technical assistance in the design of a fissile material storage facility and has since allocated $90 million to support the design, construction, and equipping of such a facility.[65] Several technical meetings have nearly completed the design phase of this project. However, the facility itself is not expected to be completed until at least 1997. The United States has also agreed to provide fissile material storage containers for plutonium or other weapons components and to give advice (and $10 million) to help establish an improved system for fissile material control and accountability; these actions are intended to enhance Russia's ability to handle plutonium (and other weapons-related materials) with requisite care.[66] These are sensible responses to serious issues, and the only snag is that the pace of implementation has not been as fast as hoped. Finally, it is probably desirable to place stored plutonium under international control; efforts should be undertaken to explore how this might work.[67]

In sum, accomplishing step one will close off one path to nuclear proliferation for Soviet successor states. Step two will do likewise for potential Russian successor states. Step three will reduce the risk of leakage or other illicit access. Steps four and five will provide safe disposition of the nuclear remnants of the cold war. Although it is not definite that any of these steps will be accomplished, the best case seems, perhaps remarkably, to be achievable. Much of the required program of international action is in place, and hastening the implementation of already agreed-upon or contemplated measures would go far in the right direction.

PRESERVING THE INTEGRITY OF THE NUCLEAR CUSTODIAL SYSTEM

The nuclear custodial system is potentially the largest source of proliferation problems. Should it erode or break down, this opens or expands a path to nuclear proliferation for states within and outside the former Soviet Union, as well as substantially raising the risk of nuclear terrorism or other unauthorized access. Hence, the continuing effectiveness of this system should be among the highest priorities for both Moscow and all other interested parties.

A primary threat to the nuclear custodial system is the possibility that socioeconomic privation in Russia will grow so acute that the relevant organizations will no longer be able to count on the loyalty of their personnel. Mounting economic distress could cause personnel to neglect their responsibilities, abandon their posts, or participate in a diaspora of the desperate. To minimize this possibility, the United States and its industrial allies should be prepared to provide financial and material support, as needed, to ensure that the necessities of life are available to the personnel, and families of personnel, of the nuclear custodial system. Obviously, the West cannot take full responsibility for the social and economic welfare of the hundreds of thousands of people in the closed cites of the Soviet nuclear complex. But it should be prepared to invest considerable resources to stave off economic disaster should it threaten. If necessary, this should be regarded as a major nonproliferation initiative.

Another potential problem is that members of the nuclear custodial system may feel that their personal fates are jeopardized in the process of substantial contraction now under way in the nuclear establishment. This could undermine their commitment to their current organizations and responsibilities. Clearly, this could increase the risk of leakage. Further, the combination of this point and the previous one has led to considerable concern that Soviet nuclear experts might sell themselves on the international marketplace—another potential blow to international nonproliferation efforts. These problems could perhaps be eased by an international program of conversion assistance aimed at smoothing the transition to a much smaller arsenal and complex.[68] One very constructive decision along these lines has already been taken. The United States, utilizing funds authorized by the Soviet Nuclear Threat Reduction Act of 1991, has committed to establishing two science and technology centers, in Moscow and Kiev, to provide rewarding and professionally relevant employment opportunities for nuclear scientists and engineers.[69] Japan, Sweden, Canada, Switzerland, and the European Community have also made contributions to the support of these centers. Once again, however, implementation of this scheme has been sluggish, and as of May 1994, neither of the two centers was actually functioning, although it is expected that both will begin to function in the not-too-distant future.

A further threat to the custodial system is civil strife in Russia. It is beyond the ken, and probably beyond the means, of Western policy to know how to prevent civil strife in current circumstances. However, the possibility of such strife argues for programs to ensure that deployment and storage sites and other nuclear-related facilities are as hostile to unauthorized intruders as possible. The United States has invested heavily in high-technology site security methods, and some of these may be useful in the context of the former Soviet Union.

Extending the Nonproliferation Regime to the Former USSR

In effect, the dissolution of the Soviet Union tore a gaping hole in the international nonproliferation regime. It produced a number of newly independent states that possess unsafeguarded reactors. Very large quantities of plutonium in spent fuel exist or are accumulating in these states, plutonium potentially available for use in the weapons programs of those states themselves, should any among them decide to exercise the nuclear option, or for sale to other states desirous of acquiring nuclear weapons. Further, some of these states may have both the means and the incentive to engage in international nuclear commerce but have not joined the institutions or formally committed to abide by the rules governing such commerce.

Thus, the present situation in the former Soviet Union is deeply inimical to the international nonproliferation regime—which is meant to discourage precisely such developments and which could be undermined if they are not corrected. Perhaps because this dimension of the proliferation problem in the former Soviet Union lacks the immediacy, novelty, and vividness of some of the other nuclear worries, and perhaps because it falls so squarely in tradition of normal nonproliferation concerns, it has not attracted much attention.[70] But no comprehensive policy for addressing proliferation risks in the former Soviet Union can afford to ignore it. And failure to remedy this situation could lead to proliferation just as surely as nuclear weapons deployed on the territory of Belarus, Kazakhstan, or Ukraine.

The remedies are straightforward and obvious. All the newly independent states should be encouraged to promptly join the NPT. This is easily done. According to Article 9 of the NPT, any state may accede at any time by ratifying the treaty and depositing instruments of accession with NPT depository governments. It is disturbing that, more than two years after the disintegration of the USSR, a number of the newly independent states have not taken this step—particularly in view of the fact that most of them have expressed a desire to join as nonweapons states.[71] If the West attached a higher priority to this matter, failure to join the NPT would inhibit or damage relations between newly independent states and the West. But although Western leaders have expressed the expectation that the successor states of the Soviet Union should join the NPT, for the most part Western behavior has not been made in any way contingent on the conclusion of the step.[72] A truer appreciation by Western leaders of the proliferation risks associated with the current state of affairs might result in more urgent efforts to bring the newly independent states into the NPT regime.

At least as important as joining the NPT is the associated step of negotiating a safeguards agreement with the IAEA, so that all nuclear reactors are subjected to international accountability. According to the NPT, this should be done within eighteen months after accession to the treaty. But in this case, both the IAEA and the newly independent states should be encouraged to proceed as quickly as possible. For the IAEA, such negotiations are routine; it has concluded safeguards agreements with dozens of states.[73] Assuming cooperation and goodwill on the part of the successor states of the former Soviet Union, there is no reason why this step cannot be accomplished quickly. For newly independent states that truly do not wish to possess nuclear weapons or to preserve a nuclear option, there should be no grounds for delay. If the effort to implement safeguards in the former Soviet Union overtaxes the resources of the IAEA, the United States and its allies should be prepared to provide additional resources, whether financial or technical. But joining the NPT without reaching a safeguards agreement does not adequately address the practical problem of nuclear reactors outside the NPT regime. The longer the delay in applying safeguards to these reactors, the greater the likelihood that at least some of the newly independent states will find themselves awash in unsafeguarded spent fuel, and the greater the risk that this fuel will be diverted to undesirable ends. It is a good sign that some CIS states, including Belarus, Kazakhstan, and Ukraine, are negotiating safeguards agreements with the IAEA; until these agreements are completed and implemented, however, grounds for concern will remain. If all the paths to nuclear proliferation in the former USSR are to be closed off, safeguards must be applied to reactors in the newly independent states.

In addition, the West should seek to ensure that any nuclear export activity by the newly independent states is in conformity with international guidelines. In part, this involves bringing those that might engage in such commerce into the relevant institutions, including not only the IAEA but also the London Suppliers Group (LSG), which has established a set of "Guidelines for Nuclear Transfers."[74] But to be meaningful, such guidelines need to be reflected in national export control legislation and behavior. The United States has already undertaken to provide assistance to some newly independent states in setting up nuclear export laws and procedures, and further efforts would be useful. To date, though, progress in bringing the relevant CIS states into the LSG and in creating effective national nuclear export control systems has not been faster, and in some cases has even been slower, than progress in obtaining NPT accession and safeguards.

To achieve the objective of incorporating the newly independent states into the international nonproliferation regime, what is primarily required is for those states to take the necessary actions, to join the appropriate institutions, and to embrace the relevant laws, agreements, and guidelines. There are no major impediments to taking these steps.[75] Indeed, joining the NPT or the LSG can be done quickly and at the initiative of the newly independent states. But so far there has been disappointingly little progress. The United States and its allies can and should do more than they have to encourage or pressure the newly independent states to take the necessary actions. A strategy to contain proliferation risks in the former Soviet Union that overlooks or neglects this set of problems will be dangerously incomplete.

PROMOTING A PEACEFUL ORDER IN THE FORMER SOVIET UNION

Finally, the likelihood of nuclear proliferation in the former Soviet Union will be heavily influenced by the character of the regional order that emerges. This confronts the issue at its most fundamental, since it pertains to the motivation that successor states will have to proliferate. Clearly, the emergence of a malign, conflict-prone regional order—particularly one in which Russia is menacing—will create conditions in which some successor states are likely to find the nuclear option attractive. Hence, concern about proliferation risks in the former Soviet Union leads directly to concern about the evolution of the post-Soviet international order.

Unfortunately, trends in the former Soviet Union since the collapse of the USSR in December 1991 have not been particularly helpful to the cause of nuclear nonproliferation. A number of the CIS states are weak and unstable. There has been a distressing amount of internal and regional conflict along the periphery of the CIS; one-third of the newly independent states have already experienced substantial violence. And perhaps most important, Russia appears to have embarked on an increasingly aggressive policy toward the other states of the CIS (the "near abroad"), with the goal of reestablishing its dominance in the CIS.[76] This policy understandably produces significant concern on the part of other newly independent states, and states with serious worries about their security are more likely to be tempted by the nuclear option. Ukraine's reluctance to move rapidly to denuclearize its territory, for example, has obviously been influenced by the deterioration in Russian-Ukrainian relations and by Kiev's fear that Moscow is attempting to subvert its sovereignty. In short, there is no clear indication that a stable, peaceful international order will emerge from the ruins of the Soviet Union.

Ultimately, the West may have little or no influence on the outcome of this evolution. Powerful internal and regional factors are clearly at work. But the United States and its allies should do what they can to promote a peaceful order in Soviet Eurasia. Existing arms control agreements—START, CFE, and the Stockholm CSBMs agreement—provide frameworks for discussion of contentious issues and for restraint in military programs. CSCE offers both codes of conduct and mechanisms for conflict resolution that may help facilitate a smooth evolution. Bilateral policies toward the successor states can be made conditional on acceptable international behavior.[77] Russia's role in shaping the new order will be particularly important, and Moscow should be encouraged at every opportunity to pursue a benign course. The main point is that Western disengagement from—or worse, disinterest toward—the international politics of the former Soviet Union would constitute a very shortsighted nonproliferation policy.

Notes

1. This analysis, particularly the discussion of possible remedies, is informed by Graham Allison, Ashton B. Carter, Steven E. Miller, and Philip Zelikow, eds., *Cooperative Denuclearization: From Pledges to Deeds*, CSIA Studies in International Security no. 2 (Cambridge, Mass.: Center for Science and International Affairs, Harvard University, 1993). Particular thanks are due to Owen Cote for detailed comments on and research assistance for this chapter.

2. For background, see Kurt M. Campbell, Ashton B. Carter, Steven E. Miller, and Charles Zraket, *Soviet Nuclear Fission: Control of the Nuclear Arsenal in a Disintegrating Soviet Union*, CSIA Studies in International Security no. 1 (Cambridge, Mass.: Center for Science and International Affairs, Harvard University, 1991).

3. In preparing this chapter, I have drawn heavily on Steven E. Miller, "Alternative Nuclear Futures: What Fate for the Soviet Nuclear Arsenal?" (report prepared for Stiftung Wissenschaft und Politik, Ebenhausen, Germany, November 1992).

4. This resulted from the relocation of all Soviet tactical nuclear weapons back into Russia. On the tactical withdrawal, and the diplomacy associated with it, see Steven E. Miller, "Western Diplomacy and the Soviet Nuclear Legacy," *Survival* 34, no. 3 (Autumn 1992).

5. This framework is adapted from Campbell, Carter, Miller, and Zraket, *Soviet Nuclear Fission*.

6. This could lead to a nuclear weapons capability in two ways. One, obviously, is that the existing warheads may be usable by whatever party gains physical custody of them. However, most of the nuclear weapons in these three states are deployed on ICBMs targeted against the United States, and the weapons themselves may be safeguarded in a variety of ways. They may not be easily adaptable for use by a new owner. In addition, the present Russian custodians may be able to disable some or all of the weapons before relinquishing control of them. The "grab and use" scenario is less straightforward than is often assumed—although some usable nuclear capability may be gained this way. There is a second scenario, however. The weapons still deployed outside Russia represent a large inventory of fissile material. This material could be removed from existing weapons and refabricated into new weapons, probably of simpler design, that would be more suitable to the requirements of the state in question. This could plausibly be done in a matter of weeks or months. See, for example, Mason Willrich and Theodore Taylor, *Nuclear Theft: Risks and Safeguards* (Cambridge, Mass.: Ballinger, 1974), pp. 20–21 and 226–27.

7. An excellent assessment of the Trilateral Statement is John W. R. Lepingwell, "The Trilateral Agreement on Nuclear Weapons," *RFE/RL Research Report*, January 28, 1994, pp. 12–20.

8. See Dunbar Lockwood, "Nuclear Weapons Developments in 1993," *SIPRI Yearbook 1994: World Armaments and Disarmament* (London: Oxford University Press, forthcoming).

9. See, for example, Dunbar Lockwood, "U.S. Reaches Understanding with Ukraine, Russia on Denuclearization," *Arms Control Today*, January/February 1994, pp. 19–20.

10. This was stated in the letters accompanying the Lisbon Protocol.

11. See, for example, Rose Gottemoeller, "Future Options for the Soviet Nuclear Arsenal: Two Scenarios," *RAND* (Fall 1991): 21, which argues that for denuclearization to work, "the non-Russian republics would have to be convinced that the denuclearization outcome would not be an overall decrement to their security."

12. See, for example, Chrystia Freeland, "Ukraine Having Second Thoughts about Giving up Nuclear Weapons," *Washington Post*, November 16, 1992.

13. See, for example, Roman Solchanyk, "Ukraine between Russian Hegemony and Western Indifference," *Strategisch-Sicherheitspolitische Studien* (Vienna: Forschungsberichte Des Ludwig Boltzmann-Institutes fur Internationale Kultur-Und Wirtschaftsbeziehungen, no. 2, 1993), p. 11, and Bohdan Nahaylo, "The Shaping of Ukrainian Attitudes toward Nuclear Arms," *RFE/RL Research Report*, February 19, 1993, pp. 21–45. For an explanation of changing Ukrainian attitudes, see Michael E. Brown, "Will START Stall?" *UNIDIR Newsletter*, nos. 22–23 (September/December 1993): 24–30.

14. See, for example, Lee Hockstader, "Ukraine Is Clinging to Nuclear Arsenal Despite U.S. Prodding," *Washington Post*, October 31, 1993, which

quotes a Canadian expert as saying, "There is widespread agreement in parliament on the wisdom of keeping nuclear arms."

15. See, for example, the comments of Ambassador Robert Gallucci, as reported in Eve Cohen, "Nonproliferation in the Former Soviet Union: The Role of International Science and Technology Centers," *Eye on Supply*, no. 6 (Spring 1992): 66–67.

16. For disturbing assessments of the trends, see Alexander Peniagin and Boris Porfiriev, "Implications of the Soviet Union's Collapse for Reorganization of the Nuclear Complex and Its Repercussions" (paper delivered to the conference on "Implications of the Dissolution of the Soviet Union for Accidental or Inadvertent Use of Weapons of Mass Destruction," Parnu, Estonia, April 23–25, 1992), which claims that the custodial system is "decaying." And see Pavel Felgengauer, "Russia's Closed Cities," *Nezavisimaya Gazeta*, June 30, 1992 (as translated in JPRS-UEQ-92-011, October 6, 1992, pp. 11–16), which reports that at nuclear production facilities, "it is possible to take and carry out fissionable materials" and that "the security system is based largely on trust" (p. 15).

17. See the thoughtful discussion of proliferation incentives and disincentives in the former Soviet Union in William C. Potter, "Proliferation Determinants in the Commonwealth of Independent States," in W. Thomas Wander and Eric A. Arnett, eds., *The Proliferation of Advanced Weaponry: Technology, Motivations, and Responses* (Washington, D.C.: American Association for the Advancement of Science, 1993), pp. 147–63. Potter concludes, "There is little hard evidence that the political leadership in any CIS member state outside of Russia actively seeks the development (or, as the case may be, the retention) of nuclear weapons" (p. 154).

18. Empirical work by Stephen Meyer found that these were the two most powerful motivations for acquiring nuclear weapons. See his "Probing the Causes of Nuclear Proliferation: An Empirical Analysis, 1940–1973" (Ph.D. diss., University of Michigan, 1978), p. 310. Meyer frames nuclear proliferation decisions in terms of the balance between motives for proliferating and dissuasive factors. The point here is that powerful incentives to proliferate are likely to exist for some successor states. But potent dissuasive factors—such as domestic opposition to things nuclear and the potential disapprobation of the United States and its industrial allies—also exist. Hence the outcome of this question in individual states is not a foregone conclusion. I am merely trying to suggest that the possibility of nuclear proliferation in the former Soviet Union should not be discounted altogether. Also addressing the sources of nuclear restraint is Mitchell Reiss, *Without the Bomb: The Politics of Nuclear Nonproliferation* (New York: Columbia University Press, 1988), pp. 247–69.

19. Russia's neighbors are unlikely to be comforted, for example, by the position expressed by the Russian Parliament's foreign affairs committee: "Russian foreign policy must be based on a doctrine that proclaims the entire geopolitical space of the former [Soviet] Union a sphere of vital interests. . . . Russia must secure . . . the role of political and military guarantor of stability on all the territory of the former USSR." Quoted in "Russia: Imperfect Peace," *Economist*, November 14, 1992, p. 60. The growing emphasis on nuclear weapons in Russia's defense policy is also unlikely to discourage the

nuclear appetites of its neighbors. See George Leopold and Neil Munro, "Russia Renews Nuclear Reliance," *Defense News*, December 21–27, 1992, p. 1. For a survey of the potential for conflict in the former Soviet Union, see "Flash Points," *Jane's Defence Weekly*, January 2, 1993, pp. 13–15.

20. On Zhirinovsky's electoral success, see Leyla Boulton and John Lloyd, "Russian Reformist Parties Fear Neo-Facist Landslide," *Financial Times*, December 14, 1993. On the wide influence on nationalist views in Russia, see, for example, Paul A. Goble, "Russia's Extreme Right," *National Interest*, Fall 1993, pp. 95–96.

21. On Russia's domineering behavior, see in particular Fiona Hill and Pamela Jewett, "Back in the USSR: Russia's Intervention in the Internal Affairs of the Former Soviet Republics and the Implications for United States Policy toward Russia," Ethnic Conflict Project, Strengthening Democratic Institutions Project, Kennedy School of Government, Harvard University, January 1994; Elizabeth Fuller, "Russia's Diplomatic Offensive in the Transcaucus," *RFE/RL Research Report*, October 1, 1993, pp. 30–34; and Thomas Goltz, "The Hidden Russian Hand," *Foreign Policy*, no. 92 (Fall 1993): 92–116. Also relevant here is Steven E. Miller, "The Eurasian Predicament: Russia's National Security Interests and Strategic Options," in Robert Blackwill and Sergei Karaganov, eds., *The New Russia and International Security* (forthcoming). On the reaction of the newly independent states, see Jill Barshay and Chrystia Freeland, "Republics Jolted by Backing for Expansionist," *Financial Times*, December 14, 1993, and Elizabeth Neuffer, "Anxious Times for Russia's Neighbors," *Boston Globe*, December 15, 1993.

22. I owe this example to Dr. William Potter of the Monterey Institute of International Studies.

23. The information in this paragraph is drawn mostly from William C. Potter, with Eve E. Cohen and Edward V. Kayukov, *Nuclear Profiles of the Soviet Successor States*, Monograph no. 1 (Monterey, Calif.: Program for Nonproliferation Studies, Monterey Institute of International Studies, 1993), which is extremely useful.

24. For the location and number of reactors in the former Soviet Union, see Thomas Cochran, William Arkin, Robert Norris, and Jeffrey Sands, *Soviet Nuclear Weapons* (New York: Harper and Row, 1989), pp. 84–85.

25. According to Potter, *Nuclear Profiles of the Soviet Successor States*, Azerbaijan, Estonia, Latvia, Lithuania, and Uzbekistan have acceded to the NPT, and the Belarus parliament has ratified the NPT, although it has yet to deposit its instrument of accession. In addition, Ukraine and Belarus are members of the IAEA. But safeguards have never been applied to facilities in the Soviet Union (or the United States), so there is no reliable way of knowing what has been going on in these nuclear power plants. See Sidney Drell et al., "Verification of Dismantlement of Nuclear Warheads and Controls on Nuclear Materials," JSR-92–331, MITRE Corporation, October 21, 1992, p. 75.

26. Ashton B. Carter and Owen Cote, "Disposition of Fissile Material," in Allison, Carter, Miller, and Zelikow, *Cooperative Denuclearization*, p. 132, uses the two hundred kilogram number. "Fuel Reprocessing and Spent Fuel Management," in Congressional Research Service, *Nuclear Proliferation Fact-*

book, Joint Committee Print (Washington, D.C.: Government Printing Office, 1985), p. 405, suggests three hundred kilograms.

27. There are minor discrepancies in published sources on Ukraine's nuclear power capacity, primarily due to the fact that some figures reflect the shutdown of the four reactors at Chernobyl, and others do not. See, for example, Cochran, Arkin, Norris, and Sands, *Soviet Nuclear Weapons*, pp. 84–85; William C. Potter and Eve E. Cohen, "Nuclear Assets of the Former Soviet Union" (CIS Nonproliferation Project, Center for Russian and Eurasian Studies, Monterey Institute of International Studies, October 1992), pp. 25–26; and Ryukichi Imai, "The Age of Plutonium: Nuclear Technology for Energy and Weapons Proliferation" (Policy Paper 99E, International Institute for Global Peace, August 1992), p. 22. Because of Ukraine's desperate need for energy, two of the three Chernobyl reactors that were not destroyed in the 1986 disaster have been restarted. See "Second Generator on Line at Chernobyl," *Boston Globe*, December 14, 1992.

28. Reactor-grade plutonium contains higher quantities of the isotope Pu-240 than does weapons-grade plutonium. This may raise the necessary critical mass for a primitive weapon design by 25 to 30 percent. This complicates, but does not prevent, the use of reactor-grade plutonium in a simple bomb. See, for example, J. Carson Mark, Theodore Taylor, Eugene Eyster, William Maraman, and Jacob Wechsler, "Can Terrorists Build Nuclear Weapons?" in Paul Leventhal and Yonah Alexander, eds., *Preventing Nuclear Terrorism* (Lexington, Mass.: Lexington Books, 1987), p. 57. An important discussion of the utility of reactor-grade plutonium for making nuclear weapons is J. Carson Mark, "Explosive Properties of Reactor-Grade Plutonium," *Science and Global Security* 4 (1993): 111–28, which concludes, "The difficulties of developing an effective design of the most straightforward type are not appreciably greater with reactor-grade plutonium than those that have to be met for the use of weapons-grade plutonium" (p. 123).

29. See, for example, Malcolm W. Browne, "Lithuania's Dangerous Orphans: Two Huge Reactors," *New York Times*, November 15, 1992, and FAS/NRDC, "Report on the Fourth International Workshop on Nuclear Warhead Elimination and Nonproliferation," Washington, D.C., February 26–27, 1992, pp. 8–9.

30. Moreover, according to one source, spent reactor fuel in the former Soviet Union was normally stored at the reactor site for three to five years before being transported to central storage or reprocessing. See Oleg Bukharin, "The Threat of Nuclear Terrorism and the Physical Security of Nuclear Installations and Materials in the Former Soviet Union" (Occasional Paper no. 2, Center for Russian and Eurasian Studies, Monterey Institute of International Studies, August 1992), p. 6. If true, this would imply that Ukraine is in possession of many thousands of kilograms of plutonium in spent fuel.

31. See, for example, "Routes to Nuclear Weapons," in *Nuclear Proliferation Factbook*, p. 304, which describes chemical separation of plutonium as "only a minor obstacle" for states with unsafeguarded reactors. William Potter, *Nuclear Power and Non-Proliferation: An Interdisciplinary Perspective* (Cambridge, Mass.: Oelgeschlager, Gunn, and Hain, 1982), pp. 78–79, makes the point that building a reprocessing capability would be affordable for most states and could be accomplished in less than a year. Ted Greenwood, George Rathjens, and Jack Ruina, *Nuclear Power and Weapons Proliferation*,

Adelphi Paper no. 130 (London: IISS, 1976), p. 18, concludes, "Almost any state with a modest chemical industry could on its own build a reprocessing plant large enough to supply plutonium to a small explosives programme." See also Robert K. Mullen, "Nuclear Violence," in Leventhal and Alexander, *Preventing Nuclear Terrorism*, pp. 231–34, which provides a detailed description of the requirements for reprocessing.

32. See Paul Szazs, "International Atomic Energy Agency Safeguards," in Mason Willrich, *International Safeguards and Nuclear Industry* (Baltimore: Johns Hopkins University Press, 1973), p. 94, who wrote, "The most serious limitation on the IAEA's safeguards is that they apply only to registered material, that is, to material of which the Agency is cognizant." For discussion of the diversion option, see Victor Gilinsky, "Diversion by National Governments," in ibid., pp. 159–75.

33. On Moscow's declining authority, see "The Cracks in Russia Widen," *Economist*, September 5, 1992, pp. 53–54. On the interest in autonomy, see Harriet Fast Scott, "The Semi-States of Mother Russia," *Air Force Magazine*, September 1992, pp. 70–74, which notes that twenty-two different regions within Russia have already asserted their sovereignty. Useful background is found in "Fact Sheet on Ethnic and Regional Conflicts in the Russian Federation," Strengthening Democratic Institutions Project, Harvard University, September 1992. See also "Siberia: Exiled No Longer," *Economist*, November 21, 1992, p. 64, which reports the strong interest in autonomy on the part of most of Russia east of the Urals. According to this analysis, the immediate goal is not independence but local economic control. But this article also notes that if negotiations between Moscow and the regions go badly, the result could be a shift from "regionalism" to "secessionism." A detailed analysis of the disintegration scenario can be found in Jessica Eve Stern, "Moscow Meltdown: Can Russia Survive?" *International Security* 18, no. 4 (Spring 1994).

34. The nuclear assets available to some of these states might not be either easily usable or suitable for their security needs—particularly if what they inherit is strategic nuclear weapons. But some might also gain custody of more usable tactical nuclear weapons.

35. This has to do, first and foremost, with the integrity of Russia's nuclear custodial system, since it inherited most of the Soviet nuclear arsenal and provides custodial arrangements for the rest under the CIS Joint Strategic Command. But should other Soviet successor states gain nuclear weapons capabilities, the reliability and effectiveness of their custodial systems would also be a concern.

36. Note, for example, Campbell, Carter, Miller, and Zraket, *Soviet Nuclear Fission*, p. 40, which comments, "A systemic disintegration of the nuclear command and control system—accompanied by a general loss of discipline or confusion of political loyalties—would lay open virtually all of the 27,000 weapons to abuse." In this context, see also Peniagin and Porfiriev, "Implications of the Soviet Union's Collapse," p. 5, which reports a "pronounced decrease of discipline among soldiers and officers that makes unrestricted access to the nuclear facilities much easier."

37. In the following discussion, I draw on William Martel and Steven E. Miller, "Controlling Borders and Nuclear Exports," in Allison, Carter, Miller, and Zelikow, *Cooperative Denuclearization*, pp. 198–215.

38. For examples, see William C. Potter, "The New Nuclear Suppliers," *Orbis* 36, no. 2 (Spring 1992): 199–210.

39. Recent developments on nuclear export controls in the former Soviet Union are described in William C. Potter, "Update on FSU Nuclear Developments," Monterey Institute of International Studies, September 28, 1992.

40. As William Potter put it, the danger is that the Soviet nuclear complex might have a "going out of business sale." See his "Exports and Experts: Proliferation Risks from the New Commonwealth," *Arms Control Today*, January/February 1992, p. 32.

41. See, for example, John-Thor Dahlburg, "Ex-Soviets' 'Loose Nukes' Sparking Security Alarms," *Los Angeles Times*, December 28, 1992, which reports at length on the growing "atomic bazaar" in the former Soviet Union; and see Jonathan Kaufman, "Smuggling of Nuclear Material from Former USSR Rising Sharply," *Boston Globe*, December 9, 1992. Other illustrations include the following: "Belarus Asks U.S. Aid on Uranium Traffic," *Boston Globe*, November 26, 1992, which reports Belarussian disclosures of multiple attempts to smuggle uranium across its borders; Jonathan Kaufman, "Poland Moves to Stop Nuclear Smuggling," *Boston Globe*, October 21, 1992; and Jonathan Kaufman, "3 Charged in Germany with Smuggling Uranium from Ex-Soviet Army Stocks," *Boston Globe*, October 30, 1992. A disturbing example of the risk of nuclear brain drain is "Moscow Reportedly Thwarts Plan by N. Korea to Hire Nuclear Experts," *Boston Globe*, December 20, 1992, which describes an incident in which Russian authorities boarded an aircraft to arrest thirty-six "nuclear experts" who were on their way to North Korea. For an extensive compendium of alleged incidents, see "A Chronology of Reported Exports or Attempted Exports of Controlled Nuclear-Related Materials from the Former Soviet Union," in Potter, Cohen, and Kayukov, *Nuclear Profiles of the Soviet Successor States*, pp. 111–54.

42. See "Iran Said to Buy Four Atom Warheads," *Boston Globe*, October 14, 1992; for denials by U.S. and Kazakh authorities, see "Kazakhstan Denies Warhead Sale to Iran," *Boston Globe*, October 14, 1992.

43. The discussion that follows draws on Allison, Carter, Miller, and Zelikow, *Cooperative Denuclearization*.

44. To eliminate all nuclear weapons in excess of the Bush-Yeltsin target of thirty-five hundred, for example, Russia will have to dismantle more than twenty thousand nuclear weapons. The dismantlement capacity of the Soviet nuclear complex may not be definitively known, but Russian authorities have claimed a maximum rate of fifteen hundred per year.

45. This passage draws on Ashton B. Carter, Owen Cote, and Steven E. Miller, "Nuclear Consolidation after Soviet Disintegration: Coping with Soviet Strategic Forces" (paper prepared for the conference on "Implications of the Dissolution of the Soviet Union for Accidental or Inadvertent Use of Weapons of Mass Destruction," Parnu, Estonia, April 23–25, 1992), and on Thomas Bernauer, Michelle Flournoy, Steven E. Miller, and Lee Minichiello, "Strategic Arms Control and the NPT: Status and Implementation," in Allison, Carter, Miller, and Zelikow, *Cooperative Denuclearization*, pp. 26–71.

46. See John Lepingwell, "Ukraine Ratifies START I—or Does It?" *RFE Research Brief*, November 19, 1993; "Ukraine: Bomb Huggers," *Economist*,

November 27, 1993, p. 55; and "Ukraine Ratifies the Missile Pact, but Delays Ending Nuclear Status," *New York Times*, November 19, 1993.

47. For a detailed discussion of the Trilateral Statement, see Steven E. Miller, "Ukraine, the Trilateral Agreement, and the Future of Denuclearization," *Strategic Comments*, IISS, no. 1 (1994).

48. This impression is based in part on interviews with officials in Washington, D.C., and Kiev, Ukraine.

49. See Dunbar Lockwood, "Former Soviet Republics Clear Way for Nunn-Lugar Monies," *Arms Control Today*, January/February 1994, pp. 28–29.

50. "U.S. Security Assistance to the Former Soviet Union," *Arms Control Today*, January/February 1994, pp. 32–33.

51. My inclusion of this point is prompted by Ashton B. Carter and Owen Cote, "Transport, Storage, and Dismantlement of Nuclear Weapons," in Allison, Carter, Miller, and Zelikow, *Cooperative Denuclearization*, pp. 98.

52. In addition to Stern, "Moscow Meltdown," see Bogdan Szajkowski, "Will Russia Disintegrate into Bantustans?" *World Today*, August-September 1993, pp. 172–76, which argues that Russia is falling apart.

53. Several U.S. participants in this process have provided informative accounts of issues and agreements reached in this process. See particularly Robert Gallucci, "Disposing of Nuclear Weapons in the Former Soviet Union," *U.S. Department of State Dispatch* 3, no. 32 (August 10, 1992): 631–34; Reginald Bartholomew, "U.S. Effort to Halt Weapons Proliferation in the Former Soviet Republics," *U.S. Department of State Dispatch* 3, no. 6 (February 10, 1992): 89–93; and the testimony of Major General William Burns (retired), House Armed Services Committee, March 26, 1992 (General Burns is head of the U.S. SSD delegation). Also relevant is the agreement on SSD assistance reached during the Bush-Yeltsin summit in June 1992. See "Agreement on the Destruction and Safeguarding of Weapons and the Prevention of Weapons Proliferation between the United States and Russia," in *U.S. Department of State Dispatch* 3, no. 25 (June 22, 1992): 496. An informative account of the early denuclearization efforts of the Clinton administration is the testimony of Dr. Ashton B. Carter, House Foreign Affairs Committee, September 21, 1993. An overview of the state of play as of January 1994 is Lockwood, "Former Soviet Republics Clear Way," pp. 28–29.

54. An extremely useful overview of existing denuclearization assistance programs is David B. Thomson, "The Nuclear Warhead Dismantling Assistance Initiative: The Nunn-Lugar Initiative," *CNSS Briefing* 4, no. 4 (November 3, 1993).

55. See, for example, Heather Wilson, "Missed Opportunities: Washington Politics and Nuclear Proliferation," *National Interest*, Winter 1993/1994, pp. 26–36, which is extremely critical of the Bush and Clinton administrations for their failure to move swiftly on denuclearization and which attributes this failure, in large part, to "Washington bureaucratic politics."

56. A good example is ibid.; discussing U.S. nuclear diplomacy toward the former Soviet Union, Wilson concludes, "Our failure to act decisively may become one of the greatest missed opportunities of this decade" (p. 29).

57. Among other things, this might facilitate the denuclearization of Belarus, Kazakhstan, and Ukraine, since it would allay their understandable concern that weapons removed from their territory would only augment Russia's nuclear capability.

58. See Frank von Hippel, Marvin Miller, Harold Feiveson, Anatoli Diakov, and Frans Berkhout, "Eliminating Nuclear Weapons" (April 22, 1993, photocopy), for an excellent discussion of the challenges associated with the dismantlement of thousands of nuclear weapons. Also helpful is Thomas B. Cochran and Christopher Paine, "Nuclear Warhead Destruction" (paper prepared for the NCI/NRDC Fissile Material Workshop, Carnegie Endowment for International Peace, Washington, D.C., November 16, 1993).

59. On this topic, see Carter and Cote, "Transport, Storage, and Dismantlement."

60. See Office of Technology Assessment, *Dismantling the Bomb and Managing the Nuclear Materials* (Washington, D.C.: Government Printing Office, 1993), pp. 125–47, which describes the Russian dismantlement process and the U.S. role in assisting it.

61. For a thorough discussion, see Thomas L. Neff, "Integrating Uranium from Weapons into the Civil Fuel Cycle," *Science and Global Security* 3 (1993): 55–62.

62. On the HEU deal, see Oleg Bukharin, "Weapons to Fuel," *Science and Global Security* 4 (1994): 179–88; Oleg Bukharin and Helen Hunt, "The U.S.-Russian HEU Agreement: Internal Safeguards to Prevent Diversion of HEU," *Science and Global Security* 4 (1994): 189–212; Oleg Bukharin, "Soft Landing for Bomb Uranium," *Bulletin of Atomic Scientists*, September 1993, pp. 44–49; and U.S. Congress, *Dismantling the Bomb*, pp. 137–43.

63. See Dunbar Lockwood, "U.S. Reaches Understanding with Ukraine, Russia on Denuclearization," *Arms Control Today*, January/February 1994, pp. 19–20.

64. For discussions of the options for dealing with plutonium, see Carter and Cote, "Disposition of Fissile Material"; and Frans Berkhout, Anatoli Diakov, Harold Feiveson, Helen Hunt, Edwin Lyman, Marvin Miller, and Frank von Hippel, "Disposition of Separated Plutonium," *Science and Global Security* 3 (1992): 1–53. An important and comprehensive analysis of the plutonium problem is the study by the National Academy of Sciences, Committee on International Security and Arms Control: *Management and Disposition of Excess Weapons Plutonium* (Washington, D.C.: National Academy Press, 1994). An extremely useful overview of the issue can be found in U.S. Congress, *Dismantling the Bomb*, pp. 70–100.

65. See U.S. Congress, *Dismantling the Bomb*, pp. 135–37, and Thomson, "The Nuclear Warhead Dismantling Assistance Initiative," pp. 5–6.

66. On the problems and dangers associated with handling these materials, see Herbert L. Abrams and Dan Pollack, "Security Issues in the Handling and Disposition of Fissionable Material," Center for International Security and Arms Control, Stanford University, November 1993.

67. Carter and Cote, "Disposition of Fissile Material," proposes the establishment of an International Plutonium Depository. Also treating the is-

sue of international control is Thomas E. Shea, "On the Application of IAEA Safeguards to Plutonium and Highly Enriched Uranium from Military Inventories," *Science and Global Security* 3 (1992): 223–36. Early in 1994, the United States and Russia reached tentative agreement to inspect one another's storage facilities; this represents a first but significant step in the direction of international control. See "U.S., Russia Agree to Permit Visits to Nuclear Sites," *Boston Globe*, March 16, 1994.

68. For a fuller discussion of this issue, see David Mussington, "Conversion and Demobilization in the CIS Nuclear Weapons Complex: Economic and Social Issues," in Allison, Carter, Miller, and Zelikow, *Cooperative Denuclearization*, pp. 176–97.

69. See, for example, "U.S. Seeks to Avert Ex-Soviet Nuclear Expert Brain Drain," *Arms Control Today*, January/February 1992, p. 40, and "Ambassador Robert L. Gallucci: Redirecting the Soviet Weapons Establishment," *Arms Control Today*, June 1992, pp. 3–6.

70. A notable exception is William Potter, whose CIS Nonproliferation project keeps a close watch on NPT and nuclear export issues.

71. Across time, this problem is gradually disappearing as more CIS states accede to the NPT. At present, eight have done so; but seven, importantly including Ukraine, have not done so. See Potter, *Nuclear Profiles of the Soviet Successor States*, p. vi, for an overview of the situation in mid-1993. Updated information can be found in *Nuclear Successor States of the Soviet Union: Nuclear Weapon and Sensitive Export Status Reports* (Washington, D.C., and Monterey, Calif.: Carnegie Endowment for International Peace and the Monterey Institute of International Studies, 1994), and in various issues of the periodical *Nonproliferation Review*.

72. See, for example, Secretary of State Baker's December 12, 1991, speech at Princeton University, which explicitly urges NPT accession. Subsequent U.S. policy was not, however, made conditional.

73. See, for example, "International Atomic Energy Agency: The Structure and Content of Agreements between the Agency and States Required in Connection with the Treaty on the Non-Proliferation of Nuclear Weapons," in Willrich, *International Safeguards and Nuclear Industry*, pp. 261–86, which describes in detail the contents of safeguards agreements.

74. The text of the original LSG guidelines can be found in William Walker and Mans Lonnroth, *Nuclear Power Struggles: Industrial Competition and Proliferation Control* (London: George Allen and Unwin, 1983), pp. 186–90. For discussion of recent efforts to strengthen LSG guidelines, see U.S. Congress, Office of Technology Assessment, *Technologies Underlying Weapons of Mass Destruction* (Washington, D.C.: Government Printing Office, 1993), pp. 191–95, which includes a description and discussion of the controls on dual-use technologies that were adopted at the Warsaw meeting of the London Suppliers Group in 1992.

75. That is, there is no impediment apart, of course, from the possibility of domestic opposition.

76. On this point, see, for example, Hill and Jewett, "Back in the USSR." Also relevant is Miller, "The Eurasian Predicament."

77. For an excellent analysis along these lines, see Stephen Van Evera, "Managing the Eastern Crisis: Preventing War in the Former Soviet Empire," *Security Studies* 1, no. 3 (Spring 1992): 361–82. Also arguing that the West should link policies toward the former Soviet Union to desirable codes of conduct is Ted Hopf, "Managing Soviet Disintegration: A Demand for Behavioral Regimes," *International Security* 17, no. 1 (Summer 1992): 44–75.

Chapter 5

North Korea

Robert Carlin

From the start, the North Korean nuclear program has not been one problem, but many: proliferation, foreign policy, and intelligence and analysis. Above all, it has called for disentangling perception from reality. Answers on one level have often seemed to contradict those on another. Frequently, the disparate strands have been pursued independently of each other, when they needed to be drawn together as parts of the whole.

The process of discovery has not been easy; in fact, it is more complex than is often realized. There has been a great deal of certainty on matters for which humility and honesty demand more caution. Finding the truth about the North's nuclear program is an example of how what we "know" sometimes leads us away from what we need to learn.

What public commentators consider the heart of the question—whether the North has the technology and material for a nuclear weapons program—is not really the issue. That has long been beyond debate. The more difficult problem has been to understand how the most important answers to the questions—and the questions themselves—have shifted as a function of time and information. In fact, one can argue that there are several types of answers: some technical, some political, some that are known in Pyongyang, and some that Pyongyang itself may not even understand.

There are various approaches to the problem. One is to take the evidence piece by piece and see where it leads—a bread-crumb or native-tracker approach. Another is to fit the pieces together into a picture—the jigsaw-puzzle approach. Whichever is chosen, the way is filled with logic bogs and intellectual loose boards. In the final analysis, what observers think about the North's nuclear program is, to a large extent, a function of what they think they know about North Korea.

The Program

At least the outlines of the North's program are relatively clear. In the early 1980s, North Korea (the Democratic People's Republic of Korea, or DPRK) began construction of a small (five megawatts electric), gas graphite reactor at Yongbyon, northwest of Pyong-yang. Yongbyon was already the site of the North's nuclear research program, centered on a Soviet-supplied research reactor that had been under International Atomic Energy Agency (IAEA) safeguards since 1977.

The five-megawatts-electric reactor began operating, according to Pyongyang, in 1986. In the mid-1980s, the DPRK started construction of a large facility for chemically extracting plutonium from irradiated nuclear fuel. The North Koreans say this repro-cessing facility was first tested in 1990. A second nuclear reactor, about fifty megawatts electric, was begun at Yongbyon around 1987; a third, much larger still, is being built in Taechon. The North also says it has plans for a large generating complex on the country's eastern coast, near Sinpo, but that is still on the drawing board.

Applications

In addition to its reactors and reprocessing facility, the North has uranium mines, ore-processing facilities, and a plant to make fuel rods. Essentially, these are the elements needed for a com-plete nuclear fuel cycle, applicable to an electric generating pro-gram or to production of plutonium for nuclear weapons. The technology is basic; the program was designed to produce civil-ian power, but it was probably conceived, planned, and con-structed in the first place for making weapons.

Without either technical problems or political pressures and the involvement of the IAEA, North Korea probably could have produced enough plutonium for a small arsenal by the late 1990s. But whether or not the North could go from plutonium to a nuclear weapon is still an open question. Recovering plutonium from irradiated fuel is largely a chemical process, and the North Koreans are good chemical engineers. Fashioning the plutonium into a bomb requires sustained precision engineering— not a strong point of the North's industry.

Proliferation

Apart from immediate security concerns on the Korean peninsula, such a nuclear program presents a potential for a further proliferation problem. The North's weapons program could put technology into the hands of a number of other countries about whom the international community is concerned. Stating a problem does not describe a solution, however. Describing the North's nuclear program primarily as a proliferation problem has, to some extent, masked the complexity involved in fully understanding it. To see the issue comprehensively, one must look past technology to politics and to a broader view of DPRK policy in recent years.

Political Prism

Though consideration of the North Korean nuclear issue often focuses on the nuclear aspect, it is important to remember that the issue is at least half "North Korean." That is, it cannot be understood apart from the Kim Il Sung regime, its domestic priorities and preoccupations, and its sometimes difficult to understand approach to the outside world.

For the North Korean leadership, the nuclear issue has been one of several, often conflicting, priorities. What appears to the outside world as a narrowly focused problem—stopping the North's nuclear weapons program—appears to Pyongyang as part of a broader political context.

For the North, the nuclear issue is viewed against what has been, since the mid-1980s—essentially when the first indigenous nuclear reactor began operating—a serious and surprisingly steady policy of economic experimentation and opening to the outside. During this same period, Pyongyang has pushed forward a dialogue with Seoul in which it has slowly recognized the legitimacy of the government of South Korea (the Republic of Korea, or ROK), redefined the nature of reunification, and moved to accept, still mostly implicitly, a long-term presence of U.S. forces on the peninsula. Since 1989, with the collapse of Eastern Europe and the unraveling of the USSR, the North has been in a struggle for survival. And if that were not enough, for more than a decade Pyongyang has been picking its way carefully toward the country's first leadership transition.

This political landscape does not alter any of the technical realities of the nuclear program, but it does provide a necessary backdrop for understanding the pace and direction of the North's policies toward IAEA safeguards and bilateral nuclear inspections, which the international community posits as key parts of the solution to the problem.

In other words, it is not as if the nuclear program is real and all else is an illusion designed to mask or distract attention from the program. Rather, the North's moves toward Seoul and Washington in pursuit of a limited accommodation and toward a guarded economic opening to the outside world provided the logic for the regime's eventual acceptance of international inspections in January 1992 and its related conclusion of a nonnuclear agreement with the ROK, a few weeks earlier, in December 1991.

Solution or Camouflage?

To casual observers, the movement toward a solution of the nuclear issue begins with the North's accession to, but laggard implementation of, the Nonproliferation Treaty (NPT). In late 1985, the Soviet Union—with which the DPRK then had recently improved relations—persuaded the North to join the NPT. We do not know what combination of pressure and blandishment Moscow used, nor do we know the North's understanding at that time of the IAEA safeguards regime. It may be that Pyongyang did not fully comprehend what being an NPT member meant for its nascent nuclear program; the North certainly could not have envisioned the post-Iraq expanded implementation of the IAEA's mandate. Most likely, Pyongyang joined the NPT expecting that its obligations would be no more onerous—or rigidly enforced—than those it accepted in the 1970s when it agreed to allow the IAEA to perform occasional inspections on the IRT research reactor Moscow had supplied.

By December 1985, the two Koreas were engaged in a slowly growing dialogue that already showed signs of transforming their relationship. This dialogue was never merely a facade but was part of a serious and much-debated policy within the North Korean leadership for a limited accommodation with Seoul. In some ways, the North's signing of the NPT, though obviously crucial in a legal sense, may be less important than the development of this dialogue—and the debate it spawned—for the eventual solution of the nuclear issue.

Though it may not have done so at that early date, the debate appears to have eventually encompassed the nuclear program, enmeshing the program in political dimensions not originally foreseen in Pyongyang. By late 1990, the North had failed to move, or had moved in a maddeningly crablike fashion, toward resolving the nuclear issue, a pace that was probably as much a function of disagreements in the North Korean leadership over relative costs and benefits of moving ahead with IAEA safeguards as a deliberate effort to deceive or stall the international community.

Through 1989 and 1990, there were steady, totally unsuccessful efforts by the international community to get North Korea to accept IAEA safeguards. Contrary to its international obligations—but entirely consistent with its own priorities—Pyongyang set two preconditions: first, the withdrawal of all U.S. nuclear weapons from the South, and second, a "negative security assurance" (NSA) from the United States, that is, a guarantee that the United States would not use nuclear weapons against the North.

In June 1978, the United States had issued a general, somewhat complicated negative security assurance, pledging not to use nuclear weapons against any nonnuclear weapons state that was a party to the NPT, unless such a state attacked the United States, its armed forces, or one of its allies and was itself allied to a nuclear weapons state. Pyongyang would not accept the general NSA; curiously, it never asked whether, having security treaties with two nuclear powers, the USSR and China, the North could even be covered. More to the point, the North raised these preconditions for political reasons. It wanted something specific from the United States as part of its quest to begin the process of engagement with Washington. It did not necessarily expect the United States to fulfill either of the two preconditions, but it did seek a gesture from Washington of willingness to begin bilateral engagement.

That effort was in full swing by 1985, as reflected in numerous DPRK proposals to deal with South Korea and address security issues in a more realistic way, as a price for getting U.S. engagement. In late 1988, with ROK approval, the United States began a slow, cautious process designed to test the North's intentions. By 1990, that process ground to a halt as evidence mounted on the North's nuclear program. Washington began to focus more and more on a solution to the nuclear issue as the key to the next steps in improving DPRK-U.S. relations. And the more Washington pressed on the nuclear issue, the more Pyongyang decided it was the lever it needed to pry loose the political engagement it sought.

In May 1991, the first signs appeared that Pyongyang was ready to accept safeguards. The North had been closely following the debate in U.S. academic and foreign policy circles over the presence of U.S. nuclear weapons in South Korea. It used the visit of a distinguished delegation from the Asia Society and an article in *Foreign Affairs* by Alan Romberg and Admiral William Crowe, Jr. (retired), to claim that the United States was demonstrating enough seriousness in considering a nuclear withdrawal to justify the North's finalizing details of a safeguards agreement with the IAEA.

This tactic became one the North would employ numerous times. U.S. actions or statements could be used as the justification for reciprocal DPRK moves. The key to progress, the North insisted again and again, was a lack of outside "pressure." The nuclear issue came to embody, most acutely, North Korean sensitivities about national will. At every step, the North cautioned that it would not move under duress.

In July 1991, the North accepted a standard safeguards text with the IAEA. There was every reason to think it would sign the agreement at the IAEA Board of Governors meeting in September. Instead, it took five more months. A careful examination of that process reveals something of the political nature of the North Korean nuclear issue and the place the problem occupies in Pyongyang's thinking.

Footprint of a Decision

The North is generally viewed as obdurate and unpredictable. At one time or another, it may be both of these. But pejoratives are too seductive and, certainly in North Korea's case, get in the way. Through its rhetoric, Pyongyang tends to perpetuate and magnify the negative stereotypes; it is its own worst enemy even when signaling its intention to move in positive directions. Yet the North Koreans have a sophisticated and, when they choose to use it, finely honed means of communicating decisions. Too often, most of the nuance is lost on the uninitiated observer, and the message tends to get drowned in the noise. This has been a recurring problem in dealing with the nuclear issue.

The expectation that the North would sign safeguards at the September 1991 IAEA Board of Governors meeting was confounded when Pyongyang responded angrily—but entirely predictably—to a resolution introduced by several countries calling on it to meet its NPT obligations. This was exactly the sort of pressure the North had warned against, and it refused to sign safeguards under these conditions. DPRK statements at the time made it clear this was not a decisive about-face and that Pyongyang intended to get the process back on track fairly soon. But it appeared there would necessarily be a cooling-off period.

The occasion to return to the question happened much sooner than Pyongyang expected. On September 21, the United States announced it was withdrawing tactical nuclear weapons from Asia and Europe. Pyongyang may have been caught off balance, but it responded with uncharacteristic speed. A Foreign Ministry spokesman's statement the next day welcomed the decision and hinted that the announcement had cleared the way for the North to sign safeguards.

Many observers nonetheless remained skeptical that the North would actually move ahead on signing, much less implementing, IAEA safeguards. But Pyongyang's signals from late September through December consistently pointed in that direction. The North made sure the process was carefully paced to extract maximum political advantage, however. The pace also apparently reflected the process of reaching and implementing the decision among the leadership.

Signs of Shift

On October 8, the North Korean party newspaper, *Nodong Sinmun*, carried a high-level article signed "Commentator." Such articles appear infrequently. They are important because of what they signal about discussion among the leadership. They do not seem to convey decisions themselves so much as reflect the fact that an issue is being seriously debated and that changes in policy are under consideration. The articles are, in effect, part of the decision-making process itself, foreshadowing, often months in advance, movement on sensitive questions.

The tone of the *Nodong Sinmun* article was curiously defensive, but the argument was clear. The North, it suggested, had been right in stubbornly refusing to accept safeguards until there was a U.S. nuclear withdrawal. But given the U.S. September 21 announcement, there was now nothing standing in the way of proceeding with safeguards. That such a position was expressed in a "Commentator" article suggested it had high-level backing but was not yet fully endorsed by all the leadership.

Umbrellas

After the U.S. announcement, many observers predicted that the North would simply pocket its gains and raise new conditions for accepting safeguards. In fact, Pyongyang moved the opposite way, paring back its conditions and redefining the nuclear problem in ways that facilitated moving ahead.

At one point, to be sure, the North did seem to create a new obstacle, arguing that the U.S. nuclear umbrella over the ROK had to be withdrawn. But a closer look showed that Pyongyang was raising this issue in the context of the North-South dialogue, not IAEA safeguards. Similarly, although the North continued for some time to suggest it still needed a negative security assurance from the United States, a more careful reading of its statements suggested it was actually dropping an NSA as a *condition* for safeguards. The logic was simple: a withdrawal of U.S. nuclear weapons obviated the need for a guarantee; with the weapons gone, no "threat" existed.

On November 25, 1991, presumably after much discussion in the leadership, Pyongyang signaled that it had reached a decision on safeguards. A Foreign Ministry statement, the most authoritative vehicle the DPRK uses for signaling changes in foreign policy, advanced a four-point proposal:

1. Signing of the safeguards accord if the United States began withdrawal of its nuclear weapons
2. Simultaneous inspections of DPRK nuclear facilities and inspections (presumably of U.S. bases, though the proposal did not specify) to confirm the U.S. nuclear withdrawal
3. DPRK-U.S. negotiations to discuss such simultaneous inspections and "removing the nuclear danger" to the North
4. North-South negotiations on the nuclear issue

The North rarely expects its proposals to be accepted as presented and no doubt did not assume this one would fare any differently. Instead, the offer was intended to sketch out a new DPRK position, providing itself with new flexibility. Most important, the proposal shifted the center of gravity on the North's stance on safeguards. Taken literally, it meant Pyongyang no longer demanded, as a precondition for safeguards, proof that U.S. nuclear weapons had been withdrawn; signing a safeguards agreement had now slipped to the "beginning" of this process. Symbolically, it meant that the North had decided it was time to blur the linkage between the entire question of U.S. nuclear weapons in Korea and its willingness to move toward an IAEA safeguards regime.

None of the other three points added any new conditions, nor did they contradict the conclusion that Pyongyang was preparing to sign safeguards sooner rather than later. The third point, calling for talks to discuss "removing the nuclear danger" strengthened the conclusion that the North was no longer focusing on the U.S. "threat" as an excuse for not signing safeguards.

In mid-December 1991, many of the strands seemed to come together—including inter-Korean dialogue, the DPRK leadership succession question, and movement on IAEA safeguards. At prime ministerial talks in Seoul on December 11–13, the two sides finished work on a basic agreement to govern their overall relations in the political, military, and humanitarian/economic areas. A few days later, ROK President Roh Tae Woo announced that there were no nuclear weapons in South Korea. The North quickly "welcomed" Roh's announcement in a Foreign Ministry statement on December 22. Further indicating that it was in a positive mode on safeguards and not interested in manufacturing obstacles, the statement declared that based "on the premise" the United States would announce a "clear position" on the withdrawal of nuclear weapons, the DPRK would sign safeguards. Those formulations were the opposite of new preconditions. They were constructed to clear away, as clearly as Pyongyang knew how, any remaining ambiguity about its decision to proceed with safeguards.

On December 24, a Korean Workers Party Central Committee plenum openly welcomed progress in the North-South dialogue. Although North Korean reports of the meeting made no mention of it, the nuclear issue probably came up. If nothing else, the plenum must have helped prepare the way within the party for accepting safeguards and for the North-South nonnuclear declaration, which was concluded on December 31.

Also at the plenum, heir-apparent Kim Jong Il was made supreme commander of the armed forces. There is no necessary link between movement toward safeguards, significant progress in North-South dialogue, and the younger Kim's formally taking control of the military. But the juxtaposition of events is probably not a coincidence. Kim Jong Il appears to have played a key role in the inter-Korean talks and in the moves toward safeguards as well. He could not hope to sustain such policies without the acquiescence of the military, potentially a source of opposition not only to these policies but also, even more important, to Kim's political succession. With the December 1991 plenum, those issues became symbolically linked. The party meeting that roundly supported progress in inter-Korean dialogue, and laid the groundwork for movement toward IAEA safeguards, also put the younger Kim in charge of the army.

The North-South nonnuclear declaration was important to Pyongyang as a key element in its move toward safeguards. The inter-Korean agreement became the second leg of its safeguards policy. Moving on safeguards was not portrayed—and could never have been sold to the leadership—as a unilateral DPRK concession. Instead, it was painted as part of a deal in which North Korea would be able to inspect U.S. bases to confirm the withdrawal of U.S. nuclear weapons from South Korea. There was no reason at the time to expect that the details of this sort of agreement would be difficult to negotiate or would seriously complicate resolution of the nuclear issue.

New Year's Address

Kim Il Sung's New Year's address was often used to prepare the way for important developments in DPRK policy, not spelling out the details but providing the formal, authoritative framework. That was the case in Kim's 1992 address, which provided the rationale for the decision to cooperate with the IAEA. The North, said Kim, would never be forced to do what it should not, nor could pressure prevent it from doing what it should. Kim is not normally so Delphic. In some ways, the torturous nature of his language may reflect the extent of the difficulty in reaching leadership agreement on progress toward safeguards. Untangled, Kim's statement meant that, at least on the nuclear issue, the North had realized that if it waited until all evidence of outside pressure disappeared, it would never be able to sign safeguards. But it could not simply drop its "independent" stance. Instead, it had to adopt a variation, a policy double-negative obscuring what was essentially a retreat from the bedrock of North Korean policy—never be seen as giving in to pressure.

Stately Pace

The North announced on January 7 that it would sign a full-scope safeguards agreement "in the near future." The announcement coincided with one from Seoul that the ROK had decided to suspend the 1992 joint U.S.-ROK military exercise "Team Spirit." On January 30, a DPRK delegation in Vienna signed the agreement, an act Pyongyang portrayed as a victory for North Korean perseverance in maintaining the country's independent policies and resisting pressure.

Over the next seventy days, observers repeatedly questioned whether the North intended to follow through, to ratify—and most important, implement—the agreement it had signed. The first problem arose with what seemed to be a totally unnecessary delay in ratification. On February 18, the Standing Committee of the Supreme People's Assembly (SPA) announced that ratification was too important for anything but consideration by the full assembly. That put off action for at least a month, probably two. It was a delay that made little sense, given the urgency with which the North knew the rest of the world viewed the situation, especially because the United States was making it clear that improvement in U.S.-DPRK ties was impossible until safeguards were implemented.

There are several explanations for the delay. One is that the North needed to move equipment or material from Yongbyon, removing evidence of its weapons program, before letting in inspectors. Indeed, it probably did need to "ready" things at Yongbyon, although it could have accomplished much the same thing by ratifying in February and then taking the full amount of time to prepare its initial declaration to submit to the IAEA. A political explanation for the delay is also plausible. Having signed safeguards, the North was under considerable pressure to ratify the agreement. Thus, it was all the more important—despite what Kim Il Sung had said about pressure no longer being an obstacle—that the ratification appear to proceed "normally." If other countries had taken their time ratifying safeguards, allowing time for their legislatures to mull over the question, it was crucial, for appearance's sake, that the North do no less.

The SPA normally meets in March or April each year to hear discussion of the budget and one or two other items. The international community waited nervously and impatiently to learn when it would begin. There is some evidence that the North Koreans, realizing it was not in their interest to drag the matter out too long, calculated whether to start the meeting in early April, before Kim Il Sung's eightieth birthday celebrations (April 15), or wait until after the celebrations. In early March, with more lead time than would normally be the case, the North announced that the SPA would convene on April 8.

Setting the Stage

The SPA ratified its safeguards agreement with the IAEA on April 9. But there remained intense skepticism over how soon the North would allow the IAEA to begin inspections. There was even some concern that Kim Il Sung, as president of the DPRK, would have to approve the ratified agreement. There are few, if any, North Korean constitutional scholars to turn to on such matters.

Fortunately, the answer came on April 12, although in typically roundabout fashion. Pyongyang television aired an hour-long documentary on the nuclear program, with details of some of the facilities in Yongbyon. For technical experts, the television presentation was too obviously propaganda. Especially noticeable was the complete silence on the key to the nuclear weapons program—the reprocessing plant. Moreover, the program portrayed the entire nuclear effort as devoted to civilian power and industrial uses.

Though unsatisfying as a source of hard information, the television program had a more important purpose. It was meant to prepare the North Korean population for implementation of safeguards and reports of IAEA inspectors coming in to and going out of the country. It was also needed to help lay the groundwork for the regime's public rationale for Yongbyon—a nuclear program still in an "experimental" phase and geared to the production of electricity through the use of technology utilizing readily available natural uranium and graphite.

On May 4, 1992, the North handed over to the IAEA its initial inventory report on nuclear material and provided design information on several facilities. IAEA Director General Hans Blix visited the DPRK from May 11 to May 16 for a tour of nuclear facilities at Yongbyon. The first IAEA inspection team arrived in Pyongyang on May 25.

The road since then has been rocky. The IAEA discovered discrepancies in the North's initial safeguards declaration, and Director General Blix requested the IAEA be allowed to visit two undeclared sites in Yongbyon, to help obtain information to resolve the discrepancies. The North Koreans refused to allow sufficient access, claiming the sites were "military" and not related to the nuclear program. In February 1993, the IAEA Board of Governors decided that the IAEA required additional access and information in order to verify the North's initial declaration, and it called for "special inspections." On March 12, the North announced it was withdrawing from the NPT, exercising its rights under Article 10 of the treaty. In April, the IAEA Board of Governors found the North in noncompliance with its obligations and referred the matter to the UN Security Council. On June 11, the day before its withdrawal was to take effect, the North suspended its withdrawal and issued a joint statement with the United States. In July, the United States and the DPRK met in Geneva; the North issued a statement in which it agreed to begin consultations with the IAEA and resume North-South talks on the nuclear issue. As of May 1994, it remains unclear how this process will end.

If one looks at the nuclear issue as having a separate existence within North Korea's policy-making apparatus, then the surrounding developments have little bearing. To some extent, it is necessary to view the program as quite distinct, with its own momentum, isolated bureaucratically and politically from many day-to-day concerns. In a country where much that is routine is treated as secret, the nuclear program has certainly been treated as highly classified and compartmentalized in the party and the government.

But there is a point in the leadership where lines of authority come together and the program is no longer isolated but must be weighed against other considerations. It is possible to make the case at each step of the way that the North Koreans have only been stalling, that they assumed they could outsmart the IAEA or never expected inspections to be so thorough. And to a large extent, the leadership did seek to put off safeguards. Yet, for Pyongyang, the process of moving toward safeguards has not been simply a case of revealing what had been long hidden and treated as highly secret.

To Pyongyang, at least by 1991, movement toward accepting safeguards fit into a larger complex of policies. The problem has been that each part of this policy is, to some extent, linked to every other. It is hard to move one forward without moving them all, or so it has seemed to a leadership unsure of which next step would prove the fatal one, the misstep onto the same steep slope of social and political disintegration that had claimed all of Eastern Europe and the Soviet Union. Even if the leadership wanted simply to dump the nuclear weapons program completely—which is probably not the case—it would have had to worry how to do so in a way that did not seem to weaken the regime or expose its vulnerabilities to the outside world.

Leadership Debates

There have been debates in Pyongyang for years—mostly in the areas of economic and foreign policy but apparently on basic politico-military issues as well. In part, these ongoing debates may have been a function of Kim Il Sung's style of leadership, allowing various proposals to contend until a final decision is reached. But increasingly, the debates appear to reflect serious leadership divisions over fundamental policies.

Since the mid-1980s, especially, there has been disagreement over an interrelated series of questions on economic policy, relations with South Korea, and ties with the United States. Real progress on the first, it was apparently understood in Pyongyang, was not possible without movement on the other two. Although the nuclear issue may not have been a central part of this debate at first, by 1991 it had become clear that movement on the nuclear issue—if not final resolution—was crucial to progress in ties with the ROK and the United States. The nuclear program thus became important not just as a part of military-diplomatic strategy but also as a crucial element in internal political struggles. By the summer of 1992, there were signs that the debate had become quite sharp.

Decision Making

North Korean decision making does not appear to be especially efficient. Though we know little of the actual mechanisms or processes, we can see the results. The normal state of affairs is near paralysis, punctuated by occasional flashes of tactically brilliant—or brutally stupid—moves. Some observers put this under the rubric of "unpredictability." There is, indeed, an element of that. No system that is ultimately ruled by one or two people is likely to have the institutional ballast necessary to prevent sudden, sharp changes in course.

Nevertheless, in many ways, the North is eminently predictable, primarily because it spends so much effort signaling its intentions and laying the groundwork for changes in approach. Explaining the rationale of a decision may be next to impossible; predicting the scope, and sometimes even the pace, of change is not.

If one assumes that the past few years have all been a charade in order for Pyongyang to hide the ongoing weapons program or, worse, to buy time to finish a weapon, then considerations of decision making and leadership debates are beside the point. Indeed, one cannot simply dismiss out of hand the possibility that the entire North Korean leadership wants a nuclear weapon no matter what, either to use for blackmail or, more likely, as a doomsday machine to hold the forces of change at bay.

But it is worth considering, with all of the other evidence, that the move toward IAEA safeguards was easy neither to make nor to implement because, fundamentally, it was part of a larger policy of reaching out to the ROK, the United States, and the rest of the world.

The "X" Factor

Approaching the nuclear issue as a political problem, as much as a proliferation challenge, is useful and necessary but still not sufficient. In the absence of definitive information about North Korean intentions, it is vital to understand the technical capabilities and limitations of the program as it exists. The laws of physics hold in North Korea. Even inspired DPRK scientists cannot make plutonium out of thin air. One can take shortcuts, apply inelegant engineering practices, and operate highly unsafe facilities in order to obtain a fuel cycle that is not world-class but that, nevertheless, delivers the goods. Yet there are limitations. A reactor of a given size with certain characteristics burns uranium at a certain rate. The amount of irradiated fuel produced yields only so much plutonium. A reprocessing plant can extract that plutonium only at a rate that is a function of its capacity. Consequently, what is unknown about the North's nuclear program is not always justification for leaping to the worst imaginable case.

Understanding the North's nuclear program, much less bringing it under control, cannot be achieved by simply imagining or planning for the worst. There is no substitute for prudent and informed integration of technical information with rigorous, intellectually honest political analysis. That is difficult in the case of North Korea but nonetheless possible, and nothing less will do.

The views expressed in this paper are the author's and not necessarily those of the Department of State or the U.S. government.

Chapter 6

China

Shirley Kan and Zachary Davis

Introduction

After criticizing the Bush administration's China policy of constructive engagement and endorsing congressional efforts to place conditions on China's most-favored nation (MFN) trade status during the 1992 presidential campaign, President Bill Clinton confronted a fundamental dilemma: can Washington use the U.S.-China trade relationship (with China's trade surplus surpassing $23 billion in 1993) to change Beijing's nuclear and missile export practices without causing serious harm to U.S. economic interests? The end of the cold war changed China's strategic relationship with the United States, prompting greater debate over policy toward China, now dominated by the three main issues of trade, human rights, and nonproliferation.[1]

The end of the cold war also changed Western security perceptions. In his January 1993 confirmation hearing, Secretary of State Warren Christopher noted, "One of the main security problems of this era will be the proliferation of very deadly weapons—nuclear, chemical, biological, and enhanced conventional weapons—as well as their delivery systems." Later in his remarks, Secretary Christopher stated that in rethinking U.S. policy toward the People's Republic of China (PRC), "we cannot ignore continuing reports of Chinese exports of sensitive military technology to troubled areas." At the Pentagon and elsewhere, the Clinton administration signaled its intention to raise the priority of nonproliferation, which President Clinton and his top officials identified as the foremost threat to U.S. national security.[2] The creation of a new assistant secretary position for nuclear security and counterproliferation at the Pentagon underscores this intent.

These developments led many to expect the new administration to take a tougher approach toward China on nonproliferation issues and to put greater emphasis on efforts to reverse China's policy of exporting technology useful in the development of nuclear weapons and missiles. What is needed is a new strategy for moving China beyond its ambiguous nonproliferation policy to full commitment to and cooperation with the international nonproliferation regime.[3] The future effectiveness of this regime depends on China's support.

Three Stages in the Evolution of China's Nonproliferation Policy

Throughout the tensest periods of the cold war, the United States and the Soviet Union cooperated to control the spread of nuclear weapons. China, however, remained isolated from nonproliferation and arms control diplomacy. Whereas Washington and Moscow perceived mutual interests in controlling the spread of nuclear weapons, China rejected the nonproliferation norm and refused to cooperate with institutions and practices that constitute the nonproliferation regime. That policy has evolved as Beijing has gradually accommodated the regime to further its foreign policy interests.

The Chinese attitude of exceptionalism toward nonproliferation is yielding to a policy of differentiation among nonproliferation commitments. A selective nonproliferation policy enables the Chinese government to deflect criticism of its nonproliferation behavior through partial acceptance of certain nonproliferation commitments while keeping others at arm's length. By signing the Nonproliferation Treaty (NPT) and agreeing to abide by the Missile Technology Control Regime (MTCR) guidelines in 1992, China moved closer to the nonproliferation regime. However, continuing reports of Beijing's nuclear- and missile-related exports and its reluctance to join the Nuclear Suppliers Group (NSG) or to require full-scope safeguards suggest that China is not yet ready to fully support the regime.

China's nonproliferation policy has evolved through several stages. From outright condemnation of the NPT in 1968, China has gradually moved to accommodate Western interests in non-proliferation.[4] How far this evolution can progress may depend on Beijing's calculation of the costs and benefits of regime cooperation.

STAGE ONE: 1968–1981

During the initial stage, Beijing condemned the NPT because it bestowed a nuclear monopoly on five declared nuclear weapons states and relegated other nations to permanent nonnuclear weapons status. Seeking to lead the Third World and chart an independent foreign policy course, China repudiated such discrimination as a vestige of colonialism and advocated the overthrow of the NPT regime. China declared it would not export nuclear weapons to nonweapons states but neither would it condemn or interfere with other nations attempting to acquire nuclear arsenals. Paramount leader Deng Xiaoping himself proclaimed the anti-NPT policy, saying that "the nuclear powers have no right to prevent nonnuclear countries from possessing nuclear weapons" unless the nuclear armed nations disarmed.[5] Other components of China's early arms control strategy included a no-first-use policy and support for regional nuclear weapons free zones.[6]

The Chinese government adopted a declared policy of not assisting other countries in acquiring nuclear weapons. However, during its post-1978 economic modernization drive, China established a pattern of exporting nuclear materials and technology to a variety of nations known or suspected to have secret nuclear weapons programs. Examples of such sales include exports of heavy water to India and Argentina, nuclear technology to Brazil, nuclear technology and bomb designs to Pakistan, possible nuclear cooperation with Iraq, Syria, and South Africa, a secret reactor sale to Algeria, and nuclear cooperation with Iran.[7] China's motivations may have been financial in part but were also geopolitical in some cases.

STAGE TWO: 1982–1991

China entered a second stage in its nonproliferation history in connection with its bid for a nuclear cooperation agreement with the United States in the early 1980s. Evidence of the change in policy included Beijing's statement of support for the norm of nonproliferation in 1982 and its joining the International Atomic Energy Agency (IAEA) in 1984.[8] Beijing continued to oppose the discriminatory aspect of the NPT but moderated its criticism with praise for the objective of nonproliferation and with denials of aiding proliferation. Beijing's denials of contributing to proliferation came in response to growing concern in the United States and elsewhere that Chinese nuclear transfers offered an alternative supply to nations that refused to join the NPT and allow inspections by the IAEA. China adopted a policy of providing assurances that it would not assist proliferation and stating its agreement "in principle" to adhere to internationally accepted nonproliferation guidelines.[9] However, such assurances, often issued by the Ministry of Foreign Affairs, were not always consistent with China's nuclear export behavior.

China's nuclear relationship with Pakistan, for example, has often been at odds with its declared policy of not aiding proliferation. The Reagan administration had evidence that China was helping Pakistan operate its Kahuta uranium enrichment plant and that Beijing provided a design for a 25–kiloton implosion device to Pakistan.[10] China reportedly supplied Pakistan with enough weapons-grade uranium to fuel two nuclear weapons. Chinese scientists have visited the Kahuta complex (in which gas centrifuges are used to produce weapons-grade uranium), and in 1986, China reportedly sold tritium (used to achieve fusion in hydrogen bombs and to increase the yield of tritium-boosted nuclear bombs) to Pakistan.[11] As evidence of Islamabad's nuclear intentions accumulated during the 1980s, China expanded its nuclear cooperation with Pakistan. As late as February 24, 1993, Central Intelligence Agency (CIA) Director James Woolsey testified, "It's unclear whether Beijing has broken off contact with elements associated with Pakistan's weapons programs."[12]

China's nuclear cooperation with Iran also has raised questions about Beijing's evolving commitment to nonproliferation. According to published reports and Chinese admissions, China—Iran's largest arms supplier during the Iran-Iraq War—

concluded covert agreements in 1989 and 1991 with Iran to provide nuclear technology. Iran also is believed to have approached Pakistan with offers of collaboration. Moreover, Iran and Syria agreed to establish joint military industries and to develop surface-to-surface missiles.[13] Such cooperation raised the issue of third-party transfers among recipients of Chinese nuclear and missile technology.

In response to growing concern about China's nuclear and missile exports, the Chinese Foreign Ministry, knowingly or unknowingly, issued false public denials of any nuclear cooperation with Iran. U.S. and European intelligence disclosed that Iranian nuclear engineers from Iran's nuclear research center at Isfahan were secretly trained in China, that China transferred technology for reactor construction and other projects at Isfahan, and that China had signed a secret nuclear cooperation agreement with Iran.[14] The Chinese embassy on July 2, 1991, stated, "China has struck no nuclear deals with Iran." Yet in early July 1991, Chinese Premier Li Peng not only visited Tehran but stopped especially at Isfahan, where he promised expanded nuclear cooperation during a visit with Chinese and North Korean missile experts there.[15] When a report said that China Nuclear Energy Industry Corporation experts were building a nuclear research reactor in Iran as part of a secret nuclear program, the Chinese Foreign Ministry denied the story on October 21, 1991, as "groundless."[16]

China finally admitted its nuclear cooperation with Iran following an October 30, 1991, report that Iran was trying to build a nuclear bomb and that China was secretly providing a calutron (electromagnetic isotope separation equipment) for uranium enrichment, a nuclear reactor, and training for Iranian nuclear engineers.[17] The *Washington Post* reported the next day that U.S. intelligence had detected China's nuclear technology transfers to Iran before June 1991.[18] On November 4, 1991, China's Foreign Ministry admitted the existence of Sino-Iranian nuclear cooperation, explaining that Chinese and Iranian companies had signed "commercial" contracts in 1989 and 1991 to transfer, respectively, an electromagnetic isotope separator (calutron) and a small nuclear reactor, for "peaceful purposes." In September 1992, China signed an agreement to build two three-hundred-megawatt nuclear reactors in Iran, although Western countries had refused to help Iran, suspecting a civilian cover for a weapons program.

STAGE THREE: 1992–?

China in 1992 signed the NPT and agreed to abide by the MTCR. Despite Beijing's continued nuclear cooperation with Pakistan and Iran, China's policy toward the NPT already showed signs of entering a third stage in 1990. China sent officials to attend the Fourth Review Conference of the NPT (and other international arms control meetings) and issued favorable statements about the treaty. China faced intense pressure from a combination of three factors: the worldwide antiproliferation sentiment stirred by the 1990–91 confrontation with Iraq; the April 1991 revelations about China's secret reactor project in Algeria, which coincided with increasing congressional willingness to use China's MFN trade status as leverage; and the announcement by French President François Mitterrand in June 1991 that France would join the NPT. The Chinese foreign minister and the premier signaled a change, stating that China had "not yet decided whether or not to join the Nuclear Nonproliferation Treaty" but that it was continuing to study the question of participating.[19]

One turning point came in August 1991 when Chinese Premier Li Peng announced China's decision "in principle" to join the NPT during Japanese Prime Minister Toshiki Kaifu's visit to Beijing. Kaifu was the first Group of Seven leader to visit Beijing after the 1989 Tiananmen crackdown. Chinese leaders promised Secretary of State James Baker during his November 1991 trip to Beijing that China would join the NPT by April 1992.[20] Although some observers expected China to delay signing the treaty, the standing committee of the National People's Congress approved the treaty at the end of 1991, and on March 9, 1992, China became the fourth acknowledged nuclear weapons state to accede to the NPT.[21]

Why did China finally join the NPT? The Chinese approach to this international agreement may shed some light on an effective strategy toward Beijing.

First, signing the NPT was a relatively painless step that enabled China to gain further legitimacy and status as a great power while pursuing various diplomatic, economic, and strategic interests. The Chinese decision might not have been perceived as a concession, since Beijing's leaders have stated since 1984 that China does not encourage nuclear proliferation and has requested IAEA safeguards.

Second, by joining the NPT, China hoped to deflect criticism of its nuclear export policy, especially in the aftermath of the Tiananmen Square massacre. In signing the NPT, China committed to few, if any, new constraints on Chinese policy or behavior but muted criticism that Beijing was leading a Third World revolt against the nonproliferation regime and remained outside international rules of conduct.

Third, signing the NPT was a step toward retaining normal MFN trade status from the United States. Joining the NPT removed the possibility that MFN could be denied if Congress decided to link MFN with NPT membership. President George Bush cited China's accession to the NPT and its increased support for global nonproliferation efforts when he recommended normal trade tariffs for China in June 1992 and vetoed legislation to place conditions on MFN status in September 1992.[22]

Fourth, signing the NPT allowed China to secure the ability to purchase nuclear goods and services, particularly in light of the increasing unwillingness of France and other countries to sell nuclear technology to non-NPT states.

Finally, without signing the NPT, China would remain the only acknowledged nuclear weapons state not party to the treaty and would continue to share non-NPT status with threshold nuclear states such as India, Pakistan, and Israel. This association not only equated China with lesser powers in a general sense but also linked Beijing with arch-rival New Delhi as the main critics of the treaty. With world interest in nonproliferation growing and the NPT Review Conference on the horizon in 1995, the prospect of attending the Review Conference with the same observer status as India was distasteful to China. Beijing found the marginal rewards of joining the NPT *as a nuclear weapons state* preferable to continued isolation and secondary status. China's place in the NPT complements its identity as a member of the nuclear "Big Five" club.

In addition to joining the NPT, China began to accommodate multilateral controls aimed at halting the spread of missiles and missile technology throughout the world. Beijing began to adjust its claim of being exempt from the voluntary guidelines of the MTCR by issuing statements supporting the principle of missile nonproliferation. During his November 1991 visit to Beijing, Secretary of State Baker announced that Chinese officials had verbally agreed to observe the MTCR guidelines and that "this applies to the M-9 and M-11 missiles." The M-9 (600 kilometers) and M-11 (300 kilometers) short-range ballistic missiles are considered capable of delivering nuclear weapons and are covered by the MTCR guidelines.[23] In return for its promise of adherence to the MTCR, China required that the United States lift sanctions imposed in June 1991 on two Chinese defense industrial companies for transfers of missile technology to Pakistan. The Bush administration effectively waived those sanctions on March 23, 1992, securing the Chinese commitment.

The Chinese promise to abide by international missile nonproliferation norms contrasted with China's formal accession to the NPT but resembled China's NPT commitment insofar as Beijing's MTCR statements did not end its controversial missile-related exports. The Chinese foreign minister gave no joint press conference with Secretary Baker but instead issued a series of statements through the official news agency. Although President Bush proceeded with a meeting with Premier Li Peng at the United Nations on January 31, 1992, he received no written assurance from Li Peng, nor did Li Peng personally state China's position on the MTCR.[24] Instead, the next day the administration received from the Chinese foreign minister a letter that reportedly confirmed the November 1991 promise in writing. The letter has not yet been released. However, reports in December 1992 alleged that China shipped M-11 missiles or equipment to Pakistan. The president's May 28, 1993, "Report to Congress" on extending MFN status also cited reports that "China in November 1992 transferred MTCR-class M-11 missiles or related equipment to Pakistan." As required by law, U.S. sanctions were imposed on August 24, 1993.[25] China responded with a threat to end its commitment to the MTCR.

During the third stage of its nonproliferation policy, China accommodated Western interests in maintaining and strengthening the nuclear and missile regimes but did not end its controversial exports to countries of concern. Beijing adjusted its declared nonproliferation policy, but its nonproliferation behavior remained inconsistent with nonproliferation norms in the post-cold war period.

Prospects for Further Steps in Nonproliferation and Arms Control

How far should we expect China to go toward closing the gap between its nonproliferation policy and its nuclear- and missile-related export practices? It remains to be seen whether the evolution of China's nonproliferation policy will end with Beijing's signing of the NPT and its pledges to adhere to the MTCR or will include further steps toward full commitment to the regime. Besides complying with its existing commitments, Beijing could take the further step of joining the Nuclear Suppliers Group (NSG), which would require China to implement full-scope safeguards on its nuclear exports, end nuclear tests, and actively support the indefinite extension of the NPT in 1995. These latter steps could be a prelude to China's participation in international arms control efforts such as a comprehensive test ban, a global ban on fissile material production for weapons, regional arms control arrangements such as those proposed for South Asia, East Asia, Africa, and the Middle East, and even discussions about limits on China's nuclear arsenal. In the past, China endorsed establishment of nuclear weapons free zones in Latin America (under the Treaty of Tlatelolco) and the South Pacific (the Treaty of Rarotonga), and during the 1980s it was increasingly active in its support for disarmament issues, particularly in the UN and in the Conference on Disarmament.[26] Beijing maintains its no-first-use policy, but its position on a comprehensive test ban is elusive. China probably does not need to produce additional fissile material for weapons, so it could afford to be flexible on such negotiations. Most important, China appears to have sufficient nuclear capability to deter potential nuclear adversaries such as India and Russia. Thus, it is possible that China's arms control and nonproliferation policy could become increasingly compatible with international efforts to reduce reliance on nuclear weapons.

One positive indication of the direction of Beijing's nonproliferation policy is its acquiescence with UN and IAEA efforts to address NPT noncompliance in Iraq and North Korea. Beijing has used its vote as a permanent member of the UN Security Council to improve relations with the West (after the 1989 Tiananmen massacre) by not blocking enforcement actions. In opting for a peaceful regional environment for its economic modernization, China also has interests in a stable, nonnuclear-armed Korean peninsula. China has cooperated with the United States, Japan, Russia, and South Korea to persuade North Korea to comply with its NPT commitments, including establishing precedents for the IAEA to report noncompliance to the UN Security Council.[27]

Evolution or Devolution of China's
Nonproliferation Policy?

There is no public evidence that China has violated its NPT obligation not to assist nuclear weapons programs in nonweapons states. However, in testimony before the Senate Governmental Affairs Committee, CIA Director Woolsey said that although China's nuclear exports to Iran, Algeria, and Syria "appear consistent with its NPT obligations," China's "relationship with Pakistan seems less benign." When questioned by Senator John Glenn about ongoing assistance to Pakistan's nuclear weapons program, Woolsey confirmed that before joining the NPT, China "probably provided some nuclear weapons-related assistance to Islamabad that may have included training . . . and equipment." Woolsey said it is "unclear whether Beijing has broken off contact with elements associated with Pakistan's weapons programs."[28] Such contact with Pakistan's weapons program, which may not in all cases be functionally distinct from peaceful applications, would violate the NPT. Specifically, Chinese assistance to Pakistan's uranium enrichment program could be interpreted as assisting Pakistan's bomb-making capability.

Despite China's formal NPT commitment, Beijing has not joined the NSG, a multilateral effort to strengthen export controls on nuclear technology, including dual-use goods. The twenty-seven members of the NSG voluntarily adopt common export control policies, including a requirement for full-scope safeguards.[29] By joining the NPT but not the NSG, China reserves its option to export nuclear technology to countries that would be barred from receiving such exports from supplier group members. Thus, China can continue to export nuclear technology to a variety of nations without violating specific commitments. Director Woolsey expressed concern that China could retransfer advanced technology it acquires from Russia and Ukraine to its clients. Discussions between Beijing and Moscow about cooperation on uranium enrichment technology raise the question of China's possible connection with Pakistan's uranium enrichment program.[30]

Some analysts argue that Chinese leaders may be unwilling or incapable of controlling the export activities of certain free-wheeling defense industrial enterprises.[31] Efforts by China's leaders since 1979 to spur economic growth has decentralized economic decision making. The problem of government control could increase when paramount leader Deng Xiaoping dies. Weak central control and/or intense political struggles would probably complicate Western efforts to encourage progress in China's nonproliferation policy. Nevertheless, the Beijing government is likely knowledgeable about any sensitive exports of missile or nuclear technology, since such exports affect U.S.-China relations and involve national defense information.

Assuming that China can control its exports, the selection of membership in the NPT without cooperating with NSG guidelines enables Beijing to claim that it has satisfied the formal *legal* requirements of the nuclear nonproliferation regime. At the same time, China responds to Western objections to transfers that would violate the stricter standards of the voluntary supplier groups on a case-by-case, quid pro quo basis. For example, China's assurances that it would adhere to MTCR guidelines were linked to President Bush's lifting of earlier sanctions. Similarly, China has linked its participation in the Perm Five arms control efforts to the U.S. sale of F-16s to Taiwan. China has also tied a suspension in its nuclear testing to ambitious global nuclear disarmament goals.

Beijing has now argued that it abides by the MTCR, that it has signed the NPT, and that recipients of its exports have either signed the NPT (like Iran and Syria) or agreed to IAEA safeguards (like Algeria). In short, China has justified the gap between its policy and its behavior by denying that it violates any international obligations. Beijing may also believe that membership in a treaty including over 160 countries is more compatible with its penchant for an "independent foreign policy" than being associated with Western-dominated supplier control groups. U.S. policy has been to encourage the evolution of China's nonproliferation policy toward closing the gap between declared policy and actual behavior. However, the debate continues over the best means to achieve that end.

Beyond Assurances, Sanctions, and the MFN Debate: Toward a New U.S. Strategy

President Bush praised China's improved nonproliferation credentials when he extended MFN status to China in June 1992 without conditions. One year earlier, the United States had determined that two Chinese arms companies had transferred missile technology to Pakistan in violation of the MTCR. The United States imposed limited sanctions that blocked sales to China Great Wall Industry Corporation (which has offered satellite launch services since 1986) and China Precision Machinery Import and Export Corporation (which marketed the M-series missiles abroad).[32] Those sanctions were lifted in March 1992 in return for China's agreement to adhere to the MTCR and not to transfer M-9 and M-11 missiles. Nevertheless, China continued its controversial missile-related exports in spite of its new commitments.[33] President Bush argued that targeted sanctions were more effective than broad MFN conditionality with undesired side effects. In August 1993, however, after Clinton extended MFN status with only human rights conditions, Washington once again had to impose MTCR-related sanctions on China and Pakistan.

It took a personal visit to Beijing by Secretary of State Baker in November 1991 to extract specific promises to sign the NPT, adhere to the MTCR, and refrain from transferring the M-series missiles. Secretary Baker finally received personal commitments from Chinese leaders but stood alone when he relayed those new promises at a press conference in Beijing. The Chinese foreign minister issued no official word at the time. The Baker visit was successful in the sense that China agreed to sign the NPT and abide by the MTCR. However, high-level assurances, even when delivered personally to top U.S. officials, have not guaranteed change in Chinese nonproliferation behavior. Such Chinese promises strengthen U.S. positions but may later be defined narrowly by Beijing as bilateral understandings.

President Bush's decision during his 1992 presidential campaign to sell Taiwan up to 150 F-16A/Bs complicated the dialogue with China about its commitment to nonproliferation. The F-16s were intended in part to maintain Taiwan's defensive capabilities in the face of new Chinese acquisitions, particularly Russian Su-27s. Nevertheless, China linked its participation in multilateral arms control efforts as retaliation for the F-16 decision. China argued the United States had violated the 1982 joint communiqué on reducing arms sales to Taiwan and boycotted the Five Power arms control talks, in which China had agreed to participate during its 1991 bid for MFN. Arms sales to Taiwan presents a dilemma for Washington, involving competing security, political, and economic objectives.

The evidence linking the imposition of targeted sanctions and China's agreement to abide by MTCR nonproliferation standards is strong. Thus, sanctions should not be excluded from a strategy to encourage the continued evolution of China's nonproliferation policy. China's accommodation of Bush administration nonproliferation objectives suggested that a tougher stance and targeted sanctions were effective, especially when combined with positive incentives such as support for China's membership in the General Agreement on Tariffs and Trade (GATT). However, some have criticized the Clinton administration's equivocal position on sanctions, which highlights continued conflicts among U.S. nonproliferation interests, economic interests, and human rights concerns. Ranking these interests and concerns according to their importance would help guide U.S. China policy.

There also need to be improvements in the bilateral relationship. Secretary Baker's November 1991 trip to the Chinese capital contains several lessons for the Clinton administration. First, agreements should be accompanied by a joint statement issued by the United States and China. Questions about China's pledges could then be directed to the Chinese leadership—not primarily to U.S. officials. Such public statements of policy would obviate the need for U.S. officials to take responsibility for explaining discrepancies between China's nonproliferation policy and its behavior and would also prevent U.S. officials from having to badger Beijing for further clarifications of its commitments. U.S. officials should not put themselves in the position of explaining China's nonproliferation assurances. Chinese promises should focus on international norms, not American demands and definitions.

Considering the issue of timing, the United States should press China sooner rather than later to commit further to international nonproliferation regimes. China's current octogenarian leaders, led by paramount leader Deng Xiaoping since 1978, are unmatched in military and political prestige, stemming in part from their participation in the revolutionary struggle. The passing of Deng and other elder leaders will likely usher in a period of political uncertainty. Although increasingly nationalistic in rhetoric (fueled by the demise of Communist ideology), the present leaders in China probably have greater capacity to make international commitments on nonproliferation—which may be criticized as concessions—than will future leaders, who will likely be preoccupied with consolidating power in a succession period.

Confidence-building measures such as a wide range of exchanges, including Clinton's November 1993 restoration of military-to-military exchanges, which were suspended in 1989, offer another way to encourage evolution in China's nonproliferation policy. By talking to leaders of China's military and defense industrial complex, U.S. officials may more accurately understand the politics of Chinese arms sales, and concepts about arms control, nonproliferation, and regime compliance may be more effectively conveyed. Although there is reason to question the utility of discussing military and dual-use sales with China's Foreign Ministry, which is often seen as uninformed and powerless in comparison with the military sector of China's leadership,[34] there may also be long-term benefits from engaging civilian leaders on nonproliferation issues. If Washington emphasizes the authority and accountability of civilian officials by providing them with greater contact with the West, those who are now making nonproliferation commitments may be helped in implementing the policies they espouse. Increased contacts could reinforce the idea that Chinese government authorities will be held accountable for actions taken by defense-industry officials, especially if such actions cause the United States to impose sanctions. Thus, Washington should continue to seek authoritative agreements from the Foreign Ministry but should also increase contacts with military, economic, and industry officials. The Clinton administration has found it valuable to expand on the engagement component of the Bush China policy.

Of course, the central issue for U.S. policy is whether, and how, to use the powerful but double-edged sword of trade to improve Chinese compliance with international nonproliferation norms. Although President Bush preferred a strategy of engagement with targeted technology sanctions and unconditional MFN, and although President Clinton has not linked MFN status to nonproliferation, some in Congress have argued that broader sanctions using U.S. leverage in trade and technology should be used. To realize the goals of modernization and political stability, China's leaders require Western, especially U.S., markets, capital, and technology.[35] Since 1985, China has enjoyed preferential treatment in technology transfers under the review procedures of the now-defunct Coordinating Committee on Multilateral Export Controls (Cocom), a group of Western countries that controlled the export of advanced items to Communist countries since 1950. Chinese leaders likely weigh carefully the economic (and political) benefits they gain through sensitive missile and nuclear sales against the costs of losing trade and technological benefits from the United States.

It is not necessary for the administration to link MFN to nonproliferation. The law has already made consideration of China's MFN status an annual event since it was first granted. The president must recommend a renewal every June. However, a repeal of the annual MFN renewal could be a significant incentive for China to accommodate U.S. interests. The Clinton administration should emphasize that China's nonproliferation practices nonetheless strongly influence debate on MFN status.

A new law included in the 1993 Defense Authorization Act, the Iran-Iraq Arms Nonproliferation Act, requires sanctions against countries that transfer to Iran or Iraq any goods or technology (including dual-use items, training, or information) that could contribute to the acquisition of weapons of mass destruction and their delivery systems. Chinese technology transfers to Iran could trigger sanctions under this law. More targeted sanctions are available to the Clinton administration, if needed.

In addition, for the United States to progress in the bilateral dialogue with China, an effective strategy would require renewed efforts on multilateral fronts. The United States retains significant leverage as a major donor to international financial institutions, such as the World Bank and the Asian Development Bank. Although Beijing by 1992 had amassed the sixth-largest foreign reserves in the world (at $43 billion in February 1992),[36] it continues to receive substantial international loans, for which it now qualifies. Washington may require nonproliferation cooperation in return for U.S. support for international loans to China, similar to the legal requirements for counternarcotics cooperation with other countries. China has also sought U.S. support for its bid to enter GATT, particularly support for its desire to join before Taiwan. Washington might require China to support UN enforcement of North Korea's NPT obligations, join the Nuclear Suppliers Group, and refrain from dual-use nuclear exports to Iran and Pakistan in exchange for its support of timely membership in GATT. The Perm Five arms control talks should be revived with vigor. Engaging Beijing multilaterally capitalizes on its desire to be included as a "great power" and to be perceived as a responsible world leader.

There is, also, a positive correlation between multilateral cooperation in efforts to influence China's nonproliferation behavior and the effectiveness of any such efforts. In other words, U.S. efforts to bring China into the nonproliferation regime are likely to succeed or fail according to the degree of allied support they receive. This is not to say that the United States should shrink from its traditional leadership in nonproliferation matters, but U.S. leverage will be reduced to the extent that China can circumvent U.S. policies and find alternative trade opportunities that are not contingent on Beijing's nonproliferation behavior. China's budding relationship with Russia is relevant in this regard. Moscow is becoming a major supplier of sophisticated weapons and technology to China. The Clinton administration should make clear to Moscow that undermining U.S. nonproliferation policy toward China is inconsistent with U.S. efforts to assist Russia. Although targeted sanctions proved to be effective, there can be no progress in greater Chinese cooperation without complementary and significant steps in bilateral and multilateral engagement.

China's membership in the Nuclear Suppliers Group would be a major step toward integrating China into the nonproliferation regime. China's full participation in the nonproliferation regime is critical if efforts to avoid nuclear confrontations or battles with chemical or biological weapons in Northeast Asia and the Middle East are to succeed. Beijing could also contribute to efforts to reverse the nuclear arms race in South Asia. Moreover, efforts to reduce the legitimacy of nuclear weapons through global arms control—including the NPT extension in 1995, a comprehensive test ban, and a cutoff of production of fissile material for weapons—are doomed without positive Chinese participation. Hopefully, Beijing will find it increasingly difficult to reconcile its nuclear- and missile-related exports with its own national security interests and, consequently, will close the gap between its declared nonproliferation policy and its dangerous practices.

Notes

1. See Shirley A. Kan, *Chinese Missile and Nuclear Proliferation: Issues for Congress*, CRS Issue Brief 92056 (updated regularly).

2. See, for example, "Excerpts from News Conference Introducing His Latest Appointments," *New York Times*, December 23, 1992, A14, in which Warren Christopher, Les Aspin, and James Woolsey each cite proliferation as a leading threat to U.S. security in the post-cold war era. Also see President-elect Clinton's speech at Georgetown University, December 12, 1992, in which Clinton cited nuclear proliferation as one of the "gravest threats we are most likely to face in the years ahead," and his September 27, 1993, speech to the UN General Assembly.

3. The term *regime* originated in scholarly research to describe "new patterns of cooperation" that some believed were transforming the international system. Policymakers, however, use the term in a more circumscribed way to describe networks of international, multilateral, bilateral, and unilateral measures to advance an international norm—in this case, nonproliferation. A landmark in regime theory is Stephen Krasner, ed., *International Regimes* (Ithaca: Cornell University Press, 1983). On nonproliferation regimes, see Zachary S. Davis, "The Realist Nuclear Regime," in Zachary S. Davis and Benjamin Frankel, eds., *The Proliferation Puzzle: Why Nuclear Weapons Spread* (London: Frank Cass, 1993), and Roger K. Smith, "Explaining the Non-Proliferation Regime: Anomalies for Contemporary International Relations Theory," *International Organization* 41, no. 2 (Spring 1987).

4. On the evolution of China's nonproliferation policies, see the following: "Chinese Statements on Proliferation Issues, 1979–1991," FBIS Special Memorandum, December 18, 1991; Timothy V. McCarthy, *A Chronology of PRC Missile Trade and Developments* (Monterey: Monterey Institute of International Studies, 1992); Robert Sutter, *China's Nuclear Weapons and Arms Control Policies: Implications for the United States*, Report for Congress (Washington, D.C.: Congressional Research Service, 1988); and Kan, *Chinese Missile and Nuclear Proliferation*.

5. Vice Premier Deng Xiaoping, quoted in *Xinhua* (Beijing), February 14, 1979; "Chinese Statements on Proliferation Issues, 1979–1991," p. 1.

6. China's arms control policy emphasized support for measures that would restrict U.S. and Soviet capabilities. Sutter, *China's Nuclear Weapons*, pp. 22–23.

7. On Chinese nuclear exports, see the following: Mark Hibbs, "Despite U.S. Alarm over Algeria, Europeans Won't Blacklist China," *Nucleonics Week*, May 23, 1991; Mark Hibbs, "Bonn Will Decline Teheran Bid to Resuscitate Bushehr Project," ibid., May 2, 1991; Mark Hibbs and Margaret Ryan, "Official Says China Developing Ability to Supply Entire PWRs," and "Sensitive Iran Reactor Deal May Hinge on MFN for China," ibid., October 1, 1992; "Bending Rules," *Far East Economic Review*, May 16, 1991; Gary Milhollin and Gerard White, "A New China Syndrome: Beijing's Atomic Bazaar," *Washington Post*, May 12, 1991; Ram Subramanian, "Second-Tier Nuclear Suppliers: Threat to the NPT Regime?" in Rodney Jones, Cesare Merlini, Joseph Pilat, and William Potter, eds., *The Nuclear Suppliers and Nonproliferation* (Lexington, Mass.: D. C. Heath, 1985), pp. 97–100; Emerging Nuclear Supplier Project, *Eye on Supply*, no. 4 (Spring 1991).

8. In 1985, President Ronald Reagan submitted to Congress the proposed agreement on nuclear cooperation with China. However, it has not been implemented, due to the lack of "peaceful use" certifications that Congress

required from the administration. See Warren Donnelly, *Implementation of the U.S.-Chinese Agreement for Nuclear Cooperation* (Washington, D.C.: Congressional Research Service, 1989).

9. "Facts about Some China-Related Issues of Concern to the American Public," factsheet from the Embassy of the People's Republic of China, Washington, D.C., May 1991, p. 13.

10. *Nucleonics Week*, May 23, 1991; Leslie H. Gelb, "Pakistan Links Peril U.S.-China Nuclear Pact," and "Peking Said to Balk at Nuclear Pledges," *New York Times*, June 22 and 23, 1984; Zachary Davis and Warren Donnelly, *Pakistan's Nuclear Status* (Washington, D.C.: Congressional Research Service, 1992). See also Seymour Hersh, "On the Nuclear Edge," *New Yorker*, March 29, 1993, p. 56.

11. Gary Milhollin and Gerard White, "A New China Syndrome: Beijing's Atomic Bazaar," *Washington Post*, May 12, 1991.

12. Central Intelligence Agency Director James Woolsey, testimony before the Senate Governmental Affairs Committee, February 24, 1993. In 1989, China helped Pakistan build a research reactor (Parr-2), which uses highly enriched uranium fuel, and assisted in fuel fabrication for the rebuilt and upgraded Parr-1 research reactor, whose capacity was doubled from five to ten megawatts in 1991. After Japanese, German, and French firms denied supporting systems and components for a power reactor, China signed a contract to build a three-hundred-megawatt reactor for Pakistan at the below-market price of $500 million (with Pakistan paying for local costs and China providing foreign exchange). *Nucleonics Week*, August 9, 1990, and January 24, 1991; Tai Ming Cheung and Salamat Ali, "Nuclear Ambitions," *Far Eastern Economic Review*, January 23, 1992.

13. *Middle East Today*, October 3, 1991.

14. *Nucleonics Week*, May 2, 1991.

15. "PRC Agrees to Complete Construction of Nuclear Reactor," *Sawt Al-Kuwayt Al-Duwali* (London), July 11, 1991, in JPRS-TND, August 8, 1991.

16. Bill Gertz, "Chinese Build Reactor for Iranian Program," *Washington Times*, October 16, 1991.

17. R. Jeffrey Smith, "Officials Say Iran Is Seeking Nuclear Weapons Capability," *Washington Post*, October 30, 1991, p. A1.

18. R. Jeffrey Smith, "China-Iran Nuclear Tie Long Known," *Washington Post*, October 31, 1991, p. A1.

19. Qian Qichen, interview with reporters during a visit to Japan, June 27, 1991, and Li Peng, interview with Chinese and Iranian journalists during a visit to Iran, July 10, 1991, both in "Chinese Statements on Proliferation Issues," pp. 6–7.

20. T. R. Reid, "China Plans to Sign Pact on A-Arms," *Washington Post*, August 11, 1991; Mark Hibbs, "Chinese Signature on NPT May Pressure North Korea," *Nucleonics Week*, August 15, 1991.

21. France did not accede to the NPT until August 3, 1992—five months after China.

22. White House Statement, Letter to Congress, and Report to Congress on Extension of MFN Status to China, *Department of State Dispatch* 3, no. 23 (June 8, 1992): 452.

23. The MTCR guidelines were revised on January 7, 1993, by the United States and the other twenty-one partners to cover missiles capable of delivering all weapons of mass destruction (chemical, biological, and nuclear). Although China has not publicly announced its adherence to the new guidelines, the original guidelines to which it committed cover the M-9 and M-11 SRBMs. Beijing is not a full MTCR "member," and Washington has said that China does not qualify in part because of its weak export control record.

24. Don Oberdorfer, "China to Reinforce Pledge on Missiles," *Washington Post*, February 2, 1992, p. A17.

25. See Kan, *Chinese Missile and Nuclear Proliferation*, and Shirley Kan, "Clinton's China Syndrome," *Far Eastern Economic Review*, July 1, 1993, p. 23.

26. Dingli Shen, *The Current Status of Chinese Nuclear Forces and Nuclear Policies* (Princeton: Center for Energy and Environmental Studies, Princeton University, 1990), pp. 14–18; Sutter, *China's Nuclear Weapons*, p. 27.

27. On February 25, 1993, the IAEA Board of Governors, which includes China, passed a resolution calling on North Korea to grant access to two sites suspected of housing materials related to spent-fuel reprocessing. Refusal to grant access is viewed as a violation of North Korea's NPT-type safeguards agreement and as grounds for the director general to report, to the UN Security Council, the IAEA's inability to verify compliance with the NPT. International Atomic Energy Agency, Board of Governors, "Report of the Agreement between the Agency and the Democratic People's Republic of Korea for the Application of Safeguards in Connection with the Treaty on the Nonproliferation of Nuclear Weapons," February 25, 1993. North Korea notified the UN of its intention to withdraw from the treaty on March 12. The three-month withdrawal period expired without resolution of the standoff. As of May 1994, North Korea had not withdrawn from the NPT but still refused to allow required inspections. The possible use of sanctions by the UN Security Council to pressure North Korea would depend on China's cooperation in the Security Council and in implementing sanctions.

28. Central Intelligence Agency Director James Woolsey, testimony before the Senate Governmental Affairs Committee, February 24, 1993.

29. Full-scope safeguards on all nuclear activities in nonweapon NPT states are not a requirement of the NPT but are required by the NSG. On IAEA and NSG safeguards, see Zachary Davis, *Nonproliferation Regimes: Policies to Control the Spread of Nuclear, Chemical, and Biological Weapons andd Missiles*, Report for Congress (Washington, D.C.: Congressional Research Service, 1993).

30. Mark Hibbs, "China Wants 200,000 SWU/Yr Centrifuge Plant from Russia," *Nuclear Fuel*, October 26, 1992, p. 4; Michael Gordon, "Moscow Is Selling Weapons to China, U.S. Officials Say," *New York Times*, October 18, 1992, A1; "Russian Official Denies Report, but Admits Military Pact with China," Associated Press, October 19, 1992; William Potter, "Nuclear Exports from the Former Soviet Union: What's New, What's True," *Arms Control Today* 23, no. 1 (January/February 1993): 9.

31. John Lewis, Hua Di, and Xue Litai, "Beijing's Defense Establishment: Solving the Arms-Export Enigma," *International Security* 15, no. 4 (Spring 1991): 87; William C. Triplett, "China's Weapons Mafia," and "Nuke Crux: 'Clans,'" *Washington Post*, October 27, 1991, p. C3.

32. The sanctions blocked exports to China of high-speed computers and satellites that were to be launched by China. The MTCR depends on national legislation for legal validity and implementation. Section 73(a) of the Arms Export Control Act (P.L. 90–629) and Section 11B of the Export Administration Act (P.L. 96–72) require U.S. sanctions if the president determines that a foreign entity, after November 5, 1990, knowingly "exports, transfers, or otherwise engages in the trade of any MTCR equipment or technology that contributes to the design, development, or production of missiles in a country that is not an MTCR adherent." The words "MTCR equipment or technology" refer to items listed in Category I or Category II of the MTCR Annex. Although the law requires sanctions for two years on foreign companies that violate the MTCR guidelines, the president may waive the sanctions if it is "essential to the [U.S.] national security."

33. In early 1992, reports revealed that China transferred missile-related chemicals (used in the fuel) to Syria, sent guidance units to Pakistan, and negotiated a sale of guidance systems to Iran. Elaine Sciolino, "China Said to Sell Parts for Missiles," New York Times, January 31, 1992, p. 1; Jim Mann, "U.S. Fears China Is Seeking Missile Deal with Iran," Los Angeles Times, April 3, 1992, p. 7.

34. Qian Qichen, the foreign minister since 1988, served without a Politburo seat until the Fourteenth Chinese Communist Party Congress in October 1992.

35. In 1991 and 1992, China enjoyed, respectively, a $12.7 billion and $18.4 billion trade surplus with the United States.

36. Central Intelligence Agency, "The Chinese Economy in 1991 and 1992: Pressure to Revisit Reform Mounts," July 1992.

Chapter 7

India

Brahma Chellaney

Nationalism, threat perceptions, and long-term strategic vision have been the most important elements in India's pursuit of advanced technology. The South Asian subcontinent is one of the most volatile regions of the world because of numerous interstate and intrastate conflicts, most of them rooted in its history and in the artificial borders created by the British in 1947. The colonially demarcated boundaries took little account of history, natural geography, or national security considerations of the states being given independence. Disputes over frontiers have sparked four major wars in the region in the past forty-five years, and border clashes remain common. Illegal cross-border movement of arms, extremists, and refugees has helped exacerbate national security concerns in the region. Transborder terrorism, which India now is beginning to cite as its foremost national security problem, is difficult to control because interstate frontiers are too porous. Underdevelopment, population pressures, limited natural resources, and ecological degradation have added to the interstate problems. One such example is the regional conflict over sharing interstate river waters, a conflict that involves India, Bangladesh, Nepal, and Pakistan.[1]

The cross-frontier movement of economic refugees, especially from Bangladesh and Nepal, is beginning to undermine the national security of India and Bhutan. The ethnic unrest in India's seven northeastern states and in Bhutan is directly linked to the refugee influx.[2] Pakistan's accord with Dhaka to take back the large number of Urdu-speaking Bihari Moslems stranded in Bangladesh since that country's 1971 war of independence has renewed ethnic tensions in the southern provinces of Sind and Baluchistan. The population explosion in South Asia is going to put growing pressure on food availability, water and energy resources, wildlife, and the environment. Bangladesh, already unable to sustain the existing population on its resource-poor landmass and facing a rising flood threat because of deforestation and soil erosion, has a population increasing at a rate of 3 percent a year. India—despite its lower population growth rate than Pakistan, Nepal, and Bangladesh—is the world's biggest contributor to the global population increase, adding 17 million people, compared with China's 16 million, in 1991 alone.[3] The human-induced environmental, economic, and social pressures in South Asia threaten to intensify political conflicts within and between states in the region. It is against this background that national security threats in South Asia are becoming increasingly internalized. Controlling domestic unrest is already the top priority of national security planners in India, Pakistan, China, and even the smaller South Asian states. Moderating the growing domestic problems of these nations is the economic liberalization drive that almost every state in the region has launched. The dismantling of licensing controls, reduction of tariffs, easing of foreign-exchange regulations to help attract investment and technology from overseas, and slashing of subsidies to make domestic industries more competitive internationally are, over the years, likely to spur faster economic growth and help raise income levels.

Threat perceptions and regional rivalries between India and Pakistan, and between China and India, provide a major stimulus to the arms competition and to the indigenous development of military technology. The wider implication of the growing military capabilities of these adversaries is underscored by their size: they make up nearly two-fifths of the world's population. The largest two nations, China and India, are engaged in building blue-water navies and acquiring other power projection force capabilities. South Asia is the world's only region where three nations, sharing disputed frontiers and torn by deep-rooted animosities, face each other with nuclear-weapons capabilities. Pakistan and India, already armed with weapons-usable fissile materials, are in the process of developing nuclear-capable ballistic missiles. China has a sizable and growing nuclear arsenal and is the only country in the world still committed to nuclear testing.

This chapter focuses on India's nuclear incentives and disincentives, domestic and external constraints on its proliferation-related activities, Indian nuclear diplomacy, and the likely security scenario in the subcontinent in the coming years.

Nuclear Weapons: Incentives and Disincentives

Unlike the dedicated weapons programs nurtured under military control in Pakistan and China, India's nuclear weapons capability derives from its civilian atomic research, and the military has no role to play in nuclear policy-making. Even in conventional defense policy, the Indian military is a limited player.[4] India, in fact, has a unique institutional setting for the conduct of weapons-related research and the formulation of policy. In theory, the atomic energy complex is under the control of the Indian Cabinet and top civil servants of the Cabinet Secretariat and is answerable to the national parliament. In practice, however, the complex operates on its own steam, and much of its dealings with the federal government focus on budgeting issues. There is really a technocratic control over the country's nuclear program, its nuclear posture, and its long-term nuclear planning. This has particularly been true since the mid-1970s when several separate component programs of a nuclear deterrent were launched in utmost secrecy by Prime Minister Indira Gandhi's government. Given a clear set of tasks to fulfill, the complex has worked on its own momentum.

The head of India's atomic program is the secretary, or top official, of the Department of Atomic Energy as well as the chairman of the Atomic Energy Commission. This position reports directly to the prime minister, who traditionally has held the atomic energy portfolio. In a country renowned for layers of complex and cumbersome intraexecutive controls over any government program, the nuclear program appears remarkably free from most such controls, although the program has spawned its own burgeoning bureaucracy. Legislative control over the nuclear program is minimal, limited mainly to the periodic official briefings on nuclear matters received by the parliamentary consultative committee on atomic energy. India's ballistic missile program, begun in 1983, also enjoys relative autonomy. Bureaucratic prerogatives have blocked interministry and interdepartment interaction and coordination on the defense production complex and the nuclear and missile programs, permitting each institution or program a considerable degree of freedom. The national parliament, which plays a weak role in shaping national security policy, has developed no structures for enforcing legislative oversight for strategic programs, some of which have no published budgets and are supported by a federal reserve fund. The uncharacteristic level of autonomy available and the lack of independent oversight carry both positive and negative elements. Although strategic programs have remarkably insulated themselves from the vicissitudes of Indian policy and political constraints, most of them, with the notable exception of the ballistic missile program, have become bloated, highly bureaucratized, wasteful, and inefficient. The nuclear program has all these characteristics.

Nuclear diplomacy is the domain of the external affairs ministry, but national *nuclear policy* is virtually the exclusive prerogative of the prime minister, who relies heavily on the country's top nuclear scientists for guidance. Contribution of other executive departments and agencies, like the intelligence organizations, to nuclear policy-making is limited. Indeed, there is little intra-executive or parliamentary debate on nuclear policy. It is the isolated and highly centralized nature of Indian nuclear policy-making that explains the country's lack of a clearly defined nuclear posture or strategy despite a weapons capability that dates back to the mid-1960s. The prime minister, India's undisputed nuclear policymaker, is usually saddled with a host of portfolios and a plethora of domestic problems. He has very little time for nuclear policy-making and is more apt to delay a crucial decision than to radically alter traditional Indian policy. This has given rise to what some Indian analysts call a "drift" in their country's nuclear policy. This drift, however, could also be seen as a masterly policy of inaction designed to buy time for the country's scientists to catch up on key technologies. India's technical capabilities at present are too limited for the development of a full-fledged nuclear arsenal, and several of its major strategic programs are lagging far behind in terms of completion schedules.

It can be argued that India's nuclear policy-making structure is such that incentives and disincentives to nuclearization are inbuilt. On the one hand, there are the relatively autonomous nuclear and ballistic missile programs, whose technological momentum appears unstoppable. On the other hand, the highly concentrated policy-making process is prone not to take a hasty political decision unless the country is pushed to the wall. India has learned to live with some harsh strategic realities without "going nuclear." China's detonation of a nuclear device in 1964, two years after it invaded India and annexed a strategic slice of Kashmir,[5] propelled New Delhi to launch its nuclear explosives program. More than two decades later, Pakistan's success in producing weapons-usable enriched uranium prompted India to accelerate work on its weapons program. But despite a weapons capability demonstrated at the Pokharan testing site two decades ago, India today still does not appear close to building a nuclear arsenal. There is little evidence of any Indian bombs in the basement. The absence of a coherent nuclear strategy or nuclear doctrine for the Indian military may reflect the absence of any clandestine nuclear arms.[6] However, the technological momentum that has been unleashed continues to incrementally strengthen India's weapons-related capabilities. Admittedly, a political decision-making process that pivots around the prime minister could be both a barrier and a facilitator to a quick decision on weaponization. If decision making in India at present finds more comfort in sticking to the present policy than in a radical departure, it could find as much comfort, given the right circumstances, in exercising the country's nuclear option. Only one major possible development in the next few years could trigger such a decision: evidence of overt weaponization by Pakistan.

Nuclear Weapons: Domestic and External Constraints

In the next decade, India's strategic vision and military doctrine will be shaped by a number of emerging internal and external factors. The most prominent domestic development is the growing internalization of security threats. The escalating ethnic, sectarian, and regional unrest in the country will increasingly force Indian security planners to look inward. The March 1993 Bombay bombing blitz that left more than three hundred dead and hundreds wounded was a grisly reminder of the menace of terrorism in India. The dangers of nuclear terrorism and blackmail in India (and in Pakistan) are now being clearly underlined.[7] Curbing conventional terrorism and controlling the influx of illegal immigrants from Bangladesh already are two major items on the Indian security agenda. The government has sought to contain terrorist violence by launching major police crackdowns in the troubled areas and by trying to cut cross-frontier supply lines of the extremists. Indian insurgents, whether in the Punjab, Kashmir, Assam, or elsewhere, are armed with sophisticated weapons such as Kalashnikov assault rifles and shoulder-fired rockets. Most of these weapons were originally intended for the anti-Communist Afghan guerrillas by Western suppliers but found their way into underground Pakistani arms bazaars and then across the porous South Asian borders. The Indian government has repeatedly accused Pakistan of training and arming Sikh and Kashmiri militants—a charge that Islamabad denies but that many of the rebels themselves acknowledge.

Terrorism is now seen by national policymakers as a major domestic menace. Indian authorities have spent tens of millions of dollars to erect a barbed-wire fence topped with lights along Punjab's border with Pakistan. The government now is considering building a similar fence along the Pakistan frontier of southern Kashmir, Kutch, and parts of the state of Rajasthan. In the mid-1980s, New Delhi proposed building a barbed-wire fence along its frontier with Bangladesh to halt the entry of illegal immigrants. The proposal, however, was abandoned after angry protests by Bangladesh, which denounced it as an "insult" to its national honor. Indian border troops have been unable to check the inflow of refugees because it is impossible to seal the frontier, made up of mainly flat delta land. The presence of millions of illegal immigrants from Bangladesh is stirring social tensions in several Indian states and undermining India's national security. An Indian security operation in fall 1992 intended to expel some immigrants in small batches was aborted after Bangladesh refused to take back the deportees, claiming they were not its citizens. Bangladesh, one of the world's most densely populated and poorest nations, is unable to sustain its burgeoning population on its existing landmass. Refugee flows from there are likely to remain a major national security problem for India.

India's future as a multinational state does not appear at stake in the foreseeable future, but the current trend of using more and more national resources to contain domestic unrest is expected to continue. Indian social unrest is likely to be exacerbated by a rising population and by issues linked to an imbalance in economic development, ecological degradation, and uncontrollable urbanization. Tensions with Pakistan and, to a lesser extent, with China will persist because there is little possibility that disputes over South Asia's colonially demarcated borders can be resolved in a satisfactory manner. However, major security threats will increasingly be internal in character. The same holds true for India's own arch-rivals, Pakistan and China.

A radical economic liberalization program launched in 1991, however, has led to a major turnaround in the Indian economy, which now is expected to grow at an average rate of at least 6 percent during the rest of this decade. The dismantling of trade and investment barriers and licensing controls by Prime Minister P. V. Narasimha Rao's government has spurred a major surge in foreign investment, boosted exports, and helped wipe out a trade deficit.[8] India, however, still faces the threat of a debt trap from its burgeoning external debt, which totaled more than $91 billion by mid-1994. The country has been self-sufficient in food since 1981, although in 1992 it imported wheat worth $400 million from the United States, Australia, and Canada to build buffer stocks and contain domestic prices. India's "green revolution" will have to spread to newer areas to cope with the demands of a growing population and the need to raise per capita food consumption.

In recent years, economic constraints have seriously affected India's conventional military and nuclear programs and strategic planning. These constraints forced India to wind down the military buildup it began in the 1980s. Although the economic pressures have started easing since the beginning of 1994, Indian security planners acknowledge that the country is unlikely to have the military resources in the next few years to take on its two largest and closely aligned neighbors, China and Pakistan. India's September 1993 border peace accord with China is an attempt to buy peace on one front, although it is a product of mutual security compulsions. Economic compulsions are also having an impact on Pakistani strategic planning. In contrast, China's military spending has ballooned since the end of the cold war, rising more than 50 percent in real terms from 1989–94.[9] Until 1990, India was the largest arms importer in the world,[10] but later it had to search for hard currency to buy even spares to keep the world's fourth-largest military machine rolling. Harsh economic realities forced a sharp decline in India's real military spending, ending a decade of rapid military growth that saw the country emerge as a regional superpower. Indian military spending increased dramatically in the 1980s; it more than doubled in an eight-year period, from $4.7 billion in 1980 to a peak of $10 billion in 1988.[11] It now stands at $7.3 billion in fiscal 1994–95 and, in constant dollar terms, is the lowest in three decades. As a percentage of gross national product (GNP), Indian defense spending declined from a peak of 4.06 percent in 1987 to less than 3 percent in 1994. It now makes up barely 13 percent of total government spending—one of the lowest percentages among major military powers.[12] The implications of its imports-based military buildup in the 1980s were not properly understood abroad. The post-1990 economic crisis helped deflate the exaggerated portrayal of the rise of Indian military power. The disintegration of the Soviet Union led to a disruption in supply of military components to India, triggering a crisis in its large defense production complex, a crisis that persists today.[13]

Pakistan's military expenditure remains among the highest in the world per capita and is underlined by the 1994 appropriation of 34.5 percent of the annual budget for defense. Economic constraints, however, have led to a slight fall in Pakistani defense spending in real terms since 1992, and the country has come under renewed International Monetary Fund (IMF) pressure to reduce its military expenditure from the current high level of more than 7 percent of GNP. For the second consecutive year, Pakistan raised its defense budget at a rate below that of inflation.[14] This marks a major departure from the steady annual increases in real defense appropriations since Pakistan achieved independence in 1947. The decline in real military spending by India and Pakistan does not mean that the two countries will stop shopping for sophisticated arms in the world arms bazaar. The lack of restraint by supplier nations in the 1980s was directly responsible for the South Asian military buildups. The present situation on the subcontinent, however, offers renewed opportunity on the supplier side to restrain the introduction of new high-technology weapons systems in the region and to help promote arms control.

With India's long-term nuclear calculations centered on China, Beijing's rising military spending and its nuclear modernization program are serving to reinforce obstacles to a regional nonproliferation regime in South Asia. China is the only country still conducting nuclear tests and committed to retaining certain classes of nuclear weapons—tactical and intermediate range— that Washington and Moscow are eliminating from their arsenals. China's biggest nuclear test at Lop Nor in May 1992 indicated that it is working on sophisticated high-yield, low-weight warheads. Beijing, defying worldwide trends, has sharply increased its spending on conventional arms. Its military spending has ballooned by more than 50 percent since 1989.[15] It is using its growing economic power to flex its military muscle, as in the case of the disputed islands in the South China Sea. The military buildup shows that Beijing is trying to project power far beyond its frontiers, with much of the additional spending being directed toward high-technology areas. It is seeking to develop a blue-water navy and an in-air refueling capability for its fighter jets. Significantly, China's arms buildup has continued despite the disintegration of its main foe, the Soviet Union. Beijing's expanding nuclear arsenal, which by 1988 was already larger than the combined British and French armories,[16] and its export of sophisticated arms and technology to two countries of proliferation concern in India's neighborhood, Pakistan and Iran, act as a barrier to Indian support for regional arms control. China also has sold intermediate-range DF-3 (CSS-2) ballistic missiles to Saudi Arabia, giving Riyadh the capability to strike targets in the Indian heartland.

Although the nuclear asymmetry with China remains a central concern among Indian policymakers, economic constraints have squeezed the budget for the country's atomic program. The government in fiscal year 1992 provided $351 million less for nuclear development than what the Atomic Energy Commission requested.[17] Paucity of funds has upset the commission's plans and affected several new projects.

Economic compulsions also have forced the Indian government to slash spending on military research and development (R&D) and general science and technology projects. In fiscal year 1992, India spent just 4.1 percent of its military outlays on defense research and development, compared with 14.8 percent in 1983.[18] At least 45 percent of the defense budget now is used for the upkeep of the 1.2 million men in uniform, putting growing pressure on the "teeth-to-tail" ratio. A committee of national lawmakers has recommended pruning the size of the Indian military to help pump more money into defense research and development.[19] Government support for science and technology also has shrunk. In the second half of the 1980s, expenditure on science and technology was about 1 percent of GNP—one of the lowest percentages among major nations.[20] But by 1992 it had plummeted to 0.9 percent of GNP.[21] The heavy slashing of research and development appropriations in 1992 due to the economic crisis spurred considerable concern among scientists. According to Director C.N.R. Rao of the Bangalore-based Indian Institute of Sciences, the decline in support for research and development raised serious questions about the future of science in India and created "a feeling of depression" among scientists.[22]

In the 1980s, there was a dramatic shift in India's priority away from industrial research and toward high-tech research in areas at the cutting edge of civilian and military modernization.[23] The fields that began receiving greater support included space, atomic energy, electronics, and biotechnology. The economic crisis, however, has also squeezed high-tech research. The Department of Electronics, which has developed a number of dual-use technologies and whose budget grew annually by nearly 18 percent in the second half of the 1980s, saw its requested funding cut by more than half in 1992. "The budgetary cut will definitely have an adverse impact on this key (electronics) program," noted V. Prasad Kodali, adviser to the Department of Electronics. "It takes years to build up strength in such an area. It will go to the dogs if it is not looked after properly."[24] In response to the mounting criticism of its science and technology policy, the government boosted R&D spending in fiscal 1993. And for the first time, it proposed in 1993 a "research and development tax" on Indian companies to encourage them to invest at least 2 percent of their sales income in developing new commercial technologies.[25] But if India is to get higher returns from indigenous research and development, it will have to do far more. The task calls for eliminating the bureaucratization of Indian science, restructuring the large state-funded research and development complex, boosting government support for science and technology, providing tax incentives to private industry to help build a culture of corporate research and development, improving national technological planning, encouraging greater interagency and interdepartment coordination and cooperation in technology development, and using economic liberalization to attract foreign capital and technology in key areas.[26]

India's severe economic constraints are unlikely to go away soon. Indeed, they have bred external constraints on any Indian move to weaponize. Recourse to multilateral institutional borrowing has brought sustained pressure on India for military restraint and regional arms control. India's radical economic reforms need the support of Western capital and technology if they are to succeed. This need, as well as New Delhi's credit dependence on Washington-based multilateral institutions, has given the United States some political leverage over India. This leverage has been reinforced by India's desperate search for new allies in the post-cold war world. In the most profound development in recent years, New Delhi has seen the collapse of its reliable friend, the Soviet Union, and with it the disappearance of a powerful balancing force to China. That countervailing force had been central to India's security planning and calculations. Now left to defend itself against two strong hostile neighbors, India is struggling to establish new strategic equations and ties in Asia and the rest of the world. In trying to strategically compensate for the loss of its Soviet card and the decline of the nonaligned movement, India has looked at the United States as a potential ally. The world's two largest democracies began developing strategic ties after India permitted U.S. warplanes to refuel on its soil during the 1991 Gulf War. Several important steps already have been planned or undertaken: joint naval exercises and simulated army maneuvers; joint military training and exchange programs; and regular meetings of senior U.S. and Indian military commanders. There is also a new recognition in U.S. policy of India's regional preeminence.

The end of the cold war eliminated the doctrinal source of friction between the United States and India: New Delhi's nonalignment had traditionally been viewed in Washington as directly opposite to the U.S. policy of containment. Now the development of bilateral relations can proceed smoothly. The emerging strategic ties will be of as much importance to India as to the United States. The current Indian economic liberalization drive, by throwing open a potentially large national market to American companies and goods, will help reinforce U.S.-Indian relations. Disputes over trade issues and protection of intellectual property rights (IPR) are unlikely to seriously affect the growing bilateral economic relationship. The warming ties with the United States make it harder for India to ignore Western pressure and chart a confrontational path toward nuclear weaponization. At the same time, there are limitations to the leverage that the United States has gained over India, which through its past policies of self-reliance retains considerable political, economic, and technological independence. Excessive U.S. pressure on India, which has always prided its self-reliant policies, could backfire, since such pressure could inflame Indian nationalistic passions.[27]

The United States may be able to persuade India not to weaponize, but such influence may not translate itself into an ability to
coax New Delhi into signing the Nonproliferation Treaty (NPT).
As Prime Minister Rao told a parliamentary committee, there is
a national consensus in India that the country needs to keep its
nuclear-weapons option open and that foreign pressure will not
be able to force a change in this posture.[28] The country has few
advocates of the NPT.

On issues of nonproliferation and safeguards, there is potential for both conflict and cooperation between the United States
and India. The degree or extent of conflict will be determined by
the level and range of political, military, and economic cooperation. A range of options for U.S. policy is proposed in table 7.1.
The types of carrots and sticks that U.S. policy seeks to apply
will obviously influence the scope of cooperation and conflict.
There is an apparent need for Washington to cooperate with New
Delhi to deter the spread of weapons of mass destruction, not
only in South Asia but also elsewhere in the world. For instance,
gentle U.S. persuasion in late 1991 succeeded in deterring India
from selling a ten-megawatt nuclear research reactor to Iran. Similarly, the United States has succeeded in swaying India to impose
export controls on many dual-use chemicals that are on the core
list of the Australia Group.[29]

India shares a number of common security concerns with the
United States. As an energy-poor country, India is heavily dependent on oil supplies from the Middle East and Iran. The Indian economy has been an important beneficiary of the low oil
prices that have prevailed in the world market because the United
States successfully foiled Iraq's plan to control a sizable share of
the global oil reserves by annexing Kuwait. China's nuclear and
military buildup is as much a threat to India as it is to the United
States. The United States, which experienced the worst terrorist
strike on its soil when New York's World Trade Center was
bombed in February 1993, shares India's concerns over terrorism.
The U.S. State Department, while placing Pakistan on a terrorism
"watch list" for about six months in 1993, revealed that it had
repeatedly raised with Islamabad at the highest level the issue
of Pakistani aid to Indian rebels.[30] India already confronts two
nuclear-capable adversaries and shares the U.S. goal to prevent
the further proliferation of nuclear weapons, particularly in the
Middle East and Southwest Asia.

TABLE 7.1   POSSIBLE U.S. POLICY CHOICES

Indian motivation	U.S. policy response
Seek nuclear weapons to deter China	Promote normalization of Sino-Indian relations and greater transparency in Chinese nuclear deployments; bring China into the international arms control arena; tacitly accept unpublicized Indian R&D work on a small nuclear deterrent but discourage overt weaponization
Seek nuclear weapons to deter Pakistan	Joint U.S.-Indian intelligence monitoring of Pakistan's nuclear program; work to slow down program by pressuring China to halt nuclear and missile assistance; support Pakistani and Indian conventional deterrence strategies; promote regional crisis-stability and confidence-building measures
Seek nuclear weapons as instruments of power and influence in world politics	Support India's addition as a permanent U.N. Security Council member; downgrade the utility of nuclear weapons in international politics; respect India's regional dominance; consult India on major regional and global issues
Seek to export civilian nuclear technology to raise funds for domestic weapons program	Persuade India to join multilateral technology regimes; offer dual-use export licensing benefits as an incentive; persuade India to incorporate, into its national law, export-control procedures and lists used by Western suppliers; encourage regime members to trade with India in components, equipment, and materials; provide technical assistance to India in matters such as reactor decommissioning and decontamination and radioactive waste management
Seek to strengthen general military capabilities by expanding nuclear and ballistic missile programs, testing new delivery systems and warheads, and building nuclear-powered submarines	Adopt universal nonproliferation measures, such as a comprehensive test ban, a halt to fissile material production and missile flight tests, and a no-first-use pact; back regional arms control; assist India in strengthening antiterrorism safeguards and physical security systems at nuclear facilities; offer high technology as an incentive for nuclear restraint

India's emergence as a potential second-tier supplier means that Washington is likely to try and bring India into the Nuclear Suppliers Group (NSG), the Missile Technology Control Regime (MTCR), and the Australia Group. India's ability, for example, to undercut Australia Group controls through exports had made it until recently a new battleground in U.S. efforts to deter developing nations from producing chemical-warfare agents. The United States had repeatedly sought New Delhi's cooperation in chemical nonproliferation efforts because India is one of the world's largest producers of industrial chemicals.[31] However, at the beginning of 1993, India clamped export controls on nineteen chemicals that have dual applications in commercial industry and poison gas manufacture.[32] Today, without being a member of the NSG, MTCR, or Australia Group, India—through its export policy—is respecting the guidelines of these multilateral technology control arrangements. The United States could succeed in persuading India to formally join those institutions by offering as an incentive a number of U.S. dual-use export licensing benefits. Such benefits could include General Cocom Trade (GCT), General Cooperating Governments (GCG), and General Free World (GFW) general licenses, a liberalized distribution license, and an expedited export-license processing.[33] It could persuade India to incorporate into its national law export-control procedures and lists commonly used by Western suppliers. New Delhi may be willing to cooperate with multilateral control regimes, even though they have consistently targeted India, if it sees no conflict with its national security interests.

Nuclear Diplomacy

India's nuclear diplomacy has been geared toward two goals: (1) deflecting outside pressure on the country to enter into regional nonproliferation arrangements or accept controls that would impinge on the country's nuclear weapons option; and (2) trying to block overt Pakistani nuclear weaponization—a development that is likely to trigger India's own weaponization. The prevailing Indian perception is that a nuclear rivalry with Pakistan based on aircraft-deliverable weapons not only would be strategically and militarily disadvantageous to India but also would be inconsistent with its long-term security interests and ambitions in the region. Premature nuclearization of the subcontinent would subvert India's superiority in conventional forces and undermine its strength as an emerging Asian power before New Delhi has acquired the technical capabilities to build a credible nuclear deterrent against its larger and mightier rival, China. An important foreign policy objective of India, as part of its efforts to deter Pakistani weaponization, has been to highlight illicit Pakistani nuclear imports and China's clandestine nuclear and missile assistance to Islamabad. Such assistance predates the nuclear cooperation agreement signed by the two countries in 1986[34] and reportedly has included the transfer of nuclear bomb designs,[35] collaboration in the development of centrifuges for uranium enrichment,[36] assistance in the development of ballistic missiles, and possibly a joint nuclear testing exercise in 1983.[37]

India appears willing to embrace *regional* measures that fall short of capping its nuclear program. And it is ready to accept *universal* nonproliferation measures even if they circumscribe its own nuclear capabilities—provided such measures are nondiscriminatory and applicable to all powers. India, for example, enthusiastically cosponsored the U.N. resolution endorsing the Chemical Weapons Convention (CWC).[38] This was in contrast to the diffidence with which its two regional rivals signed the CWC. Indian policymakers believe the CWC text provides a model for elimination of other weapons of mass destruction. The universal measures that India has pledged to support include the following:

1. A total test ban
2. A verifiable global halt to production of fissile material and tritium
3. A worldwide ban on ballistic missile flight testing
4. A no-first-use agreement among all nuclear-capable nations[39]

India, in other words, is willing to accept internationally what it refuses to embrace regionally. The universal measures it so avidly supports would, without question, stymie its own nuclear program. Part of the explanation for its abhorrence for regional nonproliferation measures is that such actions usually have been proposed in an India-Pakistan context, giving short shrift to New Delhi's legitimate security concerns over China. Western (particularly American) nonproliferation zealots have deliberately sought to underplay the China factor in Indian security calculations. This probably has to do with the fact that the introduction of China, despite its burgeoning arsenal of mass destruction weapons, into any South Asian proliferation analysis simply complicates matters and makes it extremely difficult to devise reasonable solutions. Many specialists, therefore, find it expedient to deal with China only in a peripheral way in their analyses. The fact, however, is that Indian security concerns are focused as much on China as they are on Pakistan.

Indeed, a study of the technical capabilities that India is arduously trying to develop shows that they have more to do with its desire to meet perceived Chinese military and nuclear challenges than with Pakistan. An example is the ballistic missile program. India's intermediate range *Agni* missile makes little strategic sense if it is analyzed in the context of the country's hostilities with Pakistan. The current design work by India's defense research-and-development laboratory on a longer-range ballistic missile than even the *Agni* indicates the determination of Indian security planners to develop a capability to strike targets deep inside China.[40] The motivation for the *Agni II* comes from India's disadvantage of geography in relation to China: whereas Beijing could strike India's main Gangetic plain even with short-range missiles from Tibet, the world's highest plateau, New Delhi would need missiles with a range of nearly two thousand miles to be able to hit the Chinese heartland. The *Agni*, even if fired from close to the Sino-Indian border, may not be able to reach Beijing.

If New Delhi is hostile toward the Pakistani proposal for a five-nation nonproliferation conference on South Asia,[41] it is because the proposal is centered on India and Pakistan as the main parties to the problem. Despite being adopted by the United States, the proposal has yet to define China's role in any such meeting and how China could contribute toward building a regional nonproliferation regime. China has not helped matters by saying that although it would attend such a conference, it could not be expected to make concessions on its nuclear program because it claims it has nothing to do with South Asia.[42] As the only power still committed to a nuclear buildup, China is emerging as a major obstacle to global arms control. It is still testing nuclear arms, promoting proliferation in the Middle East and South Asia through its exports, and declining to join other powers in eliminating certain classes of nuclear weapons that are destabilizing.

India has engaged in nuclear diplomacy with Washington mainly to blunt U.S. pressure. Three rounds of nuclear talks were held in 1992–93 by U.S. and Indian officials. The United States attempted to jump-start the stalled South Asian nonproliferation negotiations by proposing separate but parallel talks with Indian and Pakistan delegations in November 1992.[43] Instead, the United States had to be content with talking just to the Indians because Islamabad declined to enter into such "proximity negotiations." According to U.S. officials, Pakistan was concerned that the proposal for separate, bilateral talks would undermine its own Washington-backed, five-nation conference idea. However, if the U.S.-Indian negotiations are any indication, Washington's efforts are no longer concentrated on persuading the Indians to attend such a conference. Instead, U.S. strategy appears aimed at persuading New Delhi to accept specific regional nonproliferation controls, particularly an Indian-Pakistani ban on the production of fissile materials.[44]

Indian diplomacy has supported, with China and Pakistan, security- and confidence-building measures that do not directly impinge on New Delhi's nuclear weapons option and its vital national interests. India and Pakistan, and China and India, have taken significant steps since 1991 to reduce border tensions and build mutual confidence. Some of the credit for this ongoing confidence-building process in South Asia goes to the United States, which helped initiate it. Domestic constraints of India, Pakistan, and China also have helped propel them toward confidence building and regional crisis stability.

Since the adoption of the first confidence-building measures (CBM) in April 1991, Pakistan and India have made progress in some other areas. In 1992, they signed an agreement not to produce and deploy chemical weapons before the CWC was opened for signature. However, the accord neither prohibited research and development related to chemical weapons nor provided for verification of guarantees. An Indian-Pakistani pact not to attack each other's nuclear facilities was finally brought into force on January 1, 1992, after both sides exchanged lists of their installations. A new set of updated lists was exchanged in early 1993, per an annual requirement of the treaty.[45] Other CBMs signed by the two rivals include an agreement to provide advance notification of military maneuvers and troop movements along the frontier, periodic meetings of field military commanders, establishment of crisis "hot-line" communication links between their military operations headquarters, and common steps to deter violations of each other's airspace. There also have been some major failures in the confidence-building area. The most ominous development was the failure of the Indian and the Pakistani defense secretaries during negotiations in November 1992 to halt the fighting at strategic Siachen Glacier, located where the borders of the two nations converge with those of China, Afghanistan, and Tajikistan.[46] Hundreds of soldiers have died in the nine-year fighting at Siachen, the world's highest battlefield. Pakistan and India also have failed to reduce border deployments. Rather, India has beefed up its forces along the Kashmir frontier with Pakistan by moving in three army divisions from the northeastern Sino-Indian border. The additional deployments are linked to the growing separatist violence in Indian-ruled Kashmir and the increasingly open Pakistani support for the underground Islamic militants there.

With China, India has made more tangible progress in easing border tensions and reaching agreements on security- and confidence-building measures. However, all the progress has been in the conventional military sphere. Beijing refuses to enter into atomic confidence-building discussions or lift the cloak of secrecy on its nuclear deployments and arms production. During Indian Prime Minister Rao's visit to Beijing in September 1993, the two countries reached a general agreement on several CBMs. These measures included a ceiling on border troop deployments, allowing both sides to have an equal number of forces along their disputed Himalayan frontier; greater clarity on the present line of control to avoid confusion and deter 1987–style border skirmishes; a mutual commitment to abjure the use of force to change existing border positions; prior notification of troop maneuvers and movements; and concrete steps to prevent air intrusions by warplanes. Before that visit, a couple of CBMs ("hot-line" communication links and regular meetings of border commanders) had already come into force.[47] Technical experts from the two sides are to work out specific details to implement and monitor compliance with the other CBMs.

The Future Security Landscape

Interstate and intrastate conflicts in South Asia are likely to continue with varying intensity throughout the 1990s. Rapidly growing populations of the seven members of the South Asian Association for Regional Cooperation (SAARC) and of China are likely in the long run to undermine their national security and accentuate their intrastate and interstate conflicts. The region's colonially demarcated, imperfect borders will contribute to exacerbating such conflicts. India, the region's geographical hub that shares borders with all the other South Asian nations, is likely to see its national security seriously weakened by intrastate unrest elsewhere and the sheer impossibility of sealing porous borders. The easy availability of sophisticated arms and the spreading discontent among its own myriad castes, classes, sects, and ethnic and linguistic communities will force Indian security planners to invest sharply rising amounts of national resources in containing domestic terrorism and unrest. The growing internalization of security threats in South Asia also is expected to be underlined by the nonmilitary dimensions of national security, such as slower growth of food production in relation to population increase, ecological degradation as manifested by human-settlement encroachments on forestland and wildlife habitat, and the inability of rudimentary national health-care systems to cope with spreading HIV infection and AIDS.

Despite the domestic constraints and the pessimistic prospects for South Asia in this decade, the military-oriented technological momentum in India and Pakistan will continue unabated. India's burgeoning scientific manpower and growing military-industrial capabilities will help extend its strategic vision beyond South Asia. The Indian strategic vision will seek a greater international role and prestige for the country. India is expected to emerge by the late 1990s as an important exporter of conventional weapons systems. The already manifest economic constraints on its military modernization and expansion are likely to act as a spur to arms exports.

The South Asian nuclear genie is expected to remain unbottled despite the strenuous efforts of U.S. diplomacy. With both Pakistan and India armed with weapons-usable fissile materials and the means to deliver nuclear arms, the situation on the subcontinent has reached what may be called the postproliferation stage. The major challenge for the international community is how to manage this situation, control the degree and rate of nuclearization, and deter India and Pakistan from overtly deploying atomic arms or emerging as full-fledged nuclear-weapons states. However, there is little prospect of either India or Pakistan overtly building and deploying nuclear weapons until at least the mid-1990s.

Much of the nonproliferation literature has presented an exaggerated portrayal of the nuclear technical capabilities of the two countries. As was discovered in 1992 in North Korea, the capabilities of India and Pakistan are more limited than what has been assumed. Indian nuclear strategy is clearly not aspiring for warplane-deliverable weapons because such an arsenal, in the Indian military perspective, is likely to make the country less— not more—secure. India's missile-deliverable payload capability took a hard knock in May 1992 when design and reentry problems failed its second *Agni* test. Indian planners are unlikely to consider nuclear weaponization before the country's intermediate-range missiles have been successfully developed and have entered into commercial production. Indian scientists have made progress in many strategic projects, but it will be several years before the projects arm India with real military capabilities. These projects include the *Agni*, fuel-air explosives, and cruise missiles. In September 1992, Indian scientists successfully tested the *Lakshya*, an Unmanned Air Vehicle (UAV) that can also serve as a cruise missile.[48] *Lakshya*, like the *Agni*, is unlikely to be ready for production until at least 1997. India's nuclear-powered submarine (SSN) program, an essential element in developing a second-strike capability, is running several years behind schedule, and the most-optimistic government analysts place the completion of the first Indian SSN toward the end of the 1990s. Likewise, the component projects of Pakistan's nuclear program have all been plagued by major technical problems.

Despite the rival march toward building a nuclear deterrent, it is conceivable that India and Pakistan may never overtly produce and deploy nuclear arms or nuclearize their missiles. This could happen through a combination of factors: domestic budgetary constraints and civil unrest, external economic and political pressure, regional confidence-building and nuclear transparency measures, and global and regional nonproliferation measures. It may also be possible to achieve a straight trade-off with India, the main obstacle to a regional nonproliferation regime: security guarantees and permanent membership in the UN Security Council in return for signing the NPT and opening all its facilities to international inspection.[49] Nationalism and the desire to seek international prestige are major forces driving the Indian nuclear program. If permanent membership in the Security Council could propitiate India and turn it irreversibly from the nuclear weapons path, this may be a price worth paying for eliminating proliferation dangers in an area that, according to U.S. intelligence, presents "the most probable prospect for future use of weapons of mass destruction, including nuclear weapons."[50] Current international efforts are directed at devaluing nuclear weaponry as a currency of political and military power. But, unfortunately, the Security Council permanent membership remains synonymous with nuclear power status. By adding nonnuclear India, Japan, and Germany as permanent members, a more broadly representative Security Council would break the present umbilical cord that links big power status with nuclear power status.

Also, far more needs to be done to deter both vertical and horizontal proliferation, despite the recent progress in global arms control. There certainly is merit in the Indian argument that universal, nondiscriminatory measures like the CWC are the best way to achieve that goal. Major powers now need to work for a comprehensive test ban. The United States, the untiring champion of a South Asia free of nuclear weapons, will have to change some of its basic policy postures if such measures are to come into force. So far, it has refused to forswear the first use of nuclear weapons. There is a cardinal contradiction in its nonproliferation policy: the world's most powerful country claims it needs a nuclear weapons arsenal based on a first-use doctrine to meet its security concerns but demands that other nations forego such arms in the interests of global security. A change in U.S. policy is a prerequisite to making China, the international rogue, fall in line on arms control and export issues. Universal nonproliferation measures not only would cap Indian and Pakistani nuclear ambitions but also would block the emergence of other proliferators in the world.

Notes

1. For a full discussion, see B. G. Verghese, *Waters of Hope: Integrated Water Resource Development and Regional Cooperation within the Himalayan Ganoa-Brahmaputra-Barak Basin* (New Delhi: Oxford IBH, 1990).

2. See Myron Weiner, "Rejected Peoples and Unwanted Migrants: The Impact of Migration on the Politics and Security of South Asia" (paper presented to the 45th Annual South Asia Seminar, "The South Asian Diaspora," University of Pennsylvania, April 1992).

3. Lester R. Brown, Christopher Flavin, and Hal Kane, *Vital Signs 1992: The Trends That Are Shaping Our Future* (New York and London: W. W. Norton, 1992), p. 76.

4. The Indian defense ministry is run by career bureaucrats. Many at the senior level are members of the elite Indian Administrative Service and flit from one ministry to another during the course of their careers. A committee of national lawmakers has recommended a bigger role for the military in defense policy to provide for greater specialization and faster decision making. Estimates Committee, 10th Lok Sabha, *19th Report on the Ministry of Defense: Defense Force Levels, Manpower, Management and Policy* (New Delhi: Indian Parliament, 1992).

5. In 1962, China seized control of Indian Kashmir's Aksai Chin and Demchok areas. A year later, Pakistan ceded control of a small slice of its own Kashmir (Shaksgam Valley) to its close ally, China, so that Beijing could link its two rebellious provinces of Tibet and Xinjiang and build the strategic Karakoram Highway from the Chinese town of Kashgar to the Pakistani capital along the historic Silk Road. Today, India controls 45 percent of the 88,894–square-mile Kashmir, Pakistan 35 percent, and China the remaining 20 percent.

6. A lawmakers' panel, however, has found that India also lacks "a clearly articulated and integrated" conventional military policy. Estimates Committee, *19th Report on the Ministry of Defense.*

7. For a full discussion of these dangers, see Paul Leventhal and Brahma Chellaney, "Nuclear Terrorism: Threat, Perception, and Response in South Asia," *Terrorism* 11, no. 6 (1989).

8. Government of India, *Economic Survey 1994* (New Delhi: Ministry of Finance, 1994).

9. Brahma Chellaney, "The Dragon's Rise: Implications of China's Military Buildup," *Pacific Research* (May 1994).

10. SIPRI Yearbook, *World Armaments and Disarmament* (New York: Oxford University Press, 1991). The Indian military's dependence on imports is mainly in the area of high technology and has occurred despite India's own large arms-manufacturing capacity. Its domestic armament industries manufactured 31 percent of all major weapons produced during 1950–84 in the developing world, excluding China. Michael Brzoska and Thomas Ohlson, eds., *Arms Production in the Third World* (London: Taylor and Francis, 1986), p. 10.

11. Brahma Chellaney, "More Bang for the Rupee," *Indian Express*, August 10, 1991.

12. Government of India, *Annual Budget, 1993–94* (New Delhi: Ministry of Finance, 1993).

13. The country has been forced to cut back production of some weapons systems, including the T-72 main battle tank, and dig deep into its war-contingency spares. Brahma Chellaney, "India's Military Ties with Moscow under Stress," *Bangkok Post*, September 21, 1992.

14. Defense, the second biggest item in the Pakistani budget after debt servicing, was raised 8.6 percent in 1994 against an inflation rate of more than ten percent. About 62 percent of the entire budget was set aside for

debt servicing and defense, with a meager 23.4 percent left for national development. Farhan Bukhari, "Islamabad Prepares to Tighten Belt," *South China Morning Post*, June 11, 1994.

15. Alistar I. Johnston, "China's Arms Control and Disarmament Policy" (presentation to the Fifth International Summer Symposium on Science and World Affairs at Cambridge, Massachusetts, July 22–30, 1993); Nicholas D. Kristof, "As China Looks at World Order, It Detects New Struggles Emerging," *New York Times*, April 21, 1992.

16. John Wilson Lewis and Xue Litai, *China Builds the Bomb* (Stanford: Stanford University Press, 1988), p. 2.

17. "Lack of Capital Deters Russians from Building VVERs in India," *Nucleonics Week*, October 1, 1992, pp. 10–11.

18. *Asian Strategic Review*. The 1983 R&D spending was the highest ever as a percentage of total military outlays.

19. Estimates Committee, *19th Report on the Ministry of Defense*.

20. R&D spending peaked at more than 1 percent during fiscal 1988. Department of Science and Technology (DST), *Science and Technology Pocket Data Book* (New Delhi: DST, 1992); Department of Science and Technology, *Research and Development Statistics, 1991–92* (New Delhi: DST, 1992).

21. "Decline in Support for Science," *Statesman*, November 8, 1992.

22. C.N.R. Rao, "Saving Science in India," *Hindu*, October 7, 1992, p. 8.

23. Stephen Hill and Shantha Liyanage, *The Status of Indian Science and Technology Capabilities*, Briefing Paper for the Australian Mission to India (Wollongong, Australia: University of Wollongong, 1990), pp. 5–6.

24. "Fund Cut to Hit DoE Strategic R&D," *Times of India*, November 3, 1992.

25. Government of India, *A Draft Paper for a New Technology Policy* (New Delhi: Department of Science and Technology, 1993), p. 5.

26. See Brahma Chellaney, *Technology and Security: Implications of the Expanding Web of Technology Controls* (New Delhi: Center for Policy Research, 1993), pp. 44–68.

27. This is a point that the Carnegie Endowment Study Group on U.S.-Indian Relations makes while cautioning against excessive U.S. pressure on the Indian *Agni* program. Selig S. Harrison and Geoffrey Kemp, *India and America after the Cold War*, Report of the Carnegie Endowment Study Group on U.S.-Indian Relations in a Changing International Environment (Washington, D.C.: Carnegie Endowment for International Peace, 1993), pp. 37–39. Also, see General K. Sundarji, "The World Power Structure in Transition from a Quasi-Unipolar to a Quasi-Multipolar State and the Options of a Middle Power in the Milieu," part 2, *U.S.I. Journal*, January-March 1993. The former Indian Army chief suggests India and Pakistan build small nuclear arsenals to combat growing U.S. nonproliferation pressure. He also suggests India develop closer cooperation with its other archrival, China, to resist "U.S. arrogance" in world affairs. According to the general, if New Delhi and Islamabad openly pursued minimal nuclear deterrence, it would help create stable deterrence among the three major powers in the region: China, India, and Pakistan.

28. Government of India, *Prime Minister's Statement before the Parliamentary Consultative Committee on Atomic Energy* (New Delhi: Press Information Bureau, 1992).

29. The decision was significant because India for long had argued that export controls on dual-purpose chemicals were unfair because the chemicals are essential to the manufacture of fertilizers, petrochemicals, pharmaceuticals, and pesticides. It has contended that controls on dual-use items reinforce Third World dependency on the industrialized countries for finished products and strengthen existing trade monopolies.

30. U.S. Department of State, "Terrorism—Statement on Pakistan," January 7, 1993, published in U.S. Information Agency, *Wireless File*, January 8, 1993.

31. Brahma Chellaney, "India Is Target of U.S. Efforts to Curb Chemical Proliferation," *Washington Times*, October 12, 1992, p. A11.

32. Ministry of Commerce, *Export License Requirements for Dual-Use Chemicals* (New Delhi: Press Information Bureau, 1993). Five of the chemicals—phosphorous oxychloride, phosphorous trichloride, thionyl chloride, trimethyl phosphite, and n,n-diisopropyl-2–aminoethyl chloride—were already under export controls since 1992. *Import-Export Policy: April 1992 to March 1997, Handbook of Procedures* (New Delhi: Government of India, 1992), p. 243.

33. Under a GCT general license, India would have access to most items on the *Commerce Commodity Control List* of the Department of Commerce. A GCG general license would allow it to buy without Department of Commerce approval items controlled for national-security reasons, except for supercomputers. GFW is a general license for export of commodities at low-technology levels as identified in the Administrative Exception Notes (AEN) of the *Commerce Commodity Control List*. Stewart J. Ballard, "Technology Transfer Negotiations: Indocentric Perceptions" (paper presented to the seminar on "Dual-Use Technologies: Challenges and Choices," Institute of Defense Studies and Analyses and the National Telematics Forum, New Delhi, August 1992), pp. 7–8. India is currently a major target of national and multilateral technology export controls.

34. The nuclear cooperation agreement was signed in September 1986, during Chinese Premier Zhao Ziyang's official visit to Pakistan. "An Accord on Peaceful Uses on N-Energy," *Dawn Overseas Weekly*, October 1, 1986, p. 1.

35. The U.S. Senate Foreign Relations Committee was told in October 1991 that it was "pretty well established" that Pakistan's nuclear program had been built using designs obtained from China. That and other illicit Chinese nuclear assistance compose "one of the largest problem areas" in nonproliferation, Senator John Glenn testified before the committee. Berta Gomez, "Senators Seek to Toughen Nuclear Proliferation Controls," in U.S. Information Agency, *Wireless File*, October 17, 1991, p. 11.

36. Leslie H. Gelb, "Pakistan Link Perils U.S.-China Nuclear Pact," *New York Times*, June 22, 1984.

37. Jack Anderson and Dale Van Atta, "Nuclear Exports to China?" *Washington Post*, November 3, 1985.

38. Jacquelyn S. Porth, "Three New Nations Endorse Chemical Weapons Convention," in U.S. Information Agency, *Wireless File*, October 30, 1992.

39. India's support for universal measures is enshrined in its three-phase arms control proposal presented to the UN in 1988 by Prime Minister Rajiv Gandhi. Under the proposal, nuclear-threshold states would "undertake not to cross the threshold" if the weapons states slashed their arsenals to minimal-deterrent levels, halted nuclear testing and production of weapons-usable materials, and agreed to work toward complete nuclear disarmament by 2010. Subsequent Indian government statements have pledged support to further universal measures.

40. The *Agni II* is to have a three-thousand-mile range—almost double that of the *Agni*. Based on personal interviews with scientists.

41. Shortly before Pakistan Prime Minister Nawaz Sharif made his five-power conference proposal in mid-1991, he declared that Pakistanis would "eat one bread a day" rather than "forego or bargain on our peaceful nuclear program." "No Bargain on N-Plan: Nawaz Sharif," Official Report on Speech of April 27, 1991, *Pakistan News* 11, no. 12 (May 1, 1991): 1.

42. China's entry into a South Asian nonproliferation regime would be an "interference" and a "deviation" from its established security and foreign policy, according to an official Chinese statement at a regional nonproliferation seminar in Pakistan. "Special Issue: Nuclear Nonproliferation in South Asia," *Strategic Studies* (Islamabad) 10, no. 4, and 11, no. 1 (1987) (combined issue): 156.

43. Brahma Chellaney, "U.S. Plans Separate Talks on Indian, Pakistani Nukes," *Washington Times*, October 26, 1992, p. A11.

44. United Press International, New Delhi-datelined dispatch, November 15, 1992. The Indian team rejected the proposal but pledged New Delhi's support for a global agreement to halt production of fissile material. According to Ambassador Ronald Lehman, former director of the U.S. Arms Control and Disarmament Agency, a South Asian verifiable freeze on fissile material will not solve all the proliferation problems but may set the stage for India and Pakistan "to walk away from the (nuclear) abyss." U.S. Information Agency, *Wireless File*, October 30, 1992.

45. After the first exchange, each country admitted leaving off its list one previously unpublished facility. The Indians' list did not show a small gas centrifuge enrichment facility at Ratnahalli, in the southern state of Karnataka. The tiny plant, reportedly not completed until 1992, is expected to produce enriched uranium for India's nuclear-powered submarine project. The Pakistanis did not list their Golra facility. Mark Hibbs, "Second Indian Enrichment Facility Using Centrifuges Is Operational," *Nucleonics Week*, March 26, 1992, pp. 9–10, and Mark Hibbs, "India and Pakistan Fail to Include New SWU Plants on Exchanged Lists," *NuclearFuel*, March 30, 1992, pp. 6–7. In exchanging the new lists in January 1993, India declared that it had recorded Ratnahalli, but Pakistan declined to reveal if it had entered Golra. United Press International, New Delhi-datelined dispatch, January 4, 1993.

46. After the two sides agreed to disengage battling forces, talks broke down on the critical issue of how to demarcate a line of control at Siachen, with the Indians insisting on retaining control over the upper glacier and the Pakistanis insisting on a return to the pre-1984 positions. However, both

sides agreed to meet again in Islamabad after a joint technical team had worked out specific details on ways to disengage and redeploy troops.

47. The two sides reached an accord on these two CBMs in early 1992.

48. Ministry of Defense, "*Lakshya* Launched," press statement, Ministry of Defense, September 1992.

49. The idea of persuading India to join the NPT in exchange for big-power status as a UN Security Council permanent member was first made by Stephen P. Cohen and was supported by other scholars. See, for example, Harrison and Kemp, *India and America*, p. 42, and Ramesh Thakur, "Into the Security Council, out of the Nuclear Trap," *International Herald Tribune*, February 1, 1993, p. 6.

50. Central Intelligence Agency Director James Woolsey, testimony before the Senate Governmental Affairs Committee, February 24, 1993.

Chapter 8

Pakistan

Ali T. Sheikh

The admission by Pakistan that it has acquired a modest nuclear weapons capability, Pakistan's decision to freeze its nuclear program at the October 1989 level, and the India-Pakistan exchange of documents cataloguing their nuclear installations have moved the nuclear nonproliferation debate forward on the regional security agenda in the past few years. However, because the present weak governments of both India and Pakistan do not promise either continuity or stability, the nuclear question in South Asia continues to be especially complex and perplexing.

Both countries are faced with ethnic, communal, and sectarian strife that threatens national cohesion. Domestic politics is becoming increasingly violent in both India and Pakistan, and the military is being used more frequently to control domestic turmoil. A number of insurgencies rage along a border where India and Pakistan have fought three wars and narrowly averted one more. Armies go on alert as their governments trade charges of aiding each other's insurgents. Although there is a growing sense that the two countries need to escape this bilateral gridlock, neither country has strong lobbies seeking improved bilateral relations in an organized and vocal manner. In fact, hard-liners in both countries compose the mainstream of the national security community; maintaining a tough position against each other attracts electoral votes and bolsters domestic legitimacy.

In recent years, however, India and Pakistan have undertaken serious economic reforms and are vying for foreign capital and technology. A rapidly growing middle class in both countries has a stake in the reform process and is becoming more vocal and better organized on issues that include regional development. The security specialists in the two countries have increasingly incorporated aspects of this broader economic agenda, gained the attention of their respective civil-military establishments, and created new opportunities for dialogue.

This chapter will briefly discuss both the internal and the external factors that shape nuclear thinking and nuclear policy-making in Pakistan and will evaluate the policy directions that Pakistan is likely to take in the immediate future.

The External Context

Since India and Pakistan attained independence in 1947, super-power rivalry during the cold war years helped the two countries find friends and allies from outside the region. The cold war provided India with an opportunity to act as a moral force in the world and lead the nonaligned movement, as well as to play the two superpowers against each other. For Pakistan, the United States provided an ally and a major source of economic and military aid. Now, both India and Pakistan find themselves entangled in perceptions and policies that are relics of the cold war. Both are at a loss and are trying to learn how to manage their nuclear policies in a very different regional and international environment.

In India the end of the cold war meant the loss of nonalignment as a pillar of its foreign policy—a disturbing and disorienting shock to its worldview. Both the intelligentsia and the political leadership are still trying to comprehend the theoretical and policy implications of this sea change.

With the dissolution of the Soviet Union, India has lost its largest military supplier and most ardent diplomatic supporter in the UN Security Council, several trading partners in Eastern Europe, and political allies in the nonaligned movement from Afghanistan and Iraq to Yemen and Yugoslavia. The collapse of the Soviet Union, however, does not necessarily mean that what was previously a strong and well-entrenched pro-Soviet lobby has lost all its influence over decision making in India. Though fully gauging its influence is difficult, the lobby appears to be under strong pressure from competing interest groups. Nevertheless, it continues to wield substantial influence, albeit with waning prestige.

Further, the Indian political elite continues to be very suspicious of the West, particularly of the United States. There is a widespread view in India that a U.S.-dominated world is dangerous and antagonistic to New Delhi's aspirations. Influential members of the Indian intelligentsia seem to believe that the U.S. haste to codify a new world order dominated by Washington (nonproliferation and export control regimes, for example) betrays America's own fear that its primacy cannot last for very long. In the belief that American nonproliferation pressure will decline gradually as the Indo-U.S. bilateral relationship eventually begins to improve (as it did previously in the 1980s after very close ties between Washington and Islamabad), officials argue that India should retain its nuclear and missile programs.

Pakistan's rivalry with India and its deep sense of insecurity have survived the end of the cold war in South Asia. The Soviet Union's disintegration eliminated a perceived threat and, equally important, ended the largest source of advanced military equipment for Pakistan's adversary. The initial comfort derived from these developments, however, was diluted by the improvement in Indo-American and Indo-Chinese relations, as well as by China's decisions to join the Nonproliferation Treaty (NPT) and the Missile Technology Control Regime (MTCR), which implied a commitment not to provide assistance in the nuclear or ballistic missile fields. These problematic developments were compounded by the subsequent extension of the Indo-Russian Treaty of Friendship and Cooperation and by Moscow's willingness to continue its relationship with New Delhi in the military field.

There is widespread consensus in Islamabad that with the Afghanistan conflict removed from the East-West context and with the Soviet Union dissolved, South Asia in general and Pakistan in particular have lost their strategic importance for the United States. More important, Pakistan's "special relationship" with the United States has come under stress; Washington cut off economic aid and military supplies to Pakistan because of its nuclear program and criticized Islamabad for sponsoring "terrorism" in Indian-held Kashmir. Islamabad also fears that Indo-U.S. discussions over the nuclear issue and any understanding on MTCR could leave Pakistan "out in the cold."

Since October 1990, when the United States terminated military and economic assistance in accordance with the Pressler Amendment, Pakistan's dilemmas in the nuclear field have further sharpened: it is both unable to proceed fully with its nuclear program and unwilling to unilaterally roll the program back without reciprocal measures by India. Ironically, instead of strengthening the country's defense capabilities, the nuclear program has eroded Pakistani conventional military capabilities. The air force and navy have suffered severe blows to their operational capacities. It is believed that already half of Pakistan's F-16s, the mainstay of its air force, have been grounded, thus creating a possible military imbalance in which the air force may be unable to provide effective cover for ground forces or undertake offensive air operations if hostilities occur with India. Any serious imbalance in the region would make the current delicate state of deterrence even more fragile.

Given Islamabad's reliance on American weaponry, U.S. military aid is far more vital for Pakistan than economic aid. Islamabad continues to seek normalization of relations with the United States. In fact, Pakistan hopes "to develop a new, more mature relationship with the United States" which would seek nonproliferation "through a phased program of capping, reversing and eliminating" nuclear weapons and through U.S. help in resolving mounting tensions over Kashmir.[1] Despite additional trade restrictions now being placed on Pakistan and China as a result of the suspected delivery of M-11 missile components, relations with the United States can be improved if Islamabad continues to seize the initiative in its nuclear diplomacy with India. Pakistan's endorsement of a five-power conference on the nuclear future of South Asia and its announcement regarding the reduction of the enrichment level of nuclear fuel to October 1989 levels were motivated, at least in part, by the desire for a resumption of U.S. aid. Parts of the air force and navy now favor flexibility on the nuclear issue,[2] although it is hard to ascertain how widespread such views are and even harder to determine whether possible intra- and interservice rifts could influence nuclear decision making.

Fueled by the hawkish public posturing of political leaders for electoral gain, domestic pressure in Pakistan to continue with its nuclear program has intensified. The "bomb mentality" is ingrained in the country's political power structure. The president, the prime minister, and the chief of army staff (COAS) each pretend to control and champion the nuclear program. In this troika, former prime ministers like Mohammed Khan Junejo, Benazir Bhutto, and Nawaz Sharif had less-significant roles in nuclear decision making, in part because their tenures were brief but mainly because they never fully enjoyed the trust of the presidents under whom they served (General Zia ul-Haq and Ghulam Ishaq Khan). The president, under the eighth amendment to the 1973 constitution, enjoys the power to dismiss the prime minister and his or her cabinet. Junejo, Bhutto, and Sharif were fired, although only Bhutto's dismissal was rumored to be partly inspired by nuclear issues. Bhutto has publicly claimed that President Khan tried to keep her "in the dark" about the nuclear program and suggested that she was not even sure the president had come clean with her successor, Nawaz Sharif.[3] President Khan, an impassioned supporter of the nuclear program since the early 1970s when he was defense secretary, apparently enjoyed the military's confidence on the nuclear question, perhaps far more than did his interim successor, Wasim Sajjad.

The Domestic Context

The domestic context of India-Pakistan policies overshadows their bilateral relations, often with the result of "one step forward, two steps back." Mutual suspicions arise out of the bitter history of partition; disparity in geographical size, economic resources, and military strengths; domestic political structures and elite perceptions of each other; the rise of fundamentalist groups in each country; and their international policies and alignments.

Fears of Indian hegemony run high in Pakistan, particularly in Punjab province, which provides the main source of the civilian-military bureaucracy. These suspicions are easily translated into official policy that seeks to promote credible conventional deterrence and to secure equality with India through the acquisition of a nuclear capability. Pakistan's nuclear weapons program is expected to provide not only the "ultimate deterrent" but also the long-aspired psychological equality—not just military parity—with India.

Pakistan's nuclear program received a boost from India's nuclear explosion in 1974 and produced weapons-grade uranium within a dozen years. By its own admission, the country has accumulated enough weapons-grade material for at least one device,[4] although estimates of fissile material translate into as many as twenty devices.[5]

In an effort to address what has been described as a "credibility gap," Pakistan acknowledged its nuclear capability in February 1992 by saying it possessed "elements which, if put together, could become a device."[6] Islamabad also claimed to have "permanently" frozen production of highly enriched uranium and nuclear cores, but according to some media reports, Pakistan has refused to dismantle the existing cores without a matching gesture from India. These initiatives have not been enough either to elicit a similar Indian response or to persuade Washington to lift the ban on economic and military assistance. The Pakistani proposal to freeze its program at current levels until India agrees to attend the five-power conference to discuss the future of nuclear weapons in South Asia has also stalled. Likewise, Islamabad's offer to sign the NPT on a reciprocal basis with India, allow mutual inspection of all nuclear facilities, agree to International Atomic Energy Agency (IAEA) safeguards, and issue a joint declaration denouncing the acquisition and manufacture of nuclear weapons has failed to move the nonproliferation agenda forward in the region.

India's continued policy of nuclear ambiguity, coupled with its refusal to enter into regional and international arrangements, not only reflects India's own historical concerns but also indicates New Delhi's perception that Pakistan may be forced to accede to U.S. pressure without gaining any concessions from India. India has thus exacerbated U.S.-Pakistani relations by refusing to adopt measures that might allow Pakistan to demonstrate greater flexibility on its nuclear program. The cutoff of American economic and military aid to Pakistan under the Pressler Amendment, therefore, offers little incentive to India to show any flexibility on the nuclear question. Never before has the key to nonproliferation in the region been so clearly in New Delhi's hands.

A common view in Islamabad is that if Pakistan possesses a credible nuclear capability, India will not attack Pakistan. By acquiring nuclear capability, Pakistan has stalemated India; its nuclear diplomacy prevented an escalation of Indo-Pakistan tensions in 1990. Thus, it is argued in Islamabad, Pakistan's nuclear program has enhanced stability in South Asia. Many analysts also argue that, in the absence of a Pakistani nuclear capability, there would have been little restraint on India's nuclear program.[7] More accurately, however, a combination of regional factors, plus an elevation of the international nonproliferation agenda, obliged India to stop at a certain level of nuclear development and Pakistan to pause after acquiring a rudimentary nuclear weapons capability.

Within the Pakistani military establishment, there are currently two main views on the direction the country's nuclear program should take. First, some believe that having acquired a nuclear capability that promises credible deterrence against India, Pakistan should "lie low" and consolidate its position. There is, therefore, no urgency to conduct a nuclear explosion or expand existing capabilities, particularly under the present strained relationship with the United States. Second, others believe that for the purposes of credible deterrence in the region, Pakistan's purported know-how is not quite as good as India's demonstrated capability. To attain a reliable deterrent capability, Pakistan should continue to expand its efforts, even if this requires nuclear testing. It is hard to vouch for the strength of the first view, which is associated with General K. M. Arif, versus the second view, which is associated with General Mirza Aslam Beg, the former chief of army staff. The latter perspective finds ardent proponents among many pro-bomb civilian analysts and opinionmakers who often advocate conducting a nuclear test. In addition, the scientific community working on the nuclear program is apparently keener to expand the project than are many civilian and military analysts. Yet it is difficult to determine the degree of their influence in nuclear decision making. Such divisions, coupled with strong public opinion, make the unilateral signing of the NPT, or the acceptance of full-scope safeguards, an unlikely option for Pakistan in the short term.

Despite acquiring a nuclear capability, Pakistan does not have a publicly articulated nuclear doctrine. Many military analysts do not seem to have considered the active relationship of nuclear weapons to defense. No organizational restructuring or changes in command and control systems and conventional military doctrine have been reported in the national media, in professional journals, or other publications that would define or assign a clear mission to nuclear capability in deterrence and, if that fails, to a war-fighting role. At what stage of a possible India-Pakistan conflict would the military consider the deployment or use of its nuclear capability? What kind of targets have they identified? Conversely, what is the Pakistani assessment of Indian nuclear

planning in a conflict? How is the civilian population to be protected? Are there any plans for large-scale evacuations or nuclear
civil defense? Such questions are neither seriously raised nor
debated in any sustained manner, nor can one obtain clear answers from present and former civilian and military decision
makers. Overall, the level of debate on nuclear issues is such that
military analysts rarely discuss notions like "preemptive strike"
and "second strike capability" and their implications for a region
where both India and Pakistan have nuclear weapons capabilities.
Consequently, for many commentators and officials, having "one
nuclear explosive device" is the panacea that offers solutions to
all national defense and security problems.

It is a fairly recent phenomenon that the nuclear issue has
come to the forefront and that a true nuclear debate has begun
to occur. Although taking a public position against Pakistan's
nuclear program is unusual, some supporters of Islamabad's
signing the NPT have emerged to counter those who advocate
an uninhibited and openly declared program. This anti-nuclear
weapons group is small and remains on the sidelines of the political and security debate. However, the very fact that the issue
has recently been raised publicly and that disagreement is officially tolerated shows the growing maturity of the security debate
in the country.

The anti–nuclear weapons group draws its support from some
of the radical political parties and segments of the progressive
intelligentsia. Small but articulate, it has raised broader questions
about the utility of nuclear weapons, the rationale of an expensive endeavor in a poor society, the relevance of elite technology
in a country that lacks basic infrastructure, the military and deterrent value of weapons of mass destruction, and the secret
nature of a program controlled by the military. Its primary motivation has *not* been security or strategic considerations but domestic, economic, and social agendas that could utilize the same
resources. It does not have a uniform intellectual perspective, but
its members were perhaps influenced by the European Green
movement of the 1970s and socialist thinking that emphasized
greater allocation of resources for social welfare programs. Often
on the sidelines of mainstream thinking, these members have
traditionally been critical of the country's foreign policy in general and relations with the United States in particular.

Many of these members either changed their position or simply stopped expressing their position on the nuclear program

under General Zia's repressive rule. Remnants of these views still survive in local and regional political groups, human rights activists, and journalist and academic communities. The media has enjoyed relatively greater freedom of expression under the civilian governments of Bhutto, Sharif, and Moeen Qureshi, prompting this intelligentsia to increasingly express its opinion on national security issues.

The pro-bomb group consists of religious political parties that were previously not in the least interested in defense and strategic affairs. As Zulfigar Ali Bhutto popularized the nuclear issue in the late 1960s and 1970s for electoral purposes, the religious political parties opposed to his Pakistan Peoples Party (PPP) also began to champion the nuclear cause. Major political parties in the Pakistan National Alliance (PNA) and its successor, the Pakistan Democratic Alliance (PDA), have taken a clear pro-bomb position. This stance serves electoral purposes, particularly in the province of Punjab, where the nuclear program is most popular. This province has the largest number of representatives in the parliament and is crucial to forming and successfully running the government. The PPP, under Benazir Bhutto, on the other hand, seems to have mellowed in its position; Benazir, on the record, has claimed that she is a "non-proliferationist."

Electoral considerations apart, the Islamic-fundamentalist groups' interest in the nuclear program is also a direct result of U.S. opposition to Pakistan's program; the more Washington pushed nonproliferation, the more such groups resisted. Their viewpoint is not religious per se; these groups apparently produce no religious literature that would justify nuclear weapons from the perspective of the holy scripts. Instead, this issue is viewed more appropriately from a "north-south" perspective, whereby the West's nonproliferation efforts are viewed as discriminatory—even as a conspiracy against the Moslems—by keeping countries like Pakistan technologically backward. Inherent contradictions in U.S. nonproliferation policy, such as being harsh on the Pakistani and soft on the Indian and Israeli nuclear programs, are often cited by these groups to highlight such discrimination. With General Zia's active encouragement in the 1980s, these groups became more assertive and today constitute the mainstream opposition to Pakistan's joining the NPT. Again, their position is based on broad rhetorical posturing, with little effort to address the substantive questions of the nuclear debate. The vehemently anti-Western, anti-United States, and anti-Indian positions of such groups make rational public discourse on the issue increasingly difficult and narrow governmental options.

The Politics of Nuclear Proliferation

India and Pakistan have been developing their nuclear capabilities for over two decades. Developments on the nuclear issue between India and Pakistan have always been asymmetrical in terms of motivation, nature, goals, and achievement of their respective programs. India continues to highlight the discriminatory nature of the NPT and demands a Comprehensive Test Ban Treaty (CTBT) and global disarmament. It also cites China's nuclear capabilities and the Pakistani nuclear program to justify its nuclear endeavors. There does not seem to be a clear, coherent official Pakistani position on these issues; Islamabad does not demand a CTBT or global disarmament *as conditions* to constraining its nuclear program, nor does it feel threatened by China's nuclear capability. Likewise, Islamabad does not oppose the NPT per se and has repeatedly stated its willingness to join the NPT, if India does.

Both India and Pakistan have maintained varying degrees of ambiguity about their nuclear policies. Both countries have long recognized the advantages of achieving a nuclear capability, without actually building weapons. Islamabad is convinced that its nuclear program has also helped it obtain a measure of deterrence without suffering all the penalties of possession. But as the nuclear equation is evolving into unfamiliar territory for both countries, there are divergent views about which country has the current advantage and what dangers lurk in the future.

India and Pakistan took three years to exchange lists of nuclear installations, as required under their agreement of December 1988; these lists were finally exchanged in January 1992 and again in January 1993. They are officially confidential, but some versions have appeared in the international press. Each side is believed to have accused the other of failing to declare gas centrifuge enrichment facilities. Pakistan reportedly omitted from the list a facility located at Golra, west of Islamabad. India is said not to have listed the enrichment facilities it has built at Bombay and near Mysore.[8]

The Indian and Pakistani nuclear programs undermine each country's efforts to integrate its economy with the global market.

U.S. economic aid to Pakistan has already been terminated. India may face a cutoff of Japanese (and possibly German) aid and is suffering from restricted access to Western technology. The United States, for example, continues to withhold the sale of a Cray supercomputer because India refuses to accept conditions aimed at preventing use of the computer for nuclear weapons or ballistic missile development.

With Pakistan's disclosure of its nuclear weapons capability, the context of the nuclear debate in the region seems to have moved to a discussion of a nuclear safe zone (NSZ). The idea of an NSZ, first suggested by retired Pakistani General K. M. Arif in an off-the-record Nimrana meeting in 1991, could suit both countries (although many Pakistani participants, including Ambassador Niaz A. Naik, have reservations). The notion of an NSZ presumes that the two countries already have a nuclear weapons capability and that the aim of bilateral discussions should now be to create a political and military environment that offers stable deterrence.

Analysts in the two countries are formulating various strands of the still evolving concept of an NSZ. It is argued that after Pakistan's admission of nuclear capability, the concept of a nuclear weapons free zone (NWFZ) is meaningless, that the NPT is irrelevant to South Asia, and that rolling back nuclear capabilities is impossible. The emphasis instead should be on finding elements that make the two programs more stable and predictable through a series of bilateral agreements. It has also been suggested that India and Pakistan should agree to a pledge of no-first-use of nuclear weapons in the region. The NSZ does not include a bilateral ban on the testing of a nuclear explosive device; one does not find any willingness in either country, particularly not in India, to sign away the right to test nuclear weapons, short of a global test ban. In India, some analysts also maintain that South Asia as an NSZ will have multilateral dimensions as well; for example, the United States will have to lower its presence in the Indian Ocean, particularly in Diego Garcia.

Even if the implicit assumption of the NSZ idea is that the two countries are nuclear-capable, the idea offers opportunities for greater stability and transparency. Various elements that can be further explored in this context include follow-up agreements on the 1988 India-Pakistan agreement not to attack each other's nuclear installations; exchanges of observers to one another's nuclear facilities; cooperation in peaceful uses of nuclear energy;

bilateral consultations on nuclear doctrine, safety, and command and control; limits on the ranges of missiles and their delivery systems; and an Indian-Pakistani cooling-off period that envisions shutting down respective nuclear programs for a defined period of time, for instance six months.

As noted, Indian-Pakistani relations have been managed by their two respective governments; there is little private interaction between the security communities, intelligentsia, or nongovernmental organizations (NGOs). Supplemental or public diplomacy is one track that can play a constructive role in preparing the environment for additional confidence-building measures (CBMs). Traditionally, there have not been any forums or private initiatives that could bring together specialists in the two countries. Consequently, such exercises were government-induced, if not government-conceived, initiatives. Recently, however, some leading individuals have tried to encourage private-sector interaction. Following the lead of *Time* magazine, the Goethe Institute, and the Pugwash group, which organized meetings with analysts from both countries, the United States Information Service (USIS) initiated its "Worldnet" discussion program to link regional analysts with U.S. administration officials.

More important, Harold Saunders' idea of "supplemental" or second-track diplomacy has encouraged a private-sector initiative called Dialogue-I (also known as Nimrana). It has held a number of dialogues on various issues affecting regional security at the nonofficial level. These discussions are expected to help dampen extreme public positions and promote greater flexibility. The format has worked well, and leading private figures have now taken it upon themselves to continue the process by arranging their meetings in India and Pakistan on a rotational basis.[9]

The Nimrana process is moving ahead steadily and in fact has stimulated a parallel process, Dialogue-II, which is also believed to have official approval from the two countries. Unlike Dialogue-I, Dialogue-II has apparently raised funding from local business communities. Even though ambitious and useful, these processes are neither sufficient nor likely to go very far. Both processes have failed to meet their targets of producing "joint" or coordinated papers on Kashmir, bilateral trade, nuclear proliferation, and CBMs. Already, the two processes seem to have alienated the "doves" in India and Pakistan. Their utility has primarily been in breaking the silence and candidly exploring a range of issues.

On the whole, the nature of regional security debate is changing from sporadic comments and rhetorical generalizations to a relatively more sustained and coherent interaction. There are evolving nuances, if not identifiable positions, within mainstream thinking. Even if mainstream hawks still dominate the discourse, some political space is gradually developing in the public realm for discussion and analysis of official positions and sometimes even opposition to them. It is, nevertheless, still a dialogue of the deaf.

Both the Indian and the Pakistani governments have been encouraging these quiet, private-sector explorations. Such discussions have been taking place for three years now and have already stimulated interest in other small initiatives. Such initiatives include meetings of various professional groups like economists, arms control experts, and leaders of political parties from seven South Asian countries.

Conclusion

Given the complexities of Indian-Pakistani relations and the intricacies of their nuclear equation, there is a need to think in small steps. An ambitious all-or-nothing initiative, such as a friendship treaty or a no-war pact, has often resulted in deadlock. Bold initiatives secure propaganda points but not negotiating partners. A gradualist approach will help consolidate small gains and allow the parties to build upon them. No government in Pakistan is in a position either to unilaterally sign the NPT or to agree to comprehensive safeguards. A formula that addresses popular Pakistani sensitivities and security needs in the bilateral context is difficult but appears to be the only viable route. A series of interrelated CBMs in the conventional and nuclear fields offers the best hope for incremental progress.

India and Pakistan are overly secretive about their security issues, and one knows very little about their military budgets, procurement policies, or doctrines. Their nuclear programs are wrapped in mystery. This makes regional deterrence extremely fragile and unpredictable and the security debate fragmented, sporadic, and narrow. CBMs so far have been mostly in the military and not in the political or economic arenas. Yet the Indian and Pakistani military establishments do not seem to have adequately conceptualized CBMs; all the effort is taking place in the diplomatic arena, often at the level of foreign secretaries. The need to engage the two military establishments in the process cannot be overemphasized. Given the precarious nature of Indian-Pakistani relations, war avoidance ought to be the central objective, particularly since there is a possibility that any future conflict may escalate to the nuclear level.

The intrusive Helsinki Act model, and particularly the Conference on Security and Cooperation in Europe logic, which reduces the offensive capability of the two sides, is relevant to the South Asian context. Given the obstacles to signing the NPT, perhaps the Argentine-Brazilian experience is best suited for the region. These two Latin American countries have developed agreements for bilateral inspections and safeguards by sidestepping the NPT regime. A uniquely South Asian regime involving bilateral inspections and safeguards on nuclear installations could bring greater stability to Indian-Pakistani nuclear relations. Such a regime could be bilateral within the organizational framework of the South Asian Association for Regional Cooperation (SAARC). Given the Indian and Pakistani urge to jealously safeguard their sovereignty, a regional framework would be seen as less intrusive.

The objective of CBMs in the conventional force area needs to be as intrusive and transparent as politically possible. A sector-by-sector approach and a built-in homogenization and coordination in CBMs are required. Likewise, some analysts in the region have suggested scaling down military preparedness, beginning with offensive weapons, followed by their support systems; basing future levels of deterrence on manpower instead of technology; initiating mutually negotiated restrictions on arms transfers to the region; and restricting supplies to basic spare parts but freezing them at the present level without provisions for upgrading. All these steps may not necessarily stabilize the regional balance, and some may even be nonstarters, but they can be useful in stimulating discussion. As a promising starting point, however, Indian and Pakistani analysts need to undertake private-sector exploratory discussions on a range of issues to address the future prosperity and stability of the region.

Notes

1. "Compromise with US on N-issue ruled Out," *Dawn* (Karachi), September 17, 1993, p. 1.

2. Charles Smith, "Atomic Absurdity: Pakistan Rides the Nuclear Tiger," *Far Eastern Economic Review*, April 30, 1992, p. 25.

3. Steve Levine, "Bhutto Says Pakistan Can Build Nuclear Weapons," *Guardian* (London), September 2, 1991.

4. R. Jeffrey Smith, "Official Reveals Extent of Pakistan's Bomb-Making Program," *International Herald Tribune*, February 8–9, 1992, p. 1.

5. See, among others, David Albright and Mark Hibbs, "Pakistan's Bomb: Out of the Closet," *Bulletin of Atomic Scientists*, July/August 1992, pp. 38–43.

6. Paul Lewis, "Pakistan Tells of Its A-Bomb Capacity," *New York Times*, February 8, 1992, p. 5.

7. Personal interviews with government and military officials in Islamabad and New Delhi, April 1992, November 1992, and January/February 1993. See also Smith, "Atomic Absurdity."

8. India has operated the Mysore ultracentrifuge enrichment facility since 1985. As the Indo-French agreement on French supply of enriched uranium fuel for two U.S.-supplied reactors at Tarapura (210 megawatts each) expires in 1993, India will need enriched uranium, or even more-expensive mixed uranium and plutonium oxide (MOX), to run the two reactors, which generate about 10 percent of the electricity for its Gujrat-Bombay industrial zone. It is expected that the French cutoff will inevitably result in an acceleration of India's enriched uranium program and an expansion of its facility near Mysore. Even if initially the production in large quantities of enriched uranium may be at low-grade levels (India would need about twenty tons of uranium enriched to 2.4 percent every year for Tarapur), the enlarged facility may also be used in the future for producing highly enriched uranium.

9. The Ford Foundation has already made a commitment to fund the next four meetings of the Nimrana process.

Chapter 9

South Africa

David Fischer

South Africa's Nuclear Capability

In July 1970, Prime Minister John Vorster informed his parliament that South African scientists had invented a process, "unique in its concept," for the enrichment of uranium and was "prepared to collaborate in the exploitation of this process with any non-communist country." Vorster stressed that South Africa's "research and development program in the field of nuclear energy" was directed "entirely towards peaceful purposes."[1] Donald Sole, at that time the South African ambassador in the Federal Republic of Germany, also maintains that the United States, increasingly concerned about nuclear proliferation, "effectively discouraged other countries from responding positively to South African overtures."[2]

The South African government hoped to commercialize its enrichment process by building a large enrichment plant and by exporting enriched uranium instead of concentrates. To secure the needed capital, the South Africa Uranium Enrichment Corporation (UCOR) made overtures to French and later German firms. The South Africans were reluctant, however, to disclose details of their enrichment process until they received firm investment commitments; the French and Germans were equally reluctant to make such commitments until they were certain that the South African process was economically viable. The negotiations eventually petered out but only after South Africa had established close contacts with German scientists, in particular, with the firm STEAG.[3]

In the meantime, South Africa went ahead with the construction of a pilot enrichment plant designed to demonstrate that the process was technically feasible and to serve as a model for a larger plant. The pilot plant began partial operation at the end of 1974 and full production in 1977. At this time, according to estimates made in a UN report in 1980, the pilot plant was capable of producing fifty kilograms of highly enriched uranium (HEU) per year (i.e., the amount needed for two to three nuclear explosive devices) provided it was built and optimized for that purpose.[4] However, an International Atomic Energy Agency (IAEA) document that was released on September 4, 1992, and that drew on South African sources stated that production of HEU began only in January 1978 and was suspended between August 1979 and July 1981 because of technical problems in the enrichment plant.[5]

The University of Southampton–based Program for Promoting Nuclear Nonproliferation (PPNN) held a workshop in Harare, Zimbabwe, April 2–4, 1993, to discuss current nuclear issues of interest to Africa. Experts from some twenty African countries, including Waldo Stumpf, chief executive officer of the South African Atomic Energy Corporation, participated in the workshop. Stumpf delivered a detailed presentation of South Africa's nuclear weapons program; his comments were later reduced to writing and circulated with his approval (hereafter referred to as the Harare Report). Stumpf amplified the Harare Report at a presentation he gave at the South African Embassy in Washington, D.C., on July 23, 1993 (hereafter referred to as the Washington Report).

In 1971, the South African minister of mines gave approval for research to begin on the peaceful uses of nuclear explosives and on the development of the first "peaceful" device.[6] In 1974, the decision was taken to develop a limited nuclear deterrent.[7] Within a few weeks of taking office in September 1978, Prime Minister P. W. Botha redirected the program to military ends and envisaged the production of seven nuclear warheads.[8] Six nuclear weapons were actually manufactured, the first in 1980 and the last in 1989. If the IAEA report of September 1992 is correct, the

HEU for the first device would have been produced between January 1978 and August 1979.

Did South Africa Carry Out a Nuclear Test?

In 1977, a Soviet satellite detected and a U.S. satellite confirmed that South Africa was preparing an underground nuclear explosion in the Kalahari Desert. The United States, Britain, France, and the Federal Republic of Germany thereupon warned Pretoria that a South African nuclear test would have dire consequences for South Africa. U.S. President Jimmy Carter received an assurance from Prime Minister Vorster that South Africa did "not have and not intend to develop nuclear explosive devices for any purpose either peaceful or as a weapon, that the Kalahari test site . . . [was] not designed to test nuclear explosives and that no test [would] be taken in South Africa now or in the future."[9]

Despite Vorster's assurance, there is no doubt that in 1977 the South Africans were preparing a test at the Kalahari site; indeed, the Harare Report not only confirms this but adds that the site was "officially abandoned in 1977"[10] and revisited in 1987 "to ascertain that the bore holes could still be used if necessary and to seal the test holes."[11] Vorster's pledge to President Carter was in this respect deliberately and knowingly misleading. Nonetheless, since production of HEU began only in January 1978 (according to the IAEA report of September 1992), it is clear that South Africa would not have had the quantity of HEU needed for a nuclear test in 1977.[12] In fact, it would not have had enough HEU until much later if the Harare Report's statement that the first enrichment took place in 1979 is authentic. By that time the concerted demarches of the four leading Western powers, tacitly backed by the USSR, seem to have persuaded Vorster to delay indefinitely any nuclear test.

On September 22, 1979, a U.S. *Vela* satellite recorded a double flash (usually diagnostic of a nuclear explosion) over the South Atlantic Ocean.[13] There was widespread speculation that South Africa or Israel (or both nations jointly) had carried out a nuclear test. The HEU production schedules given in the IAEA report of September 1992 (which indicates that the pilot plant was producing HEU from January 1978 until August 1979) and the Harare Report both imply that South Africa may well have had enough

HEU for a nuclear test by September 1979. However, according to Armscor (the South African arms manufacturing corporation that was assigned the task of manufacturing the nuclear "devices"), "the first device to be provided with HEU" received its charge only in November 1979.[14]

Moreover, at his Washington conference and in subsequent correspondence with the author, Stumpf confirmed that the first charge of HEU not only was enriched to only 80 percent (the normal enrichment for nuclear weapons is well above 90 percent) but also was chemically very impure. He pointed out that if such material was used as an explosive charge, the result would have been a very "dirty" test. Indeed, if the signal received by the Vela satellite did mark a nuclear test and if the device used was similar to the six devices that the South Africans manufactured from 1980 to 1989, it would have required an explosive charge of forty to fifty kilograms of U-235, giving it an explosive yield similar to the Hiroshima warhead, that is, about ten to eighteen kilotons.[15] It is probable, to say the least, that the atmospheric testing of such a device, whether it contained "dirty" 80 percent enriched uranium or "clean" 93 percent or above enriched uranium, would have produced significant amounts of fallout; however no fallout was detected after the double flash. It is also difficult to see what reason the South African government would have had for carrying out an atmospheric test, in flagrant breach of the Partial Test Ban Treaty to which it was and is a party, when it already had a fully prepared underground testing site in the Kalahari where a test would not have been in violation of that treaty. It should also be noted that the devices manufactured by South Africa are of a type that can reasonably and confidently be incorporated in a nuclear arsenal without prior testing. Indeed, the very first device of this type was not tested before it was dropped on Hiroshima.

In his statement of March 24, 1993, President F. W. de Klerk categorically denied that South Africa had carried out any nuclear test,[16] and this denial was repeated in the Harare Report. The panel appointed by President Carter to investigate the incident concluded that the double flash had probably not been caused by a nuclear test.[17] Nonetheless, some doubts persist, especially among U.S. intelligence experts who maintain that every double flash of the type detected by the Vela satellite is caused by a nuclear explosion; they apparently suspect that the September 1977 flash was caused by an Israeli device. In support of their suspicions, intelligence experts point out that a traveling iono-spheric disturbance was detected in Puerto Rico during the early morning of September 22 and that a hydro-acoustic signal was picked up by the U.S. Naval Research Laboratory.[18]

The Harare Report describes the six warheads as nuclear devices that were "never stockpiled in their assembled form." When assembled, the devices were about 650 millimeters in diameter and 1.8 meters in length. This would make them too large for artillery shells and probably for missile warheads as well. If they were to be employed, they could be dropped only as free-fall bombs. The South African statements do not accord with the belief, widely held in the U.S. intelligence community, that the South African program included the production of artillery shells; perhaps this is an inference drawn from the assumption that the 1979 event was a low-yield test.

Did South Africa Get Help from Abroad—and How Much Did the World Know?

President de Klerk categorically denied that South Africa received help from abroad in manufacturing its six nuclear devices. That there has been very close cooperation between South Africa and Israel in other military fields is beyond doubt. For instance, the International Institute for Strategic Studies (IISS) lists South African missile craft and their missiles by their Israeli as well as Afrikaans names: "Jan Smuts (Is Reshef) with 6 Skerpioen (Is Gabriel) SSM [surface-to-surface missiles]."[19] Some observers have attributed the 1979 double flash to an Israeli or joint Israeli-South African test. However, there has been no hard evidence of Israeli-South African cooperation in the development of nuclear weapons. In fact, the two countries appear to have taken different routes—Israel with the manufacture of plutonium-fueled implosion warheads and South Africa with HEU-charged, gun-assembly-type devices.[20]

The 1980 UN report strongly suggests, however, that the South African authorities received a good deal of help from German industry in taking the South African vortex process from the laboratory to the pilot plant stage. The South African process and the jet nozzle process invented in Germany by Professor Ernst Becker are conceptually different but have been authoritatively described "as two variants of the general class of aerodynamic [enrichment] processes," and they have some features in common.[21] There were several contacts between South African scientists and Professor Becker, who visited the South African nuclear research center at Pelindaba near Pretoria. For some time, South Africa sought German help in building a large commercial enrichment plant that would use the South African technique. In particular, there was close cooperation with the German firm STEAG, which was developing the Becker process. The doors of many German research laboratories were thus open to South African scientists and technologists.

At least as early as 1980, when the UN group of experts published their report, the rest of the world has known that South Africa was capable of producing significant quantities of unsafeguarded nuclear weapons material and, in all probability, of making nuclear weapons. In fact, there were several statements to that effect by South African politicians and officials during the 1970s and 1980s. But did the governments and intelligence services of other countries know for certain that South Africa had actually manufactured six nuclear warheads and had subsequently dismantled them?

A December 1979 CIA memorandum, released in July 1990 under the U.S. Freedom of Information Act, assumed that a nuclear explosion had occurred in the South Atlantic in September 1979 and went on to speculate whether South Africa or Israel was responsible for the event. The memorandum belatedly caught the attention of a leading German newspaper, which interpreted it as a clear pointer by the CIA to a South African nuclear weapons program.[22] However, this report seems to be no more than a particular version of the conjectures already referred to above about the cause of the double flash, and it does not imply that the CIA had other, more definite information. Additional reports in recent years have noted that the U.S. government has pressed the South Africans to fully disclose information about their discontinued nuclear weapons program,[23] but this pressure may have followed a media report that the IAEA inspectors had discovered equipment that could be used in the manufacture of nuclear weapons.[24] A report in the *New York Times* immediately after de Klerk's speech maintained that the U.S. assessment of the South African program "was primarily based on an analysis of the amount of enriched uranium that South Africa had produced, and not on direct intelligence on the number of weapons. In that sense South Africa has told Washington something new."[25] If this is correct, then the U.S. "intelligence community" knew little more about the South African program than did the authors of numerous published assessments and was not aware of the subsequent dismantling of the South African warheads.

Soviet and Russian intelligence may have had better sources than the United States. In February 1993, U.S. Senator John Glenn released a CIA translation of a Russian "Foreign Intelligence Report," which stated that South Africa's first weapon was a "nuclear explosive device of the cannon type."[26] The CIA clearly obtained a copy of this report before March 24 and April 2, 1993, when de Klerk and Stumpf respectively released details of the South African design. The Russian report accords with the Harare Report's description of a gun-barrel weapon, but it implicitly contradicts the South Africans in maintaining that South Africa achieved the ability to make thermonuclear weapons during the 1980s.[27] Apparently the Russian report drew this inference from the fact that in 1987, construction activity at the Kalahari Desert site was renewed.

The Rationale for a Nuclear Arsenal

In explaining the 1974 decision of the South African government to "develop a limited nuclear deterrent capability," de Klerk maintained that "it was taken . . . against a background of a Soviet expansionist threat in Southern Africa, as well as prevailing uncertainty concerning the designs of the Warsaw Pact members."[28]

To a less partisan observer, this sounds disingenuous. It is true that the Soviet Union was supporting the government of Angola both directly and through the despatch of the troops of its Cuban ally and that it was giving support in materiel and probably military advice to Joshua N'komo's Matabele warriors in what was then Rhodesia. (In fact, most of them were based across the Zambezi River in Zambia, where they were periodically bombed by the Rhodesian air force.) But for its part, South Africa was actively helping Ian Smith in every way short of sending a division into Rhodesia; South African troops were fighting a drawn-out guerrilla war against the South-West Africa People's Organization (SWAPO) in Namibia, were backing Jonas Savimbi in Angola, and were seeking to destabilize the government of Mozambique.

Nonetheless, it was easy in the mid- and late 1970s for the hawks in the South African Defense Force (SADF) to exploit the paranoia of the white minority government and portray an intimidating array of threats to the very survival of the Afrikaner nation. The *cordon sanitaire* of white rule to the North was fast disappearing with the collapse of the Portuguese empire in 1974 and the increasingly inevitable defeat of Ian Smith's white Rhodesians, outnumbered twenty-five or more to one by black Zimbabweans. Cuban troops were beginning to pour into Angola, and there were reports of the arrival of East German troops—an Afrika Korps.[29] Pretoria saw the Cubans as a major threat to Namibia. If Cuban troops had crossed Namibia's northern border, South Africa would have been compelled to intervene, thus appearing as the "heartless oppressors" opposing the liberation of the Namibian people.[30] In 1977, Jimmy Carter, no friend of apartheid, changed the U.S. foreign policy course set by Richard Nixon and his practitioner of realpolitik, Henry Kissinger, both of whom had taken a neutral, if not friendly, stance toward Pretoria. In the same year the UN Security Council imposed a mandatory ban on all arms sales to South Africa. At home, the memory of the 1976 massacre of the schoolchildren of Soweto was still fresh. It was easy to sketch a scenario in which massed black armies, backed by fifty thousand Cuban troops and led by Soviet and East German officers, would converge on the white citadel from the North while the Soviet navy cruised off the shores of the Cape and Natal, and within the ramparts, an increasingly embittered black proletariat would rise up in revolt.

A nuclear deterrent might thus have been part of the logical response to what the SADF referred to as the "total onslaught." But was it a convincing response? Whom would it deter, and how would it do so? Where could it be used? The gravest and, in time, the most mortal threat to the minority government came not from the North but from within South Africa's frontiers in circumstances in which a nuclear weapon was irrelevant. A nuclear threat would hardly deter the African National Congress (ANC) or Pan-African Congress (PAC). If black Soweto perished, so would white Johannesburg.

Since the 1962 Cuban crisis, the Soviet Union had shown great reluctance to become directly embroiled in any military action except when one of its "satellite" neighbors threatened to defect from the bloc; it is improbable that Moscow would have seriously contemplated directly using Soviet forces in a remote and uncertain adventure in southern Africa. And to use a crude South African weapon against the USSR—even to threaten to do so—would have been national suicide. To drop it on Luanda or any other African city would have been equally unthinkable; the fury of the whole world would have turned on the white government and swept it aside.

There was only one possible use for the seven devices that Prime Minister Botha planned to build—to use them as a political weapon for putting pressure on South Africa's few remaining friends.[31] President de Klerk put the argument quite succinctly: "The strategy was that if the situation in southern Africa were to deteriorate seriously a confidential indication of the deterrent capability [i.e., a nuclear test according to the Harare Report] would be given to one or more of the major powers, for example the United States, in an attempt to persuade them to intervene. . . . It was never the intention to use the devices and from the outset the emphasis was on deterrence."[32] The Harare Report added: "In the absence of an overt threat . . . the strategy of deterrence by uncertainty was pursued in the policy of 'neither confirming nor denying' the existence of a nuclear deterrent capability." Neither the de Klerk speech nor the Harare Report sits well with Vorster's categorical denial to President Carter in 1977 of any plans for a nuclear explosion or a nuclear test.

If the ultimate purpose of the six devices built by South Africa was to persuade the United States to come to the aid of the South African government if the latter was in extremis, would this tactic have succeeded? The South African government might, for instance, have argued or threatened that if it carried out a nuclear test, this would drive other African states to stage a mass withdrawal from the Nonproliferation Treaty (NPT) and thus begin the unraveling of a treaty that was very dear to Washington.[33]

It is true that in the 1960s and early 1970s the South Africans were able to make much of the geostrategic importance of their mineral resources and of the sea lanes around the Cape of Good Hope, along which vital oil supplies flowed to the West. Richard Betts also points out that the vigorous Western reaction to the disclosure in 1977 that South Africa was preparing a nuclear test showed that the rest of the world did care a great deal about the possible emergence of a South African nuclear arsenal.[34] But within a few years, a South African threat to test would surely have been empty and indeed self-defeating. After the widespread insurrection in the townships in 1985, the response of the U.S. Congress to a South African test would probably have been to turn the screws even tighter. (Congress passed the Comprehensive Anti-Apartheid Act of 1986 in reaction to the brutal repression of township riots.) Only in the event of a direct Soviet invasion of South Africa (and only if that was seen as threatening an important U.S. strategic interest) was the nuclear test tactic likely to have succeeded—and in such a case it would probably have proved unnecessary. Test or no test, the United States would have intervened.

In short, the belief that a South African nuclear test would have prompted the United States to come to South Africa's aid in the absence of a direct threat to American national interests was probably pure self-deception. If so, the South African nuclear arsenal was a political gamble that stood little chance of success; it was a waste of valuable resources. The net effect of South Africa's calculated nuclear ambiguity was to deepen the world's suspicion of South Africa's intentions, shrink its nuclear export market, and help confirm its status as an outcast. De Klerk did well to get rid of this nuclear baggage soon after he came into office and to dispel the ambiguity about the government's nuclear program.

The Turning Point

By the end of 1989, according to de Klerk, with a cease-fire in Angola, the tripartite agreement on the independence of Namibia, the withdrawal of fifty thousand Cuban troops, and the end of the cold war, "a nuclear deterrent had become not only superfluous, but in fact an obstacle to the development of South Africa's international relations." Hence, on taking office, de Klerk believed that it was in South Africa's "national interest that a total reverse—also in respect of a nuclear policy—was called for."[35] In other words, the bombs would be eliminated along with apartheid.

De Klerk ordered the decommissioning of the pilot enrichment plant that had made the fissile material for the devices and the conversion to civilian use of the factory that had manufactured the devices. When all the fissile material had been recovered from the devices,[36] and returned from Armscor to the custody of the South African Atomic Energy Corporation, South Africa formally acceded to the NPT, on July 10, 1991. By September 16, it had promptly concluded the required full-scope safeguards agreement with the IAEA.

Since then the IAEA has carried out about 115 inspections in South Africa in order to verify the completeness of the initial report submitted by South Africa on the amount and location of all nuclear material in the country. The IAEA Board of Governors and the General Conference have been informed that the inspectors "found no evidence that the list of facilities and locations of outside facilities provided by South Africa in its Initial Report . . . was incomplete." Nor was the IAEA Secretariat "in possession of any other information suggesting the existence of any undeclared facilities or nuclear material."[37] It should be noted, however, that the CIA still has some concern about the accuracy of South Africa's initial report; the South Africans admit that production controls and accounting procedures during the first years of operation of the pilot enrichment plant were very imprecise.

This remarkable reversal of course is the first case of a nuclear weapons state divesting itself of its nuclear weapons and joining the NPT as a nonnuclear weapons state. It is an encouraging demonstration of the fact that nuclear proliferation is reversible. Will it set a precedent—as President de Klerk apparently hoped?[38]

In a sense, Argentina and Brazil have followed the same course, although quite independently of South Africa and as a result of the advent of democracy in both countries, the declining influence of the military, and a steady improvement in relations between the leading countries in the region. They also reversed course before they had actually manufactured any nuclear weapons (unless we are in for another surprise). But looking farther afield, it seems unlikely that the South African example will prove infectious.

As de Klerk made clear by word and deed, the South African decision to scrap its nuclear arsenal was not taken in isolation but was only one, albeit important, element in a complete reversal of national and international policies; this included the abolition of apartheid within South Africa and the replacement of a policy of regional destabilization by one of regional cooperation and friendship (hence South Africa's somewhat belated enthusiasm for an African nuclear weapons free zone [NWFZ]). In South Africa's case, moreover, the change of policy was almost **entirely** in South Africa's own hands (although forced on it by its black majority) and did not presuppose the negotiation of an overall settlement with hostile neighbors. In the Middle East, an Israeli commitment to dismantle its nuclear arsenal could come only as the eventual product of a tried and tested Middle East settlement in which Israel, as well as its neighbors, had complete confidence. Much the same is true in South Asia. In Northeast Asia, its seems unlikely that North Korea is at the point of jettisoning communism, converting itself into a liberal free-market democracy, and transforming its relations with its neighbors.

At the same time, one may doubt whether it was only the end of the cold war and the disappearance of a perceived Soviet threat that caused the turnaround in South African nuclear policy. As soon as de Klerk took office, it was apparent that the days of the white minority government were numbered. If South Africa was to retain the nuclear arsenal and the means of expanding it, the arsenal would relatively soon come under the control of a multiracial or purely black government (or possibly of white extremists who might make a desperate bid to seize control). There had been a few African voices that looked forward to South Africa as the first black nuclear weapons state. Dismantling the nuclear devices and the plant that made them, destroying all evidence of the technology to make them, and acceding to the NPT would preempt any such unwelcome turn of events and please those circles in the United States who looked askance at ANC President Nelson Mandela's friendly relations with Libya and the Palestine Liberation Organization.

Where Does South Africa Go from Here?

As was clear from de Klerk's March 24 speech, and from the Harare and Washington reports, the South African government wanted to close the book firmly on the past and to focus attention on a more hopeful future. South Africa hoped to play an important part in helping to create an African NWFZ and in using South African nuclear science and technology to bring the benefits of the civilian uses of nuclear energy to the rest of Africa. The reaction of other African states has tended to be positive: there is broad support for an African NWFZ; there have been several exchanges of nuclear scientists between South Africa and other African countries; and South Africa now takes part in regional nuclear cooperation organized by the IAEA.

At the same time, there has been some feeling that de Klerk's recantation of South Africa's past nuclear policies and his promise of better things to come were almost too good to be true. Most other Africans simply do not accept that there ever was a serious threat to South Africa or a justification for a nuclear deterrent; on the contrary, South Africa was a constant military threat to its neighbors. South African governments have been duplicitous in the past—how can one be sure that all nuclear material has been declared to the IAEA? The only comment that one can make on the last point is that the IAEA seems reasonably assured that the inventory of nuclear plant and material declared by South Africa is complete—the IAEA's 115 inspections have not discovered anything that would suggest otherwise, and it is difficult to see what incentive the government, knowing that its hour was coming, would have had in concealing any HEU. *Cui bono?*

However, there are some reasons for concern about future South African nuclear policy. All the hardware that went into making the South African arsenal may have been destroyed or converted to civilian use, but South African scientists have learned how to make the bomb, and this knowledge will remain with them.[39] They may never again make use of it in South Africa, but, as with the Commonwealth of Independent States, there could be a danger that some South African scientists might be prepared to offer their nuclear services abroad. The risk is small but not nonexistent.

Second, it is clear that South Africa intends to keep a portion of its HEU and operate the Safari-1 reactor at levels of enrichment higher than the current 45 percent in order to produce certain radioisotopes that, it maintains, can be made only by a reactor operating at such high levels. The fuel will be under IAEA safeguards, and in itself, the use of HEU may present little or no proliferation danger. (The fuel that the Americans originally provided for that reactor was enriched to more than 90 percent.) It also appears that South African stocks of HEU are sufficient to fuel the reactor for the rest of its working life. But stockpiling of HEU, like stockpiling of separated plutonium, is regarded by many as a proliferation risk even if the material is under safeguards.

Moreover, South African use of HEU may make it difficult, if not impossible, for an African NWFZ treaty to ban the production or possession of HEU or separated plutonium—both fissile material that can be used in nuclear weapons. At the Harare meeting, other African states also made it clear that they were reluctant to have an African NWFZ treaty renounce the production of HEU or the separation of plutonium.

Third, South Africa has reportedly made good progress in developing laser enrichment technology. This is a very sophisticated but also potentially "proliferating" process, since enrichment up to weapons grade can be made in only a few stages and in relatively small and easily hidden facilities. As soon as possible, South Africa, which is now a member of the Zangger Committee,[40] should also adopt the Nuclear Suppliers Group guidelines, which seek to impose strict controls on the export of proliferating technologies, and should become a member of the Nuclear Suppliers Group.

Finally, the Harare Report states that South Africa intends to employ and sell its enrichment technology—which is essentially "dual-use"—for other nonnuclear applications, such as dust removal. The risk that the export of this technology could lead to proliferation is another reason South Africa should be brought into the Nuclear Suppliers Group as soon as possible. Most of these problems are not confined to South Africa, and each can be addressed reasonably easily if the political will is there.

Conclusions

South Africa's abandonment of its nuclear weapons program has many implications for the country itself, for IAEA safeguards, and even more profoundly, for our understanding of the reasons nations seek nuclear weapons and what can realistically be achieved in trying to prevent their further spread or to reverse the dissemination that has already taken place.

QUESTIONS—AND SOME ANSWERS—ABOUT THE SOUTH AFRICAN PROGRAM

First, it should be stressed that South Africa's policy reversal was due not only to a perception that the external threat to its security had vanished with the end of the cold war and the withdrawal of Cuban troops or to a wish to improve South Africa's relations with the sole surviving superpower. These were, no doubt, significant factors, but the nuclear turnabout was one aspect of a much broader transformation of domestic as well as foreign policy launched by de Klerk.[41] Another of de Klerk's concerns must have been the fate of the nuclear arsenal if it fell into the hands of a successor government. This also suggests that some of the general pessimism expressed today about halting the spread of nuclear weapons may be due in part to an insufficient appreciation of the domestic constraints at work in the countries that cause proliferation concern.

Second, on the evidence available today, it is unlikely that South Africa carried out a nuclear test. If South Africa received foreign assistance in developing its enrichment program, it is likely that the main—and limited—source was German industry in the early 1970s rather than Israel, which took a different route to nuclear weapons.

As long ago as the late 1970s, foreign intelligence sources (and observers of the South African scene) were fully aware of South Africa's nuclear capability but had no direct knowledge that it had manufactured, let alone dismantled, six nuclear devices. If this conclusion is correct, we have seen another demonstration of the fact that a nation with a reasonably sophisticated scientific and technical infrastructure can build an arsenal of relatively simple nuclear weapons without detection or testing.

Several other questions remain open. First, on July 23, 1993, an act of parliament made it a criminal offense for any South African citizen to develop or help in the development of weapons of mass destruction or missile systems for such weapons. Such legislation may deter South African scientists from going abroad and helping another country acquire nuclear weapons or delivery vehicles. But in the absence of authoritarian curbs on travel, how can the country effectively prevent such a nuclear brain drain? This is, of course, a problem faced by all the nuclear weapons states, especially those that are cutting back their weapons establishments, and in a different context, by other technically advanced countries, such as Germany.

It also seems likely that South Africa will insist on operating its Safari research reactor with HEU. Stumpf has indicated that for economic reasons, the level of enrichment of the Safari fuel has already been raised from 45 percent to 60 percent and that, of the HEU recovered from the "nuclear deterrence" program, all the HEU that is not suitable for Safari fuel is being diluted to low-enriched uranium (LEU). He states that the Safari reactor must, at present, use HEU to produce certain medical isotopes and other commercially valuable materials. But he adds that South Africa would consider converting Safari to run on LEU fuel, provided that this is not at Pretoria's expense and that the technical capabilities of the reactor are not adversely affected.

Further, will South Africa maintain adequate control of the laser enrichment technology it is developing? This is not merely a matter of ensuring the application of safeguards if the technology is exported. The Nuclear Suppliers Group guidelines are today interpreted as requiring in practice a total prohibition of the export of any enrichment technology or HEU. This is another reason South Africa should be invited to join the Nuclear Suppliers Group as soon as possible.

IMPLICATIONS FOR IAEA SAFEGUARDS

Until South Africa acceded to the NPT, the IAEA had no right or obligation to apply safeguards to any of South Africa's nuclear activities. The IAEA cannot, therefore, be held responsible for not detecting South Africa's weapons program. In this context, the IAEA's role was analogous to its very limited responsibilities in India, Israel, and Pakistan (or in the five recognized nuclear weapons states), rather than in Iraq or North Korea. Nonetheless, the South African case has significant implications for IAEA safeguards.

A nonnuclear weapons state party to the NPT is required to place all its nuclear material under IAEA safeguards. However, the NPT safeguards system, which is a product of the late 1960s when Germany and Japan were the chief target countries, focuses almost exclusively on *declared* nuclear plant and material. Germany and Japan were engaged in ambitious nuclear programs; the safeguards system was concerned not with clandestine plants but rather with the diversion of nuclear material in plants that were safeguarded.

Iraq demonstrated that whereas this approach might work effectively in the industrial democracies, the risk of future proliferation would lie in countries ruled by despots that had accepted NPT obligations merely as a cloak under which they could build clandestine plants. It would be far beyond the capacity or legal authority of the IAEA to scour the territories of the more than 160 parties to the NPT in a blind search for clandestine activities. Hence it is now essential to provide the IAEA with far more comprehensive information about nuclear plants, programs, and transactions and, in particular, to provide it with the findings of national intelligence operations. The IAEA should also make use of a right that it already possesses under the NPT system but that it had had no occasion to use until Iraq, namely the right to carry out "special inspections" at any location where it has reason to suspect the existence of undeclared nuclear material or activities. The IAEA must also receive the backing of the UN Security Council if its inspectors are refused access. This has in fact been promised by the Security Council, meeting at the level of heads of government or state, in its communique of January 31, 1992.

In the abnormal circumstances of Iraq, the IAEA did indeed receive pointers from intelligence operations, was given and exercised inspection rights even more far-reaching than those foreseen by the NPT system, and received the backing of the Security Council. The first attempt to apply these three post-Iraq reforms in the context of "normal" safeguards operations was made in 1993 in North Korea, which had refused to grant the IAEA access to two suspect locations identified by U.S. satellites. When the IAEA, after formally determining that North Korea had violated its safeguards agreement, reported the violation to the Security Council, North Korea announced that it was withdrawing from the NPT. Subsequently, North Korea suspended its withdrawal, but as of May 1994 it had still not permitted access to the two suspected sites.

If North Korea remains intransigent and if the Security Council fails to enforce the IAEA's inspection rights, a severe blow will be inflicted on the credibility of the NPT and the IAEA safeguards. The jury is still out on the North Korean case, but it is already obvious that the IAEA's special inspection procedure has proved very confrontational.

The South African case has illustrated an alternative approach. For many years, South Africa had been operating an extensive unsafeguarded nuclear program, which included the production of large amounts of nuclear weapons material. Clearly, if a country with such a nuclear record reverses its policy and decides to accede to the NPT, there will be doubts in many minds whether it has indeed declared and placed under safeguards all its fissile material and nuclear plants. Under the NPT system, the IAEA has the right to verify the "initial inventory" declared by the acceding country but has no right to demand information about the activities of that country before it joined the treaty (for instance, the operating records of previously unsafeguarded plants). Neither the NPT nor its safeguards system envisaged or made any provision for the possibility that a nuclear weapons state, not party to the NPT, would decide to dismantle its nuclear weapons and accede to the treaty as a nonnuclear weapons state.

South Africa is the first nation to have confronted the IAEA with this situation and the problems it presents.[42] The only way to dispel suspicion would be voluntarily to provide the IAEA with full information about the previous operation of all hitherto unsafeguarded plants and to permit the IAEA access to any location it wanted to inspect, including nuclear test sites and any plant formerly engaged in manufacturing nuclear warheads. This was, in fact, the approach taken by the South African authorities. In doing so, they established a valuable precedent, defining the procedures that must be followed to verify the initial inventory of any other state that has carried out an extensive unsafeguarded program before joining the NPT as a nonnuclear weapons state or otherwise renouncing nuclear weapons and placing all its nuclear activities under safeguards. Had this approach not been adopted by South Africa, the IAEA may have felt it necessary to make the fullest use of the confrontational special inspection procedure.

Implications for Nonproliferation

The paramount conclusion to be drawn from the South African case is that it has demonstrated—for the first time in history—that nuclear proliferation is reversible. In a sense, Argentina and Brazil may also have done so, provided that they fulfill their commitments to place all their nuclear material under IAEA safeguards and bring the Treaty of Tlatelolco fully into force. But Argentina and Brazil changed course before they had actually acquired nuclear weapons. In the case of Iraq, substantial progress toward proliferation has been reversed by force majeure, at least for the time being. The South African (and Iraqi) cases suggest that instead of the fatalistic policy of endeavoring to "manage" proliferation, a policy proposed by some analysts, a better approach is to reverse it, as is now being tried in North Korea.

The South African reversal of policy has thus significantly helped to strengthen the nonproliferation regime and to increase the isolation of the three remaining holdouts—India, Pakistan, and Israel (or four, if one includes North Korea). Nonetheless, it seems unlikely that any of the other threshold countries, let alone any of the nuclear weapons states, will soon emulate South Africa. If North Korea has manufactured a nuclear device, it is conceivable that international pressure will compel it to dismantle whatever has been made and place all fissile material in the country under safeguards. But Pyongyang is unlikely to reverse course of its own free will, short of a revolution in its domestic and foreign policies. On a far grander scale, a comparable revolution in the domestic and foreign policies in the former Soviet Union has permitted Russia and the United States drastically to reduce their nuclear arsenals, but for the foreseeable future, both of them, as well as Britain, France, and China, will remain nuclear weapons states.

A less comforting message from the South African case is its demonstration that a nation with a reasonably sophisticated scientific and technical infrastructure can build an arsenal of relatively simple nuclear weapons without detection or testing. Moreover, even if South Africa's money was ill-spent, the cost of the program was rather low, and the first results were obtained quite quickly—in about five years from the inception of the military program. De Klerk has estimated the total cost of the South African warheads at about R 800 million (approximately U.S.$500–$600 million). (The ANC maintains that the cost was much higher than the de Klerk government claims.) This compares with estimates of U.S.$10–$15 billion for the Iraqi program over a period of ten to fifteen years—which did not produce a single bomb. The cost differential may be partly accounted for by the facts that to oil-rich Saddam Hussein, money was no object, that the arsenal he had in mind may have been much larger, that he used almost every known enrichment technology, and that he planned to make an implosion warhead rather than a gun-barrel device.

There has been some speculation about the deterrent doctrine that South Africa embraced in the 1970s and early 1980s.[43] In contrast to the meticulously detailed strategies of the five recognized nuclear weapons states that sought to demonstrate that they were willing and able to deliver nuclear weapons onto a large number of selected targets in the territory of the enemy,

South Africa planned in the first place to use its small stockpile not as weapons against enemy targets but rather as a means of inducing the United States to intervene and to prevent a Soviet attack.

But perhaps the South African program should be compared with those of other "threshold" states (if this term is still appropriate) rather than with those of the five nuclear weapons states acknowledged by the NPT. Four of the five nuclear weapons states are or were industrially advanced; their nuclear arsenals ranged from several hundred to tens of thousands of warheads; the strategic goal was second-strike capability, chiefly against counterforce targets; and in the case of the two superpowers, the goal was the ability to exercise what is obscurely described as "escalation dominance" if war should break out between them. Moreover, the nuclear confrontation had lasted for decades and had become stable, even rigid, and subject to mutual understanding.

In the geopolitical circumstances of South Africa, India, Pakistan, Argentina (?), and Brazil (?), the available means of delivery are relatively primitive and uncertain, the chief antagonist may not be clearly defined, and if it is, it may have no or at most only a few untried nuclear warheads. In these circumstances, a modest nuclear arsenal may be perceived as a not-yet-specifically-targeted "existential" deterrent, rather like the U.S. nuclear arsenal in the late 1940s. With this concept, the dominant factor is ambiguity about the deterring state's current nuclear capabilities; potential adversaries fear, rightly or wrongly, that the deterring state has or could quickly assemble a stock of nuclear warheads and would be able to mount a nuclear attack on relatively short notice. Every state that has demonstrated its ability to make nuclear explosives or that was known to have nuclear warheads on its territory (such as Ukraine and Kazakhstan today) could exercise a degree of "existential deterrence."

In seeing nuclear weapons as a tool with which to embroil "friendly" countries in defense of one's own security, rather than as a means of intimidating one's enemies, South Africa may not be unique. There were (disputed) reports that during the 1973 Middle East War, the United States stopped the flow of materiel when Israel seemed poised to conquer the Nile Valley; the Israeli response was to arm its missiles with nuclear warheads as a means of inducing Washington to resume supplies, which it did.[44] It has even been suggested that one purpose of the British and French nuclear arsenals is to ensure that if the Soviet Union ever attacked Britain or France, the victim of the attack would precipitate a nuclear war into which, willy-nilly, the United States would be dragged.

However, these can be little more than speculations. In a sense, the political value of any nuclear arsenal is that its mere existence creates uncertainty. Indeed, existential deterrence would continue to exist even in a nuclear-weapons-free world. In the event of a severe international crisis, "it will always be easy for former nuclear weapons states to lay their hands on fissile material and make a bomb at short notice."[45]

Finally, the South African case indicates that short of a major change in the strategic and political environment of an actual or aspiring nuclear weapons state, there is little, if any, prospect of persuading it to reverse its nuclear policy or roll back its nuclear weapons program. Sticks and carrots, threats of sanctions and promises of nuclear technology, are likely to be of little avail.

Notes

Copyright, *Security Dialogue* (Oslo). An earlier version of this chapter was published in *Security Dialogue* 24, no. 3 (September 1993): 273–86.

1. A semiofficial history of the first twenty years of the South African nuclear program is A. R Newby-Frazer, *Chain Reaction* (Pretoria: Atomic Energy Board, 1979). The main part of Prime Minister Vorster's speech is reproduced on pp. 82–94.

2. Ambassador Donald Sole, presentation at the Fourth Annual Arms Control and Verification Conference, John C. Tower Center for Political Studies, Southern Methodist University, Dallas, Texas, October 16, 1993.

3. The contacts between the South African Uranium Enrichment Corporation and German scientists and companies are described in "Report of the Group of Experts on South Africa's Plan and Capability in the Nuclear Field," United Nations Document A/35/402, September 9, 1980, Annex, pp. 18–19; Leonard S. Spector, *Nuclear Proliferation Today* (New York: Vintage Books, 1984), pp. 284–87.

4. "Report of the Group of Experts," p. 22.

5. "Report on the Completeness of the Inventory of South Africa's Nuclear Installations and Material," attached to IAEA Document GC(36)/1015 of September 4, 1992. In the Harare Report, Waldo Stumpf stated that "the first enrichment" occurred in 1979.

6. Mark Hibbs, "South Africa's Secret Nuclear Program: From a PNE to a Deterrent," *Nuclear Fuel*, May 11, 1993, p. 3.

7. Stumpf, Washington Report.

8. Hibbs "South Africa's Secret Nuclear Program," p. 3.

9. Edward Walsh, "Vorster Pledge on A-testing Made Public by White House," *Washington Post*, October 26, 1977.

10. Harare Report, p. 1.

11. One of the holes drilled at that time for an underground test explosion was visited by the IAEA officials in 1992. The site was destroyed under IAEA supervision in 1993.

12. Since no HEU was available when South Africa completed the non-nuclear part of the first nuclear device, it was decided to conduct a "cold test" without fitting the device with U-235 in August 1977. See Hibbs, "South Africa's Secret Nuclear Program," p. 4.

13. There is some confusion about the location of the supposed double flash, with some news reports maintaining that it was over the South Indian Ocean, near the Prince Edward Islands.

14. Quoted in Hibbs, "South Africa's Secret Nuclear Program," p. 4.

15. Ibid., p. 5. The Hiroshima and the six South African warheads were of the same "gun barrel" or "gun assembly" type. In this design, a conventional explosion causes two (or more) subcritical masses of HEU to collide with each other at a high speed, which creates a supercritical mass. This technique cannot be used if the explosive charge is plutonium. The initial presumption of many U.S. officials and scientists was that *Vela* detected a low-yield test of two to four kilotons ("Report of the Group of Experts," p. 33). If this was actually a South African nuclear test, it is contradicted by South African statements that the program manufactured only large and bulky devices. Moreover, low-yield tests are usually the result of an increasingly sophisticated manufacturing and testing program, not the first incarnation.

16. Newsletter no. 10/1993, issued on March 25, 1993, by the South African Trade Mission at Harare, Zimbabwe.

17. For a fuller discussion of the findings of the Carter panel, which was unanimous in concluding that, based on the evidence available, the double flash was not caused by a nuclear explosion, see "Report of the Group of Experts," pp. 33–35. The panel's report was reproduced in the appendix to UN document A/35/358. See also Carlo Schaerf and David Carlton, eds., *Reducing Nuclear Arsenals* (London: Macmillan, 1991), pp. 191–203, which contains a transcript of a nonproliferation lecture by Francesco Calogero of Pugwash and the subsequent discussion in which Jack Ruina, chairman of the Carter panel, participated.

18. James Adams, *The Unnatural Alliance: Israel and South Africa* (New York: Quartet, 1984), pp. 192–93.

19. International Institute for Strategic Studies, *The Military Balance, 1992–1993* (Oxford: Brasseys, 1992), p. 210. For an extensive but speculative treatment of Israeli-South African military and nuclear cooperation, see Adams, *The Unnatural Alliance.*

20. In the late 1950s, South Africa supplied Israel with ten tons of uranium concentrates; both governments reported the transaction to the IAEA.

21. Allan S. Krass, Peter Boksma, Boelie Elzen, and Wim A. Smit, *Uranium Enrichment and Nuclear Weapons Proliferation* (London and New York: Taylor and Francis, 1983), p. 20.

22. "CIA-Memorandum: Suedafrika hat ein Atomwaffenprogramm," *Frankfurter Allgemeine Zeitung*, January 9, 1993.

23. Steve Coll and Paul Taylor, "Tracking S. Africa's Elusive A-Program," *Washington Post*, March 18, 1993.

24. The statement that IAEA inspectors had "found evidence of weapons-related activities" can be found in Mark Hibbs, "Washington Wants to Purchase South African HEU Inventory," *Nuclear Fuel*, October 12, 1992, p. 3.

25. Michael R. Gordon, "Washington Welcomes de Klerk Disclosures, but Wants More Details," *New York Times*, March 25, 1993.

26. Coll and Taylor, "Tracking S. Africa's Elusive A-Program."

27. On March 24, President de Klerk said, "No advanced nuclear explosives, such as thermonuclear explosives, *were manufactured*" (emphasis added). "Speech by State President F. W. de Klerk to Parliament, 24 March 1993, Regarding the Nuclear Nonproliferation Treaty," reproduced in newsletter 10/1993 (March 25, 1993), South African Trade Mission, Harare, Zimbabwe.

28. Ibid.

29. Robert S. Jaster, "Politics and the Afrikaner Bomb, *Orbis*, Winter 1984, p. 836.

30. Sole, presentation, Fourth Annual Arms Control and Verification Conference.

31. A similar conclusion was reached by Richard K. Betts in "A Diplomatic Bomb for South Africa," *International Security* 4, no. 2 (Fall 1979): 102, and by Jaster, "Politics and the Afrikaner Bomb," p. 844.

32. "Speech by State President F. W. de Klerk to Parliament, 24 March 1993." In a 1987 chapter on "South Africa" in Harald Muller, ed., *A European Nonproliferation Policy* (Oxford: Clarendon Press for the Center for European Policy Studies, 1987), pp. 304–6, I came to the manifestly wrong, or at least premature, conclusion that since South Africa was under no visible threat of nuclear or direct "conventional" attack by a significant military force, there was little or no security incentive for it to engage in a nuclear weapons program. However, I added that in the mid-1970s "a 'Fortress South Africa,' possibly nuclear, may have seemed to some a persuasive concept of last-ditch defence," and I asked whether the 1977 preparations for a test were intended as a signal and warning to Washington and Western Europe that South Africa was "capable of making nuclear weapons and must be handled with care."

33. I have written that South Africa might have used this threat as a means of ensuring that the United States would continue to veto proposals for mandatory UN Security Council trade sanctions against South Africa; such sanctions were greatly feared by Pretoria.

34. Betts, "A Diplomatic Bomb for South Africa," p. 302.

35. "Speech by State President F. W. de Klerk to Parliament, 24 March 1993."

36. IAEA regulations do not permit the disclosure of the total amount of HEU declared by South Africa. Media estimates place the inventory at 250 to 400 kilograms at various levels of enrichment. See Mark Hibbs, "Pretoria Replicated Hiroshima Bomb in Seven Years, Then Froze Design," *Nucleonics Week*, May 6, 1993, p. 16.

37. "Report on the Completeness of the Inventory of South Africa's Nuclear Installations and Material," p. 9. If South Africa had retained any of the devices or any other nuclear weapon or explosive device or undeclared nuclear material (other than yellowcake, which is not subject to inspection under full-scope safeguards), it would have been in breach of the NPT from the moment of accession.

38. In his March 24 speech, de Klerk said, "I trust also that South Africa's initiative will inspire other countries to take the same step." "Speech by State President F. W. de Klerk to Parliament, 24 March 1993."

39. According to the head of Armscor, Tielman de Waal, more than one thousand people worked on the project and knew they were manufacturing nuclear devices. "Many have died over the years and most have been retrenched" (*SAPA* [South African Press Association], Cape Town, March 24, 1993).

40. The Zangger Committee was set up in the early 1970s to reach an agreement on the categories of nuclear hardware whose export should trigger the application of IAEA safeguards.

41. Sole points out that this meant abandoning the traditional "laager" mentality of white South Africa; the "laager" was the circle of covered wagons that served as a fort from which the Boer pioneers beat off "native" attacks as they trekked into the interior. (Sole, presentation, Fourth Annual Arms Control and Verification Conference.)

42. When the five nonnuclear weapons states of Euratom acceded to the NPT in 1975, they had been operating extensive nuclear programs that included the production of weapons-usable material, but they had never manufactured nuclear warheads, and their nuclear programs from the start had been carried out under Euratom safeguards.

43. Darryl Howlett and John Simpson, "Nuclearization and Denuclearization in South Africa," *Survival*, Autumn 1993, pp. 158–59.

44. A somewhat different version of this story, but one that also asserts that one objective of arming Israeli warheads was to force the United States to resupply materiel, is provided by Seymour M. Hersh, *The Sampson Option* (New York: Random House, 1991), p. 227.

45. David Fischer, *Stopping the Spread of Nuclear Weapons: The Past and the Prospects* (London and New York: Routledge, 1992), p. 11.

Chapter 10

Brazil and Argentina

Mónica Serrano

The rules that today regulate the nuclear interaction between Argentina and Brazil have developed within the regional nonproliferation regime established by the Treaty of Tlatelolco in 1967. This evolution has led some observers to characterize these two countries as nonproliferators, indicating the gradual transformation of their relationship from nuclear rivalry to nuclear cooperation. This chapter attempts to assess the extent to which the concept of common security could be applied to Latin America, to the regional nonproliferation regime, and more specifically to the evolving nuclear relationship between the threshold nuclear powers in the region, Argentina and Brazil. For this purpose it departs from the assumption that Latin America can be characterized as a security complex that may eventually emerge as a security community.[1]

This analysis is divided into three parts. The first part offers a brief summary of some of the main trends leading to the creation of a nonproliferation regime in Latin America. It will identify the Latin American nonproliferation regime's distinctive features that demonstrate the potential advantages offered by regional schemes and will trace the evolution of the Argentine-Brazilian nuclear interaction and the origins of Argentine-Brazilian nuclear cooperation.

Second, it will attempt to identify the role played by both domestic and external factors in the Argentine-Brazilian nuclear relationship. This section will address the following questions: What has been the role played by domestic, bilateral, and international pressures? What measures have Argentina and Brazil taken to ensure that their respective nuclear programs remain under civilian control? Does the newly created bilateral control mechanism offer sufficient reassurances to third parties? Will the nonproliferation commitment taken by these countries lead them to adhere to both the Treaty of Tlatelolco and the Nonproliferation Treaty (NPT)? What are the implications of having Argentina and Brazil as full members of Tlatelolco but not of the NPT? In other words, is their commitment to the peaceful uses of nuclear energy under international safeguards irrevocable?

The final section considers both the prospects for the regional nonproliferation regime and the extent to which the current Argentine-Brazilian nuclear rapprochement could lead both countries to retreat from the nuclear option. Adapting a policy-oriented approach, this section identifies those relevant lessons that can be derived from the Latin American experience, in terms both of wider regional security and of bilateral security mechanisms to deal with potential nuclear adversaries.

The Latin American Nonproliferation Regime

As a result of strong Latin American reaction to intervention on issues related to national sovereignty, the United States assumed a low profile on the different proposals for regional nonproliferation. The U.S. government seemed to have preferred the use of approved interlocutors to promote regional denuclearization. The idea of a Latin American nuclear free zone (NFZ) originated in the 1950s in a plan proposed by U.S. Secretary of the Treasury Robert B. Anderson and emerged as a Costa Rican proposal. In 1963, Mexico became a new force behind regional denuclearization, a role that was pursued with the full approval of and in constant consultation with the U.S. government.[2] Although it is difficult to assess fully the extent to which either Costa Rica or Mexico served as interlocutors for U.S. nonproliferation interests, what seems clear is that the bilateral relationships with these countries at the time the proposals were put forward showed a significant convergence of interests.

Changes in the wider international context influenced super-power positions on nonproliferation in Latin America. The negotiation of the treaty was dominated by the interplay of the Cuban alignment with the Soviet Union and President John F. Kennedy's unveiling, in March 1961, of a new regional security initiative known as the Alliance for Progress. U.S. support for the regional nonproliferation regime arose partly from the strong interest shown by Brazil and Argentina in the nuclear option, from the perceived advantage of insulating the region from the dangers of U.S.-Soviet competition, from a wide and genuine interest in nonproliferation, and from the advantage of maintaining overall U.S. hegemony over the region. Although a period of relative instability seemed to be approaching, given Nikita Khrushchev's ouster and the Chinese nuclear explosion in 1964, these events paradoxically had a moderating effect on Soviet foreign policy. Soviet support was complicated by the commitment undertaken by the Soviet Union to the defense of Cuba. However, it has been widely acknowledged that the Cuban Missile Crisis served as a catalyst for the emergence of an institutional framework to control nuclear proliferation in Latin America. Indeed, the eventual support that the USSR granted to the regional regime was consistent with its traditional support of plans to establish NFZs throughout the world.[3] This moderation of Soviet behavior was particularly reflected in those steps taken by both superpowers toward increasing cooperation in nuclear nonproliferation. By the end of 1964, a number of conversations between the superpowers regarding Cuba's integration in the regional nonproliferation regime had taken place.[4]

Regional developments also had an impact on the creation of an NFZ. The negotiation of the Treaty of Tlatelolco was a complicated process that took place between 1965 and 1967 in the context of the rise to prominence of a new generation of military regimes in Latin America. The negotiating process revealed the existence of contentious issues, notably Cuban participation, geographical definition, decolonization, the right to peaceful nuclear explosions (PNEs), and the nuclear powers' guarantees, all of which shaped the final agreement.

Latin American politics in the 1960s were characterized by recurrent waves of military coups. By the time the Mexican Foreign Ministry launched the formal request to negotiate a Latin American NFZ, the main obstacles that lay ahead were already clear. Significantly, it seemed that Cuba's participation in a Latin

American NFZ would be highly unlikely, given the state of U.S.-Cuban relations. Further, earlier Brazilian support for a preliminary meeting disappeared after the 1964 military coup and the inauguration of the Branco government. The new government was determined to follow a more cautious approach based on considerations of Brazil's freedom of action.[5]

The negotiating process also reflected local concern over the potential implications for nuclear energy development. The Chinese nuclear detonation in 1964 strengthened the worldwide impression that prestige could be derived from nuclear status. Latin America was not an exception to these trends. Although the Argentine and Brazilian positions endorsed the view that nuclear proliferation endangered international security, they also challenged the existing distribution of power, in which permanent nuclear hegemony favored the nuclear powers. Although Brazil's and Argentina's participation suggested a strong interest in nuclear power, the Cuban Missile Crisis generated a regional consensus acknowledging the desirability of nuclear nonproliferation. This dilemma was reflected in Tlatelolco's text.

Throughout the negotiating process, the emergence of two diverging views on denuclearization became clear. The "rigorous" view, supported by the Mexican delegation, was closer to U.S. interests. Argentina and Brazil, however, whose political character was decidedly influenced by the military, shared an interest in incorporating nuclear energy issues in their respective national security agendas. Yet, as later became clear, active participation in Tlatelolco's negotiations enabled both countries to begin the formation of an ambiguous posture toward nonproliferation commitments. In contrast, the Mexican position was less influenced by military concerns, foreclosing any option beyond the peaceful uses of nuclear energy.

Numerous procedural problems that developed during the negotiations belied deeper disagreement, which was ultimately reflected in the treaty by a compromise formula. The rationale seemed to be that nuclear proliferation would be prevented through an effective system of control and verification. As soon as Argentina and Brazil became parties to the agreement, international pressure on their respective nuclear programs would increase considerably. Despite the traditional reluctance shown by these countries toward nonproliferation and despite their clear interest in nuclear power, neither Argentina nor Brazil abandoned the regional nonproliferation endeavor.

It would be wrong to suggest that no obstacles have hindered the implementation of this regime, but it would be equally erroneous to deny the existence of those steps indicating clear progress in the direction of the original goals. Undoubtedly the more recent nuclear rapprochement between Argentina and Brazil has been one of the most important events in the process leading to nuclear security in the region. Yet this rapprochement was preceded and to a considerable extent influenced by a number of significant measures, especially the continued efforts both at the domestic and at the regional levels for better relations and the positive impact of an international consensus favoring nuclear nonproliferation. The interaction between the nuclear option and the regional nonproliferation regime is central to understanding the process leading to nuclear cooperation between Argentina and Brazil.[6]

The Argentine-Brazilian Nuclear Interaction

In the 1950s both Argentina and Brazil embarked on the development of a national nuclear capability.[7] The Argentine nuclear program was inaugurated in 1950 by President Juan D. Perón; by the mid-1950s, Argentina began steadily to pursue an independent route by developing natural uranium methods, enabling it to limit international control over its nuclear program. Although Brazil had also indicated an interest in an autonomous course, the combination of U.S. pressure and U.S. incentives led the Brazilian government to place its nuclear program under the umbrella of the "Atoms for Peace" plan.[8]

While Brazil's program gradually became dependent on and controlled through U.S. assistance, Argentina continued its silent march.[9] Priority was given to the domestic production of reactors and fuel material in order to develop a national nuclear engineering capability and an infrastructure conducive to training and testing. In 1958, Argentina emerged as the first Latin American state to operate a nuclear research reactor.[10]

The strong military component that the Alliance for Progress acquired during the Johnson years not only had a significant impact on the Latin American military but also strengthened the position of those sectors favoring nuclearization in both Brazil and Argentina.[11] In Brazil, following the 1964 military coup, previous enthusiastic support for the Latin American nonproliferation effort shifted dramatically.[12] The Brazilian nuclear program, which emphasized the use of nuclear energy to meet both energy needs and, potentially, national security requirements, continued to be conducted under the umbrella of a special relationship with the United States. Yet, as would be the case in many other areas, the nuclear issue gradually disclosed the real limits of the belief in "shared interests."[13]

Underlying Brazilian rhetoric during the negotiations was the determination to avoid a "rigorous treaty." It soon became clear that Brazil would not openly oppose Latin American diplomatic efforts but would seek to delay, if not obstruct, the course of negotiations and subsequently the treaty's implementation. Brazil was determined to keep its freedom of action on nuclear energy matters, including the right to peaceful nuclear explosions.[14]

The ambivalent character of the Argentine and Brazilian postures reflected the increasing consideration given to nuclear status. Their apparent support for the goal of regional denuclearization offered hints of what would become ambiguous policies toward nonproliferation. This attitude resembled the ambiguity pursued by certain potential nuclear powers after the 1974 Indian explosion.[15]

Both Argentina and Brazil signed the Tlatelolco agreement in 1967; however, Argentina failed to ratify it, and Brazil remained outside the treaty through its reluctance to waive the conditions attached to Article 28.[16] Indeed, delays in Argentine ratification and the shield provided to Brazil by Article 28 would soon be identified as crucial to the implementation of the regional nonproliferation regime. Just one year after the signature of Tlatelolco, Argentina's position in relation to nonproliferation became clear. In the 1968 UN debate on the NPT, the Argentine delegate stated that "Argentina could not accept remaining subject to a continuing dependence on the great powers for nuclear technology" and concluded that the "NPT would disarm the unarmed."

The interaction between the Argentine and the Brazilian nuclear programs crystallized in the 1970s with the first visible results of Argentina's excursion in nuclear energy development. In 1973, the National Atomic Energy Commission (NAEC) signed a contract for a second reactor, the Candu (Canadian deuterium uranium), and another ambitious program was announced for 1975–1985 to develop a large-scale manufacturing capacity and start construction of a heavy water plant by 1980. Early in 1974, Atucha I, a 9,320-megawatt power plant, was readied for operation. Persistent political instability continued to obstruct the NAEC's ambitious program, but these decisions laid the basis for the eventual consideration of Argentina as a threshold nuclear state. Although it would be wrong to suggest that these events were the sole motivation underlying Brazil's determination to pursue an independent nuclear route, their impact on Brazilian threat assessment should not be underestimated.[17] The Brazilian government secretly began to work on a plan for nuclear independence. Covered by their limited commitment to Tlatelolco, both countries not only continued their march toward nuclear independence but effectively resisted diplomatic pressures aimed at bringing them into the NPT. Indeed, Tlatelolco would be referred to as evidence of their commitment to the elimination of nuclear weapons.[18]

The 1973 oil shock further reinforced the interest of both countries in nuclear energy development. This was particularly the case in Brazil, where it became clear that the "Brazilian miracle" of the Medici years was dependent not only on favorable external conditions but also on inexpensive energy consumption.[19] Although German-Brazilian nuclear cooperation began in 1969, it was only after the 1973 energy crisis and the failure of the United States to fulfill its uranium deliveries that intensive nuclear negotiations between the two countries actually started.[20] In an agreement reached in February 1975, Germany agreed to provide Brazil with assistance, including technology and equipment, in the construction of eight power reactors, as well as enrichment plants and reprocessing facilities. Brazil was to acquire an independent nuclear power industry; Germany would help to discover further uranium reserves to ensure itself access and would gain entrée into the fast-developing international nuclear energy market.[21]

Although it seems difficult to assess the exact role that mutual perceptions about foreign policy and nuclear energy decisions and development played in the Argentine and Brazilian nuclear energy programs, it seems clear that they provided the grounds for potential competition. Relations between the two countries had significantly improved after the 1966 military coup in Argentina, as the result of an increasing convergence of attitudes on ideological and security issues. Yet signs of Brazil's growing interest in pursuing an independent nuclear policy awakened Argentine concern. Most analysts seem to agree that the 1974 Indian explosion, together with the opening in that same year of the

Argentine nuclear plant, had a catalytic effect on the latent nuclear rivalry between Brazil and Argentina, reinforcing Brazilian interest in pursuing an independent path after the enriched uranium crisis of that same year.

The course taken by the Argentine and the Brazilian nuclear programs, together with the position held by these countries regarding both Tlatelolco and the NPT, suggested the erosion of U.S. power and influence on nuclear and regional issues. President Jimmy Carter attempted to redress this situation. His commitment to nuclear nonproliferation, as well as the creation of a nuclear suppliers cartel, put pressure on both Brazil and Argentina. Prompted not only by the Brazilian-German agreements but also by the claims of a fifty-kilogram diversion of plutonium from the Atucha power reactor in Argentina, U.S. interest in strengthening nonproliferation in Latin America significantly increased in the 1970s. Both Argentina and Brazil came under constant U.S. pressure to adhere to Tlatelolco and the NPT.[22] Latin American reactions to American pressure were clear. As had been the case during the NPT negotiations, references to Tlatelolco were offered as proof of Brazil's commitment to "nondiscriminatory nonproliferation."[23] Similarly, U.S. pressure led Argentina to announce that it had started the process toward ratification of Tlatelolco; this process was later halted, however, by the Falklands-Malvinas War.[24] The transition to democracy in that country increased expectations of a rapid Argentine adherence, but more realistic chances of Argentine compliance did not arise until 1992, nearly a decade after the transition to democracy had taken place.

As during Tlatelolco's negotiations, international pressure became a crucial factor underlying the development of an Argentine-Brazilian common posture. U.S. pressure on both countries helped to turn earlier Brazilian concern over Argentina's nuclear aspirations into cautious cooperation.[25] This cooperation indicated the beginning of a Brazilian-Argentine rapprochement, ultimately resulting in the signature in 1980 of four agreements on the peaceful uses of nuclear energy and on nuclear research and development. Contributing factors to this process included a common interest in resisting increasing U.S. pressure, economic incentives at a time of drastic decline in external financing, and a shift in Brazil's main area of interest toward Latin America, a shift that followed General João Baptista Figueiredo's ascension to power.[26]

Formal cooperation started in 1980, during Figueiredo's visit to Argentina, with the signature of the four agreements mentioned above.[27] In the wider context of Argentine-Brazilian relations, these agreements highlighted the common interest of the parties in promoting integration in the Southern Zone. Clearly, these arrangements would grant the parties greater ability to oppose suppliers' restrictions and achieve greater access to advanced technology. But equally important was their impact on increased security through the promotion of confidence and mutual understanding of the other's actions at a time when Brazil's interest in the development of nuclear energy provided fertile ground for misperception and miscalculation.

These agreements were subsequently followed by a number of contracts under which the parties exchanged technology and technicians and jointly developed aircraft and missile programs. By 1981, three additional agreements for technological exchange were signed between Argentina's NAEC and Brazil's Nucleabras.[28] Contrary to expectations, Argentina's achievement of a uranium enrichment capability in 1983 did not inhibit the Argentine-Brazilian rapprochement.[29] Although subsequently delayed by financial constraints, differences over designs, and the reluctance of the Brazilian military regarding joint development in the high-technology sector, in 1986 these initiatives materialized in plans for a joint venture between the Brazilian company Embraer and the Argentine Ministry of Defense for research and production of civil and military aircraft and in the Argentine-Brazilian Integration Protocols of that year for the coproduction of nuclear fuel for test reactors.[30]

Other measures were also crucial in laying the foundations for what would eventually emerge as a "security community" between the two countries. These have included visits to military installations, conducted periodically since the 1980 visit by Argentine generals to Brazil. Official decisions and declarations have also been made, the most significant of which include the decision by the Alfonsín government to place the NAEC under civilian control, the 1985 Alfonsín-Sarney declaration of Foz do Iguacu leading to the signature of a security protocol, and the inclusion in the 1988 Brazilian constitution of a clause prohibiting the military uses of nuclear energy.[31] Finally, numerous protocols have been signed between the two countries, notably Protocol 11, which concerns immediate information and reciprocal assistance in case of nuclear accidents, and Protocol 17, which identifies main areas for cooperation and research and development.[32]

Three factors deserve special attention. First, by the late 1970s, Argentina's edge in nuclear energy development was being replaced by an emerging parity between the two nuclear programs. Such parity was symbolized by the capacity achieved by both countries in the 1980s to enrich uranium. Second, the transition to democracy in both Argentina and Brazil also contributed to the rapprochement. Third was the return of nonproliferation to the U.S. foreign policy agenda.

Although responding to distinct circumstances and following entirely different routes, both countries returned to the democratic path at relatively the same time, a fact that further contributed to their better relations. Elections in 1989 brought Carlos Menem and Fernando Collor de Mello to the Argentine and Brazilian presidencies, respectively. In 1990, the two presidents again decided to revive the waning integration process that had been started by their predecessors. Yet as late as 1990, these measures had not been accompanied by the creation of formal mechanisms for inspection, verification, and control, even though the transitions to democracy had raised expectations for the countries' full adherence to Tlatelolco.

Nevertheless, it has been widely acknowledged that one of the most outstanding trends in regional nonproliferation has been the Argentine-Brazilian rapprochement. Throughout the 1970s the nuclear interaction between these countries had given rise to deep international concern. Yet both the regional nonproliferation regime and the bilateral mechanisms developed between the two countries over the past decade have revealed the capacity of both countries to pursue nuclear development while ensuring political stability characterized by mutual assurances and confidence building.

The optimism that currently permeates the Latin American nonproliferation regime has also been associated with the renewed interest shown by the Bush and Clinton administrations, after a decade of relative neglect, in preventing nuclear proliferation. Partly motivated by their interest in removing a potential source of friction in their relationships with the United States, Argentina and Brazil took a number of steps that again revealed their commitment to nondiscriminatory nonproliferation: (1) the appointment of joint representatives to the International Atomic Energy Agency (IAEA); (2) their participation, for the first time, as observers during the 1990 NPT Review Conference; (3) public declarations renouncing the military nuclear option; and (4) the 1990 nuclear policy declaration of Iguacu. Iguacu committed the parties to set up a bilateral agency for accounting and control, to take the necessary steps for full adherence to Tlatelolco, to exchange lists of nuclear inventories and mutual inspections, to renounce PNEs, and most important, to start negotiations with the IAEA to agree on a safeguards system, based on their bilateral accounting system.

By December 1991, the two countries had already signed safeguards agreements with the IAEA and had jointly announced their decision to submit a modified text of the Tlatelolco Treaty to the Organizacion Para la Proscripcion de Armas Nucleares en la America Latina (OPANAL), Tlatelolco's organizational body. In August 1992, OPANAL discussed and approved the proposed Argentine-Brazilian amendments. In the words of the secretary general of OPANAL, Stempel Paris, the modifications did not affect in any way the fundamental goals of Tlatelolco.[33]

Despite the positive effect of these trends with regard to full enforcement of the Tlatelolco Treaty and the consolidation of the Argentine-Brazilian rapprochement, potential sources of instability may threaten the regional nonproliferation regime. If nuclear proliferation seems to be waning, it has also not ceased to be a problem. Four factors may raise some uncertainty. First is the perception by both Brazil and Argentina about each other's overall military capability. In this respect, it is important to mention the impact of the Falklands-Malvinas War on the consideration by these countries of nuclear submarines. Second is the fragility of the new democracies and the legacy left by military regimes in relation both to dominant national security doctrines and to the relative autonomy and prerogatives of the military regarding weapons acquisition.[34] Third is the impact of new military technological inroads by either Brazil or Argentina in their bilateral relationship. Finally, there is the increasing interaction between what the incipient security rapprochement and a more ambitious plan for economic integration embodied in the MERCOSUR plan of 1990. It is not yet clear whether these two processes will positively reinforce each other or whether lack of progress in one area will negatively affect the other.

It has been widely acknowledged that the Falklands-Malvinas War exposed Argentina's total incapacity for combined army, navy, and air force actions to sustain adequate logistical support;

it also revealed to Brazil the existence of previously unknown Argentine military capabilities.[35] The war not only had a clear impact on Argentina's decision to rearm but also encouraged the consideration of nuclear submarine programs within the region and clearly coincided with the acceleration of missile programs.[36] In 1984, Iraq, Argentina, and Egypt joined efforts to develop the Condor missile program. Brazilian industries manufactured a wide variety of rockets, some of which are capable of delivering nuclear payloads.[37] Although these missile programs have serious limitations regarding reliable guidance and motor technology, they demonstrate the problems posed by missile proliferation in the developing world and, equally important, the extent of possible cooperation among "threshold nuclear powers."[38]

Plans to develop nuclear submarines in the region date back to Brazil's 1979 decision to secretly develop a capability to enrich uranium. The disclosure of these plans in 1987 made clear the existence of what became known as the "parallel nuclear program," through which Brazil achieved secretly, and without external support, the capacity to enrich uranium.[39]

At a time of balance-of-payments difficulties, the potential export market for enriched uranium served to publicly justify what many regarded as an intention to produce fuel for nuclear submarines.[40] In unveiling the "parallel program," the Brazilian president reaffirmed the peaceful character of the Brazilian nuclear program, yet he left no doubt of "Brazil's determination to achieve full access to scientific progress and to its practical applications." At the time, the chief of the armed forces, General Paulo Campos, insisted that Brazil should not accept any international restrictions in the field of nuclear energy.[41]

The disclosure of the "parallel program" four years after the transition to democracy had taken place in Brazil highlighted the scale of the challenge posed by strong military institutions both to the consolidation of the new democracies and to the ongoing Argentina and Brazil rapprochement. Drastic economic adjustment in both Argentina and Brazil prompted the military to argue that these policies were rendering their countries "defenseless." Moreover, the "parallel program," together with previous secret arms purchases by the Argentine navy, revealed the degree of autonomy of the armed forces vis-à-vis the executive and legislative branches.[42] Although the "parallel program" played a significant role in the decision to incorporate in the 1988 constitution a clause that committed Brazil to use nuclear energy exclusively for peaceful purposes, the definite character of this clause remains unclear. In this respect, it is important to emphasize that neither the Brazilian legislature nor the Argentine legislature has a consistent tradition in investigating and controlling major defense initiatives.[43]

Nearly a decade after the transition to democracy, doubts remain as to the effectiveness of civilian-democratic control of the Brazilian military.[44] Alfonsín's efforts aimed at greater civilian control of the military had no parallel in Brazil and were subsequently abandoned by his successor. Given the previous, critical role played by the military in reinforcing the perception of nuclear issues as vital to national security, and the extent to which the military continues to assert its prerogatives and views on geopolitics and strategic thinking, the subordination of the military will remain a key factor in the consolidation of the Argentine-Brazilian rapprochement.[45]

One of the steps that could help turn such rapprochement into a durable pattern of common security is the development of an effective national safeguards systems, which in turn presupposes democratic control of the military.[46] The process started by the 1980 Argentine-Brazilian nuclear cooperation agreement raised expectations about the role of confidence-building measures and policies aimed at the reduction of mutual suspicion. Such measures were seen as setting the basis for an eventual emergence of a "security community" in which both Argentina and Brazil explicitly retreat from the nuclear threshold.[47]

The renewed international commitment to nuclear nonproliferation after the Gulf War coincided with clear signs of progress in the Latin American nonproliferation regime.[48] The suspension in 1990 by Argentina of the Condor II program, the steps taken by Itamaraty toward suspending all nuclear programs, and the decision by both countries to adopt measures conducive to full adherence to Tlatelolco had been clearly linked to external factors.[49] Moreover, the signing in July 1991 of the Guadalajara agreement for the exclusively peaceful use of nuclear energy, together with the signing in December of that year of the quadripartite safeguards agreement with the IAEA, the establishment of the Brazilian-Argentine Agency for Accounting and Control of Nuclear Materials (ABACC) in December 1992, and the full adherence of both countries to Tlatelolco, were responses not only to the need to institutionalize the Argentine-Brazilian nuclear rapprochement but also to wider international pressure demanding strict verification and higher levels of compliance. On the one hand, the unfavorable international context foreshadowing the need for closer integration with the United States highlighted the potential benefits that could be derived from a shift in nuclear policy. The external context ensuing the end of the cold war and the Gulf War enhanced the symbolic potential of those policies that could help these countries to avoid their identification with destabilizing forces and to reassert their credibility as reliable partners. Dramatic gestures—ranging from the decision to cancel both the Condor program and the Brazilian parallel nuclear program, to the increasing cooperation in UN peacekeeping forces, to Argentina's full membership in the Missile Technology Control Regime (MTCR) and their full adherence to Tlatelolco—illustrate this point. Equally important has been the impact of denial policies and external pressures.[50]

Not surprisingly, this situation has raised doubts about the extent to which the shift in nuclear policy has been endorsed by the military and some concern about the actual weight of important interests opposed to strict nonproliferation commitments.[51] Undoubtedly the steps leading toward full enforcement of Tlatelolco together with the 1991 Quadripartite Agreement have significantly reinforced the position of those who favor nonnuclear postures, yet these postures as nonproliferation commitments are far from being static and are dependent on constantly updated inducements, as the Argentine-Brazilian experience suggests. Such inducements work both at the internal and at the external levels and are linked to measures geared toward effective democratic control of military institutions and to wider international trends aimed at reinforcing the nonproliferation norm, such as nuclear powers' policies seeking to minimize the political and military utility of nuclear weapons. As Iraq's near-nuclear capability demonstrated, violations of the nonproliferation regime can also arise parallel to internationally safeguarded nuclear programs. This type of challenge will remain closely linked to the sincerity of the motivations that lie at the core of nonnuclear postures. Undoubtedly in the case of those countries that in the past have shown significant interest in the nuclear option, ongoing inducements, as well as stricter international safeguards, will be decisive.

Prospects for the Latin American Nonproliferation Regime: Argentina and Brazil as Nonproliferators?

The regional nonproliferation regime has been affected by wider international developments in the field of nuclear technology. Some developments, such as the oil crisis and the increasing availability of nuclear technology, have eroded both the NPT and Tlatelolco. In Latin America, the regional nonproliferation regime has been threatened by the determination of Brazil and Argentina to develop independent nuclear programs. Yet, as indicated by the evolving postures of these countries, formal adherence to and observance of agreed nonproliferation rules offer the only means of ensuring that these trends will not be accompanied by nuclear weapons proliferation as nuclear power spreads and as nuclear technology becomes more easily available. Even though enforcement of these rules has proved a difficult task, states normally do not accept international obligations with the intention of violating them. In the case of the Treaty of Tlatelolco, until their recent adherence, both Argentina and Brazil chose to obstruct the entry into force of the agreement rather than risk open violation. Moreover, their recent decisions, including the ratification of the Quadripartite Agreement, Argentina's ratification of the Treaty of Tlatelolco, and Brazil's full incorporation into the Tlatelolco system, have offered clear evidence of the advantages associated with denuclearization.[52]

It is difficult to assess whether international pressure on its own was sufficient to persuade these countries to move toward nonproliferation, or whether it contributed to the momentum in favor of nonnuclear status where an internal consensus in this direction already existed. What seems clear is that the evolution and the progress achieved by the Latin American nonproliferation regime illustrate a positive dynamic between domestic and external inducements.[53] Yet the perceived advantages associated with such a posture have a character that ultimately depends on the changing balance between the perceived costs and benefits of having a nuclear option.

The Latin American nonproliferation regime has highlighted the absence of nuclear weapons and therefore of nuclear targets, as well as keeping at a minimum the probability of war arising out of nuclear incidents. The role played by this regime has also reduced tensions and helped to improve relations among regional states. Nowhere has this contribution been more apparent than in the rapprochement that has characterized relations between Argentina and Brazil over the past decade. It is by no means clear if in the absence of Tlatelolco or if faced with a stricter regional regime, this rapprochement would have been possible. One can affirm with some certainty that Tlatelolco, by offering the South American states a forum to exchange their particular views about nonproliferation policies, encouraged a dialogue that alleviated anxieties about the opponent's intentions. Moreover, this regime has provided a useful framework for the peaceful transfer and development of nuclear energy; and in the light of Argentina's recent ratification and the decisions of both Chile and Brazil to waive the restrictions attached to Article 28, it again demonstrated its capacity to attract those states that have either obstructed or remained outside its regulations.

As has already been mentioned, some problems remain, but the situation today is qualitatively different from the one that prevailed during the second half of the 1970s. No doubt a latent rivalry may continue to underpin the nuclear programs of Brazil and Argentina; yet not only has open competition between them not arisen, but the two have finally agreed to set up formal verification mechanisms and to adhere fully to the Tlatelolco system.

The conditions and the progress achieved by the Latin American regime offer a solid basis for optimism. The Treaty of Tlatelolco and the control mechanisms set up by the agreement have the potential to adjust to changes and to reconcile greater flexibility with safe regulation. This favorable environment has underpinned the gradual transformation of Argentine-Brazilian relations from competition to cooperation. Yet it is by no means clear that the conditions generated by such rapprochement will remain static. The long-term prospects of stability will continue to depend on the overall balance between the perceived benefits and costs of developing nuclear weapons and between wider incentives favoring nonnuclear postures and those backing the nuclear option.

The most likely challenges to be faced by the regional nonproliferation regime in the future relate both to the effective implementation of the Tlatelolco Treaty now that the modified text has been approved and to the effectiveness of the safeguards system provided by the Quadripartite Agreement tailored to satisfy Argentine and Brazilian demands.[54] Indeed, in light of the continued opposition of these countries to the NPT, the effectiveness of the safeguards system will be crucial in assessing the commitment of Argentina and Brazil to nondiscriminatory nonproliferation. Over the past years, the governments of Argentina and Brazil have expressed their preference for Tlatelolco over the NPT.[55] Although this posture may appear contradictory, these states have insisted that it was the standard system of IAEA safeguards that represented the main obstacle to their acceptance and have also claimed that such standardization was the unfortunate consequence of having subordinated Tlatelolco to the NPT. The success or failure of the safeguards system will also be dependent on the ability of the civilian authorities to oversee the military.

The acceptance by OPANAL of the Brazilian and Argentine amendments to the text of the treaty paved the way for Argentina's ratification and Brazil's waiver of the restrictions attached to Article 28—in other words, to the two countries' full incorporation into the Tlatelolco system. The creation of the ABACC, together with the signature of bilateral agreements with the IAEA, has enabled regional states to reconcile old Argentine-Brazilian demands for "tolerable control" with genuine concerns regarding reliable safeguards.[56] Indeed, these decisions may guarantee sufficient international supervision and have already contributed to overcoming one of the main obstacles to the implementation of the Treaty of Tlatelolco. This could, in turn, allow consolidation of the regional nonproliferation regime on a basis that would enable most Latin American states to benefit.

Notes

The author would like to thank Andrew Hurrell for his comments on this chapter.

1. A "security complex" refers to that group of states whose primary security concerns link them together so that their national securities cannot realistically be considered apart from one another. Within a security community, states will neither expect nor prepare a military attack. Such an evolution may result from a combination of different factors, among which the eradication of basic fears and the solution of key conflicts are the most important. For a detailed analysis of these notions, see Barry Buzan, *Peoples, States, and Fear* (London: Harvester Wheatsheaf, 1983), and Barry Buzan et al., *The European Security Order Recast: Scenarios for the Post–Cold War Era* (London: Pinter Publishers, 1990). For a discussion of the role of norms and

rules within the context of regime theory, see Andrew Hurrell, "Teoría de Regímenes Internacionales: Una Perspectiva Europea," *Foro Internacional*, no. 130 (Summer 1992).

2. Mónica Serrano, "The Latin American Nuclear Free-Zone Established under the 1967 Treaty of Tlatelolco" (Ph.D. diss., Oxford University, 1990), chapters 3 and 4.

3. It would be wrong to take such support at face value. Indeed Soviet support served different purposes, ranging from high-sounding propaganda to efforts to arrest the rearmament of West Germany, to stop the potential deployment of tactical nuclear weapons in that country, and more generally to avoid the nuclear encirclement of the USSR. Although the Soviet interest in nonproliferation, with the exceptions of Germany and China, could be questioned, and although it is true that the interests of the USSR and regional states did not always coincide and occasionally even collided, the Soviet government not only supported most of the proposals discussed during these years but also actively promoted some of these plans. Proposals included the following: the 1956 "open skies" plan for an area of eight hundred kilometers east and west of the dividing line between NATO and the Warsaw Pact; the 1957 Rapacki Plan for an NFZ in Central Europe to expand this NFZ to Northern Europe; and equally important, Khrushchev's 1959 initiative for an NFZ in the Far East. The Soviet government also supported proposals for an NFZ in Africa.

4. National security files on nuclear proliferation, December 10, 1964, L.B.J. Library, Austin, Texas.

5. Ministerio das Relacoes Exteriores, *Textos e Declaracoes Sobre Politica Externa de Abril de 1964 a Abril 1965* (Rio de Janeiro: Departamento Cultural e de Informacoes, 1965).

6. A security dilemma appears at the core of the ambiguity pursued by threshold nuclear states. It has been defined as a "structural notion in which the self-help attempts of states to look after their security needs tend automatically (i.e., regardless of intention) to lead to rising insecurity for others as each interprets its own measures as defensive and the measures of others as potentially threatening" (Buzan, *Peoples, States, and Fear*, p. 3). Regarding nuclear weapons, a number of factors seem to inhibit open acquisition. The most important constraints underlying the military direction of nuclear energy programs include the following: (1) crossing the nuclear threshold could shift the nature of competition from one of potential capabilities to a costly arms race; (2) the probability that, as regional proliferation trends suggest, although potential nuclear status may favor a state for a short period of time, it may evolve into a source of greater insecurity for all regional states; (3) the long-term maintenance of a credible deterrent posture is highly unlikely, or at least extremely costly; and (4) the emergence of systems of nuclear deterrence, based on calculated challenges and predictable responses, under volatile and changing circumstances, is unlikely. See Mónica Serrano, *Common Security in Latin America: The 1967 Treaty of Tlatelolco*, Research Paper Series no. 30 (London: Institute of Latin American Studies, 1992).

7. These moves awakened the concern of the U.S. government. A study on the prospects for further proliferation of nuclear weapons recognized that in the 1950s the barriers to nuclear weapons by nations of middle size and

resources had steadily diminished. It included Argentina among those states that could be influenced by the general course of proliferation and by the desire for national prestige. "Memo DC1N10, Prospects for Further Nuclear Proliferation," Declassified Document, 18B-1978, LC, Washington, D.C., n.d.

8. Brazil followed the guidelines set at an international conference by limiting its thorium exports and accepting American supervision of these exports during the 1950s. Ronald M. Schneider, *Brazil: Foreign Policy of a Future World Power* (Boulder, Colorado: Westview Press, 1976), p. 48. The details of American intervention in this period were widely discussed in the context of the subsequent pressures imposed on Brazil and resulting from the 1975 nuclear agreement with West Germany. *Diario do Congresso Nacional*, August 1975, Brasilia.

9. Brazil's road toward increasing dependence continued, despite eventual recognition of the desirability of more autonomy. See Juscelino Kubitschek de Oliveira, in *Mensagem ao Congresso Nacional*, 1958 and 1959.

10. Norman Gall, "Atoms for Brazil, Dangers for All," *Foreign Policy*, no. 23 (Summer 1976): 155.

11. Reassessment of both aspects of nuclear energy took place within the new political context dominated by the military. The new politicization of the military was partly the result of the impact of revolutionary warfare on the wide and almost all-inclusive conception of national security, as well as on resulting military roles and military education. The literature on this theme is extensive. See, for example, Richard R. Fagen and Wayne Cornelius, eds., *Political Power in Latin America: Seven Confrontations* (Englewood Cliffs, N.J.: Prentice Hall, 1970), Thomas Skidmore, *The Politics of Military Rule in Brazil* (Oxford: Oxford University Press, 1988), Alain Rouquie, *Pouvoir Militaire e Societe Politique en Republique Argentine* (Paris: Presses de la Fondation Nationale de Science Politique, 1978), and Alfred Stepan, *The Military in Politics: Changing Patterns in Brazil* (Princeton, N.J.: Princeton University Press, 1971).

12. Partly motivated by Argentina's achievements, the Brazilian government again tried unsuccessfully to reach greater autonomy in nuclear energy development. See the speeches of President J. Quadros to Congress (Janio Quadros, in *Mensagem ao Congresso Nacional*, 1961).

13. During the 1960s the increased importance attached to nuclear energy was viewed as one of the main pillars of economic and scientific development. Brazilian challenges to nonproliferation postures were systematically denied on the basis of the peaceful character of its nuclear program. Humberto de Alencar Castello Branco, in *Mensagem ao Congresso Nacional*, 1965–68.

14. Report of the Course on Nuclear Energy, Brasilia, Ministerio das Relacoes Exteriores, May 17–July 14, 1966.

15. The core of this ambiguity rested on the steady development of nuclear programs with reassurances about their peaceful character and the avoidance of full commitments to nonproliferation regimes.

16. Although Brazil had signed and ratified the Tlatelolco agreement, the Costa e Silva government, protected by the shield provided by Article 28,

decided again to pursue an independent route for the Brazlian nuclear program. Article 28 allows two mechanisms for the entry into force of the agreement. A conditional choice, subject not only to the former signature and ratification by all states to whom both the treaty and its protocols were opened but also to the completion of safeguards agreements with the IAEA. In contrast, the "general rule" stipulates that the agreement shall enter into force on deposit of the treaty accompanied by a waiver of these requirements. Not only has Brazil not waived these requirements, but evidence of the shift to nuclear independence was provided by the 1967 decision to start working toward an independent nuclear fuel cycle. *Diario do Congresso Nacional*, April 1967; Schneider, *Brazil*, p. 50; Robert Wesson, *The United States and Brazil: Limits to Influence* (New York: Praeger, 1981), p. 78.

17. Although in 1961 the head of the Brazilian National Nuclear Energy Commission, Marcelo Damy da Souza Santos, tried to achieve greater autonomy by looking for French support in the construction of a natural uranium reactor, this effort ended with the resignation of President Quadros and with France's decision to give up natural uranium methods in favor of enriched uranium. This shift represented a victory for nonproliferation, since the natural uranium produces more plutonium that can be easily separated. In Argentina, the decision to pursue an independent nuclear policy explains its preference for natural uranium methods. Its choice of the Canadian Candu reactor using natural uranium, rather than U.S. reactors designed for enriched uranium, enabled this country to rely on its own uranium reserves, to escape international supervision, and most important, to eventually get access to weapons-grade plutonium. In 1968 the Argentine National Commission for Atomic Energy had already started the operation of the first chemical processing plant—on a pilot scale—for reclaiming plutonium from spent reactor fuel in the region. Wesson, *The United States and Brazil*, p. 77; Gall, "Atoms for Brazil," pp. 183–85; Margaret K. Luddeman, "Nuclear Power in Latin America: An Overview of Its Present Status," *Journal of Interamerican Studies and World Affairs* 25, no. 3 (August 1983): 381.

18. As had been the case with Argentina, Brazilian opposition to the NPT was clearly linked to concerns regarding new forms of dependency. Yet Tlatelolco utility in this respect did not prevent continued concern about its implications, as expressed in statements referring to eventual withdrawal "if new circumstances affecting Brazil's vital interests" arose. *Diario do Congresso Nacional*, June 1967 and October 1967.

19. Favorable external circumstances included the 1967–73 growth in world trade and capital availability. Brazil's Achilles' heel was its increased energy vulnerability, resulting from economic and industrial policies that assumed the continued availability of cheap imported energy. Between 1967 and 1974, oil consumption rose by 120 percent, and Brazil's dependence on imported sources of energy rose from 23.7 percent to 38.6 percent. Andrew J. Hurrell, "The Quest for Autonomy: The Evolution of Brazil's Role in the International System, 1964–1985" (Ph.D. diss., Oxford University, 1986), pp. 148–52.

20. An agreement between Brazil and the Federal Republic regarding computer methods of maximizing nuclear energy production, uranium exploration, and development of both fuel cycles and advanced reactors was

signed in 1969. Ministerio das Relacoes Exteriores, *Resenha de Politica Exterior do Brasil* (Brasilia: Divisao de Documentacao, 1975). Brazilian moves awakened U.S. concern. W. W. Rostow had stated that Brazil was "on its way to becoming a nuclear power, and consequently a danger for all its neighbors" (quoted in *Diario do Congresso Nacional*, June 1973).

21. The agreements included access to enriched uranium reactor technology. Ministerio das Relacoes Exteriores, *Resenha de Politica Exterior do Brasil*.

22. Pressures were first directed at West Germany, which reacted strongly to what was considered "harsh commercial interests" (*Diario do Congresso Nacional*, December 1976). Wolf Grabendorff, "La Politica Nuclear y de Nonproliferacion de Brasil," *Estudios Internacionales* 20, no. 80 (December 1987): 541, and John R. Redick, "Prospects for Arms Control in Latin America," *Arms Control Today* 5, no. 9 (September 1975).

23. *Diario do Congresso Nacional*, June 1975.

24. OPANAL, *Zona Libre de Armas Nucleares* (Mexico D.F.: OPANAL, 1979), p. 25.

25. Argentina's official statements condemning U.S. policies and suggesting the negotiation of a bilateral agreement on nuclear cooperation were warmly received in Brasilia. In 1977, reacting to Canada's decision to suspend the transfer of an enrichment plant to Argentina, the Argentine ambassador to the United States made public his country's interest in establishing a common front to resist U.S. opposition to the construction of enrichment plants. These declarations were followed by the first bilateral communique stressing cooperation in nuclear matters. *Diario do Congresso Nacional*, May 1975 and December 1976, and *Folha do Sao Paulo*, August 12, 1977.

26. Under Figueiredo, Argentina and Brazil reached an agreement that not only put an end to long-standing disputes over damming the Parana River but also paved the way to wider cooperation in the energy sector. *Jornal do Brasil* and *O'Globo*, October 19, 1979, and *The Times*, December 15, 1980.

27. These agreements contemplated the creation of an organization similar to EURATOM. "SUDATOM" would enable both parties to jointly demand full access to nuclear technology in international fora, to carry out research and development, and through the provision of control mechanisms, to resolve eventual differences. *Jornal do Brasil*, May 26, 1980.

28. *O'Estado do Sao Paulo*, August 12, 1980, and *O'Globo*, May 27, 1981.

29. Alfonsin's decision to personally transmit the news to Figueiredo and the meeting between the two presidents to update the 1980 agreements contributed to this development. *Latin American Regional Reports: Southern Cone*, December 23, 1983, RS-83-10.

30. *Latin American Regional Reports: Southern Cone*, January 31, 1986, RS-86-00, and December 25, 1986, RS-86-10.

31. *O'Estado do Sao Paulo*, August 12, 1980; *O'Globo*, May 23, 1981; *Latin American Regional Reports: Southern Cone*, December 23, 1983, RS-83-10; COPREDAL, G/296, May 31, 1987.

32. Fernando A. S. Henning, "Industrial and Economic Benefits of Latin American Nuclear Cooperation," in Paul L. Leventhal and Sharon Tanzer, eds., *Averting a Latin American Nuclear Arms Race: New Prospects and Challenges*

for Argentine-Brazilian Nuclear Cooperation (Basingstoke: Macmillan, in association with the Nuclear Control Institute, 1992), p. 87.

33. The main modifications were aimed at greater confidentiality. Included were the elimination of the third paragraph of Article 14, which had committed the parties to deliver their reports to the Organization of American States (OAS); an amendment to Article 15, which linked the conduct of special reports to "extraordinary events or circumstances"; and extensive modifications to Article 16, eliminating the paragraphs requesting the general secretary to communicate to his/her UN counterpart and to the UN Security Council the results of special inspections. As a consequence of these amendments, the IAEA emerges as the main and only agency capable of conducting special inspections. Two days before this meeting, the Mexican government received the French ratification of Protocol I, completing the full enforcement of the treaty, unless new guarantees are required from the Commonwealth of Independent States. OPANAL, CG/PV/E/73 and CG/385.

34. In defiance of a government-ordered freeze on arms purchases, the Argentine Navy purchased sixteen Skyhawk aircraft from Israel in a secret transaction using clandestine funds. The deal revealed a secret budget that allowed the navy to spend more than U.S.$100 million without any political supervision. *Sunday Times* (London), December 9, 1984.

35. Alfred Stepan, *Rethinking Military Politics, Brazil, and the Southern Cone* (Princeton, N.J.: Princeton University Press, 1988), p. 87.

36. Since the end of the Falklands-Malvinas War, the Argentine reequipment program has included twenty Exocet missiles, nine Super Etendard strike aircraft (some of which were thought capable of carrying Exocets), and thirty Israeli Skyhawks to replace aircraft lost in combat. *The Times*, March 30, 1983.

37. Jozef Goldblat, "Nuclear Non-Proliferation: The Problem States" (paper prepared for the joint convention of the British International Studies Association and the International Studies Association, London, March 28–April 1, 1989), p. 8.

38. One example of such cooperation: in 1980 Brazil supplied Iraq with uranium dioxide, raising international suspicion. Further, Western intelligence analysts considered the Condor missile to be a copy of the U.S. Pershing 2. Even though in 1985 the industrialized powers agreed on a Missile Technology Control Regime, the Condor development, other missile programs in Israel, India, Pakistan, South Africa, and Brazil, and the discovery of Iraq's advanced nuclear program raised doubts as to the effectiveness of both the nuclear and the missile nonproliferation regimes. Although commitments have been renewed since the Gulf War, their survival had been threatened both by export competition and by foreign policy considerations, particularly those of the United States. *Observer*, June 28, 1981, and *Financial Times*, November 21, 1989.

39. *International Herald Tribune*, September 7, 1987.

40. Personal interview with Luis Pinguelli Rosas, Rio de Janeiro, September 15, 1988.

41. *O'Estado do Sao Paulo*, September 5 and 10, 1987.

42. Stepan includes a "budgetary argument" among the motivations that led the military to adopt a strategy of political liberalization. As the acting commander of the Superior War College stated at the time, "We have been restricting ourselves in weapons requests in order to get a good image as a government . . . it will be easier to advance our legitimate claims against a government led by a civilian" (Stepan, *Rethinking Military Politics*, pp. 57, 73–81).

43. There is no evidence of any congressional involvement either in the 1985 modernization plans of the Brazilian armed forces or in the discovery in 1986 of a probable nuclear test site. Ibid., p. 106.

44. The military has been more visible in Brazil than in Argentina. Rumors of military intervention have been constant in Brazil throughout 1993. The widening of the margin of prerogatives of the Brazilian military has been particularly clear in the increase in the number of members of the military in the cabinet, from three in the Collor administration to five under the Franco administration. Frances Hagopian, "Democracy by Undemocratic Means? Elites, Political Parties, and Regime Transition in Brazil," *Comparative Political Studies* 23, no. 2 (July 1990); *Latin America Weekly Report*, July 1, 1993, and July 15, 1993; *Brazil Report*, August 12, 1993.

45. For an analysis of the dimension of military prerogatives in both Argentina and Brazil, see Stepan, *Rethinking Military Politics*, pp. 93–127.

46. This issue was constantly referred to in the discussions in Leventhal and Tanzer, *Averting a Latin American Nuclear Arms Race*. See especially the chapters by William Higinbotham (on nuclear confidence-building) and Milton Hoenig (on verification arrangements).

47. Following the 1985 Foz de Iguacu declaration, the Permanent Argentine-Brazilian Committee on Nuclear Policy was set up in 1988 and started discussing proposals for the creation of national safeguards systems and models of safeguards agreements with the IAEA. However, these were temporarily abandoned in favor of "mutual trust" agreements. Undoubtedly, the need to provide the Argentine-Brazilian nuclear rapprochement with control and surveillance mechanisms was increasingly recognized, and pressures in this direction evidently increased in the 1990s. This was a constant theme and apparently a deliberate goal of the articles collected in Leventhal and Tanzer, *Averting a Latin American Nuclear Arms Race*. Spector also emphasized that full-scope safeguards were the best protection against nuclear proliferation in a situation in which political instability could lead Argentina and Brazil to reassert the nuclear option. In contrast, Argentine and Brazilian observers continued expressing their preference for informal confidence building over verification and raised attention to a sequence that followed the inverse pattern to the one advocated in international forums since the cold war, namely, cooperation/confidence building/transparency/verification. See, Leonard Spector, "Nuclear Proliferation in the 1990s: the Storm after the Lull," in Aspen Strategy Group Report, *New Threats: Responding to the Proliferation of Nuclear, Chemical, and Delivery Capabilities in the Third World* (Lanham, Md.: University Press of America, 1990), p. 37; Julio Carasales, "Goals of Argentine-Brazilian Nuclear Cooperation," in Leventhal and Tanzer, *Averting a Latin American Nuclear Arms Race*, p. 59; and the comments of Dr. Estradea Ojuela, Dr. Coelho Pontes, and Dr. Quintana in the same

volume and of George Lamaziere and Roberto Jaguaribe, "Beyond Confidence-Building: Brazilian-Argentine Nuclear Cooperation" (mimeo, 1992).

48. Indeed, with the end of the cold war and the lessons of Iraq, in Latin America as in many other areas of the world, the margins of acceptable levels of compliance with the nonproliferation norm significantly narrowed.

49. At the time of the Condor suspension, Argentina's defense minister mentioned political and financial considerations. *Financial Times*, April 23, 1990, and *Latin American Weekly Report*, April 25, 1991, WR-91-15.

50. Argentina's cooperation with both the nuclear nonproliferation and the missile control regime has already been rewarded. Evidence of this is provided by the negotiation of several nuclear cooperation agreements, including the nuclear cooperation agreements between Argentina and the United States of 1992, the ongoing negotiations between EURATOM and Argentina, and equally important the signature with the United States of an agreement on the protection and transfer of sensitive technology. "Informe sobre política en materia de no-proliferación de la República Argentina 1993"; Lamaziere and Jaguaribe, "Beyond Confidence-Building," p. 8.

51. Important military figures in both countries have made their opposition clear. Suspension of the Condor missile was strongly criticized by the former chief of staff of the Argentine Air Forces. In Brazil, the navy minister openly protested the Foreign Ministry's plans to suspend all nuclear programs in exchange for U.S. concessions in other areas. The continuation of the navy's plan to build a nuclear power submarine was arduously defended. *Financial Times*, April 10 and 23, 1990, and *Latin American Weekly Report*, April 25, 1991, WR-91-15, and July 11, 1991, WR-91-22.

52. Argentina deposited its ratification of the Treaty of Tlatelolco on January 18, 1994. On that occasion, Chile deposited its waiver of Article 28. Similarly, although Brazil had ratified the treaty in January 1968, it finally waived the conditions attached to Article 28 on May 30, 1994.

53. Feelings of obligation are not restricted to the international level. In fact, the internalization of norms could have important effects. First, this process reinforces the linkages between international law and domestic legal frameworks, and second, it generates domestic costs associated with violations of international norms. To the extent that the signature of Tlatelolco created international obligations binding both Brazil and Argentina (at least to respect the spirit of the treaty), it also had an impact on their domestic arenas. As Hurrell has observed, "A good deal of the monitoring of international regimes is carried out by domestic groups acting either within one country or transnationally." Evidence of domestically generated pressure can be found in the activities of concerned scientists and in the demands of these societies for greater scrutiny in the assignation of public funds and accountable governments. Hurrell, "Teoría de regímenes," p. 666. See also Hans Blix, "The Role of the IAEA in the Development of International Law," *Nordic Journal of International Law* 58 (1989).

54. The provisions for the creation of an agency that has independent control but linked to the IAEA were included in the Guadalajara agreement for the Exclusively Peaceful Use of Nuclear Energy, signed between Argentina and Brazil in July 1991. ABACC was officially established in December 1992 with its central office in Rio de Janeiro. Its main task is the implemen-

tation of the Argentine-Brazilian Common System for Accounting and Control on nuclear material that has not been covered by the IAEA system of safeguards. Negotiations with the IAEA on an acceptable regime for common safeguards started in March 1991 and led to the signature of a safeguards agreement in December of that year. The Quadripartite Agreements are divided into two parts. The first section requires the parties to place all nuclear material under the IAEA systems of safeguards. ABACC bears primary responsibility for the conduct of safeguards that the IAEA, through additional safeguards, can in turn verify. A sophisticated dispute-settlement mechanism was also created. The second part of the agreement specifies the safeguards procedure, including inventories of material and IAEA inspections. Formal links have also been established between ABACC and OPANAL through an agreement endorsed by the latter's General Conference in May 1993. Throughout 1993, ABACC's efforts have been devoted to drafting the reports on accounting and control for each installation listed in the register. The reports of the enrichment plants have already been completed. *ABACC News*, January–April 1993; "Informe sobre política en materia de no-proliferación de la República Argentina, 1993," OPANAL, CG/390.

55. There is little doubt that the creation of ABACC and the provision of full-scope safeguards represent a positive step for both the regional and the global nonproliferation regime. Indeed, the prospects for having Tlatelolco fully enforced are significantly greater today than before. Although ABACC has partly satisfied demands for independent verification, despite Argentine and Brazilian aspirations for a SUDATOM, ABACC is essentially a bilateral mechanism as opposed to the multilateralism embodied in EURATOM. Clearly, the prospects for authority delegation, as is the case in Europe today, do not seem quite promising in the case of two threshold nuclear powers that have recently rolled back the nuclear option. Moreover, and to the extent that ABACC has introduced a bilateral dimension, in the long term there is some risk of instability in the regional multilateral regime. This would be a paradoxical outcome at a time when the vulnerability of the global regime to accusations of discrimination has again come to the surface, when increasing responsibilities put greater pressure on the IAEA, and perhaps most important, when the advantages of regional schemes to implement the nonproliferation regime have been increasingly acknowledged. On the relative fragility of the global nonproliferation regime, see Adam Roberts, "Law, Lawyers, and Nuclear Weapons," *Review of International Studies* 16, no. 1 (January 1990): 80–83.

56. At the time of signing the NPT in 1969, Germany made its ratification conditional on "tolerable international control . . . based on agreement between the IAEA and Euratom." Martin Wight, *Power Politics*, ed. H. Bull and C. Holbraad (London: Royal Institute of International Affairs, 1978), p. 288.

Part II

*New Technologies and
Institutional Responses*

Chapter 11

The Impact of New Technologies on Nuclear Weapons Proliferation

Amy Sands

Technology obviously plays a key role in determining the military systems that states rely on in their pursuit of specific policies, strategies, and tactics.[1] The introduction of new technologies during a crisis has at times dramatically shifted the course of events, often deciding a crisis in favor of the group controlling the new technology. However, new technologies, although initially creating tactical or local shifts in power, may also be quickly and effectively countered with measures and modifications in defensive and offensive doctrines and strategies. The historical record does not necessarily justify the assumption that new technologies will be a determining factor; the impact of new technologies, though significant, will depend to a great degree on the specifics of their development and use and the response they engender.

The problems emerging from the spread of nuclear weapons have largely been addressed with strategies and policies aimed at controlling the impact of new nuclear-related technologies, such as those involved in fissile material production or nuclear-capable delivery systems. Initial efforts to prevent the spread of nuclear weapons focused on limiting the use for military purposes of particular technologies, such as reprocessing and uranium enrichment. Access to these technologies was limited, and information about nuclear weapon designs was restricted. The delays created by these technology control activities, although not fully successful, in certain cases provided the critical time for changes to occur that reversed a state's march toward nuclear weapons. Scientific achievements over the past few decades, however, have increased concern that today's advances in technology will provide the technical basis for the next generation of nuclear weapons states. New technologies will have a significant impact on the spread of nuclear weapons but will actually serve more strongly as *inhibitors* than as facilitators of nuclear proliferation.

Before examining the impact of new technology on nuclear proliferation, it is important to distinguish the meanings of the phrase *new technology*. New technology for the developed states in the 1940s and 1950s may still be new technology to the developing world in the 1990s. Meanwhile, the developed states have continued to develop ideas, methods, equipment, and materials that are at today's cutting edge; in addition, scientists throughout the developed world are researching technologies that may not be available until sometime in the next century. Thus, the phrase *new technology* needs to be defined to clarify its role in relation to nuclear weapons proliferation. In this chapter, *new technology*, *advanced technology*, and *emerging technology* will relate to recently developed technologies beginning to become available or still undergoing testing and experimentation.

When efforts to internationalize the control of nuclear weapons technology failed immediately after World War II, tight controls were placed on the technologies central to nuclear weapons development, even to the point that the United States excluded its closest allies. By the early 1950s, when the spread of nuclear technology appeared inevitable and commercially lucrative for U.S. companies, President Dwight Eisenhower's "Atoms for Peace" program was designed to promote the use of nuclear technology while also requiring a pledge of peaceful use. The International Atomic Energy Agency (IAEA), also proposed by President Eisenhower and created during this period, attempted to incorporate a similar strategy, namely providing states access to the technologies associated with nuclear energy only after they committed to its peaceful application and to safeguards to ensure proper use. Controlling militarily critical technology, such as uranium enrichment, as a means to control the spread of nuclear weapons was thus embedded early in the philosophy of nonproliferation efforts.

In ensuing years, the objective of controlling nuclear technology has come to dominate efforts to control nuclear weapons proliferation. Despite rhetorical comments about the limitations of this technology-denial approach, the effort to enforce these technology controls effectively or to address the proliferation threat in other ways was, until recently, minimal.[2] The reasons for not pursuing other strategies more forcefully are complex and, to a large degree, stemmed from cold war politics that gave nonproliferation efforts, in general, a low priority. For example, both Pakistan and Iraq benefited from America's focus on perceived threats associated with the cold war and Islamic fundamentalism, rather than on the threat of nuclear weapons proliferation.

Technologies developed in recent years could conceivably speed the spread of nuclear weapons, but they may also enhance ways to prevent and counter nuclear weapons proliferation by improving our ability to detect nuclear weapons-related activities, verify nuclear weapons-related arms control agreements, and respond to the increased number of countries having a nuclear weapons option. Until the end of the cold war and Desert Storm, scant attention was devoted to increasing technical capabilities to meet proliferation threats and concerns. Now, numerous initiatives are aimed at making gains through developing technologies in the areas of intelligence collection, detection, verification, and counterproliferation military systems.

Examining the relationship between different categories of recently developed technology and nuclear weapons proliferation may help clarify the role of technology denial and technology development in addressing the threat of nuclear proliferation. The first part of this analysis will explore the role new technologies may play in countries attempting to develop nuclear weapons, in light of the ability (or inability) of these states to absorb and make effective use of new technology. The second part will briefly describe new technologies that improve collection, verification, data integration, and response capabilities. The final section will discuss the continued effectiveness of technology denial and the new role of emerging technologies in preventing nuclear proliferation.

New Technologies and Nuclear Proliferation: The Past Record

Significant changes in the world since the end of the cold war necessitate reexamining how technology influences the development of nuclear weapons, how the advance of technology might affect the spread of nuclear weapons in the future, and what the implications of such an impact are for U.S. policy. For example, cutting-edge technologies related to fissile material production may not play a significant role in facilitating the spread of nuclear weapons, but dual-use technologies might. Thus, past technology-denial policies may require modifications to include all technologies of concern (old but still sensitive nuclear technologies, any emerging nuclear-related technologies, and certain dual-use technologies) *and* all potential suppliers.

In the early days of exploring the possibilities for nuclear energy, its allure as the critical technology of the future and one that a state needed both to spur its economy and to symbolize its position as an advanced technological society created pressures for making nuclear technology easily available. At the same time that civilian applications were becoming evident, so was the concern that these technologies could be a means to develop nuclear weapons. The Atoms for Peace program and the IAEA were outgrowths of efforts to disseminate nuclear technology while safeguarding its peaceful uses. These efforts were partially successful in slowing the spread of sensitive fuel cycle technology, namely, the technology that would facilitate the acquisition of fissile material needed for nuclear weapons. However, states like Israel and China, which gave the development of nuclear weapons a high priority, obtained sufficient access to nuclear technology during the 1950s and 1960s to construct the necessary indigenous infrastructure to sustain an ongoing effort.

During the 1970s, the demand for nuclear energy increased dramatically, in part to counter the effects of the Arab oil embargo. Several countries vied to supply parts of or the complete fuel cycle. The upsurge in interest in nuclear technology and the Indian nuclear test in 1974 renewed concerns about the extensive spread of sensitive nuclear technology. With U.S. leadership, several initiatives were undertaken to tighten the controls on nuclear fuel cycle technologies. France, for example, stopped the transfer of reprocessing technology to Pakistan, and West Germany slowed the pace of nuclear technology transfer to Brazil. At the same time, the Zangger Committee's "trigger list" of sensitive nuclear items for export controls was expanded, and the London Suppliers Guidelines were developed as an additional set of sensitive technology export regulations.

With this tightening of export controls, states with questionable commitments to nuclear nonproliferation and hostility to the West have found it difficult to obtain sensitive nuclear technologies, even as part of the commercial fuel cycle. For example, a reasonably effective international effort has limited Libya, despite its status as an NPT signatory with full-scope safeguards, in its access to nuclear technology because of concern about its nuclear weapons ambitions.[3] For the same reasons, Iran is currently having difficulty finding external suppliers to help develop its nuclear infrastructure, including the completion of two safeguarded nuclear power plants at Büshehr. Thus, export controls and technology denial have delayed, if not prevented, the development of nuclear weapons by certain states.

New Technologies and Nuclear Proliferation: The Future Impact

The question for the future is whether states interested in developing nuclear weapons can obtain new technologies that might improve their development efforts.

Technology influences several aspects of nuclear weapons development. In developing a nuclear weapons capability, states have to accomplish the following steps (although not necessarily in this order): first, they have to acquire the technology to produce fissile material; second, they have to build and operate fissile material production facilities; third, they have to develop a viable bomb design (i.e., a bomb design that is effective and deliverable); fourth, they have to manufacture the components of the bomb; and fifth, they have to weaponize the bomb and integrate it into an appropriate delivery system. In many of these steps, the scientific principles, such as the chemistry involved in reprocessing or the physics behind a nuclear explosion, may be well known and understood, but the engineering required to develop the capability is not. For example, limiting the availability of information on how to make gaseous diffusion barriers or of certain types of equipment (such as hot isostatic presses) may impede the ability of a state to move from scientific theory to actual capability.

Thus, the effect of a specific technical advance on nuclear weapons proliferation will vary depending on the role of the technology in developing nuclear weapons, the access to it, and the ease of absorption. In a discussion of such new technologies, three categories emerge: (1) technology directly related to developing nuclear weapons, such as new methods to obtain fissile material or to improve nuclear weapon designs; (2) dual-use items, such as high explosives, numerically controlled machines, computers, and components of firing systems; and (3) delivery systems, particularly ballistic missile technologies.[4]

The first category does not seem to offer the potential proliferator much help in facilitating its nuclear weapons development. New advances in enrichment technologies, such as laser enrichment or chemical enrichment, may be too sophisticated for most developing states to exploit. These technologies have not been fully proven even in the advanced industrial states and could require years of research and development before producing significant quantities of enriched uranium. Most states may dabble in emerging technologies, in part because of technical discussions in the open literature and the exposure of their scientists to new techniques during their training, but probably will not focus their efforts on these technologies. Given their generally weak infrastructures, potential proliferators choosing these new technologies as their primary method of enrichment would more likely be slowing, not quickening, the pace of their progress.

Additional advances in fissile material production and nuclear design are unlikely to occur extensively in the future. States that have the technical expertise to develop advanced technologies in these areas do not currently have an incentive to do so. The end of the cold war not only removed the incentive to build and design better nuclear weapons but also created a glut of fissile material that adds to the existing glut of low-enriched uranium. Thus, advanced states will probably not expend many resources on developing new technologies in this first category.

The second category, dual-use equipment, may offer more help to the potential proliferator. The United States, Switzerland, the United Kingdom, Japan, Germany, France, and Russia (to name a few) continue to make advances in technologies for machining, computations, diagnostics, robotics, and chemical processing. Such technologies have both military and civilian applications, and many may be available without strict export controls. Access to computer numerically controlled machines, faster oscilloscopes, and more powerful computers could facilitate a state's nuclear weapons development. Unlike the first category, there will be dual-use technology advances that could help a state develop nuclear weapons and improve its nuclear capabilities. An example may be the availability of increasingly powerful computers to simulate aspects of weapon design and questions of physics. The challenge for developing states will be whether they can fully exploit and maintain these new technologies without either significant foreign assistance or a strong infrastructure.

Another area in which new technologies might play a role is delivery systems. Most states of proliferation concern already have delivery systems, such as aircraft, capable of delivering nuclear weapons. Many have older ballistic missile technology, such as Scuds. The basic technologies involved in these systems are not new, nor are they necessarily difficult to master if a state has an adequate infrastructure. As with nuclear technologies, utilizing the more advanced technologies, such as those improving guidance or propulsion, will depend on a country's infrastructure, foreign technology, and often, ongoing foreign assistance.

These advanced delivery-system technologies will improve the capabilities of an advanced proliferator. Exploring expensive, advanced technologies for delivery, however, will probably be a secondary concern for a state whose first-generation nuclear weapons can be delivered by aircraft it already possesses. Countries wanting to develop nuclear weapons in the next decade will likely stress fissile material production and improvements in nuclear weapon designs and rely on currently available ballistic missiles and aircraft for delivery. Although potential proliferants may continue to upgrade their ballistic missile capabilities, the speed, scope, and direction of their advancement will be constrained by their weak technical base and limited access to external technical expertise.

In general, proliferators (except for Israel) may find it difficult to take advantage of many of the new nuclear weapons-related technologies, especially without significant foreign assistance. In some cases, the advances in technologies may be too complex for a state to use effectively at this point in its development. In others, the advances may reflect specific security or safety requirements of an advanced weapons state (such as insensitive high explosives) and add unneeded complication in a proliferator's process or design.

Iraq's success in electromagnetic isotope separation (EMIS) to enrich uranium demonstrates that some older technologies may be better suited to the more rudimentary technical capabilities of certain countries of proliferation concern, especially a country that can handle the high capital and energy costs of EMIS. It also shows how advances in engineering and machining, both capabilities that the Iraqis developed with external assistance, may have improved the efficiency of an old technology.[5] Updating and modernizing thirty- to forty-year-old technology might help potential proliferators more than today's advanced enrichment technologies. Advances in dual-use technologies, however (such as in machining, computations, and diagnostics), may facilitate some aspects of nuclear weapons development but probably not the most difficult and central ones.

The greatest technological threat for nuclear proliferation results from an improved scientific, technical, and industrial infrastructure in the developing world. The inevitable economic and technical progress of a state, albeit slow at times, and the general spread of information and technology will provide a potential proliferator the basis with which to develop nuclear weapon capabilities using thirty- to forty-year-old science, adapting others' technologies to fit its own needs and developing technologies and methods based on its own requirements. Israel has already passed this point, as have South Africa and Taiwan; South Korea, Brazil, and India, which was slowed considerably by the cutoff of Western nuclear technology after its 1974 nuclear test, are well on their way. In ten to fifteen years, several more countries of proliferation concern may have reached development levels that will permit them to take advantage of old nuclear technologies more effectively.

New Technologies and Nonproliferation Efforts

Although the advance of technology may play a marginal role in facilitating the spread of nuclear weapons, it may become a major component of efforts to prevent, contain, and respond to such a spread. With increased priority given to the nuclear proliferation threat, attention is now being directed to technologies that can assist nonproliferation efforts. The successful development of new technologies for collection, detection, monitoring, and analysis may significantly limit the ability of states to pursue clandestine nuclear weapons programs or otherwise violate their nonproliferation obligations.

NEW TECHNOLOGIES AND THE PREVENTION OF NUCLEAR WEAPONS PROLIFERATION

During the cold war, much effort was put into developing technical means to improve collection, detection, monitoring, and analysis related to the Soviet threat. With that threat removed and with nuclear proliferation emerging as a major U.S. foreign policy concern, increased effort is being directed toward the development of new technologies to assist in nonproliferation efforts. Areas of new technologies include surveillance and safeguards hardware, remote sensors, improved imagery, accurate thermometry, laser radars, and forensic analysis.[6]

The Department of Energy's national laboratories are already engaged in numerous efforts to identify new technologies that will provide information vital to achieving nonproliferation objectives.[7] Advanced airborne and space-based remote sensing systems, including both active and passive systems, such as laser radar and near-infrared reflectance, are examples of such efforts. Additionally, land-based remote sensors will be upgraded to improve measurement capabilities, and ground-based sensors that use radiation detectors, optical detectors, or imagers will be developed to verify observables difficult to see from the air or space, such as underground facilities. In the area of treaty verification and safeguards technology, new electronic identification devices and fiber-optic seals may provide methods to monitor objects and activities with more certainty.[8]

These systems offer hope of detecting and identifying minute levels of chemicals emitted from a suspect site. Small amounts of chemicals in soil, water, or air can be detected (e.g., using an integrated gas chromatograph and mass spectrometer), but miniaturizing and packaging these technologies for rapid deployment, remote access, or airborne use will be a challenge. The advances in collection and detection technologies may improve our capability not only to obtain and identify signatures of proliferation-related activities, such as reprocessing, enrichment, and high explosive testing, but also to determine certain critical information such as the type, scale, and history of operation. If these potential advances become reality, they could result in less-intrusive methods to increase the transparency of a state's nuclear activities.

Current technology already provides the means for detecting nuclear tests. The United States has developed a global seismic monitoring network to verify compliance with nuclear test limitations. Upgrading this capability so that it can differentiate between an attempt to conceal a test through masking or attenuation and the various types of seismic events that regularly occur is one of the challenges being worked on. At the moment, the United States has technologies it could employ to improve its ability to detect possible nuclear tests worldwide or regionally, whether they are above ground, underground, or in the ocean. Such a comprehensive or regional nuclear test detection system would require additional funding, resources, and access to establish and then maintain.

In addition, advances in the technologies related to data integration and processing will help nonproliferation efforts. At the moment, analysts are overwhelmed by a wide variety of information that needs to be sorted, culled, and evaluated. Improving the tools available for these tasks will result in more effective utilization of information. In the future, analysts and policymakers will be able to exploit information more comprehensively and quickly using electronic information-network systems. They will be able to access more data, communicate with each other more efficiently, and eventually process all types of data with new software and hardware tools. Increasing analysts' access to information will not by itself prevent the spread of nuclear weapons but will likely lead to better-informed assessments that can provide the basis for nonproliferation policies and activities.

These new technologies, when applied to nonproliferation activities, will make the nuclear-related activities of states more transparent, strengthening efforts to monitor compliance with international and regional nonproliferation obligations. The information derived from these new technical collection, detection, and data-integration methods will provide the basis for unilateral U.S. policies toward specific states and possibly for international activities, such as IAEA challenge inspections and sanctions. These new technologies will also improve verification capabilities, facilitate confidence-building measures, and possibly, because of fear of being discovered, inhibit nuclear weapons development programs.

New Technologies and the Response to Nuclear Proliferation

A final area in which new technologies will affect the spread of nuclear weapons involves responding to threatened or actual use of nuclear weapons. Advances in technology may improve not only the military systems available for defenses and interdiction but also the capabilities for real-time searching, seizure, and destruction of sensitive nuclear materials and nuclear weapons. Eventually, with improved sensors and forensic capabilities that facilitate chemical and material identifications, it may be possible to locate and disable clandestinely positioned nuclear explosives and to identify the source of unattributed nuclear explosions or devices. Finally, advances in communications and data-analysis technology will be critical to comprehensive contingency planning, accurate threat assessment, and quicker operational support.

Achieving some of these capabilities, however, may be quite costly and may involve tackling some extremely difficult technical problems. For example, determining the state responsible for a nuclear explosion involves answering a variety of technical questions against the backdrop of significant intelligence information. To make a certain identification requires a thorough understanding of any state's nuclear weapons activities, including explicit nuclear weapon design information and the processes or sources used in obtaining fissile materials. Equally important will be the ability to collect and evaluate as quickly as possible all relevant information from such an explosion, then to integrate this event data with all other pertinent information in a timely and credible analysis. Just one of the technical challenges involved in this complex question will be the development of sensor platforms that are globally available, cannot be easily spoofed, and provide consistent access and accurate data.

The impact of these emerging technologies will, in general, be to improve the response capabilities of the United States and others to potential proliferator threats. Advanced technologies, as discussed in the previous section, are now being developed to improve the quality and quantity of information available about nuclear weapons-related activities. Understanding the nuclear capabilities of a possible adversary will allow appropriate plans, strategies, and military systems to address the specific threat envisaged. In addition, during a crisis, new technologies relating to data integration and analysis will provide better real-time intelligence and more efficient analytical support. Defense planners will have better information earlier about an adversary's capabilities, intentions, and overall threat.

Advances are also expected in military technologies involved in responding to the threats posed by nuclear proliferation. Advanced conventional capabilities already provide precision targeting, as demonstrated in Desert Storm. With additional improvements, precision-guided munitions and missiles could be used to selectively destroy or otherwise neutralize foreign nuclear weapons stockpiles and facilities. Satellites, which support both planning and operational activities, will continue to improve their capability to provide critical intelligence and reconnaissance information before, during, and after crises. Ballistic missile defenses that provide area protection to population centers or military targets may also be developed.

These advancements in detection, analysis, planning, and military options will result in more effective responses to incidents in which nuclear weapons may be used. As countries recognize the depth and sophistication of the technology being arrayed against them, they may be deterred from developing nuclear weapons or at least from using them. For example, one impact of the massive display of American advanced technology in Desert Storm may have been to discourage states from pursuing nuclear weapons.[9] If they do develop such a capability, they may not be willing to deploy or use them except as a last resort because of fear of preemption or retaliation.

New Technologies: Key to Nonproliferation, Not Proliferation

New technologies will not significantly increase the threat of proliferation in the next ten to fifteen years. States with strong motivations will continue to progress toward a nuclear weapons capability; their progress will probably not be the result of new technologies, however, but of success with old ones. Although improved computers, machine tools, and diagnostics may help proliferators' programs, these advances will not provide any state with a great leap forward. For many states, attempts to use advanced technologies might actually impede their progress because they will not have the infrastructure required to absorb and use the new technologies effectively.

With proliferation becoming a high priority for the United States, additional resources—human, financial, and technical—are already becoming available to spur the development of technologies to support nonproliferation policies, including detection and verification technology, integration and analysis of data, interdiction capabilities, defenses, and deployment support. As observed by the *Economist*, "If the democracies will expand their research-and-development budgets, their technological advantage can be made even bigger."[10]

Does Technology Denial Still Make Sense?

Preventing the diffusion of sensitive nuclear technology has been a primary aspect of nonproliferation activities for the last two decades. Denying certain sensitive technologies completely, such as reprocessing and enrichment, has been combined with efforts to control other aspects of the nuclear fuel cycle through peaceful-use pledges, regular inspections, and safeguards. Technology denial has been most successful when combined with other efforts that include diplomatic initiatives, security guarantees, and regional arms control.

Despite the importance of technology controls, defining the issue of nuclear weapons proliferation only in terms of its technical aspects provides a too narrow focus and could result in an inadequate response. Technology denial not only did not prevent proliferation in the 1950s and 1960s, when the United Kingdom, France, and China all became declared nuclear weapon states, but also was only part of the solution in dealing with Germany and Japan and later with South Korea and Taiwan. Security guarantees and economic and military leverage were more significant than restricting access to technology. At present, the decision concerning nuclear weapons for states such as Germany, Japan, Sweden, and probably Taiwan is not technical but political, determined by each state's perceived security requirements.[11]

Technology denial has not reversed the nuclear weapons programs in states that strongly perceive their security as requiring nuclear weapons, although it has slowed progress in programs forced to rely on indigenous capabilities and covert activities. In cases such as Pakistan, technology denial alone has proven inadequate to prevent nuclear proliferation—such a technical approach was overwhelmed by the central motivations for acquiring nuclear weapons. In cases where security motivations were less critical, the policy of technology denial may have played a more direct role in dissuading some countries from attempting to develop nuclear weapons. Argentina and Brazil are obvious cases in which technology denial may have slowed technical advancement until domestic political changes resulted in a reversal of their nuclear programs. Note that even in this example, the role of technology denial was probably secondary to the coming to power in both states of civilian leadership interested in gaining access to advanced technologies and Western trade.

New technologies will not markedly change the significance of technology denial or technology-use management. For the next ten years or so, most states of proliferation concern can use "old" technology to develop nuclear weapons more effectively than they can exploit new technologies. Nonproliferation efforts must, therefore, continue to control both old and new technologies and be given high priority if technology controls are to influence the pace of nuclear weapons development. Without high-level attention, other interests (economic or geopolitical) may influence the manner in which technology controls are implemented. Efforts should be made to include all potential suppliers in discussions involving technology controls to lessen as much as possible their potentially discriminatory nature and to integrate these technology controls with other activities, such as regional arms control and conflict-resolution efforts, increased worldwide transparencies of military technology development and transfers, and multilateral security guarantees. Integrating technology controls into broader nonproliferation and foreign policy objectives will strengthen their impact and help address all aspects of the proliferation threat.

As long as nonproliferation continues to receive high-level attention in the United States and elsewhere, states will find it difficult to develop nuclear weapons, although they may be able to develop a nuclear infrastructure. In the next twenty years, more states will probably reach a technological threshold from which they will have a short-term nuclear weapons option. At this point, new technologies will probably not be critical to a state's decision to progress toward nuclear weapons, but they may play a central role in the prevention and containment of their spread and use.

Notes

The views expressed in this chapter are those of the author and do not necessarily reflect those of the Lawrence Livermore National Laboratory, Department of Energy, or University of California.

1. I would like to thank Bert Weinstein, Paul Chrzanowski, John Illige, and Neil Joeck for their helpful comments on earlier drafts of this chapter.

2. The Nonproliferation Treaty, the Zangger "trigger list," the Nuclear Suppliers Group guidelines, and the Missile Technology Control Regime reflect the policy emphasis on technology denial as a means to thwart the spread of militarily sensitive nuclear technology. These policies notwithstanding, states such as France, Israel, India, and China demonstrated that indigenous nuclear weapons development is possible.

3. Despite Libya's wealth, it has not been successful in finding foreign suppliers to assist in the expansion of its nuclear infrastructure. Although the Soviet Union provided some assistance, as did Belgium, their contributions have been limited to narrowly defined areas of nuclear research. In addition, Libya has signed nuclear cooperation agreements with several countries, such as Brazil, Argentina, and India, but none of these agreements have resulted in significant technology transfers. See Leonard S. Spector, *The Undeclared Bomb* (Cambridge, Mass.: Ballinger Publishing Co., 1988), pp. 196–201.

4. These three categories are not meant to be mutually exclusive, since equipment and materials used to develop nuclear weapons and delivery systems may include dual-use technologies. They provide, however, a useful framework to discuss areas of technological improvements that might facilitate the spread of nuclear weapons.

5. The Iraqis used unclassified data from the Manhattan Project to develop calutrons in which a strong magnetic field applied to an accelerated beam of uranium ions causes the ions to separate into U-235 and U-238 isotope streams. The Iraqis are believed to have made modifications, such as incorporating modern microprocessors, fiber optics, and computer-aided manufacturing controls, to improve reliability and precision; however, these changes were never proven in full-scale production, so they may not be as effective as first believed. See Jay C. Davis and David A. Kay, "Iraq's Secret Nuclear Weapons Program," *Physics Today*, July 1992, pp. 22–23.

6. Forensic analysis in this context involves identifying indicative materials and chemicals associated with nuclear material production or weapons development. Chemical analysis of effluents in air, soil, and water, for example, may help characterize the processes (such as gaseous diffusion for enrichment or spent fuel reprocessing) employed within a targeted facility.

7. "Livermore Combats Spread of Nuclear Arms," *Aviation Week and Space Technology*, November 2, 1992, pp. 60–61.

8. "Advances in Treaty Verification Technology," *Energy and Technology Review*, January-February 1992, pp. 49–51.

9. It is also possible that states may have taken another message away from Desert Storm, namely, not to challenge the United States without nuclear weapons. This chapter argues that it will be increasingly difficult for a

country to reach the stage of having nuclear weapons without the United States being aware of it and prepared to respond, if such a policy is adopted.

10. "Defence in the Twenty-first Century: A Survey," *Economist*, September 5, 1992, pp. 8–9.

11. Leonard S. Spector, *The New Nuclear Nations* (New York: Random House, 1985), pp. 65–77, 85, 271–73.

Chapter 12

Responding to Proliferation: A Role for Nonlethal Defense?

Joseph F. Pilat

Iraq's invasion of Kuwait and the ensuing U.S.-led multilateral military response dramatically demonstrate that regional threats pose formidable challenges to the United States in the 1990s and beyond. Although the old Soviet threat to the West has disappeared with the Soviet Union, and even though a fundamental transformation of East-West relations has occurred, new threats, direct and indirect, are developing. The ethnic, religious, political, and military rivalries in the Middle East, South Asia, East Asia, and perhaps other regions are being, or have the potential to be, aggravated by the acquisition of advanced weapons systems.

The post–Gulf War revelations of the advances achieved in the Iraqi nuclear weapons program, as well as questions about the nuclear inheritance of the former Soviet Union, have highlighted the threat of spreading nuclear capabilities. The proliferation of advanced conventional weapons (including missiles) and weapons of mass destruction will continue over the next decade, becoming militarily more significant and posing a threat to U.S. interests, friends, allies, and power projection forces (but not to the continental United States). Developments such as increased opportunities for nuclear terrorism or greater instability in the former Soviet Union could fundamentally change this situation for the worse. But the military significance of proliferation will be more challenging in any event.

The proliferation of advanced weapons capabilities gives developing nations the means to pose serious threats to U.S. interests and armed forces overseas, to allies and friendly nations, and perhaps eventually to the continental United States. The United States and its allies must be able to respond to regional conflicts, as well as to incidents of terrorism, hostage taking, drug trafficking, and interference with navigation and shipping. Yet there may be constraints on such responses, and perhaps far higher thresholds for intervention, if nuclear and other weapons of mass destruction have proliferated in the regions of concern. This growing proliferation danger in the context of post-cold war regional conflicts has enhanced the priority of nonproliferation efforts and raised questions of unilateral military responses. Clearly, this issue is now on the agenda in the context of managing or containing nuclear proliferation and will have to be addressed.

Military action can never provide the basis of nonproliferation policy, and the prospects for military actions that genuinely remove a proliferation threat without creating an international backlash, an environmental disaster, or some other unintended consequence are in any event limited. But options must be available. Among the more promising of the options are those presented by a suite of technologies known as "nonlethal defenses" or "disabling technologies," which could create a new arena for action and, if proven technically feasible and appropriately used, could ameliorate some of the problems associated with military responses *without being any less effective.*

Military responses and nonlethal defenses in particular must be understood in the context of the proliferation threat and broader nonproliferation efforts. Accordingly, the following discussion will consider first the new threat environment and then new responses. It will then turn to a discussion of the difficulties of utilizing military measures and the possibilities of nonlethal defenses as a means of addressing those difficulties.

New Threats

In contrast to perceived wisdom, the problem of the proliferation of weapons of mass destruction is not spiraling out of control.

Although we may be surprised in the future about one or another country's interest or achievement, there are only a few countries with an undisputed nuclear weapons capability and only a limited number of countries with programs or interests. Of these states, those whose possession of nuclear weapons would be most destabilizing and most threatening to U.S. interests are farthest away from developing nuclear weapons either because of virtually nonexistent indigenous capabilities (e.g., Libya and Iran) or because of international pressures or actions (e.g., Iraq). In this context, persistent rumors of Iran's acquisition of former Soviet weapons and of Chinese willingness to assist proliferators indicate wild cards.

In recent years, there has been more interest in chemical weapons (CWs) and biological weapons (BWs), especially among states viewed as potential adversaries. But CW capabilities do not appear as threatening as they did before the Gulf War, and BWs, while a frightening prospect, are difficult to weaponize and employ effectively. It is clear that BW-CW programs complicate the nuclear proliferation issue, as do the proliferation of delivery systems and other advanced conventional capabilities. The linkages among the types of proliferation are an obstacle to dealing with the proliferation problem in the Middle East and other conflict-prone regions, and the mix of these capabilities is making proliferation, where it is occurring, more militarily significant, to the extent that weapons of mass destruction are mated to delivery and support systems.

In the years before developments in Iraq and the former Soviet Union galvanized concern about nuclear proliferation, the growing interest in nonproliferation was primarily fed by fears of chemical and biological weapons, as well as missile proliferation. Of course, the long-standing interest in nuclear nonproliferation, which successive U.S. administrations have regarded as a fundamental national security and foreign policy objective, had not disappeared. On the contrary, it was generally assumed that the problem was relegated to a few rogue states that refused to accede to the Treaty on the Nonproliferation of Nuclear Weapons and to comprehensive International Atomic Energy Agency (IAEA) safeguards and that a mature, functioning nonproliferation regime had succeeded reasonably well in stemming the problem elsewhere.

What is new is the nature of the challenges to the nonproliferation regime evident in the Iraqi and post-Soviet nuclear devel-

opments and an assumption among many observers that the
regime will be unable to handle them. First, it is believed that
the regime is too narrowly focused and thus not responsive to
states that are proceeding toward nuclear weapons on the basis
of dedicated programs. Such programs are not covered by verification mechanisms under the Nonproliferation Treaty (NPT),
that is, by IAEA safeguards, to the extent that they are undeclared and based on a sophisticated, indigenous defense industrial base and imports (legal and illegal) of dual-use items that
are far removed from direct nuclear uses. Second, it is assumed
that the regime, which was designed during the cold war and
reflects the mutual interests and influence of the United States
and the former Soviet Union, is ill-equipped to deal with problems arising from the breakup of the Soviet Union. These assertions cannot be dismissed, but they do not foreshadow the demise of the regime.

The regime is being challenged in a dramatically changing
world, and in the next years, we shall see whether it meets its
challenges. The following are key issues in the nuclear arena:

1. Whether the international community continues sanctions
   and long-term monitoring of Iraq's military-industrial infrastructure
2. What lessons will be drawn by potential proliferators from
   Iraq's behavior and its consequences
3. Whether the international community's response to problems that have arisen in North Korea over IAEA safeguards
   will be strong and sustained
4. The perceived credibility of safeguards in South Africa, given
   inherent uncertainties about stocks of weapons-usable materials in the country and the difficult problem of ensuring
   that South Africa's nuclear weapons and associated facilities
   have been destroyed or are no longer operable
5. The behavior of Israel, India, and Pakistan, as well as other
   problem countries

These are believed to be the most pressing of the traditional
proliferation challenges now facing the international community.
Nuclear weapons tests by proliferators, overt weapons declarations, further safeguards violations, and nuclear theft, sabotage,
or terrorism could also challenge the regime, as could differences

on Article 6 of the Nonproliferation Treaty, which could undermine the treaty as it faces extension in 1995.

One emerging challenge that has the potential to undermine the regime more severely than any that has commanded attention in the last four decades is the collapse of a powerful nuclear weapons state, the Soviet Union. Nuclear weapons, nuclear scientists, engineers, and technicians, and associated nuclear capabilities may spread to other countries. Further, unrest in the Soviet successor states, including the possible disintegration of Russia, may result in nuclear theft or sabotage, and terrorism or use cannot be ruled out. Such problems may also arise with advanced conventional, chemical, and biological weapons and capabilities. And it is possible that a similar situation may develop with the passing of the old order in China, whose willingness to export advanced military capabilities has been a serious irritant in the past. These dangers are serious but remain largely prospective.

If these dangers are not realized, the near-term proliferation threat will largely be limited to those developing countries of concern over the last ten to twenty years, especially problem countries in the Middle East, South Asia, and Northeast Asia. Indeed, there are already signs that the list may be declining rather than growing due to positive developments in areas such as Latin America and southern Africa. In the longer term, the "delegitimization" of nuclear weapons, along with developments in the international security environment and in the international arms and high-technology markets, could lead to an expansion or contraction of this level of threat. These longer-term trends, if they continue, will reduce the perceived utility of nuclear weapons (with the possible exception of regions with intractable conflicts) but will also undermine even further the barriers to their acquisition.

Responses: Old and New

It seems clear that the new threats are not only different from those that have appeared in the past but also more difficult to address. The United States will continue to rely on both multilateral and unilateral approaches to nonproliferation. The United States will continue to use political incentives, technological constraints, bilateral export controls, and multilateral treaties, insti-

tutions, and arrangements, including the NPT and IAEA safeguards. However, the cost of these approaches can be expected
to increase in coming years if they are to be strengthened and
their scope is to be expanded.

U.S. nonproliferation policy will be pursued through efforts
to support and strengthen the international nonproliferation regime. In particular, the United States will strongly support
strengthening the IAEA-administered system of safeguards and
will support the indefinite extension of the NPT. U.S. nonproliferation policy will also be pursued through diplomatic efforts. In
the past, demarches to, and bilaterals with, major suppliers (and
allies) dominated the diplomatic agenda. Building a nonproliferation consensus, especially during and after regional crises, may
dominate the agenda in the future.

The United States has been and will remain committed to
reducing states' motivations for acquiring nuclear explosives. To
this end, the United States will continue to seek to improve
regional and global stability, to strengthen alliance systems,
and to promote the legitimate security interests of states
through economic and security assistance and by other means.
Of course, each of these objectives has other defense and diplomatic rationales, which at times work at cross-purposes with
nonproliferation.

Export controls will remain an essential element of U.S. nonproliferation policy. Multilateral controls are being strengthened
in the aftermath of revelations about the Iraqi programs to develop weapons of mass destruction and the means to deliver
them. Yet the significance of export controls is already eroding
as technologies inevitably spread and new suppliers emerge. This
is presumably the case more in the chemical and biological than
the nuclear spheres, but this process will continue across the
board. Moreover, the control of dual-use items has economic
costs and can pose serious impediments to developing economies, impediments that could undermine the commitment of supplier and recipient states to implementing these controls and raise
North-South tensions, among other consequences.

The United States will continue to seek to strengthen such
traditional elements of U.S. nonproliferation policy. Especially in
light of the Gulf War and its lessons, however, the United States
will be committed to an incremental improvement of these traditional responses to the nuclear weapons proliferation threat,

along with efforts in CW, BW, and missile nonproliferation, including the following:

1. Strengthening the NPT and IAEA safeguards
2. Rapidly bringing into force and implementing the Chemical Weapons Convention and strengthening the Biological Weapons Convention
3. Promoting regional arms control and openness, transparency, and confidence-building measures
4. Enhancing enforcement and compliance mechanisms by building on the UN experience in Iraq (e.g., sanctions, inspections)
5. Strengthening and expanding export control measures, particularly in dual-use areas, including the Missile Technology Control Regime
6. Improving intelligence and increasing intelligence sharing

In the new threat environment, such traditional responses, ranging from diplomacy and intelligence to export control arrangements and treaties, are no longer wholly adequate, even if strengthened. New approaches, from arms control to military options, are being considered. The United States is undertaking further limitations on nuclear testing and has announced a cutoff in fissile material production, in part in the belief that these actions will enhance nonproliferation efforts. A nuclear no-first-use policy, more formal negative and positive security assurances, and other such actions may also be explored as means to inhibit proliferation.

These "arms control" approaches to nonproliferation have primarily been put forward in the context of strengthening the NPT. Whatever their security rationale, which is different now from the rationale before the end of the cold war, such trade-offs are unlikely to affect the behavior of proliferators. These approaches will not have a decisive impact on the future of the NPT, though there is a widespread belief that they will.

The United States will also explore the difficult avenue of unilateral or internationally sponsored responses to proliferation. What might such responses entail? There are potentially wide-ranging options for military and other responses to various proliferation contingencies. At one end of the spectrum are possible covert actions or special operations to prevent certain exports or assistance, to delay a proliferator's program, or to eliminate nuclear weapons and other weapons of mass destruction or related facilities and capabilities in the proliferator's possession. Conventional military actions could be undertaken to preempt weapons or capabilities or to respond preventatively to the threat or use of nuclear weapons or other weapons of destruction. It has been argued that nuclear responses are necessary here, but this is unlikely and, given current and prospective threat levels, unnecessary. Developing and deploying defenses against missile attacks with nuclear and other unconventional payloads may also be required, along with creating capabilities for U.S. forces to operate in a proliferated environment.

At the other end of the spectrum are responses to nuclear accidents or use to mitigate environmental consequences and the like. A first-order requirement would involve strengthening and expanding the role of existing U.S. capabilities, including the Nuclear Emergency Search Team (NEST) and the Accident Response Group (ARG), to ensure that they are responsive to emerging threats. NEST and ARG offer capabilities that might possibly be used, for example, to disable a proliferator's nuclear device or to respond to a nuclear accident in a proliferator country.

If realized, this range of responses would reduce the threat, increase the costs of proliferator behavior, and reduce the military benefits of possessing weapons of mass destruction. Such responses could actually mitigate the consequences of the threat or use of these weapons.

The precise response would depend on a host of circumstances, including, first and foremost, the question of whether the perpetrator can be identified by intelligence available to the United States or the international community. The scope, nature, and level of development of the program, and the regional and global security environment, will also be critical in determining the response. A key factor may be whether the response was undertaken during a conflict or whether it occurred in peacetime.

Counterproliferation?

The undeniable problems of undertaking military actions in response to proliferation, or counterproliferation in contrast to nonproliferation, have often been raised. Unless military responses are undertaken in unequivocal self-defense or are sanctioned by the UN Security Council, they constitute challenges to national sovereignty and raise questions of international law. Certainly, unless they are undertaken against a pariah state or a state that has engaged in an act of naked aggression or whose weapons program presents an overwhelming, urgent, and recognizable threat, they will be criticized in the "court" of world public opinion.

The Gulf War demonstrated that it is possible to win approval for military actions against proliferators if a direct threat to peace and security exists. Yet the Iraqi case, which was not originally a nonproliferation action and which has provoked negative responses in the developing world, also showed how difficult it is to reach consensus on such matters. Indeed, most proliferation programs do not pose clear and present dangers. Without a sense of urgency deriving from the proliferator activity itself or from other related objectionable international behavior, there will be no international consensus for responses such as warnings, embargoes, or the like, let alone military action. Such problems are highlighted by recent U.S. efforts to control the transfer of sensitive technologies to Iran.

If no UN action is feasible, will the five nuclear weapons states act in concert, or will the United States (or another state) consider unilateral action? If UN action is not possible, it is unlikely that they could agree to take action outside the UN framework. Some of them may agree to action, but it will not be seen as legitimate. The Israeli strike on the Osirak reactor in 1981 was one of the few cases in which unilateral actions have been taken. But the legitimacy of the Israeli action was widely assailed, even though many of Israel's critics quietly approved of the result.

The bombing of targets of proliferation concern during the Gulf War would seem to suggest that during a widely approved conflict, there are opportunities for military nonproliferation measures. The difference between the negative reaction to the Osirak attack and the silence after or support for similar actions during the Gulf War is astounding. Yet there has been some criticism over the appropriateness of these actions, criticisms that have a North-South dimension that is critical of the regime.

Any military action, even if sanctioned by the United Nations, has effects on the international nonproliferation regime. Such action highly publicizes the failure of the regime and gives succor to its domestic and international opponents. Moreover, because such action is likely to be carried out, for the foreseeable future, by the United States, by its Western allies, or by a U.S.- or Western-led multilateral force, it will have an air of serving the interests of these states and thereby enhance discrimination. Military action can be undertaken in these circumstances, but it must be done only in extreme cases and only rarely if it is not to fully bring down a weakened regime that has been criticized in many quarters. However, the effects of inaction may be just as damaging.

Military measures are difficult not only politically but also militarily. The intelligence requirements for actions against proliferators' programs are particularly demanding, whether those actions are designed to disable or to destroy research and development and production facilities or weapons and materials while minimizing collateral damage. The attacks on suspected Iraqi BW and CW facilities during the Gulf War apparently did not result in any significant releases of agent into the atmosphere, and in any event, the targeted facilities were not located near large population centers. Nonetheless, strikes against such facilities in the future will require extensive intelligence to guarantee that buried or other concealed facilities are located and that the design, status, and other matters are known, to ensure both that the facility is no longer operational and that the release of chemical and biological agents and the exposure of the population are limited.

Precision-guided munitions will have to be improved and perhaps specially tailored for such tasks. Even the use of "smart" weapons against targets such as a nuclear materials production facility can have unintended consequences, resulting in the deaths of noncombatants, damage to collocated and other civil facilities, and adverse environmental consequences. The challenges of theater or strategic ballistic missile defenses are well known, but the ability of systems to deal with tactical ballistic missiles carrying weapons of mass destruction is particularly daunting. If, for example, a CW warhead was intercepted in the lower atmosphere, atmospheric conditions (e.g., precipitation) could result in the unintentional dispersion of most of the agent near the original target.

The very presence of nuclear weapons complicates the projection of U.S. power, but arguments that suggest that such a presence would necessarily prevent U.S. actions are not compelling. Operational challenges, from detection to destruction of special nuclear materials and weapons, are critical. It will be necessary to undertake these actions in a manner that minimizes the prospect of effective retaliation against the United States or U.S. interests, that limits adverse political effects, particularly international criticism or condemnation that could undermine the nonproliferation regime, that minimizes human casualties, and that avoids or limits serious collateral damage or environmental effects.

A full response capability will require developments in advanced conventional ordnance, as well as defenses, but an opportunity to meet the political and military challenges of responses to proliferation that have a military dimension may be offered by nonlethal defenses.

Nonlethal Defenses

"Nonlethal defenses" or "disabling measures" go well beyond efforts to prevent or respond to proliferation. In the view of proponents, they may be applicable across a continuum ranging from preconflict to high-intensity conflict at the strategic level. In all of these areas, nonlethal defenses may be able to play a significant role by enhancing current capabilities and perhaps creating new ones, especially in the area where diplomacy and military force meet. The highest payoffs would probably be before the engagement of major lethal force.

Nonlethal defenses, as they are now being discussed in the policy and academic communities,[1] involve a suite of technologies designed to disrupt, degrade, or destroy a wide set of targets, with minimum physical damage and no intentional casualties. Electromagnetic, acoustic, materials, information, and other technologies are being explored for nonlethal applications. Those potential applications would respond to wide-ranging military contingencies. They might, for example, involve disruption of information, communications, command and control, and other systems by advanced computer viruses, electromagnetic disturbances, and deception; disruption of advancing forces by jellifying fuel and inhibiting combustion in the engines of tanks and armored personnel vehicles, crystallizing the tires of military vehicles and stalling the vehicles with antitraction polymers and lubricants; and destroying air forces by embrittling or otherwise weakening airframes and spraying polymer adhesives on runways. Certain technologies being considered for these and related nonlethal applications are proven and available; others will require long-term research and development.

Although the concept of nonlethal defenses is not new, the maturation of critical technologies, along with new military requirements at the end of the cold war, has created new interest in the academic, policy, and military communities. Former Undersecretary of Defense for Policy Paul Wolfowitz reportedly called for increased research and development of nonlethal technologies, stating to Secretary of Defense Richard Cheney at the end of the Gulf War, "A U.S. lead in nonlethal technologies will increase our options and reinforce our position in the post–Cold War world."[2]

As Wolfowitz's statement suggests, nonlethal defenses are in principle applicable to a wide range of emerging contingencies. Counterproliferation, along with many other new military scenarios that may be confronted in the post-cold war world, will require controlled execution and minimal force. With a decline in the importance of formal alliance structures and the emergence of ambiguous threats and a more complex and unpredictable environment, changes in force structure and forward presence (to enhance flexibility) and greater reliance on crisis response are inevitable. Power projection is critical in this environment, and more options to project power are required, especially for contingencies short of open warfare, including crisis management, peacekeeping operations, hostage-rescue operations, and such operations as counterdrugs, counterterrorism, and counterproliferation. The use of nonlethal capabilities, perhaps along with precision-guided and other smart munitions, would help to minimize the negative consequences of military actions and thus avoid a potentially negative international backlash against the cause for which the United States is fighting.

If required, the preemption of proliferation programs with minimal cost and the least amount of damage is critical. Amid global changes, there may be the requirement to disable or recover nuclear weapons or weapons-usable nuclear materials, for example, that are stolen from the former Soviet Union, either after a request from Moscow, Kiev, Minsk, Almaty, or another authority or on a unilateral basis.[3] But preemption can occur at any stage along the various routes to nuclear weapons, from exports to deployed weapons themselves. Preemption may be undertaken overtly or covertly and by the United States alone or in concert with other powers or regional or international organizations.

In light of the wide-ranging aspects of this potential mission, substances to corrode or change the chemical composition of various materials used in weapons of mass destruction or to undermine the tensile strength of metals in the weapon or the delivery system could conceivably fulfill military requirements. In similar fashion, the introduction of a computer virus in the process-control system of a nuclear weapons production facility, or any number of electronic disruptions, could also be useful in achieving certain nonproliferation objectives. Operations at high explosive (HE) testing sites could be delayed if the HE stores were detonated by microwaves.

Another preemptive application may involve interdicting or degrading nuclear capabilities before or during a possible conflict, presumably creating new conditions for action that may not have existed during peacetime. Storage and launch sites could be effectively neutralized during a crisis or in conflict if the electronics were disrupted or destroyed by nonnuclear pumped electronic pulses or microwaves. The electronic triggers of weapons themselves may also be destroyed. Such actions might effectively neutralize an adversary's small, centralized nuclear forces, making them unavailable during a conflict.

A larger mobile force would pose more formidable challenges, as U.S. difficulties during the Gulf War in destroying mobile Scud launchers demonstrate. Intelligence requirements would be high. Even if one had flawless intelligence, certain actions may be nearly impossible to execute. Others may be too risky.

Nonlethal defenses also can be used to support various operations, including incursions into a proliferator country to emplace untended sensors designed to monitor nuclear or other weapon activities, to disable or destroy facilities or sites for the production or storage of weapons of mass destruction, or to seize or neutralize weapons, nuclear materials, or chemical or biological weapons or agents. It is believed, for example, that such measures might deal with the adversary's security system and forces (e.g., optical munitions to blind sensors) or delay the arrival of military forces (e.g., combustion engine inhibitors, antitraction polymers and lubricants for railroads, adhesive polymers for runways) and allow the U.S. forces to perform the mission and leave the country without a major engagement.

All of these potential uses of nonlethal defenses have received some attention and discussion in various quarters, including in the military services and the Joint Staff. But these possibilities are not the only ones and may not ultimately prove to be feasible or appropriate. Whereas any such action holds dangers, the physical impact of an action using direct lethal force would be far more damaging. Moreover, the nonproliferation regime implications might be expected to be greater in the event of the use of lethal force.

If the benefits appear greater than the costs, such approaches as have already been put forward and other promising approaches will need to be extensively addressed. This must be done on a high-priority basis by nonproliferation officials and military planners, along with the intelligence community, if the promise of nonlethal technologies as part of U.S. efforts to prevent and manage proliferation is to be realized in the future.

Conclusion

Developing and adopting new nonproliferation and counterproliferation measures, from arms control to military responses, would augment the old approaches that remain the foundation of current nonproliferation efforts. None is truly an alternative to those approaches; genuine alternative measures are unlikely to be posed as such without some extraordinary event, such as the collapse of the NPT in 1995, when the treaty's extension is to be reconsidered. Even now, the revival of the Baruch Plan (which proposed a rigid international control regime for all nuclear activities), the conclusion of some overarching nonproliferation treaty, and other grandiose concepts are being put forward. However, the very appearance of lesser measures suggests that the old regime has problems and loopholes and that these are being increasingly recognized.

Clearly, direct military activity, even if it can be undertaken by nonlethal means, is only a matter of last resort. It shows the regime has failed in some aspect, and it challenges regime structures in the best case. But there may be no choice. The Osirak attack and the Gulf War demonstrate that military responses can be used without apocalyptic consequences. Although any response capabilities in the future may be largely constituted on a national basis, they may be used in the context of multilateral action, perhaps even under international authority.

Are we moving exclusively to multilateral or international approaches to proliferation? U.S. nonproliferation policy has long relied on both unilateral and multilateral approaches, although the balance (or imbalance) between them has changed over time. Today, to develop domestic and international support for nonproliferation actions, to reduce costs, and the like, multilateral efforts are desirable in principle but are not always possible. The capability to act alone, if needed, is essential. It is necessary to have options. Few countries will be able to develop, for example, interdiction capabilities. One can imagine many scenarios where unilateral action will be supported domestically (and perhaps welcomed internationally).

In the future, as in the past, unilateral capabilities would augment multilateral approaches, and both will be important to U.S. nonproliferation efforts. Growing interest in and possibilities for multilateral action, along with declining opportunities for unilateral action, appear likely in the new world we are entering. However, the last resort to proliferation dangers may well be U.S. military capabilities. In order to address military proliferation challenges of the future in a manner that best serves the interests of overarching nonproliferation policy, it will be necessary to investigate nonlethal defenses for counterproliferation contingencies. If some technologies prove feasible, they should be included with other arrows in the country's nonproliferation quiver.

Notes

The views expressed in this chapter are those of the author and do not necessarily reflect those of the Los Alamos National Laboratory, the Department of Energy, or the U.S. government.

1. See, especially, John B. Alexander, "Anti-Material Technology," *Military Review* 69 (October 1989): 29–41 and "Rethinking National Security Requirements and the Need for Non-Lethal Weapons Options," Los Alamos National Laboratory Report, LA-UR-9Z-3773 (1992).

2. Thomas E. Ricks, "Nonlethal Arms: New Class of Weapons Could Incapacitate Foe Yet Limit Casualties," *Wall Street Journal*, January 4, 1993, p. A4.

3. See Lewis A. Dunn, "Fifty Years since Stagg Field: Nuclear Nonproliferation Challenges and Opportunities" (paper prepared for symposium on "Proliferation Issues: Past, Present, and Future," University of Chicago, December 3–5, 1992), p. 23.

Chapter 13

Can the Intelligence Community Keep Pace with the Threat?

Jeffrey T. Richelson

On November 25, 1991, President George Bush signed National Security Review Directive 29, "Intelligence Capabilities 1992–2005." The directive required over twenty government agencies to specify their intelligence requirements and priorities for the next thirteen years. Among the highest priorities specified were intelligence on the proliferation of nuclear, chemical, and biological weapons.[1]

Few, if any, would disagree with the proposition that monitoring nuclear proliferation activities should be a major task for the U.S. intelligence community in the years ahead.[2] In addition to monitoring those countries that have not acknowledged their nuclear weapons capability (e.g., Israel, Pakistan, India), there is the need to monitor those who, at various times, seek to develop or acquire such a capability (e.g., North Korea, Iraq, Iran, Libya).

At the same time, many would also point to the post–Gulf War discoveries concerning the Iraqi nuclear program, as well as internal intelligence community disputes over Iranian nuclear intentions, as troubling signs that the U.S. intelligence community may not be able to adequately monitor such nuclear weapons programs.[3] Among the gaps in U.S.-UN knowledge about the Iraqi program was the identity of the program's director. In July 1991, five months after the end of the Persian Gulf War, the UN officials responsible for destroying Iraq's nuclear weapons were searching for an unidentified "mastermind" who they believed had overall charge of the Iraqi program. The belief in an unknown mastermind, possibly a foreigner, resulted from the perception that none of the Iraqi scientists who had been interrogated had a full grasp of the complex program.[4]

It wasn't until September that the UN inspectors discovered secret Iraqi documents that indicated that the program's director was Jaffar Dhia Jaffar, the deputy head of the Iraqi Atomic Energy Commission (IAEC). Although the inspectors had been aware of Jaffar's existence and position in the IAEC since July, they had dismissed the possibility that he was in overall charge of the nuclear weapons program.[5] Nor was the identity of the program's director the only aspect of the Iraqi program that escaped U.S. intelligence. The significance of the Al Atheer scientific research installation, a complex of buildings about forty miles south of Baghdad, was misunderstood. The complex, which was not linked to the Iraqi program until a week before the end of the war, turned out to be the nerve center of the Iraqi nuclear program. Likewise, the purpose of another installation (at Furat) that was secretly building centrifuges for enriching uranium to a weapons-grade level was apparently not discovered until after the war.[6] But possibly the biggest surprise concerning the Iraqi nuclear program was its reliance on calutrons, considered to be an outmoded technology. The Iraqi development of the huge, inefficient devices went undetected by U.S. and other Western intelligence agencies for years.[7]

In the face of such post–Gulf War discoveries, one nuclear proliferation expert observed, "The revelations about Iraq's clandestine nuclear activities also raise questions about the adequacy of nuclear intelligence gathering by the United States and other concerned states."[8] Further, the experience of the UN inspection team in Iraq could be taken as another indicator of the great difficulty of monitoring a foreign nuclear weapons program. Despite their mandate to conduct intrusive inspections, and the aid of the U.S. intelligence community, the UN inspectors often found themselves involved in a game of hide-and-seek with the Iraqis.

However, there are reasons to believe that the situation is not as bleak as it might appear. Although it is impossible, at least on an unclassified basis, to precisely assess how well the U.S. intelligence community might be able to monitor foreign nuclear weapons programs, it is possible to examine the challenges faced by the U.S. intelligence community in effectively monitoring such programs and to explore ways in which the probability of successful monitoring can be (or possibly *is being*) increased.

It would be helpful to begin by examining the different collection targets associated with foreign nuclear weapons programs.

Collection Targets

Any nation's nuclear weapons program consists of several distinct elements. One key element is the thousands of skilled scientists and technical workers employed in any program. Secret Iraqi documents seized by the UN inspection team in the summer of 1991 indicated that more than ten thousand nuclear workers, technicians, and scientists were involved.[9] Such individuals are the one element that are likely to survive a concerted attack on a nuclear weapons program and provide the basis for regenerating a damaged program. Thus, the head of the inspection operation of the International Atomic Energy Agency (IAEA), Maurizio Zifferero, noted: "You can remove the equipment. You can remove fissile material. You can destroy instruments, but you cannot take out the know-how."[10] Monitoring the activities of such individuals can provide valuable clues to the course of a nuclear program. David Kay, who led the UN inspection teams in Iraq, observed, "If you identify 10 people and they end up all working at some place labeled a dairy research institute, you'd want to go out and find out what they were doing."[11]

A second key element is, of course, the facilities—which may include research and power reactors, uranium mining sites and mills, enrichment facilities, centrifuge production facilities, laboratories, weapons assembly and storage sites, and nuclear test sites. The function of only some of the facilities is apparent from their appearance or emissions. Thus, as noted above, the United States did not discover the role of the Furat centrifuge production facility until after the war.[12] A crucial question concerning these facilities is exactly *what* is inside them—how sophisticated is the equipment, and what are their capabilities?

Just as it is important to investigate what is inside the facilities, it is also vital to monitor what leaves the facilities—specifically, communications and emissions. Successful monitoring may help answer some of the questions as to what is inside a facility. Reactors discharge heat, reprocessing facilities that extract plutonium emit krypton-85 into the air, and enrichment plants leak radiation into the surface. Facilities also must communicate with some related facilities and the nuclear program's nerve center.

In addition to people and facilities located within the proliferating nation, there are the foreign governments, corporations, or groups that supply key technologies and material, sometimes covertly or unknowingly, for nuclear programs. Thus, Iraq received key nuclear-related equipment and material from Britain (plutonium), Switzerland (metal casings), France (research reactors), Italy (plutonium separation utility), Finland (copper coils), South America (uranium ore concentrate), Japan (carbon fiber), Africa (uranium ore concentrate), and the United States (power supply units).[13]

German corporations have provided key nuclear technology not only to Iraq but also to Pakistan. Pakistan acquired the special steel electronics and processing vessels needed to produce nuclear weapons material from German firms such as NTG, PTB, and Leybold-Heraeus. It also acquired a multimillion-dollar plant to convert natural uranium to gaseous form—an essential step in enriching it to weapons grade.[14]

Various international banking institutions also play a significant role in the proliferation effort by funding and directing the financial activities of companies involved in proliferation activities. Thus, an investigation by the Italian Service for Information and Military Security (SISMI) identified twenty-two companies that "might have benefited from the financial operations that were 'steered' by the Banca Nazionale del Lavoro (BNL) in Atlanta."[15]

Additionally, unacknowledged and emerging nuclear states—including Pakistan, Iraq, India, and Israel—have shown an inclination and ability to acquire crucial material and technologies by illicit means. Thus, Israel and Pakistan have sought to illegally acquire krytrons from sources in the United States. And, in 1989, West German investigators uncovered a Pakistani smuggling network that apparently assisted Pakistan's uranium-enrichment efforts by providing specialized containers for the transport and storage of uranium hexafluoride. In 1990, Iraqi agents attempted to illicitly acquire U.S.-made military-grade capacitors.[16]

A recent concern is the smuggling of nuclear material stolen from former Soviet and East European nuclear facilities. Although the material so far seized by authorities would be of little immediate value in developing atomic weapons, the activity does create a new concern.[17]

Just as there are a variety of targets, there are also a number of different collection methods and strategies.

Collection Methods and Strategies

Various means exist to gather intelligence on nuclear weapons programs—including nuclear intelligence (NUCINT), imagery intelligence (IMINT), signals intelligence (SIGINT), communications intelligence (COMINT), and human intelligence (HUMINT).[18]

The most direct technical means of collecting intelligence on other nations' nuclear weapons programs is through the variety of sensors that fall in the NUCINT category. Such sensors, which detect radiation and other effects resulting from radioactive sources, can be deployed on spacecraft, aircraft, ships, small boats, and helicopters; they can even be placed in an attaché case.

Fuel reprocessing plants can be monitored by the releases of krypton-85 gases, which are sufficiently large to be detectable at long distances. In the early 1950s, the krypton-85 level was the key to U.S. estimates of the Soviet Union's plutonium production and nuclear weapons production rate.[19] Plutonium production reactors can be detected by satellite infrared sensors. Thus, the outflows of hot water from the Savannah River production reactors are easily visible in thermal infrared photographs taken from an altitude of 1.2 kilometers and are so broad that they are also detectable from satellite altitudes.[20]

But NUCINT certainly does not play as great a role in evaluating the nuclear weapons programs of emerging nuclear states as it did in monitoring the Soviet nuclear weapons program. The United States was concerned for over forty years not with how the Soviets would attempt to acquire an A-bomb or whether they had succeeded, but with how many warheads they were producing and the characteristics of those warheads. The constellation of nuclear intelligence aircraft, ground stations, and Sound Surveillance System (SOSUS) arrays provided a valuable means of providing answers to such questions.

Naturally, NUCINT sensors are of much lesser value when the questions involve a nation's nuclear intentions, its efforts to acquire nuclear material and technology, research and development, or production work, none of which give off signals detectable by such sensors.

In spite of the massive intelligence-gathering means at the disposition of several nations, including overhead reconnaissance and electronic intercepts, there seem to have been serious deficiencies in the general assessment of Iraq's nuclear program.[21] It has been suggested that such deficiencies were due to an inadequate devotion to human intelligence collection and an overreliance on technical collection, particularly imagery and signals intelligence.[22] And it has recently been reported that "U.S. intelligence professionals who have been stymied in their attempts to monitor and curb proliferation through satellite intelligence gathering and export controls are turning anew to developing networks of agents and informants." In particular the report claimed that the CIA was working "at a frenzied pace" to establish human intelligence networks in hard-to-penetrate countries such as Iraq and North Korea.[23]

Potentially, HUMINT can be applied to foreign nuclear weapons programs to provide a level of understanding that would probably be unavailable from technical collection. Human sources not only can provide information on intentions but also can provide an integrated overview of a program (its people, facilities, suppliers, and progress), an overview that could be extraordinarily difficult to piece together by relying on technical collection. Further, human sources can report on what is inside facilities and can acquire and pass on documents and hardware of great value in helping to understand a foreign nuclear weapons program—for example, a master list of foreign suppliers. In addition, certain smuggling networks may not rely on any form of interceptable communications in conducting their operations. Human sources can also scoop up soil samples around a suspected nuclear installation to be examined for traces of uranium hexafluoride.[24]

It is easy to provide examples in which HUMINT was or would have been of tremendous value in evaluating the status of a foreign nuclear weapons program. At least one penetration of the Chinese government has involved someone with access to information concerning Chinese nuclear relations with Pakistan. That source reported on the following:

1. China's nuclear exports to Argentina and South Africa

2. Chinese technicians who helped at a suspected Pakistani bomb-development site
3. Chinese scientific delegations who were spending a substantial amount of time at a centrifuge plant in Kahuta where Pakistani scientists were attempting to produce enriched uranium
4. Pakistani scientists from a secret facility at Wah who showed a nuclear weapons design to some Chinese physicists in late 1982 or early 1983 and who sought Chinese evaluation of whether the design would yield a nuclear blast
5. The triggering mechanism for the Pakistani bomb design that appeared to be very similar to one used by China in its fourth nuclear test[25]

Information about the Taiwanese nuclear program was also provided by an informant, Colonel Chang Hsien-Yi, who worked in a Taiwanese research institute. This information indicated that the Taiwanese were in the process of building a secret installation that could have been used to obtain plutonium. Further, U.S. Army human intelligence reports on the Pakistani presence at Chinese nuclear test sites and on Iraqi-Chinese discussions about construction of a nuclear reactor also indicate the value that can be played by human sources.[26]

Aside from the significant new information provided by Iraqi defectors after the Persian Gulf War, the Mordechai Vanunu case certainly illustrates the potential value of HUMINT. According to *The Samson Option*:

> Vanunu's *Times* interview and his photographs of many of the production units in the Tunnel, or Machon 2, provided the American intelligence community with the first extensive evidence of Israeli capability to manufacture fusion, or thermonuclear, weapons. . . .
>
> One American official who has been analyzing Israel's nuclear capability since the late 1960s depicted Vanunu's information, which includes a breakdown of the specific function of each unit inside the Tunnel, as stunning: "The scope of this is much more extensive than we thought. This is an enormous operation."[27]

It is important to acknowledge the potential value of HUMINT and the value of improving HUMINT collection on proliferation activities. In addition to attempts to penetrate the actual or potential nuclear programs, there is also an obvious value to penetrating portions of the suppliers' network and smuggling operations.[28]

However, there is a real danger in viewing HUMINT as *the* answer to monitoring proliferation activities. As desirable as it may be, it may be impossible to attain sufficiently reliable human intelligence, particularly from nations such as Iraq, North Korea, and Iran. It should not be forgotten that along with notable U.S. HUMINT successes, there have been some significant failures. Thus, it has been reported that the CIA networks in East Germany and Cuba were heavily penetrated by those nations' security services. Local conditions—including the isolation of the country as well as the thoroughness and brutality of the security service—and the nature of a country's relations with the United States may preclude sufficient successful recruitments. Recruiting a source in the Pakistani nuclear program will not be as difficult, probably by several orders of magnitude, as recruiting a source in the North Korean program. Thus, according to one U.S. intelligence official, the United States did have some human intelligence sources reporting on Iraq. But he added: "With North Korea, we had nothing. Zip."[29]

In addition, an excessive preoccupation with HUMINT may divert attention from enhancing other activities, including technical collection and analysis, which may yield significant benefits.

Certainly, imagery and COMINT can provide significant hard information (and a valuable check on HUMINT) on many aspects of foreign nuclear weapons programs. Imagery intelligence can and has provided information valuable in monitoring nuclear weapons programs. Gaseous diffusion plants are reasonably conspicuous because of their large size (and heavy power demand)—due to the fact that each passage of uranium hexafluoride through a diffusion barrier increases its enrichment by only a very small percentage.[30]

Satellite imagery can show the presence of completed reactors, cooling towers, and power lines, as well as facilities under construction and their external characteristics. Whereas the United States has apparently learned "zip" about the North Korean program from human sources, it has learned a great deal from satellite imagery. In the 1970s, satellite imagery alerted the United States to the existence of a research installation, roads, railroad tracks, power grids, housing, and storage areas. In 1980, a satellite returned imagery that indicated that a new reactor was going up at Yongbyon. Further photos showed a thirty-megawatt, graphite-moderated, gas-cooled machine that burned natural uranium. During 1988–89, additional satellite imagery revealed a second large building that seemed perfectly suited for reprocessing plutonium.[31] In the winter of 1991, U.S. imagery satellites detected North Korean workers digging trenches in frozen ground between Yongbyon's principal facility for reprocessing nuclear fuel and one of two facilities suspected of storing nuclear wastes. The conclusion drawn by the CIA was that the North Koreans were planning on burying the pipes between the two facilities and thus concealing their connection from IAEA inspectors.[32] U.S. imagery satellites also detected trucks pulling up to the reprocessing plant before the arrival of IAEA inspectors in 1992, possibly to haul away equipment. Similarly, U.S. imaging satellites monitoring Iraq have detected uranium-enrichment machinery being moved around on trucks or buried to evade detection by UN inspectors.[33]

Communications between the different elements of a nuclear program and between the different elements and higher authority are subject to interception by space and other COMINT systems. Although there are virtually no specific examples in the open literature of the contribution of COMINT to nuclear proliferation intelligence—the only exception being a report of National Security Agency intercepts of South African–Israeli communications after the September 22, 1979, *Vela* incident—it is safe to assume that there are a number of classified examples of the contribution of COMINT. It has been noted that Pakistani officials regularly use the telephone to relay information about their nation's nuclear weapons program.[34]

But clearly, the U.S. technical collection effort directed against Iraq left significant gaps. And it is clear that several nations, including Iraq, North Korea, and South Africa, have made or examined the feasibility of denial and deception efforts to hide aspects of their nuclear weapons programs from U.S. reconnaissance activities.[35]

Thus, in a report circulated to several governments, Hans Blix, the director general of the IAEA, noted that the North Koreans may have built a "pilot plant" to process plutonium, out of satellite view, before taking the risky leap and building at Yongbyon.

Likewise, Iraq pursued, with China, possible plans to build a nuclear reactor that would be camouflaged to defeat satellite surveillance.[36]

In the aftermath of the Persian Gulf War, it was discovered that Iraq had constructed underground facilities for nuclear weapons development and had buried related power lines. In addition, a strict communications security program prohibits Iraqi officials from discussing the nuclear program over the telephone. It has also been reported that North Korea was working on aspects of its nuclear weapons program in Bakchon County at a secret underground site designed to avoid satellite detection (and international inspection). The United States reportedly first became aware of the facilities after a North Korean diplomat defected in May 1991. U.S. imagery satellites detected the digging of deep tunnels around the nuclear site at Yongbyon in early February 1992. The tunnels are believed to be part of a program to harden the facility against a possible attack. They may also be part of a program to hide nuclear weapons components from international inspectors.[37]

At the same time, it should not be assumed that gaps are inevitable or that denial and deception measures cannot be defeated. Due to launch failures, the U.S. imagery satellite constellation in the 1987–88 period was quite limited compared with today's constellation—consisting of one KH-11 visible-light electro-optical spacecraft through October 1987 and two KH-11s through November 1988. Since that time, the United States has launched approximately three Advanced KH-11s and two LACROSSE spacecraft. The increased number of imagery spacecraft in orbit is, in itself, significant. But the new spacecraft have additional capabilities; in addition to its visible-light imagery capability, the Advanced KH-11 is capable of producing infrared imagery, and the LACROSSE is a radar imagery spacecraft. As a result, the circumstances under which the United States can monitor certain activities or their effects—such as heat discharges, nighttime construction, and activities taking place under cloud cover—have increased dramatically.

Further, the size of the U.S. space SIGINT constellation has increased since 1987–88. In addition, with the launch of two VORTEX and two MAGNUM geosynchronous SIGINT spacecraft, a new heavier SIGINT spacecraft is scheduled for launch in late 1994.

Also, the "take" obtained from constructing and deploying U.S. technical collection systems is a function not only of their number and technical characteristics and capabilities but also of how they are employed—of human decisions concerning the areas and facilities to be covered and the frequency of coverage.[38]

Until recently, the primary focus of U.S. technical collection efforts was the former Soviet Union. Although Iraq, North Korea, and other potential proliferators were not ignored in imagery and COMINT collection plans, they certainly did not receive as much attention as they might have and as they are receiving now. Increasing imagery and COMINT coverage means increasing the probability of detecting new facilities and new developments.[39]

Imagery coverage can be increased in several ways—by scheduling images of targets already on the target list to be produced more frequently, by increasing the frequency and area of missions devoted to searching for new facilities, and by devoting more attention to anomalous or suspicious facilities. Thus, the United States has recently stepped up satellite reconnaissance of Iran's nuclear-related facilities in response to evidence of a "suspicious procurement pattern" of nuclear-related technologies.[40]

Likewise, COMINT coverage can be increased by more frequent monitoring (and/or processing) of communications links known to be associated with nuclear weapons programs, as well as more frequent searches for new frequencies that might be associated with such programs. In addition to increased attention to the communications links of a particular proliferator, increased coverage of supplier communications links may reveal valuable new information.

Defeating denial and deception measures may depend on a variety of strategies, including more frequent imagery coverage at night and when cloud cover is present. In the days before the launch of the first U.S. reconnaissance satellites, some believed that it might be imperative to obtain photography of Soviet missile silos while they were under construction because once construction was completed they would be camouflaged. Although that was not actually a problem, the attempts by Iraq and North Korea to construct underground facilities suggest that it may be necessary to detect some nuclear facilities in the construction stage. Increased nighttime coverage (employing Advanced KH-11 and LACROSSE spacecraft) and increased coverage in the presence of cloud cover (relying on LACROSSE spacecraft), along with coverage of more territory, increase the chances of detecting construction of underground facilities before they have been completed.

But improvements in collection are only one means of enhancing the ability to monitor the activities of emerging nuclear powers. Improved analysis is another.

Analysis

Improving the ability to monitor attempts at nuclear proliferation requires more than enhanced collection operations—whether human or technical. This is particularly true when dealing with an intelligence problem such as proliferation, which makes the intelligence problem of monitoring Soviet nuclear weapons developments simple by comparison. The analytical component of the proliferation monitoring effort can improve the chances of successful monitoring.

A fundamental condition for analytical success, before even the proper analytic strategy, is to focus analytic resources on the problem. The staff of the Senate Select Committee on Intelligence found only one finished intelligence community assessment of the Iraqi procurement network in the 1983–89 period.[41] Clearly, more attention to the issue would have been justified.

Aside from the multitude of potential proliferators, there are distinct alternative paths to the production of nuclear weapons, paths that are the product of numerous choices (e.g., the choice between plutonium and highly enriched uranium). And for any particular path or paths chosen, there are a number of suppliers for the resources required. Furthermore, given the constraints facing potential proliferators, often including the desire to achieve the capability covertly, the most direct, least costly, and most "rational" method may not be the one chosen. Hence, the logic that "if they were pursuing a nuclear capability, they would do X, and since they are not doing X, they are not pursuing such a capability" may have little validity. As a result, it is necessary to evaluate information against a variety of models of nuclear proliferation.

It appears that the surprise that resulted from the discovery that Iraq was employing calutron technology to produce nuclear material stemmed from the dismissal of the method as being obsolete. Instead, analysts had concluded that Iraq was seeking to enrich its uranium through the use of delicate fast-spinning centrifuges that separate the heavier and lighter isotopes of uranium gas. It was subsequently discovered that Iraq was pursuing both approaches.[42] Similarly, U.S. analysts apparently considered it unlikely that some Iraqi facilities detected by satellite reconnaissance were involved in the nuclear weapons program because of a lack of visible security around the facilities. However, the extensive nature of the program resulted in security fences being placed so far from those facilities that the fences went unnoticed.

Recognizing the variety of paths a nation may pursue to achieve a nuclear weapons capability can also improve the value and efficiency of the collection effort. Models of alternative proliferation paths can be (and presumably are) employed to direct collection activities, as well as to simply evaluate the meaning of data already collected.

Conclusion

Although the postwar discoveries concerning the Iraqi nuclear weapons program raise legitimate concerns about the ability of the U.S. intelligence community to monitor nuclear proliferation activities, they are not cause for despair—for even though it may be desirable for the United States to know *everything immediately*, this is not generally necessary to put a brake on proliferation. Knowledge of select procurement attempts or other actions, and measures to block such procurement attempts or actions, may suffice. Hence, in 1992 the United States was able to persuade China and Argentina to cancel planned transfers of key technologies to Iran.[43]

In 1977, following a tip from the Soviet Union, a U.S. imagery satellite photographed a suspected nuclear test site in the Kalahari Desert. On the basis of that imagery, the United States began working with France, Great Britain, and West Germany to develop a concerted response to a possibly impending test. That pressure, at the very least, may have discouraged a South African test in the Kalahari, then or in the future.[44]

But as the aftermath of the Persian Gulf War showed, there is considerable room (and need) for improvement. The overall performance of U.S. intelligence in the proliferation area can be improved by a number of means.

Improving HUMINT collection is one of those means, for such collection may provide information that would be of tremendous value and that is unobtainable from other sources. However, it should not be seen as *the* answer. A near exclusive focus on improving HUMINT may divert attention from other areas of possible improvement. For in addition to improving HUMINT collection, U.S. intelligence should be able to improve the effectiveness of technical collection, as well as analysis.

Technical collection has already improved due to the increased sensor capabilities of U.S. imagery satellites and the increased number of those satellites in operation. The development of an improved broad-area search capability would further enhance imagery capabilities. But beyond improvements in sensor capabilities and the number of spacecraft in orbit, it is also necessary to improve imagery collection strategies—by devoting more time to (1) searching for new facilities, (2) examining suspicious or anomalous facilities, and (3) reexamining known nuclear facilities.

COMINT collection can also be improved in similar ways. More frequent monitoring and processing of nuclear weapons programs, suppliers, and financial communications links known to be associated with nuclear weapons programs would increase the probability of discovering relevant information. Increased searches for relevant communications could also produce valuable information.

Finally, among the most important and necessary improvements are those that lie in the area of analysis. As with collection activities, some improvement would come just from an increase in effort—in other words, the hiring of more analysts or the devotion of more analytical time to proliferation problems. But it will also be necessary to make better use of the analytical resources already available. Better integration of the analytical effort presently being conducted by several distinct intelligence organizations may produce better analysis. In setting intelligence collection requirements and in analyzing data, analysts also need to consider the numerous alternative paths that can be used to produce nuclear weapons.

Notes

1. Remarks by Director of Central Intelligence Robert M. Gates to the Association of Former Intelligence Officers, November 14, 1992, Boston, Massachusetts, p. 2.

2. The most prominent organizations in the U.S. intelligence community involved in monitoring foreign nuclear programs are the DCI Joint Atomic Energy Intelligence Committee, the Central Intelligence Agency, the Defense Intelligence Agency, the Department of Energy Office of Intelligence, the Air Force Technical Applications Center, and the Z (Special Projects) Division of Lawrence Livermore National Laboratory.

3. Elaine Sciolino, "Iraq's Nuclear Program Shows the Holes in U.S. Intelligence," *New York Times*, October 20, 1991, p. E5; Elaine Sciolino, "CIA Says Iran Makes Progress on Atom Arms," *New York Times*, November 30, 1992, pp. A1, A6.

4. Paul Lewis, "U.N. Officials Seek Mastermind in Charge of Iraq's Nuclear Effort," *New York Times*, October 1, 1991, p. A11.

5. R. Jeffrey Smith and Glenn Frankel, "Saddam's Nuclear-Weapons Dream," *Washington Post*, October 13, 1991, pp. A1, A44–A45; Paul Lewis, "U.N. Aides Discover Atom Arms Center Concealed by Iraq," *New York Times*, October 8, 1991, pp. A1, A9.

6. Lewis, "U.N. Aides Discover Atom Arms Center"; Eric Schmitt, "U.S. Says It Missed 2 A-Plants in Iraq," *New York Times*, October 11, 1991, p. A6; R. Jeffrey Smith, "Nuclear-Related Plant Discovered in Iraq," *Washington Post*, August 8, 1991, p. A30.

7. David Albright and Mark Hibbs, "Iraq's Quest for the Nuclear Grail: What Can We Learn?" *Arms Control Today*, July/August 1992, p. 3; Anthony Fainberg, *Strengthening IAEA Safeguards: Lessons from Iraq* (Stanford: Center for International Security and Arms Control, Stanford University, 1993), pp. 11–14.

8. Leonard Spector, "Threats in the Middle East," *Orbis*, Spring 1992, pp. 181–98.

9. Rowan Scarborough and Bill Gertz, "U.N. May Destroy the Hardware, but Iraqi Nuclear Workers Remain," *Washington Times*, November 16, 1991, p. A3; Michael Wines, "U.S. Is Building Up a Picture of Vast Iraqi Atom Program," *New York Times*, September 22, 1991, p. A8.

10. Smith and Frankel, "Saddam's Nuclear-Weapons Dream."

11. Scarborough and Gertz, "U.N. May Destroy the Hardware."

12. Schmitt, "U.S. Says It Missed 2 A-Plants."

13. Smith and Frankel, "Saddam's Nuclear-Weapons Dream"; Michael Wines, "Iraq's Nuclear Quest: Tentacles in Four Continents," *New York Times*, December 23, 1990, pp. 1, 10.

14. Gary Milhollin, "Asia's Nuclear Nightmare: The German Connection," *Washington Post*, June 10, 1990, pp. C1, C2.

15. SISMI, "Subject: BNL Affair-Atlanta Branch," n.d.

16. Leonard S. Spector with Jacqueline R. Smith, *Nuclear Ambitions: The Spread of Nuclear Weapons, 1989–1990* (Boulder: Westview, 1990), pp. 29, 33–34.

17. Steve Coll, "For Sale: Nuclear Contraband," *Washington Post*, November 29, 1992, pp. A1, A36.

18. It should be noted that HUMINT comes in two varieties—overt and clandestine. Overt collection includes interviewing selected individuals, such as businessmen and travelers, who may have relevant information.

19. Frank Von Hippel and Barbara Levi, "Controlling Nuclear Weapons at the Source: Verification of a Cut-Off in Production of Plutonium and Highly Enriched Uranium for Nuclear Weapons," in Kosta Tsipis, David W. Hafemeister, and Peter W. Janeway, eds., *Arms Control Verification: The Technologies That Make It Possible* (McLean, Va.: Pergamon-Brassey's, 1986), pp. 338–88, at p. 377; "Memorandum for Director of Intelligence, DCS/O, Subject: (Uncl.) Determination of Proper Security Classification," November 26, 1954, RG 341, Entry 214, Files 4-4459 through 4-4592, Military Reference Branch, National Archives and Record Administration, Washington, D.C.

20. Von Hippel and Levi, "Controlling Nuclear Weapons at the Source," p. 377.

21. Fainberg, *Strengthening IAEA Safeguards*, p. 18.

22. James Adams, "Help Wanted: Bring Cloak, Dagger," *Washington Post*, February 9, 1992, p. B2.

23. David A. Fulghum, "Advanced Arms Spread Defies Remote Detection," *Aviation Week and Space Technology*, November 9, 1992, pp. 20–22.

24. Rodman D. Griffin, "As Intelligence Needs Change, So Do CIA Recruits' Resumes," *Washington Times*, December 28, 1992, p. A5. The standard argument for the benefits of HUMINT is that it can provide information on intentions, which technical collection systems cannot provide. This is a fairly poor argument for the value of HUMINT. Intentions are detectable by a variety of collection methods, with communications intelligence being a very significant means. The unique ability of human sources to acquire documents, hardware, or soil samples seems to be a far better example of its potentially great value. In addition, and particularly regarding proliferation, knowledge of intentions may have only a limited impact on U.S. actions. Thus, although intelligence analysts may, and should, seek to determine Iran's present nuclear intentions, it is not clear that their conclusions should influence U.S. actions in attempting to limit Iran's acquisition of nuclear technologies—given the nature of that regime and the fact that intentions can change overnight.

25. Jack Anderson and Dale Van Atta, "Nuclear Exports to China?" *Washington Post*, November 3, 1985, p. C7; Patrick E. Tyler and Joanne Omang, "China-Iran Nuclear Link Is Reported," *Washington Post*, October 23, 1985, pp. A1, A19; Joanne Omang, "Nuclear Pact with China Wins Senate Approval," *Washington Post*, November 22, 1985, p. A3; Patrick E. Tyler, "A Few Spoken Words Sealed Atom Pact," *Washington Post*, January 12, 1986, pp. A1, A20–21.

26. Stephen Engleberg and Michael R. Gordon, "Taipei Halts Work on Secret Plant to Make Nuclear Bomb Ingredient," *New York Times*, March 23, 1985, pp. A1, A15; U.S. Army Operational Group, "Nuclear Power Plant Development Plans," May 12, 1986 (Sanitized/Declassified); 500th MI Brigade, "Pakistani Use of Chinese Nuclear Weapons Test Facilities," June 19, 1991 (Sanitized/Declassified).

27. Seymour M. Hersh, *The Samson Option: Israel's Nuclear Arsenal and American Foreign Policy* (New York: Random House, 1991), p. 198.

28. Overt HUMINT collection may prove fruitful for some segments of the international suppliers network. Under what circumstances the United

States would attempt (or has attempted) to recruit clandestine sources in German, Italian, or other West European corporations makes for interesting speculation.

29. David E. Sanger, "Journey to Isolation," *New York Times Magazine*, November 15, 1992, pp. 28ff. (source of quotation); "Saddam's Nuclear Secrets," *Newsweek*, October 7, 1991, pp. 28–35; Jack Anderson and Dale Van Atta, "Cuban Defector Impeaches CIA Spies," *Washington Post*, March 21, 1988, p. B15; Bill Gertz, "Stasi Files Reveal CIA Two-Timers," *Washington Times*, September 12, 1991, pp. A1, A11.

30. Von Hippel and Levi, "Controlling Nuclear Weapons at the Source," p. 375.

31. Don Oberdorfer, "North Koreans Pursue Nuclear Weapons," *Washington Post*, July 29, 1989, p. A9; John J. Fialka, "North Korea May Be Developing Ability to Build Nuclear Weapons," *Wall Street Journal*, July 19, 1989, p. A16; Sanger, "Journey to Isolation"; William E. Burrows and Robert Windrem, *Critical Mass* (New York: Simon and Schuster, 1994).

32. R. Jeffrey Smith, "N. Korea and the Bomb: High-Tech Hide-and-Seek," *Washington Post*, April 27, 1993, pp. A1, A11.

33. Sanger, "Journey to Isolation"; Paul Lewis, "U.S. Shows Photos to Argue Iraq Hides Nuclear Material," *New York Times*, June 27, 1991, p. A12; Bill Gertz, "Satellite Spots Iraq Burying Atomic Gear," *Washington Times*, July 10, 1991, pp. A1, A10.

34. Stephen Green, *Living by the Sword* (Brattleboro, Vt.: Amana Books, 1988), pp. 128–29; Sciolino, "Iraq's Nuclear Program Shows the Holes in U.S. Intelligence."

35. R. Jeffrey Smith, "South Africa's Sixteen-Year Secret: The Nuclear Bomb," *Washington Post*, May 12, 1993, pp. A1, A26.

36. Sanger, "Journey to Isolation"; U.S. Army Operational Group, "Nuclear Power Plant Development Plans." Presumably, by "out of satellite view," Blix meant in a location not likely to be the subject of coverage. North Korea is located well within 30 to 50 degrees north latitude, making it easily accessible to all U.S. imagery satellites. To be literally "out of satellite view," the plant would have to be in the Arctic.

37. Sciolino, "Iraq's Nuclear Program Shows the Holes in U.S. Intelligence"; Michael Breen, "N. Korea Goes Underground with Nuclear Plants," *Washington Times*, October 25, 1991, p. A11; Bill Gertz, "North Korea Digs Tunnels for Nuclear Arms," *Washington Times*, February 21, 1992, p. A9.

38. Decisions concerning the targeting of space imagery and space signals intelligence systems are made by the DCI Committee on Imagery Requirements and Exploitation (COMIREX) and the SIGINT Overhead Reconnaissance Subcommittee (SORS) of the DCI SIGINT Committee.

39. After the Iraqi invasion of Kuwait, the United States sharply stepped up its technical collection operations directed at Iraq. One measure of the value of more intense coverage might be how much additional information the United States acquired about Iraqi nuclear programs due to increased technical collection in the period between the Iraqi invasion and the beginning of the air campaign.

40. Steve Coll, "U.S. Halted Nuclear Bid by Iran," *Washington Post*, November 17, 1992, pp. A1, A30.

41. U.S. Congress, Senate Select Committee on Intelligence, *The Intelligence Community's Involvement in the Banca Nazionale Del Lavoro (BNL) Affair* (Washington, D.C.: Government Printing Office, 1993), p. 9.

42. Michael Wines, "U.S. Is Building Up a Picture of Vast Iraqi Atom Program," *New York Times*, September 27, 1991, p. A8.

43. Coll, "U.S. Halted Nuclear Bid by Iran."

44. Leonard S. Spector, *Nuclear Proliferation Today: The Spread of Nuclear Weapons, 1984* (Cambridge, Mass.: Ballinger, 1984), p. 292. Some U.S. government and private analysts are skeptical that South Africa had enough fissionable material for a bomb in 1977. Of course, given reports of close Israeli-South African links, it is possible that such a test was planned in 1977 with Israeli help. And the South Africans confirmed, in 1993, that two shafts had been dug at the site for a potential nuclear blast. See Smith, "South Africa's Sixteen-Year Secret."

Chapter 14

The IAEA: How Can It Be Strengthened?

David Kay

The context within which the nuclear nonproliferation system—
and it must be remembered that the International Atomic Energy Agency
(IAEA) is only one part of that system—must operate has begun to
shift fundamentally in the last few years. For the sake of logical
rigor, and not because I believe that these observations are necessarily novel, I would like to identify the major events and processes that are affecting the nuclear nonproliferation system.

To begin, however, I would like to emphasize the fact that I
believe the threat of nuclear proliferation today is undiminished
and is, in fact, greater than four years ago when Saddam Hussein
launched his attack on Kuwait. Simply repeating old nostrums
and marginally reinforcing old policies will not meet these challenges. Indeed, to the considerable extent that efforts immediately following the discovery of the Iraqi nuclear weapons program have focused on doing just this, they may undermine the
remaining shreds of viability of the current nuclear nonproliferation system in the eyes of both those states intent on or considering the acquisition of nuclear weapons and those policymakers
most concerned with controlling the further spread of nuclear
weapons.

First, the event that initially signaled the inadequacy of the
existing nuclear nonproliferation system was the discovery that
Iraq had been able to pursue for a decade a broad-fronted, multi-

billion-dollar, clandestine nuclear weapons program.[1] Iraq did this while maintaining its status as a signatory in good standing of the Nonproliferation Treaty (NPT) and a frequent member of the International Atomic Energy Agency (IAEA) Board of Governors. Iraq's program was not detected by IAEA safeguards inspections or, as far as the public record shows, by national intelligence agencies. The extent of the Iraqi program is now, largely, on the public record, so it is unnecessary to detail it here. It is, however, necessary to understand the nature of the threat Iraq posed to the nuclear nonproliferation system.[2] Iraq managed to carry out a broad nuclear weapons program, with three major uranium-enrichment programs, twenty thousand employees in the clandestine program, a worldwide clandestine procurement network, and design, development, and testing of weapons components and delivery systems—all while remaining a member in good standing of the Nonproliferation Treaty and successfully "passing" two IAEA safeguards inspections a year.

Second, a development increasing the prospects of the spread of nuclear weapons is the breakup of the former Soviet Union. Although much has been justifiably made of the dangers posed by the prospect of Soviet nuclear scientists selling their skills to the highest bidder, much less attention has been paid to the more immediate dangers of nuclear bomb material and associated hardware being smuggled across the porous borders of the collapsing empire. In the case of Iraq, the greatest barrier to nuclear ambitions was not any lack of technical skills; this they readily acquired from the West, either surreptitiously or quite openly from the mass of declassified material now available and from the training and technology that the West was eager to sell. Iraq's greatest difficulty was in obtaining fissile material and some of the associated electronics necessary to ensure that a nuclear explosion takes place.

To gain an appreciation of the size of this problem solely as it relates to special nuclear materials in the inventory of the former Soviet Union and how it is changing, consider the following: it is now estimated that the nuclear weapons inventory of the former Soviet Union consisted of approximately 10,900 strategic warheads and about 22,000 tactical warheads. Its inventories of special nuclear materials, both in warheads and in strategic stockpiles, is now estimated to amount to more than nine hundred tons of weapons-grade plutonium (Pu-239). By way of comparison, and without the use of any esoteric weapons design concepts, it can be calculated that twelve to fourteen kilograms of highly enriched uranium or four to seven kilograms of Pu-239 would be sufficient for a nuclear weapon comparable to the Hiroshima weapon. In a world in which drug smugglers routinely move cocaine around the world in amounts of hundreds of kilograms and marijuana in ton quantities and in which European border controls are being dismantled, the task of illicitly moving small amounts of nuclear materials is not very daunting.

In the last five years in Afghanistan and in East Europe and in even Russia itself, Soviet and now Commonwealth of Independent States (CIS) troops have been quite willing to sell an extraordinary range of military equipment. The economic chaos that engulfs the former Soviet Union should give pause to Western policymakers as to what is now or may in the future be offered by poverty-struck employees, many of whom are not the high-ranking researchers that current Western proposals aim to employ. The once trumpeted Soviet national nuclear material safeguards have been revealed to be as hollow as the rest of the facade of Soviet modernity that was shown to the West during the cold war.[3] Both Russia and China are officially offering for sale a range of military and dual-use equipment that, unless soon checked, will make the acquisition of nuclear weapons and effective delivery vehicles a much less daunting and less expensive task than Saddam faced.

Third, although Saddam's nuclear program represented a "gold" medal try for nuclear weapons, an attempt that should have been, but was not, detected, we should be more worried by the world of "bronze" medal attempts that are more likely to be the route taken by other states and that will be even harder to detect.[4] Weapons designs that the United States would not consider putting in its own inventory, even ones that might be considered fundamentally unsafe or with a high probability of not giving the calculated yield, might still be considered quite adequate for a Third World state that could see its purposes achieved by any yield, even a fizzle yield. Saddam sought a large nuclear inventory requiring a considerable amount of special nuclear material and was already considering design evolutions involving fusion boosting. Others may believe that they can achieve their purposes with even a gun-assembly design or an over-large implosion design that might have to be delivered by a 767 instead of by a ballistic missile.

Fourth, although it is easy to believe that having stopped Saddam and having "won the cold war," we are now free of the nuclear threat, Iraq and even more recent developments in North

Korea should warn us that there remain potential and potent motives—both military and symbolic—for states to develop and threaten to use nuclear weapons. If we fail to understand the evolving incentives for proliferation, how can we hope to devise effective barriers to nuclear proliferation? (We have not yet even fully plumbed the calculations that made it seem rational to Saddam to develop such a massive nuclear program in the face of clear evidence that Israel would not hesitate to launch a preemptive attack to stop an even smaller program, or the rationale for Saddam to try to provoke an Israeli attack during the Gulf crisis, which might well have been nuclear if the extent of his nuclear program had been suspected.)

Fifth, we are now able to speak more openly about past nuclear proliferation. It is clear that Israel, India, Pakistan, and South Africa crossed the threshold and that North Korea, Iraq, Argentina, and Brazil had programs moving toward weapons acquisition. We are still inhibited, or just plain uncertain, when it comes to Iran, Libya, Algeria, and others. But enough is known to be certain that the basic "secrets" of classic nuclear weapons design, and the material and technology required, are accessible to a broad range of industrial developing countries and to an even larger range of developed industrialized states.[5]

Export control programs have until now been largely nationally administered and have been more concerned with advancing national trade interests and other foreign policy objectives than with preventing states from acquiring advanced military capabilities. There has been a most uneven pattern of international coordination of these separate national export control regimes and essentially no on-the-ground inspection to ensure that stated end uses turn out to be actual end uses. This "system" clearly did not work in the case of Iraq.

Even the best export control regimes can hope to accomplish only three objectives. First, they can buy time and delay a determined proliferator. Second, they can add to the expense of a clandestine nuclear weapons program. And third, they may increase the probability of early detection of a clandestine weapons program if nations will share the information gained through their individual export control programs. All of these are worthwhile objectives, but none are a panacea for preventing, or even detecting, further nuclear proliferation. The Iraqi program would have proceeded even if more effective export controls had been applied—but it would have cost Saddam more, delayed the program, and most important, raised the probability of timely detection of this program's massive scale.

Sixth, the collective security system that dominated the post-World War II age, a system that was based on overwhelming U.S. military power, much of it forward deployed in Europe and Asia, and that was harnessed to a security posture intolerant of military action across national borders, is now being fundamentally reshaped. It is not clear what the resulting system will look like, how it will be governed, or to what sort of threats it will be sensitive. Unless steps are quickly taken, however, to give concreteness and confidence to a post-cold war collective security system, there is a strong possibility that a number of states, in reviewing their own national defense postures, will at least consider whether nuclear or other weapons of mass destruction have a role to play in a defensive or deterrent posture.[6]

It has been largely forgotten that at an early point in the cold war, before the stability of the mutual deterrence system became apparent, Sweden and Switzerland actively considered the development of nuclear weapons—and in the case of Sweden, it has been publicly acknowledged that this consideration went well beyond the stage of academic policy reviews.[7] We are now entering a period as fraught with mistrust and danger as the early, uncertain days of the cold war. Unless the United States and its allies act quickly and with wisdom, there will be growing concern as to the extent and continuing durability of the international security structure. This is occurring at a time when the required technology to produce nuclear weapons is much less costly and difficult to obtain than in the 1950–80 period. In such circumstances, one should not be surprised if more states revisit the nuclear option, starting with exploring the nonnuclear components of a nuclear explosive device and extending to the acquisition and/or development of effective delivery systems. The control of special nuclear materials can be left to near the end of this process and need not be a necessarily difficult task.

The IAEA and the Nonproliferation System

Any discussion on how IAEA safeguards can be strengthened rests on at least three assumptions:

1.   IAEA safeguards are too weak at present to accomplish their mission. Or, to put it slightly differently, Iraq has made it clear that there is a mission that, if it is to be effectively addressed by the IAEA, will require the strengthening of safeguards.
2.   There is an important task for which a strengthened IAEA would be the most suitable and effective instrument.
3.   Strengthening IAEA safeguards is within the scope of realistic policy options that make the topic worthy of consideration.

These three assumptions are reasonable, although much ink has already been spilled in trying to apply different nuances to each and to defend or attack the proposition that before Iraq, there was no reason to fundamentally question the efficacy of IAEA safeguards.

Iraq demonstrated that the IAEA's previous policy of exclusive concentration on material balance accounting could not effectively address the issues of detecting even a large-scale clandestine program centered physically and managerially within Iraq's declared civilian program. Contrary to assertions now made that "IAEA inspectors were very familiar with its *declared* civilian program,"[8] the IAEA inspectors who visited Iraq's Tuwaitha Nuclear Research Center every six months never looked beyond the narrow confines of the three "material balance areas" where declared nuclear materials were held, never even asked what might be going on in the other seventy-plus buildings on the same site, never attempted to visit any but the three areas where declared nuclear materials were held, never tried to sample the radioactive waste areas, and on and on, in a display of lack of curiosity that we now know emboldened the Iraqis to an extraordinary level of brazenness. If safeguards are to address the possibility of detection of clandestine programs that do not depend on a proliferator's diversion of declared nuclear material—a very foolish proliferation strategy—then indeed they need to be strengthened.

The advantages of building on IAEA safeguards are clear. The agency exists; it has a trained core of about two hundred inspectors and four hundred support staff; it has agreed-upon inspection arrangements with more than fifty countries, covering about nine hundred facilities, 35 thousand tons of enriched uranium, and about 370 tons of plutonium; and it is the designated inspection service for the NPT. Even if it was decided that the IAEA should have no role in a strengthened nonproliferation system beyond its narrow pre–Gulf War role of verifying no diversions of declared nuclear material, the IAEA would have to continue, since this is an essential task on which the world's peaceful nuclear programs are built. Economies both of time—it would clearly take a great deal of time to negotiate the creation of a new inspection institution—and of resources call for at least beginning with an attempt to strengthen the IAEA.

Equally clear is the case that a *reinvigorated IAEA* could significantly raise the hurdles that a proliferator would have to jump and increase the probability of detection. From what we now know about the Iraqi program, this must be so, since Saddam and his colleagues, in developing their nuclear weapons program, completely discounted the possibility of detection by existing IAEA safeguards. In these circumstances, even marginal improvements—and a lot more than this is possible—in safeguards would seem a worthwhile investment in giving pause to other proliferators. This is true even if one believes that a substantial effort should now go to strengthening non-IAEA-centered nonproliferation efforts.

Is it a realistic policy option to believe that governments and the international bureaucracy will, in the face of the Iraqi revelations, turn to a genuine effort to increase the effectiveness of safeguards? Although one would be much less sanguine if the question were "Will such an effort succeed in establishing more effective safeguards?," there is no doubt that the attempt is within the envelope of realistic policy options and is one that must be pursued—even if one thinks it will ultimately not fully succeed—along with support for other actions.

Before turning to the priority and realistic areas in which improvements in safeguards can be made, let me, at the considerable risk of repetition, reiterate that the IAEA—either its unimproved version or a new strengthened one—will remain only one element of the required global effort to halt nuclear proliferation. Left to itself and without the required actions, individually and cooperatively, by states, the IAEA will not be able to stop nuclear proliferation. In the period we are now entering, halting the spread of nuclear weapons will demand that national export policies, coordinated export controls of major supplier states, national intelligence resources, regional and international security schemes, and perhaps most of all, diplomatic efforts to remove major sources of insecurity all focus on avoiding further nuclear proliferation. If this is not done, we will no doubt see another conference on the "failure of safeguards and the nonproliferation system" and, even worse, another (or the same) Saddam, who may well obtain nuclear weapons before the world reacts.

Opportunities for Strengthening IAEA Safeguards

Organizational Culture and Management Change

The first priority in any effort to strengthen safeguards must be to begin with a change in the organizational culture and management ethos of the IAEA. Until the discoveries were made in Iraq, the IAEA was optimistic and very self-congratulatory in describing safeguards and was firmly wedded to the belief that ensuring the nondiversion of declared nuclear materials was the be-all and end-all of an effective safeguards program.[9] Even as sympathetic a commentator on the IAEA as Lawrence Scheinman recently wrote:

> Nevertheless, there is a certain sense that the IAEA is perhaps more conservative, more cautious, and less aggressive than it should or needs to be—that it is an inherently conservative institution that cannot easily adapt to a radically changing environment and an upgraded agenda. It cannot be denied that over the past twenty years, the agency has experienced restraints on its right of access, on the intensity and frequency of inspection efforts, and even on the extent to which it could exercise its discretionary judgment in planning, scheduling, and conducting inspections.
>
> The events and circumstances that account for this evolution do not need to be elaborated; only the results need to be noted. Certain patterns of expectation and behavior appear to have set in among IAEA staff. Conservatism and self-constraint became internalized to the extent that the agency occasionally gave more ground in negotiating subsidiary arrangements that regulate the operational side of safeguards than perhaps was necessary. Thus, inspectors were not encouraged to raise questions about activities or structures outside defined strategic points when conducting

routine inspections. Mind-set was based on verification of what was declared by states being inspected as literally specified by legal agreement. Asking too many questions was said to lead to difficulty with the state, and ultimately at headquarters.[10]

That even the events of Iraq have not completely washed away the former "mind-set" and organizational culture is obvious from the way the IAEA has reacted to a growing volume of allegations about undisclosed nuclear activities in Iran. In early February 1992, a group of four senior IAEA staff members, headed by Jon Jennekens, the deputy director general for safeguards, but also including the director general's own special assistant who handles safeguards matters, spent less than a week in Iran visiting various facilities. This was an opportunity to demonstrate that the agency had learned the following lessons from its Iraq trauma:

1. To look beyond the narrow confines of safeguards data
2. To seek out and use information from the press and intelligence sources
3. To be sensitive to the many opportunities that a skillful proliferator has for engaging in deception activities
4. To indicate that it understood that safeguarding only declared facilities was inadequate
5. Above all, to be careful about drawing sweeping conclusions of innocence from quick, superficial visits

And yet here is how Jennekens, on behalf of the team, described the results of this mission:

> Well, as you know, as I know from my own experience with the media over many years, almost 30 years in the nuclear field, the media transmits what it sees, what it hears. Sometimes what it hears comes from certain unreliable sources, is incorrect. We have reviewed some of the media coverage of the activities alleged to take place in Iran and we are very pleased to confirm that there doesn't seem to be a shred of evidence of any of these misleading misrepresentations. Everything that we have seen is for the peaceful applications of nuclear energy and ionizing radiation. . . . So I think that it's an important fact of life that when the media is not in a position to confirm the correctness of certain

information that is provided to it, that it is understandable that some of the media coverage may not be correct, and that's why for us it is particularly important that we have this opportunity to transmit to you the results of our six days in Iran, and we are very happy to do that.

Our task is not to go and bang on doors of anyone who might not be friendly towards Iran. Our task is to report to our Director General on the results of our visit, our findings, our conclusions, and our recommendations, and our Director General, in turn, will, I'm quite confident, report to the Agency's Board of Governors—the 35 Member State Board of Governors, which is like the Board of Directors. His report then to the Board hopefully will provide the kind of convincing information that will enable all Member States of the Agency to come to the conclusion that the peaceful uses of nuclear energy and ionizing radiation, and thereby, hopefully, the sensitive part of your question will be addressed in a more positive sense.

As to the possibility of the non-peaceful use of Bushehr, we are very confident that the existing safeguards systems of the Agency is fully adequate to provide convincing evidence on a continuing basis that declared facilities are being used only for the stated purpose. So by making that statement as firmly as we can—that two part statement—we hope that we will be able to convey the conclusion to the Member States of the Agency that the Bushehr plant should in fact proceed.

We came having already indicated to your Government through your Government's mission in Vienna the various places that we wanted to see. We saw all of them. There was absolutely no restriction, no limitations on access.[11]

The content of this press conference is evidence enough of the enduring power of a safeguards culture that seems to have survived, unchanged, the debacle of Iraq. As if to add insult to injury, it later was reported that one of the places the IAEA team had visited with "no restriction, no limitations on access" was, in fact, a place completely different from the place to which they had asked to be taken. This really should not have been a surprise, since it was a stratagem that Iraq frequently sought to employ during the post-Gulf War UN inspections but without success. The teams in Iraq, conducting inspections under UN

Security Council Resolution 687, have always insisted on carrying the small handheld Global Positioning Satellite (GPS) instruments that give one's location with an accuracy of ten meters or less. But the prevailing IAEA safeguards culture had criticized this practice as indicating "a lack of trust" in the country being inspected. This culture still seems to prevail over experience.

Unless there is strong leadership from within the IAEA Secretariat—specifically the director general and the head of the Safeguards Department—and from the IAEA Board of Governors, the prevailing cultural ethos of safeguards will not change. For twenty-five years this culture has been dominated by a drive to achieve greater accuracy in accounting for declared nuclear material rather than by a desire to understand the totality of a nation's nuclear activities and to determine whether any of these are directed toward nonpeaceful ends. I do not underestimate the difficulty of changing the culture of safeguards, particularly since changing will require that the agency's management stake out positions that may not have the general support of its Board of Governors. This is a board, for example, whose members throughout the 1980s have included states such as India, Pakistan, China, Argentina, Brazil, Iraq, Iran, Libya, and Syria, and it is the same board that elected Libya and Syria to its membership in September 1992.

The difficulty in bringing about a change in organizational culture is that it cannot be achieved simply by proclaiming a new culture or a few speeches from the top—if it were that easy, the United States would now have a world-class automotive industry. Over the last eighteen months, Hans Blix, the IAEA's director general, has made a number of presentations on the need for a new focus for safeguards activities. These presentations have outlined what he sees as the new resources and support that must be given by states to the IAEA if safeguards are to become more effective, and they have detailed the new tasks—controlling the nuclear weapons material that is becoming available from the breakup of the former Soviet Union—that he believes safeguards can carry out.[12] Most of these presentations, however, are singularly devoid of any mention of changes that the Safeguards Secretariat can, and must, make on its own to justify being given additional resources or responsibilities. The result is a refrain that seems to indicate that the situations in Iraq, Iran, and North Korea are primarily the result of the failure of states to provide the resources and support necessary for the IAEA to be the type of inspectorate that it has always wanted to be. The record does not support this, and more important, this refrain does not communicate that a change within the agency is necessary or that, unless such changes take place, the agency will have a reduced role in controlling proliferation and that more challenging tasks will not be offered to it.

The director general and the senior management of the Safeguards Department must communicate by word and deed, internally more often than in outside speeches, that the old pattern of compromise—in the interest of not offending or challenging an inspected state, of not asking too many questions beyond the narrow nuclear material accountancy brief, and of not actively seeking out from all sources any information that would make inspections more effective—will no longer be tolerated. It would also help if when the "old" habits appear to become dominant (as they did in the Tehran press conference or even more recently in announcements concerning the "zeroing of the Iraqi program because the Iraqis told them so"), heads were made to roll (rather than simply sending out press releases "clarifying" the statements), making it clear both *internally* and *externally* that such attitudes will no longer be rewarded.[13]

Although the required change in the safeguards culture must originate and be driven from within the Secretariat, starting at the top, there is a strong supporting role that can—and should— be played in this process by the member states, particularly the United States. In the last twelve years, the United States has generally seen its role in the agency's safeguards program as one of speaking quietly behind the scenes and in private to the director general while funding a greater emphasis on technical rigor for materials balance accounting. One will look long and hard through the records of the board's deliberations, the records of the SACSI (the Standing Advisory Committee on Safeguards Implementation), or the records of the various groups of "wise men" that have been periodically assembled to assess safeguards, without finding any strong U.S. opposition to what is now, even by the agency's most fervent supporters, called the overly "mechanically quantitative" orientation of safeguards. Indeed, the British, Swedish, and Japanese governors, not those of the United States, have been in the vanguard in the board and in informal efforts outside the board in seeking to sharpen safeguards. This must change. Without an adjustment in the organizational culture of safeguards away from this mechanically quantitative approach, the IAEA's future role in halting nuclear proliferation will be sharply diminished. Without greatly intensified U.S. leadership, there is unlikely to be a culture adjustment, as opposed to simply an adjustment in rhetoric.

SAFEGUARDS PROCEDURES AND APPROACHES

Safeguards have up until now focused on accounting for declared nuclear materials on the assumption that if any clandestine activities were to be undertaken, they would most likely begin with diversions from declared nuclear materials.[14] The implicit further assumption, although not one that the IAEA often mentioned before Iraq, was that any large clandestine effort or one that did not rely on a diversion of declared materials would be detected by national intelligence efforts. The lack of clarity on this assumption led, in the case of Iraq (and there have been other cases as well), to Iraq's using the fact that it "passed" IAEA safeguards inspections to "prove" that it had a "clean" peaceful program.

In the days before the Gulf War, the IAEA, in confirming that the material under safeguards had not been diverted, often got hung up in seeming to validate that the Iraqi program was peaceful. The IAEA failed to communicate clearly the more limited assertion that the material it was charged to look at was in fact still there but that it could not speak authoritatively about anything else in the country. This directly contributed to the troubling first postwar inspection under UN Security Council Resolution 687, where agency inspectors seemed to concentrate on declared materials and were criticized for being too timid. Speaking of this carryover of old attitudes, Lawrence Scheinman wrote, for example, "It was not surprising thus to hear concerns about how vigorously agency personnel might prosecute the mandate under security council RES/687 in Iraq, or reports that they were too circumspect on the first mission."[15]

IAEA safeguards now must come to terms with an expectation that they will be able to usefully contribute to the effort to detect clandestine nuclear programs or at least raise the hurdles over which an aspiring proliferator would have to jump.[16] There is no shortage of good suggestions as to how this might be done.

More targeted inspection effort.   Currently 55 percent of the IAEA inspection budget goes to just three countries: Germany, Japan, and Canada. This is because the amount of inspection effort is determined solely by the amount of declared nuclear material and the type of nuclear activities under way in a country. There is little role left for managerial judgment as to where the dangers of proliferation and clandestine programs might be greatest.[17]

Indeed, the mechanistic criteria that are applied work perversely to make it easier for a state like Iraq to lower the level of inspection effort to which it is subjected. Based on the aggregate amount of nuclear material in prewar Iraq, it should have received monthly instead of semiannual inspections. However, Iraq was allowed to "divide" this material into three material balance areas—all within the same facility and only meters apart—which then resulted in a calculated required inspection rate of one inspection a year. Iraq then agreed to accept two inspections a year to demonstrate their "openness." When a safeguards official was asked why Iraq was allowed to use such an artificial division to reduce the frequency of inspection, he replied: "That is what we allow the Germans and Canadians to do and therefore we must do it for Iraq. And, if we denied this right to Canada and Germany, the increased frequency of inspections would break the safeguards budget."[18] The fact that in the 1980s, Canada and Germany seemed not to be leading proliferation suspects, whereas considerable doubts were expressed in open literature and by governments about Iraq, seems to be a "soft" factor that could not be taken into account.

There are no shortages of suggestions as to how various weighting factors could be used to better direct safeguards efforts. The most comprehensive proposal is that by David Fischer, a former IAEA official.[19] Fischer would use openness bonuses to award those states that give greater freedom to the IAEA to conduct inspections in any manner the agency sees fit. Such bonuses would be used to reduce the inspection effort in "open" states and increase it in "closed" states. I think that a sounder basis would be to gear the inspection effort to regional levels of tension or growth of military forces, particularly the acquisition of launch vehicles, such as Scuds and nuclear-capable aircraft, and imports of key dual-use items.

Use of equipment and methods more likely to detect undeclared programs. The current safeguards practice severely limits the equipment that an inspector may bring to a site, and inspectors have been discouraged by the agency from taking samples and measurements at locations other than the strategic points set out in the individual facility attachments.[20] This has meant, for example, that inspectors have not tried to take samples even from their own clothing and equipment once they leave a facility. There is an irony in this—one of the tip-offs to the Iraq clandestine program came from sampling clothing of several of the hostages, "guests of the state" in Saddamspeak, held by Saddam at the Tuwaitha Nuclear Research Center in the days before the Gulf War began. These hostages traveled much the same route covered by inspectors, and the data could have been available to the IAEA years earlier with the use of the right methods. Inspections need not necessarily become more confrontational, but they clearly need to become more focused on trying to address issues larger than the balance of declared material.

Special inspections.   This has probably been the most widely discussed and misunderstood suggested improvement in safeguards procedures. Its roots are quite simple. The post–Gulf War inspections carried out under the Security Council mandate were widely viewed as successful—and there is no dispute that with their greater freedom of movement and methods, these inspectors found out in short order much more about the Iraqi nuclear program than either the IAEA or national intelligence efforts had before the war. It seemed to many that a panacea for the ills of safeguards might be to enshrine the inspection rights under UN Security Council Resolution 687 as more generally available inspection rights for the IAEA. It quickly became clear, however, that very few states would be willing to grant a general right to the IAEA to act in unspecified other states the way the Security Council had mandated was acceptable in the special case of Iraq.

This had led to the consideration of whether the broad, but previously unexercised, rights of the IAEA under basic NPT safeguards agreements could not be used to carry out inspections beyond the routine inspections directed toward known declared activities. The Secretariat, after examining this issue, concluded that all along this right had indeed existed, and the Board of Governors in February 1992 agreed with this finding. It is not certain yet whether this is more than a symbolic victory, since no such inspections have been carried out. In the abstract, lacking even one such inspection, it is impossible to know what rights such an inspection will assert—go anywhere, with anything, and at a time of the inspectors' choosing, or something considerably less sweeping—or how effective such inspections might be.

There is much more leverage to be gained in making routine inspections "special"—that is, endowed with more freedom of choice of methods and with greater curiosity—than there is in hoping that a few lucky special inspections will nail the proliferator. In the case of Iraq, inspections have been frequent and with no certain end in sight; that has been the unheralded key to their success. Unsuccessful inspections have quickly been followed by others, and it is the relentlessness that has been crucial. Given the politics of the IAEA and the Board of Governors, it is difficult, for example, to imagine that the director general would have authorized seven successive special inspections to Iran in three months if the first three had found nothing. Far better to ask how you can make the routine IAEA safeguards inspections have more of the characteristics that made the UN inspections in Iraq special.

Greater information on nuclear activities within countries and nuclear-relevant exports between countries. Over the years, the agency allowed the practice to develop of requiring that design information on new facilities capable of using or producing nuclear materials be supplied only 180 days before such facilities were to receive nuclear materials. This is a classic case of the IAEA's tying its own hands, since the statutory basis for requiring design information states in Information Circular 153 that design information be provided "as early as possible before nuclear material is introduced into a new facility." After Iraq, the Secretariat decided that this particular barn door should be bolted and came forth with a proposal, now endorsed by the Board of Governors, that "as early as possible" should be understood to mean that such information be provided to the agency at the time of the decision to construct, or to authorize construction of, or to modify any nuclear facility.

If this change is to have any real bite, it will have to be vigorously enforced. The old 180-day rule was, in more than one case, openly flouted. It will be necessary also for the Secretariat to exercise its right to verify such design information through inspection during the course of construction—a right that has not previously been vigorously exerted. Such inspections should also draw on technical experts from outside of the Secretariat, particularly experts from the nuclear weapons states.

After it became clear how large a role foreign imports played in allowing the Iraqi program to reach the scale it did, the IAEA sought to push legal conventions that would provide for mandatory universal reporting of the production and export of a comprehensive range of nuclear materials, sensitive equipment, and nonnuclear materials. The proposals reeked more of legalisms than of practical nonproliferation efforts and met with almost uniformly negative reactions from the Board of Governors. Some states were concerned that the costs of collecting, reporting, inspecting, and analyzing such a mass of materials would be disproportionately high and might give a false sense of security; others feared that this process would undercut the already valuable, and more practical, efforts by the Zangger Committee and the Nuclear Suppliers Group to improve coordination; and some states feared that such reporting would be used as an excuse to restrict valuable exports.

National export controls need to be improved and better coordinated, and the IAEA needs to be made aware of such information as it relates to proliferation concerns in specific countries and regions. About this there can be no doubt. There is, however, considerable doubt about whether the way to achieve this is through a formal international legal convention. The IAEA, in many areas of its activities, not just safeguards, has in the last few years developed a preference for binding international legal conventions as opposed to seeking less formal—and usually quicker and more effective—means of getting action under way. In the fight to prevent the further proliferation of weapons of mass destruction, and particularly in the complex and sensitive area of exports, international legalistic prescriptions are less likely to be effective than is a shared commitment to making national export mechanisms more effective, to cooperating, and to informally sharing sensitive information.

RESOURCES AND INFORMATION AVAILABLE FOR SAFEGUARDS

The IAEA, like the UN system as a whole, has labored under more than nine years of imposed "zero growth," as member states have insisted that more be done without increasing resources. In the last two years, even "zero" has taken on new meaning as the former Soviet Union has not met its almost 12 percent assessment. The agency's regular budget for 1992 is approximately $207 million, of which safeguards account for about

$65 million. However, the budget crunch caused by CIS nonpayment has forced a uniform 12 percent reduction of all programs, including safeguarding.

Although some efficiency gains, beyond those already achieved, can certainly be made—for example, reducing the 55 percent of the safeguards budget that is spent on safeguarding activities in Canada, Germany, and Japan and increasing the fifty days of inspection effort that is the goal for each inspector—there is no doubt that the program needs more resources. Safeguards analytical capabilities, based at the Seibersdorf Laboratory outside Vienna, urgently need to be upgraded if the agency is to have any hope of playing a significant role in detecting clandestine efforts. Just as the frequency of inspections should not be determined by ritualistic resort to standards of "equity" that ignore the objective of halting proliferation, the number surely should not be limited by budget concerns. Commercially available satellite imagery—from the French Spot, U.S. Landsat, and Russian systems—now offer a potentially useful adjunct to classic safeguards methods. Their use can be pursued without any access to intelligence data. All that is needed is the money to buy the imagery and to hire the skilled analysts to interpret it.

In the immediate aftermath of the Iraqi discoveries, there was an upsurge of enthusiasm for making national intelligence data available to the IAEA so that it could improve its inspections. The director general was quoted as being in favor of setting up an intelligence unit in his own office, although this was soon changed to the more acceptable formulation of an "information" unit.[21] For a variety of reasons, this proposal is unlikely to lead to a substantial long-term increase in the flow of high-grade national intelligence information to the IAEA. National intelligence communities will continue to be reluctant to provide, on a continuing basis, information to an international bureaucracy that does not even perform background checks on its own staff before or after hiring, has no real communications security, does not have document storage that measures up to national secure storage standards, and lacks any counterintelligence culture or capability. For its part, the agency's insistence that it must evaluate national intelligence information before it can act implies that it has the skills and capabilities to do so. It does not—and is unlikely to be able to—hire such capabilities.

It is clear that the agency must have better information if it is to be able to conduct more effective inspections. Indeed, this requirement for better information is not unique to the IAEA. It lies at the heart of the effort to improve UN efforts to meet the proliferation of all types of weapons of mass destruction and to meet crises such as those in Bosnia, Somalia, and Cambodia at an early enough stage so that peacekeeping can work. The UN itself will, in my view, be no more successful than the IAEA in institutionalizing direct access to national intelligence data.

On the other hand, the UN Charter does provide an institutional mechanism that holds considerable promise for harnessing national intelligence efforts to international objectives. This is the Military Staff Committee established by Article 47. This body, which was rendered moribund by the cold war, is composed of representatives of all five permanent members of the Security Council and can be supplemented by other countries if needed; it can also create subsidiary bodies. Now is the appropriate time to consider creating, under the Military Staff Committee, a Joint Intelligence Staff (JIS), which would be the focal point for screening, analyzing, and reporting to the appropriate UN bodies those developments that might lead to threats to international peace and security. The JIS would be the body responsible for protecting the sources and methods involved in collecting the information and for providing the Security Council and the IAEA with the necessary interpretative skills for understanding the data. In the case of information relating to nuclear proliferation, such a Joint Intelligence Staff could relay the information to the IAEA after having screened the information for its relevance and quality.

Necessary Actions outside of the IAEA

As has been emphasized several times above, the IAEA is only one part of the nuclear nonproliferation system, important but not sufficient in itself to meet the threat of greater nuclear proliferation. There are other actions that must be taken and that, if done well, will themselves strengthen the contribution that the IAEA can make.

Security Council action to make it clear to all that from now on any further efforts by states to acquire nuclear weapons will be viewed as a threat to international peace and security within the meaning of Chapter 7 of the UN Charter. The UN Security Council, on January 31, 1992, recognized in a nonbinding statement that the proliferation of weapons of mass destruction "constitutes a threat to international peace and security," and it committed the council to take action to halt such proliferation.[22] This was an important first step in recognizing that the further spread of nuclear weapons and other weapons of mass destruction represents an intolerable threat that demands an international response. The next step, and one that should be taken now, is to translate this statement into a binding Security Council resolution to put all states on notice that in the future, any attempt to embark on the acquisition of nuclear, chemical, and biological weapons and long-range ballistic missiles will face the certainty of Security Council action.[23] One positive benefit of such a move would be to abolish the benefit that states now derive from not signing the NPT or the advantage that some think they may gain from blocking the extension of the NPT when it is reviewed in 1995.

Unlimited extension of the Nonproliferation Treaty.   The NPT comes up for review and decision on its extension in 1995. It is imperative that the treaty be extended without any limitation as to its term. Rather than something to be feared, governments should approach the 1995 review conference as an opportunity to reaffirm the international community's commitment to the objective of halting the spread of nuclear weapons and to explicitly affirm that the IAEA is mandated to ensure, by all appropriate means, the observance of this principle.

The establishment of a comprehensive nuclear test-ban treaty.   States seeking to develop a clandestine nuclear weapon will not be hindered significantly by a comprehensive test-ban treaty. "Bronze" medal nuclear weapons designs of several types are already in the public domain, and computer simulation codes are now sufficiently accurate and available that early design solutions can be simulated with confidence as to workability, if not to exact yield. It is also sometimes forgotten that none of the known nuclear states ever had a failure on their first tests. It is now apparent that some nuclear states have, either clandestinely or through the failure of their own security systems, allowed design and test data to become available to others. On the other hand, a test ban would be politically significant as a signal that the nuclear weapons states—and this would include even the nondeclared nuclear states—are prepared to accept limitations on their own arsenals. When coupled with the deep cuts now under way in the nuclear forces of the United States and the former Soviet Union, a test ban should provide the necessary trade-off to ensure the support needed to strengthen the NPT and the IAEA.

Positive and negative security assurances.   We are now entering a period when the weak and largely implicit negative security assurances that accompanied the approval of the NPT need to be strengthened and stronger positive assurances need to be considered.[24] The cold war security system is changing in ways that make it difficult for a number of states to accurately assess the risks they will face in the future. Dependable security assurances that would give states reasons to believe that nuclear weapons—and ideally other weapons of mass destruction as well—are one threat that they will not face would enhance international security in this uncertain period. Such assurances are not easy to construct, particularly if they are to be believable. They represent, however, an important issue on the diplomatic agenda of the post-cold war world and one whose achievement will strengthen efforts to address security concerns in the Middle East and South Asia.

The task of establishing an effective nuclear nonproliferation regime must be at the forefront of today's diplomatic agenda. Iraq was a failure of vision, priorities, policy, and execution, the consequence of which was nearly calamitous for the Middle East and perhaps the world. Those leaders who in August 1990 recognized the necessity of meeting the challenge presented by Saddam's invasion of Kuwait and mobilized an international coalition to stand firm and repel this aggression deserve appreciation and respect. But the nature of weapons of mass destruction, particularly nuclear weapons, means that such a second chance to correct a failed policy is not guaranteed. If we are not to depend on just the hope that such failures can always be corrected, then we must urgently turn to the task of ensuring that there is an effective nuclear nonproliferation regime. This task will have many fronts: our national intelligence efforts must be better focused and better directed; our leaders must ensure that the prevention of the further spread of nuclear weapons is recognized as the threat that it is and not routinely subordinated to short-term trade and policy objectives; defense and security postures must be directed toward the twin goals of fighting proliferation and offering security to those countries that choose not to seek weapons of mass destruction; and the IAEA must be effectively directed toward and supported in efforts to ensure that the clandestine proliferator does not receive the same free ride that Saddam enjoyed.

Notes

1. "The revelation in the aftermath of the Gulf War of an extensive and previously unknown Iraqi nuclear weapons program has raised difficult questions about the efficacy of the nonproliferation regime and its supporting international safeguards system. What happened in the case of Iraq was a systemic failure of that regime. National intelligence failed to detect ongoing clandestine activity. National export control policies fell short of closing down the possible export of components that could contribute to a nuclear weapons program. Finally, the International Atomic Energy Agency (IAEA) safeguards system was not only focused and implemented in such a way as to reduce the likelihood of detecting a range of unauthorized activities, but also lacked some of the capabilities necessary to deal with clandestine activity. . . . Today the central concerns for IAEA safeguards are how loss of international confidence in them as a result of the Iraqi situation can be restored, and how their effectiveness and credibility can be strengthened." (Rozanne L. Ridgway, foreword to "Assuring the Nuclear Non-Proliferation Safeguards System," by Lawrence Scheinman, Occasional Paper, Atlantic Council, p. i. Scheinman's paper takes the view that the NPT system *pre-Iraq* was never meant to detect unauthorized or clandestine activities and that everyone should have known that IAEA "safeguards traditionally were intended to—and do—assure that declared safeguarded material is not being diverted.")

2. See, for example, Jay C. Davis and David A. Kay, "Iraq's Secret Nuclear Weapons Program," *Physics Today*, July 1992, pp. 21–27; "Testimony by Robert Gates, Director of Central Intelligence," Hearings before the House Armed Services Committee, Defense Policy Panel, U.S. House of Representatives, 102d Cong., 2d sess., March 27, 1992.

3. "Nuclear materials physical protection and accounting in the Commonwealth of Independent States (CIS) remain inadequate to prevent smuggling of nuclear materials out of the countries of the Commonwealth, a German government report has concluded." (Mark Hibbs, "Bonn Agencies Say Safeguards, Protection Nearly Absent in CIS," *Nucleonics Week* 33, no. 34 [August 20, 1992]: 1–10.)

4. This very useful distinction has been used by Peter Zimmerman, senior fellow for arms control at the Center for Strategic and International Studies, Washington, D.C., to distinguish between "gold-medal" military technologies, represented by the latest in designs and hardware in the inventory of the United States and other first-rank military powers, and "bronze-medal" technologies, represented by designs and hardware no longer—if

ever—considered adequate for first-rank military powers. A classic bronze-medal technology is Scuds, which differ only marginally from German V-2s used in World War II. These so-called bronze-medal technologies are, as Zimmerman points out, more than adequate for many quite credible military uses by Third World countries—the more so when mated with nuclear, biological, or chemical warheads.

5. If you doubt how much is in the public domain, just read Tom Clancy, *The Sum of All Fears* (New York: Putnam and Sons, 1991). In the afterword to this technically interesting novel, writing about the task facing a proliferator today, Clancy noted: "I was first bemused, then stunned, as my research revealed just how easy such a project might be today. It is generally known that nuclear secrets are not as secure as we would like—in fact the situation is worse than even well-informed people appreciate. What required billions of dollars in the 1940s is much less expensive today. A modern personal computer has far more power and reliability than the first Eniac, and the 'hydrocodes' which enable a computer to test and validate a weapon's design are easily duplicated. The exquisite machine tools used to fabricate parts can be had for the asking. When I asked explicitly for specifications for the very machines used at Oak Ridge and elsewhere, they arrived Federal Express the next day. Some highly-specialized items designed specifically for bomb manufacture may now be found in stereo speakers" (pp. 1029–30).

6. See Rolf Ekeus, "The Iraqi Experience and the Future of Nuclear Nonproliferation," *Washington Quarterly*, Autumn 1992. "Even if no one laments the passing of the Cold War, the global security structures in place during it tended to help contain the spread of nuclear weapons. The character of the security structures now emerging tends to be more regional than global. This process contains a potential for proliferation even if 'only' on a regional scale. The Iraqi example and some of its repercussions send a warning signal to the international community. It can be argued that, in the absence of concerted international countermeasures, the spread of nuclear weapons will become a fact in a not too distant future" (pp. 68–69). "The emerging international security structures imply a risk of nuclear weapons proliferation that is both permanent and considerable. There can be no guarantee that Iraq's nuclear ambitions are an isolated phenomenon" (p. 73).

7. See Mitchell Reiss, *Without the Bomb: The Politics of Nuclear Nonproliferation* (New York: Columbia University Press, 1988), pp. 37–77.

8. Hans Blix, "Verification of Nuclear Nonproliferation: The Lesson of Iraq," *Washington Quarterly*, Autumn 1992, p. 57.

9. See, for example, Jon Jennekens, "IAEA Safeguards: A Look at 1970–1990 and Future Prospects," *IAEA Bulletin*, 1/1990, p. 10. "Thus, the future prospects for IAEA safeguards are quite bright, albeit with a not unexpected degree of uncertainty. The continuing importance of IAEA safeguards as a bulwark of the nuclear nonproliferation efforts of the world community is beyond question. States which have undertaken comprehensive safeguards obligations firmly believe that IAEA safeguards provide the only broadly international and therefore credible means of verifying the peaceful nature of their nuclear activities. . . . The two decades of the 1970s and 1980s have provided striking evidence of the near universal belief in the value of IAEA safeguards. Hopefully, the decade of the 1990s will see the joining together

of all States in a truly universal undertaking of a system of verifying the non-diversion of nuclear materials to non-peaceful purposes. Or, stated in a more positive way, a system of verification which will provide the necessary confirmation of the solely peaceful use of nuclear materials."

10. Scheinman, "Assuring the Nuclear Non-Proliferation Safeguards System," pp. 26–27.

11. IAEA-supplied transcription of English portion of tapes made during the press conference held on February 12, 1992, Tehran, by Jon Jennekens, deputy director general for safeguards.

12. Blix, "Verification of Nuclear Nonproliferation."

13. "It is clearly important that management throughout the IAEA safeguards department accept and promulgate these beliefs so that the values of and commitments to the system can be fully realized. Many IAEA safeguards professionals are willing and anxious to take on the more challenging tasks that have resulted from basic political change. They share the views about not being mechanically quantitative, and they place value and importance on qualitative approaches to enhance the overall effectiveness of safeguards. It would be imprudent to make the predictive statement that, 'Of course everybody will fall in line.' With commitment and determination at the top, however, there is no reason why this should not be the case and, where it is not, that those unwilling to follow the precepts of leadership be replaced. On the other hand, it should be emphasized that in the absence of cultural adjustment by the inspectorate and the agency as a whole to the political environment in which safeguards will operate in the future, the IAEA could have a much curtailed role in nonproliferation." (Scheinman, "Assuring the Nuclear Non-Proliferation Safeguards System," p. 29.)

14. Myron Kratzer, "How Can International Non-Proliferation Safeguards Be Made More Relevant?" (draft prepared for the Atlantic Council, August 27, 1991). "International safeguards now in use were designed to verify the peaceful use of nuclear material in declared nuclear facilities and activities. Clandestine activities are outside the present scope of 'classical' safeguards" (p. 1).

15. Scheinman, "Assuring the Nuclear Non-Proliferation Safeguards System," p. 27.

16. "Nevertheless, we cannot overlook the fact, as the Iraqi experience exemplifies, that virtually all of the activities generally regarded as 'proliferation threats' have been brought to light not by safeguards but by other means." (Kratzer, "How Can International Non-Proliferation Safeguards Be Made More Relevant?" p. 2.)

17. A secondary, but not unimportant, effect of this overconcentration of inspection efforts on countries in which proliferation concerns are minimal is that it has further reinforced the dominant safeguards culture of lack of curiosity. Why be curious and investigative about countries for which there is no plausible reason to believe that they have any intention of engaging in clandestine nuclear activities? And yet the distribution of inspection effort tells the inspectors that these are the countries with which the IAEA is most concerned.

18. Conversation between the author and a senior safeguards official, April 1991.

19. David Fischer, "Consequences of the Iraq Case for Non-Proliferation Policy," *Arbeirspapiere zur Internationalen Politik*, October 1991, pp. 29–44.

20. "'Subsidiary arrangements' for the purpose of giving states a good-faith indication of how safeguards will normally be implemented are called for by the system. It is important, however, that these arrangements not be allowed to become, as they have tended to, a de facto limitation on the Agency's rights." (Kratzer, "How Can International Non-Proliferation Safeguards Be Made More Relevant?" p. 5.)

21. At the time, I found this newly discovered, and short-lived, enthusiasm of my IAEA colleagues for intelligence data amusing, in light of their earlier reaction to it. "A second vital function performed by the Special Commission has been legitimizing the passage of national intelligence information to an international activity. In the early days of the Iraqi inspections, I often wondered which would stop us first: the fear of national intelligence services that sources and methods would be compromised if valuable intelligence passed into the hands of a group of international inspectors or the fear of my superiors in the IAEA and the UN that their moral purity would be ruined if they allowed the inspectors to have access to intelligence gathered by national intelligence communities. That these mutual barriers have largely been overcome owes much to the tact and intelligence of Rolf Ekeus and his colleagues." (David A. Kay, "Arms Inspections in Iraq: Lessons for Arms Control," *Bulletin of Arms Control* 7 (August 1992): 6.

22. UN Security Council Resolution 536, January 31, 1992.

23. The UN Security Council could set a date by which those states—such as Israel, India, and Pakistan—that are widely assumed to have already acquired nuclear weapons, but are not nuclear weapons states in the terms of the Nonproliferation Treaty, would have to declare that they possess nuclear weapons if they want to avoid coming under the provisions of this declaration.

24. A negative security assurance simply asserts that a nuclear weapons state will not threaten or use nuclear weapons against a state that does not possess nuclear weapons. A positive security assurance would go beyond this to provide guarantees that states would come to the assistance of any state threatened by another state with the use of nuclear weapons.

Conclusion: Nuclear Proliferation after the Cold War

Mitchell Reiss

Careful readers may have detected an ambiguity in the title of this volume, an ambiguity that is purposely repeated in the title of this chapter. In one sense, "Nuclear Proliferation after the Cold War" indicates merely that the time frame for considering this issue should be updated. But in another sense it also suggests that the nature of proliferation after the cold war has somehow changed. That there should be some differences is not surprising. With the disintegration of the Soviet empire and with the U.S. search for a new international role commensurate with its values, history, and resources, the current state of world affairs is characterized by flux and uncertainty. With the transformation of the previous bipolar international system, the problem of nuclear proliferation has altered as well.

The interesting question is, of course, how has the issue changed? Is the spread of nuclear weapons more likely than before? Has preventing nuclear proliferation become less difficult in a post-cold war environment? Essentially, is the situation better or worse than in the past?

Finding satisfactory answers to these questions requires addressing two related sets of additional questions. The first set concerns incentives. What factors motivated countries to acquire nuclear weapons during the past forty-five years? Are these motivations still present today? Are they stronger or weaker than before? Are there any new incentives that favor proliferation in the post–cold war world? And how much influence does each exert?

The second set of questions deals with the other side of the ledger. What disincentives persuaded countries not to acquire nuclear weapons during the cold war? Are these disincentives present today? Do they possess greater or lesser vitality than before? Are there any new factors concerning nuclear weapons development in the post-cold war world that were not present earlier? And how much influence does each exert?

This matrix of incentives and disincentives, both during and after the cold war, provides a helpful analytical framework for evaluating the prospects for nuclear proliferation during the 1990s. This model is set out in figure 15.1.

Incentives during the Cold War

Traditionally, four general factors have motivated countries to seek nuclear weapons. All these factors were present in countries' decisions to acquire nuclear arms, although some motivations were more influential than others.

Security is a primary reason countries have acquired nuclear weapons and is most responsible for the original decisions by the United States and the Soviet Union to build nuclear weapons. Many countries, even including some that chose to remain non-nuclear, perceived that nuclear weapons enhanced a country's security by deterring aggressive behavior and actions.

Some countries have also sought status through nuclear weapons development. Nuclear arms have traditionally been thought to symbolize modernity and prestige. A nuclear stockpile has been seen as the ultimate political symbol, all the more potent because of its rarity.

The other two motivations are more difficult to isolate, but there is little doubt that they exist. A third motivation has been termed "technological determinism," which can be described as the momentum that becomes an inexorable force in confronting, and conquering, technological obstacles. The colloquial expression "If something can be done, it will be done" neatly summarizes this motivation.

The fourth factor derives from certain scientific or bureaucratic elites' single-minded determination to acquire nuclear weapons.

FIGURE 15.1

	Cold War	Post–Cold War
Incentives		
Disincentives		

This motivation has received very little attention, although it may be more responsible for proliferation than commonly realized.[1] India was one example of this highly personalized preference for nuclear arms. Homi Bhabha toiled for two decades, until his untimely death, to preserve India's nuclear weapons option. Similarly, in the United States, Edward Teller zealously advocated development of the "super" (hydrogen) bomb during the early 1950s, contrary to the recommendation of J. Robert Oppenheimer and the government's General Advisory Committee of the Atomic Energy Commission.

Incentives in the 1990s

All the motivations for acquiring nuclear weapons during the cold war are present in the post-cold war world, although some have become stronger and others weaker than before.

Multipolarity, the diffusion of power and technology, and the deterioration of the cold war security architecture have fostered greater national insecurity than before among many countries. NATO's uncertain future, the termination of the Warsaw Pact, the cutoff of American military and economic assistance to Pakistan, and Russia's refusal to ensure India's security are only some of the disruptive changes in alliances and bilateral relationships in the past few years. More generally, the Clinton administration's emphasis on domestic affairs, the inability of the UN to substitute for a strong U.S. internationalist role, and an increasingly imperialist strain in Russia's foreign policy may force many countries to rethink their security requirements.[2] Although it is unlikely that any country will soon acquire nuclear weapons, many may hedge their bets. Their unease may manifest itself in behavior that at best questions and at worst undermines the international nonproliferation regime. Specific actions may include treaty members' rejection of the indefinite extension of the Nonproliferation Treaty (NPT) in 1995 in favor of a fixed-term extension period, countries' redoubling of their efforts to obtain security assurances and guarantees from the five acknowledged nuclear weapons states, or countries' attempts to alleviate the sources of their insecurity through appeasement.

With the end of the cold war, the question of whether nuclear weapons necessarily enhance a country's security has come under greater scrutiny. The main impetus for this reevaluation was the disintegration of the Soviet Union. Moscow's possession of thirty thousand nuclear weapons proved totally useless in preventing the end of Soviet rule.[3] Similarly, nuclear weapons could not sustain the apartheid system of white rule in South Africa.

It is unclear how, or if, nuclear weapons have improved the security of certain other countries. India's "peaceful nuclear explosion" in May 1974, for example, only energized Pakistan, which by the late 1980s had also developed a nuclear weapons capability. For the first time since independence, Pakistan now possessed the ability to place at risk India's viability as a sovereign state. However, Pakistan's nuclear ambitions in turn alienated its most important strategic ally, the United States; in October 1990, Washington terminated all economic and military assistance to Islamabad because of Pakistan's nuclear weapons program. In these instances, it is difficult to see how nuclear weapons increased national security. For the most part, they proved either irrelevant or counterproductive to the country's larger foreign policy objectives.

Is it still possible that these weapons might retain some application on the battlefield? This too seems unlikely, at least for the five declared nuclear weapons states. Would any American president, or any leader, be willing to use nuclear weapons for only the second time in history? How much more unlikely would this be if use was directed against an adversary that had not used nuclear weapons first and perhaps one that did not even possess nuclear weapons?[4] Some sense of Washington's reluctance to use nuclear weapons first was conveyed in Robert Kennedy's memoir on the Cuban Missile Crisis. Kennedy described his opposition to a first use of *conventional* weapons by the United States against Cuba: "I could not accept the idea that the United States would rain bombs on Cuba, killing thousands and thousands of civilians in a surprise attack. . . . America's traditions and history would not permit such a course of action . . . if we were to maintain our moral position at home and around the globe. Our struggle against Communism throughout the world was far more than physical survival—it had as its essence our heritage and our ideals, and these we must not destroy."[5]

Anecdotal evidence from individuals who have participated in war games staged by the Defense Department reinforces this point; even when assigned to play the role of Soviet leaders, participants have been extraordinarily reluctant to be the first to use nuclear weapons. Moreover, the end of the cold war's super-power rivalry has eliminated the one global power that threatened U.S. national interests and offered the most likely scenario for using nuclear weapons.

Despite the nonexistent or negligible political and military utility of nuclear weapons in contemporary international relations, they have traditionally been perceived to confer a certain degree of prestige. This too appears to have changed somewhat in the post-cold war environment. The acquisition of nuclear weapons was once seen as the sine qua non for modernity, evidence of superior engineering and scientific expertise. Nuclear technology actually dates from the 1930s and 1940s and is best viewed as similar to the use of keypunch cards to program the first generation of computing machines. Today, a country that constructs nuclear weapons is performing a proven and not-too-complicated technological feat; Iraq demonstrated that even a preindustrial society can master this technology. To place nuclear weapons acquisition in proper historical perspective, how much prestige would a country reap today from the successful assembly of a rotary-dial telephone? The measure of political power and prestige in the twenty-first century promises to be grounded in economic prosperity, financial acumen, and critical technologies, such as high-performance computing, materials science development, and superconductivity applications, rather than in the ability to manufacture a nuclear explosive.

Recent arms reduction agreements by the United States and the Soviet Union (and now Russia) have further reduced the status associated with nuclear weapons and undoubtedly strengthened the perception that nuclear arsenals are expensive and elaborate anachronisms. The 1987 Intermediate-range Nuclear Forces (INF) Treaty eliminated an entire category of ballistic missiles, and in the START I and II agreements, the United States and Russia pledged to reduce their nuclear stockpiles by two-thirds, to 3,000–3,500 weapons each, including the elimination of all land-based multiple, independently targetable reentry vehicles (MIRVs).

Further, in September 1991, President George Bush announced that Washington's ground-based tactical nuclear weapons would be dismantled, that such weapons would no longer be deployed overseas or on naval vessels, and that air-delivered tactical nuclear weapons would be reduced by 50 percent. The next month, President Mikhail Gorbachev announced similar reductions in the Soviet Union's tactical nuclear arsenal; all remaining tactical nuclear weapons were consolidated in Russia by May 1992. Britain declared that its policy would follow that of the United States, and France stated that it would reduce its tactical missile modernization program. The United States decided in July 1992 to freeze the production of fissile material for weapons purposes.

To be sure, the nuclear weapons states disagree on the role and legitimacy of nuclear weapons in the post-cold war world. Yet Washington, Moscow, London, and Paris collectively took a positive step with their unilateral declarations of a moratorium on nuclear weapons tests. The Clinton administration favors a comprehensive test ban and is negotiating such a treaty in the Conference on Disarmament in Geneva. All these measures have helped turn the flank of a cold war mentality that persistently exalted the importance of nuclear arms for over four decades.

Interestingly, though, it is not the positive but rather the negative example provided by the superpower nuclear rivalry that has possibly exerted the more persuasive influence. As a full accounting of the Soviet-American nuclear arms race is tabulated and more widely appreciated, the enormous economic sacrifice— including the opportunity costs of having talented scientists, engineers, and technicians devoting their professional careers to expanding the nuclear stockpile instead of enlarging the gross national product—and the significant environmental damage associated with the nuclear weapons complex at first shocks and then saddens.[6] Nor has the cost of this arms race ended with the termination of the cold war; nuclear weapons dismantlement costs and environmental cleanup expenses furnish a bitter nuclear legacy for future generations. Cost estimates for environmental remediation in the United States range from $30 billion to $300 billion; given the strained financial circumstances of Russia and the other newly independent states, it is highly unlikely that funds will even be made available to adequately repair the widespread environmental damage caused by the Soviet nuclear weapons complex.

The third and fourth incentives—technological determinism, and scientific and bureaucratic determinism—are both still present after the cold war. If anything, these motivations are stronger than before because technology is more widespread and because there is greater scientific and technical competence generally throughout the Third World today.[7]

Another factor, new to the post-cold war world, also needs to be considered. This may not really be an incentive in the traditional sense; it is simply the increased *opportunity* for the spread of nuclear weapons and nuclear technology. This new opportunity derives from the Soviet Union's breakup, which is the single greatest source of proliferation anxiety today. The sheer magnitude of dismantling much of the former superpower's nuclear arsenal and the particular difficulties associated with storing the special nuclear material safely and securely introduce unprecedented proliferation problems.

Entropy in the former Soviet Union also presents new and alarming possibilities for proliferation. A weakening of the nuclear custodial system, the possibility of nuclear terrorism, emigration of talented nuclear weapons design and engineering personnel,[8] a growing sense of personal desperation amid domestic disorder and instability, the expanding reach of the mafia, and the collapse of export controls on nuclear materials and technologies could seriously compromise the nonproliferation regime. This precarious situation could persist for the next decade or longer. The ambivalent nuclear posture of Ukraine introduces additional uncertainties, especially when viewed against the larger context of simmering tensions and growing turmoil within and among the former Soviet republics.

Disincentives during the Cold War

Four general categories of disincentives hindered the spread of nuclear weapons during the past forty years. Foremost were nuclear weapons states' bilateral or multilateral security guarantees to come to the defense of nonnuclear weapons states. The earnestness of this commitment was demonstrated by the presence of foreign armies, usually (although not always) supplemented by nuclear weapons, on the territories of insecure countries.

NATO was the preeminent example. The United States guaranteed, through its declarations and actions, that it would defend its European allies, thereby making national nuclear forces less necessary and less attractive. The Soviet Union's role in the Warsaw Pact had the same effect (if not serving as the primary purpose of that alliance).

Bilateral security guarantees, such as those between the United States and Japan, and the United States and South Korea, similarly reassured countries and dissuaded them from acquiring nuclear weapons. And some countries that were outside any formal alliance structure or bilateral security relationship were convinced, by the concept of extended deterrence, that a national nuclear arsenal was unnecessary. For example, Sweden's belief that it fell within the penumbra of America's nuclear umbrella influenced its decision not to pursue a nuclear weapons capability.[9]

Another disincentive to nuclear weapons acquisition was the policy of technology denial through export controls. The concerted effort by many nuclear supplier countries to restrict trade in sensitive nuclear technologies started with the Zangger Committee in the early 1970s, which was originally designed to interpret the safeguards provisions of the NPT.[10] Export control efforts were expanded and informally organized in the mid-1970s in the Nuclear Suppliers Group, which agreed on a list of items whose transfer should automatically trigger the application of international safeguards.[11] Although the policy of denying certain technologies to suspect countries did not necessarily prevent them from acquiring a nuclear weapons capability, it raised the cost of obtaining these items and increased the amount of time and effort needed to develop nuclear arms. In other words, technology denial was a hurdle that delayed the nuclear ambitions of countries, rather than an absolute barrier that prevented these ambitions from ever being realized.

The peaceful uses of nuclear technology, first promoted by President Dwight Eisenhower in his December 1953 "Atoms for Peace" speech at the United Nations, attempted to channel the nuclear activities of countries away from military uses. An interlocking web of atomic energy cooperation agreements, often supported by scientific exchanges and nuclear technology at concessionary prices, legally obligated countries to use nuclear materials and facilities solely for peaceful purposes. Bilateral pledges with nuclear suppliers, primarily the United States, were later multilateralized after the establishment of the International Atomic Energy Agency (IAEA) and implementation of its safeguards system. This safeguards system formed an integral part of the NPT, which in turn was the centerpiece of the international nonproliferation regime. Together, the NPT and the IAEA safeguards agreements permitted member countries to reassure others of their commitment to use nuclear technology only for peaceful purposes.

All these factors contributed to the fourth disincentive: the general international norm against nuclear weapons. This norm had both an ethical and a strategic dimension. During the cold war, many viewed nuclear weapons as immoral instruments whose use could never be justified, even in retaliation. In many instances, countries also viewed nuclear weapons as antithetical to their larger political and economic objectives and questioned the legitimacy of any country's possession of nuclear arms. Nuclear weapons were thought to aggravate regional tensions and threaten international security; both their vertical and their horizontal dissemination should therefore be curbed. The "tradition of nonuse" of nuclear weapons evolved during the cold war and reinforced this norm.

Disincentives in the 1990s

After the cold war, these same disincentives are largely still present, although their influence is uncertain. NATO has survived the dissolution of the Warsaw Pact and the Soviet Union, but its future mission and composition are unresolved. American troops and nuclear weapons are still based in Europe, albeit at much lower levels than during the cold war. No one has recently questioned the U.S. commitment to Europe's defense, primarily because there are few, if any, threats on the horizon to defend Europe against.

Although the United States under the Clinton administration has placed greater priority on redressing some of its domestic problems, there is no call for the wholesale abandonment of America's European allies or the termination of important security relationships, such as those with Japan and South Korea. Even if Washington places less emphasis on its overseas responsibilities than before, this by itself should not induce countries to take the momentous step of acquiring nuclear weapons.

In this more fluid international environment, nuclear deterrence will still operate. There is no cogent reason why deterrence should not work in the post-cold war world in the same manner as it did during the cold war. Admittedly, it may not work. The specter of crazy states or unbalanced leaders is not new; they have always existed and will exist in the future. Good luck, which played a helpful role, may turn. But there is no *new* reason why nuclear deterrence should not continue to operate successfully.

Of course, some countries will still not be covered by another state's nuclear umbrella. Negative security assurances along the lines of those extended to all nonnuclear weapons states party to the NPT may not be sufficient to reassure certain countries. The most prominent and worrisome example is Ukraine. Washington has unequivocally refused to extend a NATO-type security guarantee to Kiev, which apparently has settled for security assurances contained in the UN Charter and the CSCE Final Act. Ukraine's security dilemma poses a particularly vexing nonproliferation problem. How, or whether, it is resolved will have ramifications far beyond the international nonproliferation regime.

Another disincentive, technology denial through export controls, remains in place. The network of formal and informal arrangements that govern international nuclear commerce was strengthened in the aftermath of the Persian Gulf War. In March 1992, the Nuclear Suppliers Group (NSG) tightened its guidelines by prohibiting the export of nuclear-related dual-use technology and requiring the application of full-scope safeguards as a condition for significant new nuclear technologies and components.[12] The twenty-nine NSG members meet annually to review and update these guidelines. The Zangger Committee also reexamined and refined its control list. The Missile Technology Control Regime (MTCR), which was formally established in April 1987, expanded its membership and strengthened many of its export policies.[13] Even though, clearly, much has been accomplished in this area, more can be done. A key concern is that nuclear suppliers such as the United States and Germany will attempt to boost the international competitiveness of domestic industries by ignoring or minimizing their nonproliferation responsibilities.

The IAEA has acknowledged some of its past shortcomings and has taken steps to redress them. Significantly, safeguards procedures are more rigorous than before, and the IAEA has won from a number of key states, including South Africa and

Iran, an agreement that it can inspect "anywhere, anytime." Although this is not identical to complete nuclear transparency, it is a large step in the right direction. The IAEA continues to perform a vital role in providing an independent method of monitoring nuclear activities, even, perhaps especially, if a country is not also a member of the NPT. The IAEA will soon perform this valuable function in Argentina and Brazil; both accepted full-scope IAEA safeguards in December 1991.

The biggest constraint on the IAEA's effectiveness, at least in the near term, is budgetary. Funding for safeguards has remained frozen in real terms for almost a decade. Whereas fiscal austerity initially forced the IAEA to eliminate waste and improve efficiency, that time is past. With the IAEA now being asked to assume greater safeguarding responsibilities than ever before, its future institutional effectiveness will require increased funding for safeguards activities. Complicating this issue is the fact that many IAEA members want any new money for safeguards to be matched with new funds to support peaceful nuclear assistance and technology transfers. Yet given the large return that a minimum financial investment in the safeguards budget will bring, it is near scandalous that this state of affairs exists.

The NPT has been strengthened in recent years as well. Two nuclear weapons states, China and France, joined the treaty in 1992. Another important holdout, South Africa, had acceded the previous year. At the beginning of 1994, over 160 countries were members. The treaty's future will be decided in April 1995 at the NPT Review Conference. At this conference the treaty may be extended indefinitely or, more likely, for a fixed period of time.

Three new disincentives may deter or defeat countries from building nuclear weapons. The first is the maturation of advanced technologies that can actually help prevent the spread of nuclear weapons. These capabilities will permit the nonproliferation regime to strengthen its ability to detect nascent nuclear weapons programs. Improved surveillance and imagery abilities, remote sensors, data-processing efficiencies, and seismic monitoring capabilities are just some of the areas in which new advances could assist nonproliferation efforts. If combined properly with an array of lethal and nonlethal defense options and enhanced intelligence gathering and analytical capabilities, these technologies should make it highly unlikely that a country will ever again be able to surreptitiously construct a nuclear weapons program and surprise the international community, as Iraq did during the 1980s. The sophistication of the IAEA and the United States in determining that North Korea misrepresented the scope of its reprocessing activities provides some indication of the current state of this forensic technology.[14]

The second disincentive is the Defense Department's counterproliferation strategy, which Secretary of Defense Les Aspin officially unveiled in December 1993.[15] The doctrine in still being developed and clearly means different things to different people and departments. One of the most controversial aspects of the doctrine is its apparent contemplation of unilateral, preemptive military strikes by the United States against the nuclear activities of certain countries. If these countries believe that Washington may attack their nuclear programs, it remains to be seen whether this perception will deter countries from proceeding down the path to a nuclear weapons capability or if it will accelerate nuclear development by providing further justification for countries that believe themselves already threatened by the United States. The U.S. strategy may simply force them to adopt countermeasures (such as burying critical elements of their nuclear complex) to frustrate or defeat the strategy. In this case, it will nonetheless raise the costs and increase the time required to build a nuclear arsenal.[16]

The treatment Iraq suffered in the aftermath of the 1991 Gulf War, when it became certain that Baghdad had violated its international nonproliferation commitments, may have real nonproliferation benefits for the future. Although the casus belli of the UN coalition was Iraq's invasion of Kuwait, the destruction of Baghdad's nuclear weapons program (and other programs for weapons of mass destruction) was nonetheless a wartime objective and, due to U.S. leadership, became a primary objective of the postwar settlement. More effectively than any counterproliferation strike, Baghdad's nuclear infrastructure is being dismantled in accordance with UN Security Council Resolutions 687, 707, and 715.

Though difficult to quantify, the greater priority that the international community appears to have placed on nonproliferation is a third disincentive that may dampen nuclear ambitions. Resources and attention formerly devoted to the Soviet-American competition have been redirected to combating the spread of nuclear weapons. That this may be for budgetary, institutional, or purely career reasons is immaterial. The result is a proliferation of proliferation expertise both in government bureaucracies and in nongovernmental organizations. Many of the constituent parts of the international nonproliferation regime have been reexamined, revised, and reinvigorated. For example, the UN Security Council declared for the first time in January 1992 that proliferation constitutes a threat to international peace and security. Perhaps most meaningful, awareness in capitals around the world—especially in Washington, D.C.—of the importance of preventing nuclear proliferation is at its highest since the time of the Baruch Plan in June 1946.

Conclusion

The state of international efforts to prevent the spread of nuclear weapons after the cold war evokes the opening lines from Charles Dickens's *A Tale of Two Cities*—it is both the best and worst of times. On balance, then, is the current situation better or worse than before? Despite the severity of recent blows to the international nonproliferation regime and opportunities for future failure, efforts to prevent the spread of nuclear weapons stand at least as good a chance as before. Disincentives have generally been strengthened and reinforced, whereas incentives have generally weakened. A completed framework of incentives and disincentives, before and after the cold war, is set out in figure 15.2.

Whether and how well other countries learn from these lessons, or whether they can even be persuaded to acknowledge them, remains to be seen. Regardless of these lessons and the active efforts of the international community to discourage nuclear programs, a small number of countries will undoubtedly persevere in seeking to acquire nuclear weapons—countries that will tolerate the price of being hated in return for being feared. For them, nuclear weapons will still be perceived as a way to ameliorate their security dilemmas and elevate their status. Although clearly unwelcome, this continued interest should not be surprising; the problem of nuclear proliferation is nonlinear, that is, there is no "final" resolution.

More important, efforts to further strengthen the many aspects of the nonproliferation regime should continue. The task of preventing the spread of nuclear weapons after the cold war

FIGURE 15.2

	Cold War	Post–Cold War

Incentives	1. insecurity
	2. status
	3. technological
	   determinism
	4. scientific and
	   bureaucratic
	   determinism
		1. insecurity
		2. status
		3. technological
		   determinism
		4. scientific and
		   bureaucratic
		   determinism
		5. "increased opportunity"

Disincentives	1. security guarantees 2. export controls 3. NPT/IAEA 4. international norm	1. security guarantees 2. export controls 3. NPT/IAEA 4. international norm 5. nonlethal technologies 6. counterproliferation 7. "higher priority"

will be very much like it was during the cold war—a pattern of quiet, gradual, and incremental successes punctuated by a few very public failures. The battle to prevent the spread of nuclear weapons has to be waged anew each day. Yet this should not unduly dismay us. Although the problem persists, our knowledge and resources are greater than before. As has been true throughout the nuclear age, the key variables will be the energy, leadership, and wisdom we bring to this problem.

Notes

1. For an explanation and discussion of "nuclear myth makers," see Peter R. Lavoy, "Nuclear Myths and the Causes of Nuclear Proliferation," in Zachary S. Davis and Benjamin Frankel, eds., *The Proliferation Puzzle: Why Nuclear Weapons Spread (And What Results)* (London: Frank Cass, 1993), pp. 192–212; for how this motivation influenced South Africa's nuclear program, see Mitchell Reiss, *Bridled Ambition: Why Countries Curtail Their Nuclear Capabilities* (New York: Columbia University Press, forthcoming).

2. See Benjamin Frankel, "The Brooding Shadow: Systemic Incentives and Nuclear Weapons Proliferation," in Davis and Frankel, *The Proliferation Puzzle*, pp. 37–78; John J. Mearsheimer, "Back to the Future: Instability in Europe after the Cold War," *International Security* 15, no. 1 (Summer 1990):

5–56; and John J. Mearsheimer, "The Case for a Ukrainian Nuclear Deterrent," *Foreign Affairs* 72, no. 3 (Summer 1993): 50–66.

3. The minister of atomic energy for the Russian Federation, Victor Mikhailov, has claimed that the Soviet nuclear inventory peaked in 1986 at forty-five thousand nuclear weapons, approximately twelve thousand more than some U.S. intelligence estimates. See William J. Broad, "Russian Says Soviet Atom Arsenal Was Larger Than West Estimated," *New York Times*, September 26, 1993. Reportedly, Mikhailov later recanted this statement.

4. Lewis Dunn has argued that the United States would even be reluctant to use nuclear weapons *second*. See Lewis Dunn, "Rethinking the Nuclear Equation: The United States and the New Nuclear Powers," *Washington Quarterly* 17, no. 1 (Winter 1994): 12–14.

5. Robert F. Kennedy, *Thirteen Days: A Memoir of the Cuban Missile Crisis* (New York: W. W. Norton, 1969), pp. 37, 38, 39.

6. For a description of the environmental damage in the United States from its nuclear weapons complex and various cost estimates for cleanup, see Michael D'Antonio, *Atomic Harvest: Hanford and the Lethal Toll of America's Nuclear Arsenal* (York: Crown, 1993); U.S. Office of Technology Assessment (OTA), *Complex Cleanup: The Environmental Legacy of Nuclear Weapons Production* (Washington, D.C.: OTA, 1991); U.S. Department of Energy (DOE), *Environmental Restoration and Waste Management Five-Year Plan, Fiscal Years 1993–97* (Washington, D.C.: DOE, 1991); and National Academy of Sciences, National Research Council, *The Nuclear Weapons Complex: Management for Health, Safety, and the Environment* (Washington, D.C.: National Academy Press, 1989). For an accounting of the environmental damage in the former Soviet Union from its nuclear power and weapons programs, see D. J. Peterson, *Troubled Lands: The Legacy of Soviet Environmental Destruction* (Boulder: Westview, 1993), and Murray Feshbach and Alfred Friendly, Jr., *Ecocide in the USSR: Health and Nature under Seige* (New York: Basic Books, 1992).

7. See Peter D. Zimmerman, "Proliferation: Bronze Medal Technology Is Enough," *Orbis* 38, no. 1 (Winter 1994): 67–82.

8. To a lesser degree, this pressure is present in South Africa and even in the United States as it downsizes its nuclear arsenal and weapons labs.

9. This was one of a number of factors that dissuaded Sweden from acquiring nuclear weapons. See Mitchell Reiss, *Without the Bomb: The Politics of Nuclear Nonproliferation* (New York: Columbia University Press, 1988), pp. 69ff.

10. The Zangger Committee was established in 1971 to assist NPT parties in arriving at a uniform interpretation of Article 3(2). See David Fischer, *Towards 1995: The Prospects for Ending the Proliferation of Nuclear Weapons* (Aldershot, England: UNIDIR/Dartmouth, 1993), pp. 98–99.

11. On January 16, 1978, the IAEA announced that the director general had been informed that fifteen countries had harmonized their export policies on nuclear material, equipment, and technologies. See IAEA Press Release 78/2, January 16, 1978. The original members of the Nuclear Suppliers Group—the United States, the Soviet Union, West Germany, France, Britain, Canada, Japan, Belgium, Czechoslovakia, East Germany, Italy, the Nether-

lands, Poland, Sweden, and Switzerland—had convened secretly in London since 1975.

12. See *IAEA Newsbriefs* 7, no. 2 (April/May 1992): 7. In addition to the original fifteen members, the NSG includes Argentina, Australia, Austria, Bulgaria, Denmark, Finland, Greece, Hungary, Ireland, Luxembourg, Norway, Portugal, Romania, and Spain. Czechoslovakia is now represented by the Czech Republic and Slovakia, the representation of West and East Germany has been consolidated, and Russia has assumed the seat of the Soviet Union. The Commission on the European Communities attends meetings as an observer.

13. See The White House, Press Release, April 16, 1987. "In deference to the political sensitivity of more formal arrangements, the regime was not designated as a treaty but as a consensual agreement, asking states to incorporate its guidelines into their national export codes and abide by them as sovereign countries." (Janne E. Nolan, *Trappings of Power: Ballistic Missiles in the Third World* [Washington, D.C.: Brookings, 1991], p. 28.) The original eight MTCR members were the United States, the Soviet Union, Canada, France, Germany, Italy, Japan, and Britain. Argentina, Australia, Austria, Belgium, Denmark, Finland, Greece, Hungary, Iceland, Ireland, Luxembourg, the Netherlands, New Zealand, Norway, Portugal, Spain, Sweden, and Switzerland subsequently joined, bringing membership to twenty-six. The MTCR guidelines were revised in January 1993. See U.S. Department of State, Press Release, January 7, 1993.

14. To make this determination, laboratory technicians analyzed minute quantities of radioactive isotopes from North Korea's Yongbyon facilities. See R. Jeffrey Smith, "N. Korea and the Bomb: High-Tech Hide-and-Seek," *Washington Post*, April 27, 1993.

15. See text of Secretary Aspin's talk before the National Academy of Sciences, Washington, D.C., December 7, 1993. See also Michael R. Gordon, "Pentagon Begins Effort to Combat More Lethal Arms in Third World," *New York Times*, December 8, 1993, and John Lancaster, "Aspin Vows Military Efforts to Counter Arms Proliferation," *Washington Post*, December 8, 1993.

16. A critique of the foreign policy, military, and legal implications of the Pentagon's counterproliferation strategy is beyond the scope of this chapter. However, as of mid-1994, questions exist both within and without the U.S. government over the definition of "counterproliferation" and its ramifications.

Editors and Contributors

ROBERT CARLIN is Northeast Asia Division Chief, Office of East Asia and Pacific Analysis, Bureau of Intelligence and Research, U.S. Department of State.

BRAHMA CHELLANEY is Research Fellow at the Center for Policy Research, Delhi, and UPI Bureau Chief, South Asia. He is the author of *Nuclear Proliferation: The U.S.-Indian Conflict*.

SHAHRAM CHUBIN is a specialist on strategic studies and the international politics of the Middle East. His recent publications include *Iran's National Security Policy* and *Germany and the Middle East* (editor).

ZACHARY DAVIS is Analyst, International Nuclear Affairs, Environmental and Natural Resources Division, Congressional Research Service, Washington, D.C., and coeditor of *The Proliferation Puzzle: Why Nuclear Weapons Spread*.

SHAI FELDMAN is Senior Research Associate at the Jaffee Center for Strategic Studies, Tel Aviv University, and is director of the center's Project on Security and Arms Control in the Middle East. He is the author of *Israeli Nuclear Deterrence: A Strategy for the 1980s*.

DAVID FISCHER writes widely on international nonproliferation matters. He is former Assistant Director General for External Relations of the IAEA.

SHIRLEY KAN is Analyst, Foreign Affairs and National Defense Division, Congressional Research Service, Washington, D.C.

DAVID KAY is Assistant Vice President at Science Applications International Corporation. From 1983 until January 1992 he was with the IAEA and served as Chief Inspector for three of the

351

early post-Gulf War nuclear weapons inspections in Iraq that uncovered the extensive Iraqi clandestine nuclear program.

ROBERT S. LITWAK is Director, Division of International Studies, at the Woodrow Wilson International Center for Scholars, Washington, D.C. He is the author of *Détente and the Nixon Doctrine* and *Security in the Persian Gulf.*

STEVEN E. MILLER is Director of the International Security Program at the Center for Science and International Affairs, John F. Kennedy School of Government, Harvard University, where he is also Editor-in-Chief of *International Security.* He is coauthor of *Soviet Nuclear Fission* and coeditor of *Cooperative Denuclearization.*

JOSEPH F. PILAT is on the staff of the Center for National Security Studies, Los Alamos National Laboratory, Los Alamos, New Mexico. During 1993, he was Visiting Associate Professor in the Department of Government and Visiting Fellow in the Peace Studies Program at Cornell University. He is a coeditor of *Beyond 1995: The Future of the NPT Regime.*

MITCHELL REISS is Guest Scholar at the Woodrow Wilson International Center for Scholars, Washington, D.C. He is the author of *Bridled Ambition: Why Countries Curtail Their Nuclear Capabilities* (forthcoming) and *Without the Bomb: The Politics of Nuclear Nonproliferation.*

JEFFREY T. RICHELSON is a consultant based in Alexandria, Virginia, where he writes on intelligence issues. He is the author of *America's Secret Eyes in Space* and *A Century of Spies* (forthcoming).

GARY SAMORE is Acting Director, Office of the Proliferation of Nuclear Weapons, Bureau of Political-Military Affairs, U.S. Department of State.

AMY SANDS was head of the Proliferation Assessment Program at the Lawrence Livermore National Laboratory when her chapter was written. Dr. Sands is now Assistant Director, Bureau of

Intelligence, Verification, and Information Support, U.S. Arms Control and Disarmament Agency.

MÓNICA SERRANO is Assistant Professor at El Colegio de Mexico in Mexico City.

ALI T. SHEIKH, who has served as a consultant to the Rockefeller Foundation, writes widely on South Asian security issues.

Index